Active Voices
IV

Active Voices
IV

James Moffett

with Miriam Baker and Charles Cooper

BOYNTON/COOK PUBLISHERS, INC.
UPPER MONTCLAIR, NEW JERSEY 07043

Library of Congree Cataloging in Publication Data

Main entry under title:

Acitve voices IV.

1. College readers. 2. College prose, American.
I. Moffett, James. II. Baker, Miriam. III. Cooper, Charles Raymond, 1934 –
PE1417.A313   1986   428.6   85-27996
ISBN 0-86709-115-0

For information address Boynton/Cook Publishers, Inc.,
52 Upper Montclair Plaza, P.O. Box 860, Upper Montclair, NJ 07043

Printed in the United States of America
86   87   88   89   90   10   9   8   7   6   5   4   3   2

Acknowledgments

This book was actually written by students, so it's to these authors that we are most indebted. Their names appear under the titles of the selections and in the Contents. Many thanks to them for giving of themselves, often in kinds of writing they had never done before, and for giving permission to use their work.

The "teaching assistants" who actually teach many of the composition courses in this country are very much unsung. They do what may well be the hardest job in a college, but do it as birds of passage, enjoying little status or security and learning mostly on the job, a job they will soon leave. The following instructors in the Third College Writing Program of the University of California at San Diego, directed by Charles Cooper, supplied a substantial portion of the papers from which final selections were made. In most cases they took on assignments or sequences of assignments that they had not dealt with before, and we are deeply grateful to them all.

Cherryl Armstrong	Igor Korneitchouk	Peggy Stamon
James Degan	Tom Larson	Dawn Tebor-Lettau
Richard Finn	Carol Mavor	Alan Timmerman
Sheryl Fontaine	Cezar Ornatowski	Carol Vernallis
Katherine Gardner	Clive Roberts	Eric Watkins
Keith Grant-Davie	Judith Shushan	

Of the many selections from Dowling College on Long Island those not from Miriam Baker's own classes were contributed by her colleague Paul Takis. Special appreciation to Steve Kowit for offerings from his poetry class at San Diego State University, and many thanks for help also from Karen Carlton at Humboldt State (CA) and from

Janice Chernekoff and Douglas Boettiger at San Diego State.

The remaining selections came from classes of Charles Cooper at UCSD and of James Moffett at Middlebury College's Bread Loaf School of English in Vermont and at San Diego State.

The more difficulty we had obtaining samples of writing not commonly done for college courses, the more grateful we became for those students and teachers who came through for us. May their work make it much easier in the future to find such a variety of writing on college campuses.

Contents

INVESTIGATION (Looking Into)

Introduction

The writing collected here was done in college classes by students of various ages and abilities. It's meant to illustrate the many kinds of composition actually practiced in the non-school world that you need to experience, whatever your course of study. Practice them yourself and become a writer among writers.

We made no effort to run a national contest or seek elite students. We wanted the writing to represent what most students can match in originality and quality. Most of the selections were written by freshmen in required composition courses. Some were by students in advanced composition courses, a few of whom were M.A. candidates. From previous experience, we felt confident that most students writing from authentic experience and interest, and benefiting from feedback and revision, would supply us with plenty of entertaining material. They did. So while the selections aim to show what these various sorts of writing look like when done by your peers, we offer this anthology also as a good book to read.

We recommend that you begin doing right now what nearly every writer does—keep a notebook of possible material. You don't have to be a novelist or a poet; many professionals have to keep field or lab notes just to stay on top of their jobs. You'll find it much easier to start composing if you have accumulated jottings on this and that— observations, random thoughts, dreams, recollections, images, over-heard conversations, story ideas, or the stray phrase that unaccountably intrigues you. Don't count on remembering these; get them down on paper for future use. Writing begins with the discovery of subject matter you care about. You don't have to stare at a blank page and scratch your head. Store up *too much*, and savor an embarrassment of riches.

A kind of writing is going on all the time in your mind as you register experience, recollect it, reflect on it, and recombine it in imaginative ways. By processing experience this way, you're constantly making your own knowledge. Writing intensifies and raises to awareness this ongoing process. It externalizes thinking so we can better guide it. Any material is fair game when the range of writing is opened across the whole spectrum. At any moment, look inside, look around; stuff is everywhere.

The organization of this book brings out how kinds of writing correspond to kinds of thinking. We start with a section on journals called NOTATION, which includes a segment of a diary that a student kept while participating in an air meet. The section also offers samples of journal entries expanded into compositions. NOTATION corresponds to the registering of experience. The other four sections group composition according to what the writer has to do to turn up and work up material. They feature the *processes* that yield the *products*. They are:

RECOLLECTION—**looking back,** to produce autobiography and memoir.

INVESTIGATION—**looking into,** to produce reportage and research, biography and chronicle, case history and profile, and factual articles.

IMAGINATION—**thinking up,** to produce plays, fiction, and poems.

COGITATION—**thinking over** and **thinking through,** to produce personal reflective essays, editorials and reviews, and the various thesis essays based on documentation and argumentation.

Organizing selections this way puts them into relationships to each other that can help you gain insight about how to work with each kind.

Take the major groupings themselves. The material of RECOLLECTION is already stored within us, in some ways already composed as well. Working with it requires something different than does INVESTIGATION, for which you have to go look (visit), go ask (interview), and go look up (consult books or records). In looking back, you *re*-discover, whereas when you look into, you discover something new. To your past experience, INVESTIGATION adds not only new firsthand experience but the secondhand experience of other people as well. **Looking Back** and **Looking Into** form together a kind of data base for **Thinking Up, Thinking Over,** and **Thinking Through.**

In contrast to the more concrete, more factual writing of RECOLLECTION and INVESTIGATION, the writing of IMAGINATION and COGITATION departs further from physical experience to create second-order experiences of the mind. To fashion more general knowledge, we recombine and transform first- and secondhand experiences. Imagination does this figuratively and implicitly; reason does it literally and explicitly. (But *all* writing is idea writing.) So the processes of the last two groups depend on those of the two before, as generalities are abstracted from particulars. All depend on registering experience (NOTATION).

This order of derivation is not necessarily a writing sequence, however. Often the processing of certain material may occur only in the mind up to a certain point, and it may not be picked up in writing until a later stage, where the composition will seem to begin. Although a sensible order in which to practice different kinds of writing does partly follow this building from more concrete to more abstract knowledge, there are other factors affecting growth and difficulty. Most people find RECOLLECTION and INVESTIGATION easier than COGITATION—stating facts easier than arguing general propositions—but people vary considerably in how difficult it is for them, for example, to deal with facts as compared with inventing fictions. Still, the main groupings do break down writing into five important areas to practice in and should prove useful in sequencing selections for a program.

Within a single group the positioning of selections is also important. Sometimes the kinds of writing presented first may be simpler than those to follow. For example, either a Visit or Interview is easier than the later types of reportage that combine both with each other and eventually with other sources. Similarly, a single two-person scene (Duolog) makes good preparation for a play of several scenes and several characters.

But the order of assignments within a group isn't always meant to suggest a sequence. Sometimes it's to array and differentiate closely related kinds of writing. For example, RECOLLECTION is broken down into Autobiography and Memoir. Each in turn is further divided: Autobiography into Incident and Phase; Memoir into Memoir of Another Person, of a Group or Place, of an Eyewitness Incident, and of Nature. All these variations in focus affect how the author goes about selecting and shaping recollections. If you have a certain memory in mind, you might aim directly at, say, Memoir of an Eyewitness Incident, but you might very well just want to delve into memories and see what comes up. In that case, you would do Memories, a "scatter" assignment that could, when finally composed, take any of the focuses above. But perusing the array of possibilities aids final choice and refines your composing process. Each grouping opens with one or so "scatter" assignments that could go in any of the directions indicated by following, more specialized assignments. One kind helps find subject matter, and the other kind helps find a form and focus for subject matter already in mind.

It's usually a certain subject matter that makes us want to write something. But what form should we cast it in, and what focus would be best for it? Let's say you want to deal with teenage suicide. Maybe you're not even sure which group this would fall under. So consider the total array of the whole book. Can you write your piece from memory? Or would you have to do some investigation? Considering your purpose and audience, do you want to communicate through facts, reasoning, feelings, or imagination? Would it be better to detail the story of one suicidal person and let it represent the entire issue (Case: Individual), to narrate several suicidal episodes of different people (Thematic Collection of Incidents), to document the trend as a current problem (Generalization), to *explain* why this trend is occurring (Causal Analysis), or to make up a short story in which the mental life of a suicidal teenager is contrasted with that of another family member (Third Person: Dual Character Viewpoint). In general, the array should help you perceive possibilities and make realistic decisions.

Knowing the kinds of writing and how they relate to each other is, of course, only part of the picture. The rest—the actual processes of composing—concern what goes on *inside* you as you think and write and what goes on *between* you and your instructor and classmates. Writing is personal *and* social.

Take the *inside* part first. As a writer, you need to be conscious of what you feel and think when you experience, recall, or observe something. (Keeping a notebook helps fix your responses in awareness.) What's on your mind? What's under your mind? You can find out by taking a little time each day to sit still and relaxed in a quiet place, close your eyes, and focus attention inward in one or more of the following ways:

- Let your mind romp wherever it wants but witness it like a bystander instead of being swept away obliviously.
- Or try to slow down and perhaps even suspend the inner chatter and buzzing concerns. What comes into your mind then?
- Or review the day's events. How do you respond to them?
- Or choose some subject you want to understand better, perhaps some problem you want to solve, and focus just on that by concentrating on some image or phrase or idea

that represents it for you. Such a subject might be one that recurs when you try to still or witness your thoughts, or it might just be some situation, person, object, place, or idea that attracts you. Follow through in this way by giving full attention to whatever is already asking for more attention.

Inner material is not necessarily about *you;* it's what you think and feel about *anything.* It's the prime source of what you can write about. If you learn to tune into it and cultivate it, you'll not only find writing easier and more satisfying but you'll probably understand yourself and your world better.

Now the *between* part. Unlike many writers who toil alone, you have ready access to an appropriate trial audience—your classmates. You and they don't have to be experts to help each other. And you don't have to play teacher. All you have to do is respond as readers. If you can keep reasonably good track of what you're thinking and feeling as you read or hear a composition, you can help the author a great deal to know how close she or he came to the mark. In return, your partners will give you the same useful feedback before you revise so that you can benefit from a realistic trial before handing compositions in to the instructor. Most writers do a draft, try it out on whatever nearby audience they can scare up, and then revise (usually more than once). Of course, your instructor provides very important feedback, but he or she rarely has time to respond between drafts as well as after the final version—if indeed ever.

Working with classmates has other advantages too. Your group may smoke out a particular composition problem not only in a single paper but across your accumulating portfolio of papers, because partners in a writing workshop group get to know traits and trends in each other's writing. Finally, help can begin even before the drafting stage, when you're trying to get started. Telling a story aloud to someone, or talking over some tentative ideas, can be a useful way to sort out your thoughts and decide how to proceed, especially if both you and your listeners ask questions.

Here are several ways that members of a small workshop group can help each other:

1) Depending on the kind of writing and on other circumstances, you can all either read aloud your own drafts, read aloud each other's, pass around your papers to read silently and discuss later, or pass out copies to annotate as you read silently.

2) As you read or listen to a paper, think of a title for it and jot this down on a scrap of paper and compare later with others'. (The author should have a title but not place it on the paper.)

3) Let the author say what he or she wants help with or is wondering and worrying about.

4) Describe what you thought or felt at various points in the draft without necessarily advising.

5) Ask the author questions on what you don't understand or are curious about.

6) Play with other possibilities. Tinker. Ask the group creative what-if questions about someone's draft. What if things were changed around or expressed in some other way?

While thinking of your workshop group as an immediate audience and your class and instructor as a still wider readership, consider as you write who else you may be addressing. Where might the finished piece *go*? What might it *do*? Scripts, for example, or how-to directions, are meant to be performed or carried out. Many other compositions, like stories and poems, serve well as material for rehearsed readings. Nearly all the types of writing in *ACTIVE VOICES* are publishable somewhere because they illustrate what can be found in various publications. Consider local newspapers and newsletters and regional or specialized journals. Look and ask around. Exchange suggestions with classmates.

Now read and enjoy. See how some other college students have done kinds of writing practiced in the world at large. Try your hand and practice too. Enjoy being a writer among writers.

James Moffett
Mariposa, California

Active Voices
IV

Notation

(Taking Down)

Journal and Diary

Writer's Journal

Keep a writer's notebook in which you jot down all sorts of things you might want to save and use in your writing—not just events of the moment but also thoughts and feelings that come to you, memories, dreams, imaginings, and so on. Date your entries, and try to make at least several a week. Notes are for yourself; you can choose what others read.

Besides having value in themselves, your notes are a source book for material you can write up later for others however you see fit. You may draw on only a fraction of it for writing, but if you keep it well-stocked you'll have plenty of choice. Rereading it will probably help you go over some things in your life from a longer-range perspective, and this also prompts ideas.

Journal Greeting [*first entry*]
John Carey

So how ya doing, Journal? I'm John, and I am about to create you. What do you think about that? I know you're not going to answer back, but just let me tell you what's going on. Whenever we have English I'm going to write on your pages. I'll probably be writing pure nonsense in you, but that's the way it's gonna be, I'm telling you that right now. I really don't like you too much, but we're going to have to learn to live with each other for the next five months. Most of the paper in you will probably go to waste, but you're required for the

1

class. So do you have any ideas for me? I know it sounds like I don't like you much, but any ideas you have for me I'll write down just to fill up space. Wait! Why am I asking you for advice? You're just a book. My life is more interesting than a black and white notebook worth $1.70. I've got plenty of interesting friends. I meet some strange people every once in a while. I even work at an airport where some funny things happen at work. You know, Journal, I said I didn't like you much, but I guess you gave me some pretty good ideas from your muteness. So hold onto your binding, buddy, this is my life!

Rewritten Journal Entry

Select an entry, or a portion of one, from your writer's journal and compose on the basis of it any kind of writing that you think will interest some other people. Expand or re-cast some idea, image, or event into whatever form seems appropriate—a true story, fiction, essay, poem, or script, according to the kind of value you feel the material has. Or if you're working within the framework of one of the four kinds of writing represented in the following four sections of this book, browse through your journal and select some entry that naturally lends itself to Recollection, Investigation, Imagination, or Reflection.

(To illustrate the process, the following samples include both the original entry and the composition based on it.)

Journal Entry 3-9-83
Stephen Ebinger

The weather really has deteriorated lately. I think we're going to run into the "Flood Age" before we hit the "Ice Age." The past week has been nothing but rain. Yesterday was my 21st birthday and it poured all day. I still had a great day. My girlfriend and her family are really nice. They went out of their way to make me a nice little birthday party. Everyone of her brothers and her mom and dad bought me presents. And of course Donna got me a gorgeous gold herringbone bracelet. Her mom made $40 worth of prime ribs for dinner, what a feast. They're such great people.

I've been having a problem writing a paper that's due today in this class. I never talk to anyone about my oldest brother's tour of duty in Da Nang, So. Vietnam. I'm very inhibited about writing or talking about it. I've never quite been able to accept the fact that he was never the same after those 18 months. The matter is highly personal. You see, before he went to Vietnam he was like a father to me since my father is so much older than me—47 years older to be exact. Now instead of being a father figure he's my brother in Jersey whom I see once a year, if I am lucky enough to be graced with his presence that often. The whole situation has been a great personal loss to me.

Big Brother

One memory that has always been present in my mind, when I ponder it, is that of the horrible experiences my oldest brother Frank had in Vietnam.

Frank was only sixteen when he graduated from high school and went off to college, a lot of responsibility for such a young boy. He attended SUNY at Oswego and studied biology, living on campus his first semester. It was tough adjusting to dorm life but he pulled a solid 3.0 grade point average. By the time his second semester came around he was bored with dorm life so he moved into a house off campus with friends. He liked this idea and partied the semester away to celebrate his brilliant move. Needless to say he flunked out of school and returned home, which he couldn't stand, and soon signed his life away to the U.S. Navy.

After completing training and specializing in martial arts and field medicine, they sent him to Da Nang, South Vietnam during the height of U.S. involvement in the war. Eighteen long months in the battle-field with mauled bodies and incoming shells ended abruptly when a certain incident occurred.

My brother and his buddy in the field were cruising in a jeep when they were hit by a grenade. Both men were thrown clear from the jeep. My brother was semi-conscious but not moving, and his buddy was dead. The gook who threw the grenade came over to check the victims and loot their persons. First he saw that Frank's buddy was dead, and then he approached Frank. As he bent over and reached for him, Frank instantly snapped his hand up at the gook and ripped his windpipe right out of his throat and passed out with the gook's larynx clenched in his hand. The doctor at the M.A.S.H. unit had to pry it out of his hand. That moment completely changed his life. He was never more to be the same. For five years he pumped gas for a living, wasting his life away. Finally he returned to college and obtained his nursing degree and began to work in a hospital. It took him almost ten years, a wife and two children before he got his life going in some direction, and, sad to say, it still isn't going straight. It's a shame to see how a war could so shatter a man's life irreparably. It made a very disturbed young man out of a very brilliant young man.

Journal Entry
Jennifer Zipkin

I don't even feel like I belong here.

Who, Me?

I don't even feel like I belong here. I have felt like this so many times that I have stopped counting. The time I started high school I felt like I should be back in seventh grade. I just didn't feel old enough to be there. Another time was at my high school graduation. I kept saying to myself, "This isn't really happening, don't worry, in September you'll be back." But it didn't happen.

Now I'm in college and sometimes I feel I don't belong here either. I register for all my classes and go to them just like everyone else, but something happens to me somewhere along the way that creates this weird sense of being lost inside of me. I know that I'm just as smart as my classmates because after all I get A's and B's in most of my classes. Yet sometimes I feel lost in those classes. Usually I just sit back and let the other people in class do all of the talking. They always sound so grown up and mature that it frightens me. I just don't see myself as being like that.

Then every once in a while, when I will open my mouth and say something and people actually respond to my comments, I get a wave of "mature" feelings inside myself. It's like when I'm in a group of people talking about a piece of writing, I will give a comment that people listen to and react to. I feel as if I have contributed to someone else's education for a change. Maybe I am ready for all of this. Perhaps

I just need to open up a bit more because what I have to say really does mean something to others.

Journal Entry 5/9/83
Gregory Janusz

Well, here it is Monday again. Wow, just saying that reminds me of the comic strip Garfield. He hates Mondays but they're not so bad. Mother's Day was good. I got my mom a plant, and I hand-raked the front lawn. She loved them both. I got a blister on my hand from raking. Boy, was my sister in a silly mood yesterday. She was acting like a little kid. You know, she must have been in a good mood. I told her that I got a blister on my hand, and she said "Ah, poor baby, my little baby brother got a blister on his hand." The house and yard is really going to look good this summer because I'm going to take care of it. You know, I can't figure my mother out. She gets all upset when I leave beer in my car and room, which is wrong for me to do. But when I was raking I had two beers and she didn't say anything. That's so strange.

Mother's Day

Well, here it is Monday again. Wow, just saying that reminds me of the comic strip *Garfield*. He hates Mondays but they're not so bad. Mother's Day was good. I got my mom a plant and I raked the front lawn for her. She loved them both. I also got a blister while raking! Aw, poor baby. My mom is the greatest. I love her so much. I mean, what other lady could raise three kids and own a house on a waitress's salary. I'm going to try and make the lawn look dynamite this summer. I mean, after all she's done for me it's the least I could do for her. I am the baby in the family so I get treated a little different than my brother and sister. My mother has done so much for me alone, not to mention what she's done for the rest of the family. When I was in high school and I just got my driver's license, my mother and I went looking at cars and she cosigned a loan for my first live car. Not only did she do that but she paid for my insurance. I was working close to full time during school so I was able to pay off at least half of the loan. When I graduated from school she took over the payments for a graduation gift. Anytime something would go wrong with the car my mom would always be there to help out for any of us. This may sound like it's a little difficult to believe, but she still buys me clothing every year. Now that I'm in college she's always trying to help me in whatever way she can. It sounds like I'm a spoiled brat, but it's just not that way. My mom just wants me to have the things she didn't when she was a kid. My mom hasn't had a drink in 7 or 8 yrs. and she quit smoking altogether about 2 or 3 years ago. I have to say that without a doubt I'm the proudest son around to have a mom love and do so much for me. I just hope one day I can pay her back.

Journal Entry 4-19-83
Bruce Trimble

The bad weather came and went today in massive proportions. John and I took the jeep out for a little drive and came back 5 hours later. You name it and whatever it was that broke a rule we did it. The mountains and canyons were incredible. The weather broke and off into the wild blue we went. Thunderstorms forced us back but it made Colorado mean a lot more to me. Mother nature is awesome. I saw 3 rainbows side by side. I flew around them almost out of respect so as not to disturb them. Things naturewise happen so drastic here. We have flatlands and huge mountains. The weather moves in and out faster than you can tell.

By Land and By Air

When I got accepted on the flying team for Dowling College, I never thought that I would be making a two-thousand mile trip, from New York to Colorado, to compete in the national tournament. No one on the team really knew what to expect, as far as flying conditions around the Rocky Mountains were concerned.

We woke up early our first morning in Colorado Springs, and as the fog rolled through the mountains, I anticipated a good morning ahead for the team. My hopes dwindled, however, when 10:00 a.m. came around and the weather turned from bad to worse. My teammate and good friend, John Stanton, suggested we just pick up and leave for a while.

Our initial plan was to drive up into the mountains in our Jeep and get on top of the clouds. We never made it, however. When the two of us go out together it's like two babies at playtime in nursery school. We have to experiment and investigate everything. After driving around in the mountains for a while it seemed our only motive was to find uninhabited dirt roads, each one being in worse condition than the last as we progressed. We finally hit "paydirt," and wound up on a road that turned into a stream. The jeep was doing great so we hung in there until we drove into a huge canyon. There were rocks, caves, wild animals and, best of all, sheer wilderness. It was an eerie feeling to be in such wilderness with no apparent life. Everything was kind of sedate, which gave us the feeling that everything was just barely existing. If we had not been there I thought none of it might exist at all. We walked around for a while in what seemed a prehistoric habitat.

It wasn't long before I noticed the weather was clearing, so we decided to make a start out to get back to the rest of the team. The afternoon cleared up reasonably well and we decided to try our first trip in the area. We picked an easy trip to fly since the terrain was tough to follow. Landmarks from the air are few in this portion of the country.

The most apparent landmark we had available to us was the eastern edge of the Rocky Mountains. The mountain ridge was our helping hand to wherever we flew. Pike's Peak was like a beacon that I could simply fly to whenever I was heading home. I was kind of starstruck by being around such a display of architectural genius on the part of mother nature. Everything seemed as if it were placed piece by piece by some incredible force. Each mountain top seemed to be looking up at Pike's Peak, which is the highest peak in the entire mountain range. It almost seemed as if they were worshipping the granddaddy of all mountains.

We started to head out towards the east and noticed a remarkable change in the terrain, from incredible sized mountains to low sweeping plains. Then it just got extremely flat and spread out. It was a totally desolate area. Towns were spread from fifty to one hundred miles apart. Every now and then you might see a house out in the middle of nowhere. Seclusion took on a whole new meaning for me on this trip. I couldn't actually picture myself living like that. Some of these places were an easy twenty miles away from any type of civilization.

After flying for a while, I decided the only way to get a good visual fix on my position was to look at the whole area at once. The customary procedure is to simply look straight down and pick out different points that can be recognized with ease. Taking a wider scope of the area opened my eyes to something new I wanted to check out.

Forty miles off was the largest rainbow I had ever seen. I started to fly closer to it and two other rainbows popped out right next to it. Each one was exhibiting a full spectrum of colors that lit up the sky. The whole scene kind of made me respect mother nature in such a way that I flew around it all so as not to disturb anything. In the next few minutes we encountered a thunderstorm that turned us back to home.

Mother Nature gave us her best that day. I think that I couldn't have been in a better part of the country. It all seems to stem outward from the Rockies as if there was some controlling force making all of these miracles come out to play at once. Weather changes drastically in Colorado because of the radical wind currents in the mountains. Very soon after landing we found ourselves smack in the middle of a blizzard. This slowed our flying down somewhat, but at least we knew what we had to look forward to in the days to come.

Journal Entry 4-4-83
Diane Sagesser

Well, it's first time in a long time I write because of the vacation. I didn't do anything exciting the past week. I fertilized the lawn, and I had a fight with my aunt. She annoys me so much. She lives with my family, and I don't know if I can stand it much longer. She is such a picky person, she thinks she knows it all. One of these days, all my anger I feel towards her, I'm going to let out and then she'll really be sorry for trying to run my life. Anyway I have three mid-terms coming up and I really didn't study for any of them too good. I would like to get at least a B on all the tests. I found out I might be going to California for three weeks in the summer, I can't wait! Well, all in all I think my vacation was pretty good. Oh, on Thursday I'm going to Shea Stadium. My neighbor has season tickets and he asked me to go because he knows I like the Mets.

In April, Not in May

My aunt is divorced and recently moved from California to New York. She lives with us in our downstairs apartment. My Aunt Sally never had children, so the only thing she ever had to worry about was her house and how spotless the inside was and how well her outside grounds were. On the other hand, I am a very disorganized person. I do mow the lawn, fertilize the lawn, and weed the lawn. I also clean inside the house, but I shove things around, overstuff closets and drawers, and I don't worry about if I missed a spot or patch of the lawn. I don't have time to worry about nonsense like that because I have two jobs, go to school full time, and have to watch two younger sisters when my parents go to work. Now, my aunt has nothing better to do than pick at me all the time. My aunt tells me how to mow or fertilize, or when the right season is to fertilize, also she yells at me for over-stuffing the closets. Let me tell one argument we had! California weather is different than New York weather. People fertilize their lawns in May. But in New York most people do it in April. She took charge and ordered me not to do it until May. I said a few choice words to her and did it in April!

Aunt Sally not only thinks she's a professional at household chores but also at styles in clothes. She's forever telling me I still have my younger years ahead of me. Aunt Sally tells me I should stop wearing jeans and start wearing mini skirts. I should stop acting tough when a guy asks me if I need help, and I should start wearing makeup because I'm nineteen years old and I'm in college. Maybe she has a point on some things. Maybe I should get dressed up once in a while. Maybe I should wear makeup once in a while. I feel I should not do things I don't believe in. I have this theory that Aunt Sally wants me to be interested in the things she was interested in when she was younger. But I have different likes and dislikes and beliefs than she did or still does. I'd rather go to a ball game than go out to dinner, and rather play softball then get dressed up. My complexion is good most of the time, so I don't believe I need make-up. And why should some guy help me if I don't need help?

Maybe I should give in a little on some things. Maybe I shouldn't be so stubborn, just to ease up the tension a little that is between the two of us. It seems she'll be living with us for a while, so I'm going to have to learn to deal with her.

Journal Entry 3-7-83
Joanne Albertsen

Mrs. Fauth is another era. She does not rush around and compete with the craziness of today. She slows the world down to her pace. She is so supportive of me, she makes me feel good about myself. She encourages me to go to school when others feel it's a folly. She has sort of an elegance and charm most people seem to lack today. The funny thing is that she has singled me out for friendship. Isn't that great! She says "I march to the tune of a different drummer." I guess I do.

Another Era, a Different Drummer

As I pass Argyle Park, the gardens are in bright bloom. Water is gently flowing down the terraced falls with swans and Canadian geese gliding around the lake in the background. I turn at Argyle Avenue, a narrow, winding road with old trees sometimes causing traffic to flow into one lane. The town has often considered widening the road in past years but always met with opposition from the aged residents, and so it has remained for fifty years. As I pull up to number 43, I am always awed by the sight of this stately Victorian house with ornate trim in various stages of decay. The path to the front door is difficult to maneuver because of the healthy growth of lilacs barring my way. As I get closer I notice the white shingles are starting to flake and the trim is blistered and peeling. The green shutters are fading and the large old windows have screens that are slightly warped from countless summers and winters and don't quite set into the trim. Around back, the large sun porch, with wicker furniture still covered, looks out over the beautiful lake.

My knock is finally answered, and I am let into the comfortably decorated living room, twice the size of the efficient, compact rooms of today. My eyes are drawn to the delicate treasures displayed on mantle and tables. Mrs. Fauth, the lady of the house, seems as fragile as the lace curtains on the windows. Her naturally white hair is tinted grey and waves elegantly around her face. She has not been well this year and the dark circles under her eyes only accentuate her pale face. She is tall and thin and in the past few years, I notice the gentle sloping of her shoulders.

In a hoarse whisper she invites me to have tea, a weekly ritual for us. Although she only serves tea and biscuits, they are served on two little white trays, with lace doilies. The flowered china is chipped with fine cracks that don't somehow detract from its elegance. To Mrs. Fauth's eyes they are perfect and treated with care. We sit in the living room and I feel I am part of her past. She talks about the yacht club races and how she cheered on her son and husband, of parties on her lawn with lights and music, and her face lights up in the telling. She loved to entertain in the twenties; her parties were famous throughout the town. She always hired a band and made sure that everyone got up to dance. She loved being a trend setter and shocked everyone one summer by being the first to wear a flapper dress.

But all too soon she stops and I see her tire. I make my visit short today; she is not too well. This gentle lady has become a dear friend over the past eight years. Many of her friends have stopped by during our visits, and she has had a kind word for each of them. She has a unique talent for making people feel they are special.

As I leave today, I feel I am losing something wonderful from my life. Although she is still alive, she is fading slowly like her home before my eyes.

To watch this inevitable evolution is painful, but not to be a part of her life would be much worse.

Diary

Keep a diary for a number of weeks, making at least four or five entries a week. Allow ten to fifteen minutes to write down whatever seems important for that day or the previous. This is meant to record events and how you feel about them. It can be general or you can use it to focus on some speical pursuit or aspect of your life. Write with enough explanation so that you—and possibly someone else, if you want—will be able to understand it later. Although you may want to offer all or portions to others as is, one purpose is to provide details of the moment that you can summarize from the vantage point of the completed events. Often the complete diary, or a slightly edited version, such as the following, is readable and interesting enough to deserve an audience for its own sake, whether or not you also summarize it.

The Nationals

JOHN KOENIG

I remember looking at the flying team tryout results, not thinking I would make it—but I did. Sitting on Eastern's red eye to Los Angeles for the National Flying Competition, I was very excited and gung-ho like the rest of the team. I was thinking of palm trees, Universal Studios, Hollywood, and what a great time we're going to have—ten free days in California. (Little did I know what Bakersfield is like.)

I finally got to bed after being up for twenty-four hours. Flying out here, getting a rent-a-car, and finding a hotel made the day feel so long. My father, who flew out with us, left me at L.A. airport and went to our cousin's house in Santa Ynez. (We were to meet later in the week at Bakersfield.)

Day one, like all the rest, we were up at the crack of dawn. We rented two Cessna 152's in L.A. and flew them to Bakersfield. This is the first time I had ever flown over mountains. These mountains are 9,000 feet high and the planes can only fly 12,000 feet high. This is a situation where you don't want anything to go wrong—even in the slightest way. But, sure enough, on run-up before take-off the plugs were fouled or the mags were bad. We had the plugs cleaned and were off. Going over those mountains into the valley was absolutely beautiful but I always had a little insecure feeling in the back of my head— hoping the plugs wouldn't foul again.

Day two. Bakersfield is the pits. It's a big dust ball town with a bunch of oil fields. The only thing good about it is the weather.

Day four. The only thing I've been doing is practicing touch and goes. Our team attitude is bad. Ray says forget it, have a good time, we're no competition in the nationals. "We're going to get blown away." This disturbs me, I'm working very hard, trying hard to get used to the thermals in this hot weather. I'm learning how to fly all over again. I'm worried, I'm not being consistent.

Day five. Major Smith is due tomorrow so we all decided to have a vacation before he came. When he gets here the days will get longer and we will work harder. We decide to fly to the coast just south of Santa Barbara. What a beautiful day. When we flew back to Bakersfield, a few more teams had shown. The traffic patterns are getting crowded, making it harder to practice. Tension among the team is building, we need time away from each other.

Day six. I spoke to my father. He is in Santa Ynez. I made plans to fly in and get him. I was looking forward to seeing him. I was also starting to feel lonely. I left at 9 a.m. and visited a beautiful town of Santa Ynez. On our way back the clouds were starting to close in on the west side of the mountains. I got on top and my vacuum pump went. This caused all my gyro instruments to go on the blink. Thank goodness it was nice weather or I would have had some trouble—to say the least. My father stayed for two days and helped us practice our bomb drop. It was good to have him around. Dad took us out to dinner that night. He left the next morning for a friend's house in San Diego.

When he left I started crying and feeling very empty. I know I still have not begun to get over my mother's death.

Day eight. Major Smith's presence helps the team morale. The competition is only two days away. We are all starting to fall into the groove.

Day nine. Ray and I found a river valley. The next thing I knew I was chasing Ray through it. I never had such an exhilarating feeling in my life. I felt as if the airplane was an extension of my body. It was nice to fly around the valley for a change; it helped let off some steam.

Day ten. The competition went very fast. We were tense and ready. The other teams from our region were very friendly, like we were all one team, unlike the Regional Competitions, last fall. Their rivalry couldn't have been stronger.

Day eleven. Competition is over. We are on our way to the banquet. I was thinking in the back of my head, I wonder if I won something. Everyone else in the car was joking and talking about the prizes. I was in another world in anticipation. But I knew that if I didn't win anything I wouldn't be too disappointed. When the awards dinner was over we didn't do as well as we thought. Ray had a good score on his cross country event. But later, it turned out the judges mixed up the papers and Ray had won first place in navigation. That caused a lot of problems. It also put our team in second place. Ray won top pilot. Most disturbing of all we missed out on the awards acceptance.

Day twelve. Time to go home. It's Sunday, and we have to catch the 8 p.m. flight which would get me home Monday in time for English. We spent our last day touring L.A.. We were all proud of ourselves. I think Major Smith was the most excited. I don't push myself that hard very often. Bakersfield is probably the worst place to spend a vacation, but I wouldn't have passed this trip up for the world.

Diary Summary

Write an account of the material covered by the diary. Eliminate the dates; summarize so that you blend things into one continuous whole. Feature what seems most important to you and what you think will most interest some audience you have in mind. You're free to cut and add material and to reorganize according to your purpose as you look back. Fit length to whatever the main subject seems to require and choose your audience according to the direction this takes.

Down to Reality
CINDY BOONE

College-life activities—parties, dances, close friendships—are just a few of the expectations of university life. I never realized that I had those dreams until looking back through the pages in my diary. Over the last five weeks it seems that I summed up my life at college—hard work and not much play.

My greatest disappointment was the quantity and relationships of friends, which I thought would be abundant and close. I never realized how difficult it would be to find just a few who were special. Most are just people to talk with in passing. Class time does not permit time to meet people. Everyone is too busy listening to the professor and taking notes. Most of my time after class is spent doing homework. All the friends I have now I met during the first week of the fall quarter, welcome week.

My friends are warm and good companions but not ones to lean on for emotional support. They are there for good times, going to a movie or throwing a birthday party, and also they are willing to help with homework problems. But they are not to be counted on in times of trouble. For this I would have to relie on myself and my friends back home.

It is easy to become lonely and feel like an outsider. At the beginning of this quarter I felt much like the Sun God, so alone, on the outside. Spring break was so relaxing, but then coming back here was a shock, especially when I found out that I got a "D" in chemistry. I felt my whole world collapsing around me. I thought I would have no chance to go into nursing, my intended major, but slowly I've accepted the poor mark and have been getting back into the swing again as my calculus mid-term showed—ninety-eight out of a hundred!

The work load is incredible. Monday through Friday, plus all day Saturday and Sunday. Nights are spent doing homework or cramming for exams. Sure, there are a couple of parties on the weekends, but these are only enjoyable if you are fond of getting drunk, which I'm not. In the last five weeks I've gone to a few school events—a square dance, a Monty Python movie, and the Sparks' concert. The dance and concert were especially fun, letting me be able to get a release from the week. At events such as these I really do enjoy myself, but sitting through "Monty Python Live at the Hollywood Bowl" was a waste of time for me. Sure, it was humorous but would have been more so if I were a Python follower. So I wasn't too thrilled with it.

There has been only one weekend in which I was off campus. My parents came to visit and took me to Los Angeles to go shopping. I spent Saturday night and Sunday relaxing at my room-mate's house in Palas Verdes after my folks flew back to the Bay Area.

What keeps me going now is my dreams of summer vacation, being able to see my close friends again, my boy friend, and have a summer job. I've already applied for several and have had one long-distance interview over the telephone. I'm hoping to get a job working with children. There has always been a special place in my life for them. There seem to be too many people who don't care for youth, so I want to show that I do care. With my summer dreams and busy schedule with school, time should pass quickly for me.

From reading over my diary I see the reality of college life, the bed of roses that it isn't. I see my disappointments from the disillusion that is caused by hearing only the memorable events from others at college who neglected to tell the hardships too. But when I compare myself now with when I just got to UCSD I can't regret ever coming. My maturation is enormous. As long as I got something out of being here it was well worth while.

Taking Stock
PETER WILDHORN

As I looked through my "diary" to try to assemble all of the entries on education in some kind of cohesive, understandable manner, I became amazed at the extent to which I wrote about the negative aspects compared to the positive on this subject. My amazement lies in the basic reason for which I chose to attempt to write on the subject of education. At this point in my life, school has the biggest influence on my day-to-day activities. I feel like I am in a minority, because I actually *want* to learn. This is the reason for which I am in college. When quarters end, I find myself almost bored, because of the sudden lack of responsibilities. I never thought I would feel this way about school. Also, the more I learn, the more I realize just how little I know. This makes me want to learn more and more. It is for these reasons that I was so amazed that my diary entries were so negative.

A lot of problems that I found were ones that took effect before a person began his education. First, high school does not prepare the student for college. Even the so-called "college level" classes (Advanced

Placement) fail to give one a good idea of what is required in a class in college. A student going to a college like UCSD is usually in the top ten percent, or so, of his graduating class. Also, in high school, a resourceful person could get by with a minimal amount of work and still graduate and get into a good college. Therefore, it can be very difficult for such a student, when he gets to college and finds himself working hard and maybe only getting C's. This can really upset a student's motivation and self-confidence.

Another problem is the lack of importance placed on a good education, except to the end of getting a well-paying job. College seems to have become a place to train for a job, instead of a place to learn. Thus the importance of being intelligent is relatively little. The "famous" people all seem to have nothing to do with intellect. The people most talked about and idolized are sports figures and performers (film and music) with the small exception of some politicians who may or may not possess some intelligence. Whatever happened to the days when the respected people were the intellectuals (like Aristotle, or any of the other philosophers, theologians, or prophets)? People see the "easy way" to "get ahead" and that is what they want to do. Why work when you don't have to? And as a result of this minor role of education, those who want good educations may be deprived in that money allocated to education is decreasing proportionately rather than increasing. An example of what this lack of funding does occurred when I was almost unable to continue my math sequence. There were about 150 people waiting for this class. The rooms were available, but there was not enough money to pay a professor and a few TAs to do one more class. As a result, over a hundred people were forced to discontinue—due to no fault of their own. It is hard to believe that an advanced society such as ours would show so little concern for its future. It is sad.

This problem affects a student's college education in other ways. The basic problem is that the student feels a great pressure to take classes needed to get a degree as soon as possible so that he can either continue the education or go to work. This pressure is the basis for most of the problems encountered in college.

To begin with, this pressure is most evident when one takes a test. When you take a class where the grade rests solely on your performance on one, two, or three tests, there is no room for mistakes. If anything is wrong when you are taking one of these tests, like sickness, or any other valid reason, you are out of luck—your grade suffers. The solution is to give more tests, to leave more room for error. In this way, there would be less pressure, less disappointment, and less giving up.

Another negative is the pressure put on the student to find a major, take the necessary classes, and graduate in four years. School is made more difficult if you don't know in what you want to major. You need to take classes in all different fields so you can find something you like. Plus, you have to do well in all of them in case you decide to study them in more depth. It makes it hard to get a "well-rounded" education if it is important to graduate in four years.

Another result of the pressure is the feeling of having to keep up with the next guy. Many professors seem to be oblivious to the fact that you have other classes. Maybe they love their field so much that they think everyone will want to do a huge amount of work for that class. As a result, work tends to pile up despite the valiant tries to keep up. There are times in every quarter when a lot of things happen to be due very close together. All one can do is give up needed sleep and become anti-social.

Lastly, this great competition (of trying to *stay ahead* of the next guy) creates a population of robots instead of people. These robots are those who get so tied up in competing for good grades (this is especially true in the sciences) that they become completely mechanized. They eat, sleep, study, and go to class—and that is it. Any social skills are lost. This may seem a bit extreme, but I have seen it many times.

From reading the foregoing criticisms, one might conclude that I feel there are no redeeming qualities to college. If I believed this, I wouldn't be here. One can have a good experience—they are just getting rarer. An example is my psychology class. The teacher *and* the TAs are really interested in helping you learn the material. They do a lot of work to help the students. It is a good feeling to see someone cares.

One of the best parts of college is the contact that one has with all different people. I feel I have learned more from the people around me, thus far, than in all my classes put together. You get exposed to different views on almost every subject. Each argument has its validity and its faults and one can learn from both on any issue.

There are good and bad things about these aspects of college. First, I will explain the bad. The pressure seems to enhance people's desire to drink alcohol and take drugs. They are able to loosen inhibitions *and* not have to worry about how badly they are doing. It's so easy.

The worst part is that students seem to get "tunnel vision." They study their subject and that's it. Many become insensitive to what is going on in the world. There's nothing in this country that resembles the hundreds of thousands of people who gather to protest social issues in small towns in countries like Germany. There needs to be a higher value placed on knowledge and awareness here. But the question is, is it possible? I think not.

The problems with the college system do have their positive

fallouts. For one, college helps the maturity process. There is a huge increase in responsibility. Suddenly, one must take care of all of his/her needs. There is no one to buy the food, cook, drive places, pick things up, clean, help with homework, and most importantly, there is no one to push you to do your work. *You* have to motivate *yourself*. If you don't do it, it won't get done. This brings me to the other positive result of the negative aspects of college; you must learn to manage your time, and to concentrate on what you are doing. You need to be able to plan your time and then stick to what you have set out to do. This means being able to concentrate on what you are doing in each time period so that you will be able to stick to a schedule when it is needed. This becomes very important when you have things to do other than huge amounts of homework.

In conclusion, I feel that the problem lies in the misinterpretation of the function served by a college education. This education has come to be thought of as a tool that gives you a future in some field. Actually, this education should only give you the tools with which you can shape your future to what you would like it to be. It (education) is not a training camp for a job, but a foundation to find what is best for you, and then you may apply it to further study in the field. In short, a college education is only what you make it. It can be a one-sided view of one subject, or it can be a well-rounded education that gives insight into the human condition from many different perspectives.

Recollection

(Looking Back)

Memories

Look around at your surroundings until something you
see reminds you of an event or person or place from your past.
Write that down. What does that memory in turn remind you
of? Keep the chain of memories going. Write pell-mell without
worrying about completeness or correctness. Get down a lot of
material to choose from later.

With the help perhaps of partners with whom you talk
over these notes, you can go a couple of ways at this point. One
is to pluck out a single memory that seems to have promise and
expand it by jotting down more details about it. A second is to
look for threads or themes across a number of apparently
jumbled or unrelated memories and to make notes on the
continuity or connections you now see among them.

Now compose a memory piece comprehensible and interesting to some audience you fix in mind. Use your notes, but
feel free to go as far beyond them as you need to to do justice to the
memory or memory thread that has emerged. Starting to
compose may trigger more details or more ideas about a theme.
Try out a draft on partners and revise for a final version to
print up with other memories by you or others, or deliver as a
reading to some audience.

[The following samples include the notes from which they
were written.]

Memory Train
Paul Barrera

windshield wipers
airport
my mother
Dad taking us home
the way we fought
Edward's fault
my fault

I hit him
my mother gone
my father left
my father's wife
tricks we played
I hate divorce

Divorce and Revenge

Probably the most devastating thing that can happen to a family, besides a death, is divorce. It hit my home with a bang. The whole mess really didn't make any sense to me. I mean I couldn't imagine not seeing Dad any more. I was twelve when it happened. I wasn't even there actually. I was in Milwaukee, where every American kid is when his parents are getting a divorce.

Over the summer of 1975, what a bad year. I remember coming home from the airport. My father came to greet me. All seemed to be normal. On the way home I recall the rain hitting the hood and the wipers going back and forth and back and forth and my father telling me that my mother wasn't going to be home when I got there.

Well, we finally got home after a car ride that seemed so, so long. The whole time I was wondering how could Mom not be there. We stepped in the door, and just as he said it would be, it was motherless.

I can't explain how empty I was. My three brothers and I used to be frequently caught by my father, blaming each other. It was Frank's fault, he was seven, because he was always complaining. It was Edward's fault, he was ten, because he was Edward, and it was my fault because I used to bring mud in the house from playing soccer. The only thing we could agree on was that it wasn't Anthony's fault, he was fourteen, because he was so wonderful—and could beat us up!

I suppose after everything was final and done the only thing to do was to find out whose fault it was. Well, to shorten the investigation we discovered it was my father's. I guess that's pretty normal. I think that we understood what life was to be like from that day on, but it wasn't. It turned out my mother got custody of us and my pop had to pack his bags.

Before my father left the house my brothers and I wondered where my mother had been all this time. As it turned out it was not only that my mother was in the hospital but that she was there because of a nervous breakdown.

As far as Anthony and I were concerned my father could have gone straight to hell. Personally I lost most of my respect for my father that day that I heard about this. I just couldn't believe that my own father would do such a thing to my mother, his "wife." While my mother was recovering from this illness it was housekeeper after housekeeper. It was sickening!

Now that I think about it I realize how lousy we really were. The housekeeper would cook something and one of us little terrors would dump a touch of garlic or something else just to make the food taste so bad we wouldn't eat anything and my father would have to fire her. I can't believe some of the things we used to pull on these defenseless employees.

We used to give them the silent treatment, make a total mess of the house just before my father got home. The worst thing we ever did was tell Frank to go over his friend's house for the day and tell the housekeeper that he disappeared and we couldn't find him. She'd go crazy! It was great! Then when my father got home she'd tell him that Frank was missing, and all of a sudden we'd remember that he was over at a friend's house. We had to have some fun; it was hard, but we had to do something to avenge, as it were, my mother's situation.

When my mother came home and my father was gone it was much better. As young children, and as a "teenager" as he (Anthony) liked to be called, we needed a mother. It was so much easier to get to sleep and wake up knowing your mother was going to be there.

Years went by and my father remained away. And my mother, the saint that she is, still takes good care of her four kids. We see my father as little as possible. And we never bend over backwards for his wife. Sometimes I laugh at the table at their house in New Jersey when I think of what we had done to those poor housekeepers, and how I wish we could do the same things to this new "housekeeper" of his.

People say that if your parents smoke, the children will smoke. If the parents drink, the children will drink. And if the parents divorce the children too will divorce. When I get married, if I do at all, I will do everything in my power to prevent anything from falling apart. I wouldn't want my kids to go through what I had to go through. That would be very, very cruel.

Notes Expanding One Memory
Susan Swift

The photographs on the small hand carved table, pictures of family, friends. Wedding pictures and pictures of nieces and nephews.

The one picture that really sparks the memory is the one in the ceramic frame with the small pink flowers. This reminds me of a day when myself and my two cousins, Dot and Peggy, went to visit a great-aunt and uncle with my grandmother. We were about 5 years old and it was such an adventure. We had never been there before. Aunt Jo made it so special. She had the table set as if it were a party and we ate candy and cookies before lunch, which is every childs fantasy. I can remember how all their home was decorated so frilly and fancy, old fashioned. At the time I could not help but feel a little frightened because I remember that Uncle Eddie was a massive man and always had a cigar in his mouth. I felt it strange that they had no children and that maybe Uncle Ed was bad or something. Aunt Jo showed us all around the house. Although it was so pretty it was also lonely. At that age I was somewhat frightened of older people. But they made the day so delightful. All the bed spreads and curtains were lacy and light. She had little figurines that you knew were just to look at and not to handle. Her china had little flowers and was ever so fragile and we felt like three little princesses. There was a festive feel about the day and Aunt Jo made it that way. She always dressed so flamboyantly and gay and gives one the impression that she doesn't take life too seriously. Her hair jet black and always smiling, never sits down and talks to you as if she were a social director when she told us what she had planned for our day. Uncle Eddie, I learned later was a sweet, gentle man. I can remember once later, after the time we visited them that he brought Aunt Jo over to our house one day and he sat in the car and waited. I walked over to the side walk and we had a conversation of sorts. Because of the cigars he would discharge of the bits of tobacco that came off the end and got in his mouth. In other words he spit a lot. Brazen as I was at 5 I suggested that he not do it anymore for it wasn't polite. He cheerfully humored me, (5 year olds are very sincere), and stopped at once assuring me that I was absolutely right. I think it's a shame that two such loving people deprived themselves and their unborn children of all the love and fun that I imagined they could have had.

The Porcelain Frame

It's the end of the day, and I'm sitting on the sofa winding down and just letting thoughts come and go as they please. I'm in an almost dream-like state when my glance falls on the small ceramic picture frame, the one with the tiny pink flowers, which we received for a wedding gift. I find myself trying to recall who gave it to us, and my thoughts drift to a day, a good many years ago. Myself and my two cousins went to visit a great-aunt and uncle who lived somewhere in Queens. They lived in an old house, and it seemed as though no one really lived there. Everything was so elegant and looked like a picture on an old fashioned post card. There were lovely little nick-nacks everywhere and they were exclusively for the eye to behold and not to be handled, fragile figurines of ballerinas and courting couples, beautiful tea cups and saucers with delicate little flowers. All through the day we were distracted as we noticed each and every treasure.

None of us had ever been there before and we were quite giddy. Our grandmother guided the excursion and also served as our security in this social outing.

The table was set as if it were a party, and we ate cookies and candy before lunch, every child's fantasy. Aunt Jo made it so special as though she were entertaining three little princesses. She always dressed so flamboyantly and gay. Her hair was jet black and she constantly smiled. She flitted about and spoke as if she were a social director as she told us of her plans for the day.

Uncle Eddie, sweet and docile as always, had a cigar clinging to his lips. It seemed to me that he did little else but adore his wife, and they did adore each other. I could not understand why two people with such lovely things and such love to give never had children. Although their home was so lovely, it was lonely, a museum of sorts. It would have been a wonderful place for them to share with a child.

We laughed and played games all day, and I think they persuaded us to stay for dinner. It's funny, I can't remember what, if anything made up the meal. I do know that Aunt Jo prepared little packages of candy for each of us to take home.

Although the day had been exciting I found myself anxious to go home. I missed my mother and father and even my two brothers. It's nice to be treated specially, but it's also nice to have a family, to wish them away when you want but to be sure they are always there.

Aunt Jo hasn't changed much. She's still wearing flashy outfits and getting the kids involved at family gatherings. Uncle Ed is gone now. Although my Aunt has married again, and still has her menagerie of exquisite finery, I can't help wonder if it's enough. Does she ever wish she had had a child, a part of her departed husband, to keep his memory alive?

Memory Train
Kathleen Kenney

Sister Carlotta	Fear of speaking
Hate	Fear
Silence	swollen face
gray building	stomach in a turmoil

humiliation
Sixth grade
my place
the sisters

reading
speaking
fear

Speaking Out in Class

Communicating with others is very difficult for me. I have problems speaking out loud. It's not that I have nothing intelligent to say. I do. It's just that I start to recall many horrible experiences growing up in a Catholic school as a child. I know I have to overcome my fears, but it's not easy, for it took a long time to understand what has happened to me. Going back in time I tend to shut out the bad incidents in my mind. It's like shutting off the running water of a faucet.

Being in Sister Carlotta's class in the sixth grade was devastating for me. I can recall many agonizing moments of feeling confused and defeated. Being stripped bare of self-worth is putting it mildly. The everyday suffering I had to endure at times was more than one small person could stand.

However, like most middle-class Catholic families in our neighborhood, we all belonged to the parish. You had no choice if you were Catholic. You belonged; your children went to their school. You lived and abided by their rules and commands, or else you were damned, and of course you would surely burn in hell for eternity, as we were all told.

The nuns and priests at that time when I was growing up were supposed to be the sacred, blessed people, followers of God, put here on this earth to preach the holy gospel, to teach and show children and adults the divine path to follow, the newer philosophers of our time like Aristotle in his.

In school I felt we were brain-washed day after day. I would listen with tender young ears to tales and settings I couldn't quite visualize, my mind absorbing the aftermath of a bad flood. They just poured it in and in. Day after day I read from the catechism the messages and passages that showed only the good, Christian Catholic people crusading for one thing or another.

Sr. Carlotta was great for this; she would be preaching on and on about the ten commandments and about the humanities of life. Looking back now, what a sad, sadistic joke to have played on the young, to have had Sr. Carlotta in charge of ethical studies.

It's ironic, I think, to have had this sister of the faith teaching gullible frightened children. It's funny though, when a horse becomes old and sick we put it out to pasture without regrets. Why the parish pastor kept her in class to teach was beyond me. I know for a fact that she is long dead, but if there is a God I know where she is today and all the prayers in the world could not save her wicked soul.

The parish I belonged to was a prison and I was the prisoner. The tall two-tone grey brick building with its six-foot iron picket fence around still stands today. My dues though are paid today in full for my innocent crimes.

I can still recall the cold eerie feelings I would get inside me, always hesitating before walking through the entrance. Even if the sun was shining bright the day always felt like darkest winter. The minute my foot crossed that thin line on the pavement, a heavy weight, an unseen cloud entered my body and mind. To me it always felt like the end and not the beginning. This feeling stayed with me each and every day of my sixth-grade school year. How I ever survived is beyond me.

Once inside I knew I was not safe, for I knew Sr. Carlotta was indeed lurking in the halls, waiting impatiently, with a wooden ruler in hand for her students to come to class. The minute I saw her I wanted desperately to run. There was no mistaking her for someone else. Her face was chubby; her eyes a cold dark stare. You never saw her hair, but it must have been black, for she had a faint dark moustache and a few black unruly strands of hair on her double chin. She was truly ugly inside and out. I used to think she was a man under all that garb. Even her hands were huge and masculine. Maybe she lifted weights in some deep dark part of the convent.

Upon entering her classroom I would run to my special seat. I'm surprised she didn't nail us to our desk like Christ to his cross. Usually seating was assigned according to last name, height, or medical problems. But not Sr. Carlotta's class. She had her own method. She divided us up by our intelligence, or should I say our lack of it, and she made it known to all.

Sr. Carlotta would humiliate us, disgrace us and call us names that fit our I.Q. She would call us words like "dummy," "stupid," and "imbeciles." Her words raped us of our pride. Her words were sharper than the stings of a hundred wasps, and the pain lasted longer than time itself.

She would wear this funny grin on her swollen face to remind us all she hated kids. I appalled her, and she was aware of this. Because I was slower than most, I would daydream and wish I were somewhere else. My stomach was always in a turmoil and my body weak with emotions. She would continually harass me, and she would never let up. Instead of helping me she continued to inflict pain on me.

One day that I recall like yesterday Sr. Carlotta called on me to read out loud. She really enjoyed hearing children make mistakes just so she could make fun of us.

Each of us had a spot next to our desks where we would kneel to say the rosary on hard wooden floors, where we would kneel to receive punishment, or where we would stand to recite our lessons. It was our personal place. That day while standing frozen in the spot that I knew so well, with my book in hand I started to read.

I was not even out of the first paragraph when she complained I was not reading fast enough for her. As I tried to find my place and began to read again she banged her wooden ruler on her big mahogony desk. I jumped with fear as she yelled that I was not reading loud enough for her. Again I began reading faster and louder. I began to shake inside. I wanted to die right then and there. By then I was reading just words, words that had no meaning for me, just plain black marks on white paper in a book. I just wanted to get done. That was my mistake because I started to lose it and I started to mispronounce the words. She was so angry. She stood screaming and saying how stupid of me to fumble over such simple words.

Sr. Carlotta went on and on, her words harsher and harsher, and my classmates started to giggle softly. By this time I started to go into my secret hiding place. In my mind I had to shut out the laughter of others and her mean harsh voice. I had no more feelings. My body stood there frozen, but my mind slipped away until I heard nothing but only saw ugly moving lips and angry gestures.

Needless to say this happened many more times until the end of my sixth-grade class. Sr. Carlotta saw me unfit to be promoted.

Still to this day this stigma still stands firm in my mind, but I honestly can deal with it, and one day I will overcome my fears of speaking out in class and sharing my voice.

Memory Notes
Maria Whitnum

Chalkboard—all kinds of formulas that make no sense.
Early class—in fact the first one.
Dreaded the class.
Constantly watched the clock.
Stern teacher who had very little hair.
Text book thick and written in some unknow language.
Subject giving me a headache.
Devoted much time to it.
Sitting in class. Teaching something new—
    something to do with Δx's and Δy's.

Puzzled by the whole procedure and just kept jotting down what was on the board.

Remember getting a chill when the teacher called on me and asked me the answer to the example he just had given.

I said very low that I didn't know. Told me to go through the steps. Humiliated. I couldn't begin. Started saying how I should pay more careful attention. Felt like crying. Time seemed to stand still. Couldn't get away. He made me do the problem with him echoing behind me.

After class I approached him and told him I didn't appreciate him putting me on the spot and suggested that I would like to drop out of course. He told me bluntly no! I decided to go home and go back to bed.

Two Teachers

The chalkboard in the center of the room reminds me of my twelfth grade calculus course. It was the first class of the day and the hardest one I was taking. I had a very stern teacher who wore a crew cut all year long. The book for the course was a very thick one written in some unknown language.

I always had trouble with the course, but on this one particular day I couldn't get started at all. I remember sitting in the classroom at 7:30 on a dreary cold morning. The teacher was demonstrating a new formula, something to do with delta x's and delta y's. Actually I think we were working with some kind of derivatives. I was totally puzzled by the whole procedure and decided to jot down every piece of information whether it was written on the infamous chalkboard or spoken by my drill sergeant. As I was writing down the formula, I got a cold chill and with that the teacher called on me to give the answer for the first example. I said in a very low tone that I didn't know and continued writing down the formula. If nothing else, it kept me from looking at everyone looking at me. But he wasn't going to leave me alone.

He said abruptly to go through the steps and derive the answer. I looked at the board with despair and just didn't know where to start. I felt so humiliated and wondered why he was doing this to me. I felt like crying, and all the arrows and x's and y's seemed to be all over the place. I felt like running as far as I could. Time just seemed to stand still. He began yelling and made me do the problem with him pointing to each step I had to do. Finally the bell rang. Everybody ran to the door and left.

I decided that I was going to tell this teacher what I thought of his teaching methods. I approached him slowly, remembering the ordeal he just put me through. He looked up at me with anger and asked me impatiently what I wanted. I told him that I didn't appreciate being humiliated like that. He told me without hesitation that I should pay more attention. I explained to him on the verge of tears, but as calmly as I could, that I just did not understand this topic. I suggested that maybe I should drop the course and he bluntly told me no way. I decided to go home and go back to bed after this because I just couldn't face any of my peers.

At the end of the year I took the final exam and failed by one point, which resulted in my failing the course. Later I took the course for my benefit at Stony Brook, hired a tutor and earned an A. The calculus course had no effect on my graduation because it was an elective, but I'll never forget that awful day.

This brought back memories of my eighth grade Iowa tests. They had a section on graphs which I didn't do well on. It was the only section I didn't score well in the 90's. It was because of this that I got to know my guidance counselor very well.

I was summoned to her office to go over the results of my tests. When we got to the section of the graphs, I was astonished that I did very poorly on it. She must have realized that and made a joke about it, which made me feel more comfortable. While she was talking to me, I noticed the surroundings of her office. It was very small but it had so much love in it. It actually made the room seem bigger. She had many plants in this tiny room, and her desk was cluttered with all sorts of papers.

We started talking about my future plans, and at that time I wasn't sure what I wanted to do because of my fear of leaving junior high. She picked up on this and started talking to me about herself at my age. She sounded like a close friend talking about her past experiences. She encountered the same fears and feelings I was having and more. She was a poor student and since she didn't have the kind of money you need to go to college, she just about gave up the idea.

She'll never know, but from the moment she told me that, I had the greatest respect and admiration for her. She began talking to me about the possibilities of college. We talked a long time about many things and the guidance counselor was no more. She had become a close friend of mine that day. The only thing I wasn't pleased about, was that I didn't get to know her sooner, because I could have used a friend like her in seventh grade.

Memory Notes
Roger Bly

    -Stupid questions
    -want for understanding

-want to talk
-Critical/sceptic
-Sour/old
-Rebelious/young
-Merv the pervert
-William Catt
-foreigners (Mexicans/Japs/Europeans)
-Cash Control
-employee interaction (girl w/Mercedes)
-lunch break
-Supervisor (lax)
-Rush vs. Slow periods
-discust for people

The Scene
-scream/crying kids
-beer-reeking Mexicans
-Catalina Island
-Sky tower
-reek of ocean (damp-fishy smell)

Marineland

I never looked forward to summer jobs. This was because all the jobs I had been able to get during past summers were the same— unskilled (not that I really had a skill), boring, and inhumanly repetitious. From cooking hamburgers to stocking warehouses, I had done it all, and it was all the same. But it was something I had to do, for two reasons.

"Every college-bound highschooler should work hard in the summer to put money away," my parents would scream against my threats to become a beach bum, probably because they didn't want to pay as much, and I immensely enjoyed having a $100 pay check at my disposal each week. I enjoyed the end, but not the means. The summer before college I hoped would be different. I started work at Marineland, aware that a job at this "fish zoo" probably would be as dull and monotonous as any other minimum-wage summer job, but I was certain it had to be more interesting than making french fries at McDonald's.

Since I had been hired by the merchandise department, I had expectations of working in some dismal souvenir shop, selling plastic whales to mobs of Japanese kids, but fate dealt me a kind hand that day, and I found myself working in games. The games department really wasn't much of a department. It consisted of a dime-toss, a ring-toss, a hoop-toss, and a semifunctional water-race game. I and about six other employees would stand dressed in blue and white sailor suits, collect money, and watch for obvious cheaters, the ones that would lean over the counter and almost drop their ring on the bottle.

"Sorry sir, you can't do that!" I would say in a casual voice.

"What d'ya mean? Can I lean just a little?" the guy would say, thinking he was a real comedian.

"Can you read?" I would sneer back, pointing to the large sign directly in front of him: "NO LEANING."

None of it was really that hard; if by chance, someone won, I was supposed to act excited and make as much noise as possible when I handed them the prize. If they lost I would force a smile and utter, "Oh...you were pretty close" or "It is pretty windy right now"; the idea was to give them a scapegoat, some way to justify their losing, and if you didn't ask them to, they would probably play again.

Water Race was the game we drew straws for; the loser had to work it. The entire game was shooting water at stupid sea horses and trying to get yours to the top first. The real problem was that the game had degenerated to a point well beyond repair. Only half the guns worked, and even those malfunctioned now and then. At first I felt bad every time someone's gun didn't work right and would give them a refund or let them play again, but I soon learned it was easier to not do anything unless they complained, to stand there with a hardened heart, insensitive to the whole mess. They wanted us to talk like horse-race announcers on the microphone, but I kept my speech short as possible. Over a hundred times a day:

"OK you're aiming at the red dot in the middle of the star... ready, get set, and fire!" I'd reach up to hit the red button which started the game, waiting for a second after I said "fire" so they would realize who was in control.

"And they're off...Number two's in the lead with five and six close behind...two, five, six, and fourteen all neck to neck...it's going to be a close race...and number fourteen wins it by a nose!"

"Fourteen won again! fourteen always wins! this game is fixed!"

"No, this game is computer-controlled, all the guns are the same," I would reply in the most authoritative voice I could muster. I often had to bite my tongue in order to keep a straight face when I said this. "Computer controlled" was stretching things a bit, but it seems when-ever people hear the word "computer" they instantly back down, "Oooh...I see, computer, eh."

One good thing about Water Race, in fact the only good thing about it, was that you had an excellent view of the sea lion petting tank. Not that sea lions were that exciting, but to see some of those girls in their summer clothes, leaning over that tank wall, getting all excited over touching a smelly "seal," it was heaven!

"Hey mister, where's my prize?"

"What?" I would say, slipping back to reality.

"I won, where's my prize?"

"Oh...I already gave you a prize." I didn't think I had, but most of these little Mexican kids were great con artists; you had to bluff, just in case.

"No, you didn't, I just won!"

"Well ok, what color would you like—white, pink or blue fish?"

"I want a Shamoo!"

"We don't have Shamoo here; if you want a Shamoo you'll have to go to Sea World." I hated it when people called our whales Shamoos. Why would you name a killer whale "Shamoo" anyway? As soon as everybody had left, I would slip back and adjust the control labeled "14," and of course practice a few games to make sure things were working ok.

If Water Race was the worst, then without a doubt, Dime-toss was my favorite game to work. I would stand in my place, arms crossed, one leg bent back behind me to lessen the weight on my feet, observing from this spot the barrage of activity around me. They would dart around with child-like energy from this to that, from show to show, from restaurant to shop. They were here not to observe, but to be entertained, to look on in a mindless, consumptive state. To be led by the hand, to be smiled at, talked to, and made happy. But what this mass of tourists never realized, as they scurried from here to there, criticized our games, and complained about our food, was that they were also on exhibit; they were our school of fish, our entertainment. And they were indeed a show, as well trained and predictable as the seals and dolphins for whom they cheered; only now we were the audience. Dime-toss was in fact a curious game, to some as addicting as the one-armed bandits of Vegas. I had seen men spend $20 in dimes trying to win one of the huge St. Bernard dogs. But even Dime-toss had its trying moments. Occasionally when a group of Japanese tourists would be walking by, one of them would become excited over our display of stuffed animals and drag the whole group over. As they approached, dressed in loose cotton pants, white shirts, sailor hats, and cameras dangling from their necks, they resembled a small army marching toward us.

"JAP Attack!" I would yell to the employee next to me. They would stand for several minutes in a semicircle around us, oooing and awwwing, yipping back and forth in their native tongue. Finally one of them would pop the inevitable question—remember, I said they were predictable.

"How much does cost?"

"It's ten cents, ten cents a throw," I would say sarcastically, "that's why we call it the Dime-Toss."

"Oh, how you play?" another would interject in a strong accent and nervous expression.

"Well...all you have to do is get one of your dimes to stay on one of these here plates and win a dog," I would say in my best red-neck voice, probably too fast for them to fully comprehend.

"One dime...on plate?"

"Right!"

"And you win dog?"

"Yep!" Now they were pushing it.

"One of those big dogs?"

"Sure do." I wanted to say "No! we have smaller ones under the counter that we give as prizes, these big ones are out just to attract people like you," but I didn't want to be too harsh. When you think about it, a large part of their impression of America rested in my hands.

"Here...which is dime?" One of them would jut a hand full of American and Canadian coinage into my face.

"There, that one a dime," I would say in an unconciously mocking voice. They all would search through their change, looking for Roosevelt's face. Soon a barrage of dimes would be dinging and donging around me.

Dime-Toss wasn't really that hard to win at. It's just that most people were so convinced the odds were against them that they couldn't help but lose. What's funny is that when someone really concentrated and won, it attracted many other people, who, seeing that it could be done, were for some strange reason able to win where they hadn't been able to before. The strangeness of human nature never ceases to astound me.

For a summer I passed the time and escaped boredom by observing people. But even this entertainment, after a while, turned to boredom in itself. My communication with the guests was limited to twenty-odd phrases which I used almost unconsciously. The people were all the same; and such predictability in repetition makes the most exciting show boring after a single viewing, be the performers people or dolphins.

Autobiography and Memoir

Autobiography: Incident

*Tell an incident that happened to you some time in the
past, an incident being a specific occurrence that took place only
once, on a certain day or mostly on one day. Think of who
might want to hear or read this and where or how.*

A Sunday Night

LAURA HITCHCOCK

I remember playing with my father in our kitchen, playing toss
and catch with a little rubber super ball, which when thrown had a lot
of energy. As Dad threw I lunged toward the tiny ball; and when I did
I felt a quick jolt of pain as the raw edge of the cupboard sliced
through my ankle. I jumped into my father's lap. Blood splattered on
the floor. My brother said that there had been a puddle, but I only
remember seeing a spatter on the floor out of the corner of my eye. I
was taken to the doctor, stitched up and sent home. When we got
home Urban, my brother, told me about the mess. I wasn't impressed
nor grossed out. I figured it probably took him longer than it had to
because he's so slow and methodical.

I marched into school the next day as any other brave soldier
would. Pain never fazed me then. After I came home my brother
seemed concerned about me. I thought that was pretty weird. He
offered to read to me out of one of his school books. In the middle of
the line he stopped and quickly placed a hen's peck on my hand. I
bellowed a loud "yucky" and quickly wiped the "germs" off my hand. I
was seven, and if you kissed me I would have belted you, as one grade-
school boy found out. He hid his face; I was immediately sorry that I
had embarrassed him. I hadn't meant to.

He never showed affection; at that age we ignored each other. He
was immersed in books, I in boxball and jungle gyms. I could never
remember him without an armload of school books. When in fourth
grade it seemed his life's calling was to be a chemist. Before he became
Urban to me, he was the mad scientist, Gilbert Chemistry set and all.
He eventually did go off to college to make fizzles and booms, and
through those years we seemed to drift into each other's life more and

more. We fought as brothers and sisters do, but we became friends rather than brother and sister. I began to realize that he really wasn't so distant and really did have some of my interests.

Now he's concerned with my college life, and I dabble in his love life. I never thought I would tell him about some of the jerks I've gone out with. But then I seem to become better friends with boys than girls. So why shouldn't my best boy friend be my brother? When he becomes my best friend I ought to be sure to let him know. He's defended me when my parents wouldn't, told Mom not to worry about me when she did. Actually he told her I was a pretty level-headed kid for my age. He respected and listened to my viewpoint when nobody else would. We're not ever totally open with each other. We don't run to each other first with every piece of news, but we find out stuff.

When I was seven I never thought I'd miss him like I do now. Even during college when he came home for fifteen minutes he was fun. "I've had my quota, let's ship him back to Ithaca." He went to college and became the extrovert. He was painfully shy in high school. I came to college and became the introvert. I had my fun in high school; now it's time to get serious.

That day way back when my brother showed me that first piece of himself, I began to realize I must not be just the pesky little sister I usually was. It was a momentary but permanent alteration in our friendship.

My mom removed that cupboard from the kitchen and replaced it with a set of wooden drawers. It sits in the shed to this day, and I notice I'm always cautious around it. I wonder why my mom never threw it out?

The Present

CHAN MAI MAI

I always felt lonely when I was a young kid, about eight years old. I found it difficult to express my feelings and what I wanted at that time. Because I was always sick, I behaved stupidly compared with the other six children in my family. I used to get angry easily and to be scared by small events, even a sudden noise made by a small cat. There seemed nobody in the world who cared about me, so I used to cry to attract attention.

My father was a very successful businessman who gave us a very good living standard. Because he was always away from home, at business, sometimes we couldn't see him for more than three months or half a year. I remembered once I saw him only a week for the whole year. But I loved my parents, I wanted to stay with them, to see their smiles, to hear their voices and to touch them as often as possible. Fortunately we had maids to take care of us.

One day, when I went out with my brothers and sisters to play in a garden, one of our servants came to us and said that our father wanted to see us. I suddenly felt that the weather that day was so fine and comfortable. When we lined up in my father's room to meet him, he seemed extraordinarily happy. Nobody knew the reason why. Even to this day, I don't know why he was so happy. He was always very serious, there was never any smile on his face. He might have been concerned about business. I can just remember that after he talked to us, suddenly he turned to me and said that he wanted to give me a present, I could have whatever I wanted. I didn't know how to answer him, and at that moment I suddenly recognized that I didn't understand myself, because when my dear father asked what was my favorite thing, and what did I want to have, I didn't know. But my father said that I had to decide and to answer him, whether it was to be a small thing or a big thing. And I was given a certain time to think about that. After an hour, I told my own maid what I wanted to have, and she talked to my father.

My father laughed when he heard my request and looked at me with his eyes full of interest, wonder and questions about why I would like to have as my present the toy gun that he had brought from Japan for my brother. He thought since I was a girl, what I might like to have would be a beautiful dress, a golden bracelet, or a big ice-cream or chocolate instead of a boy's toy. This gun was my brother's favorite. He didn't want anyone to touch it. In our old Chinese tradition, boys don't like to play with girls and never like them to touch any of their things. But my father gave it to me, and he said he was going to buy another one for him.

When I touched the toy, I had a feeling which I still cannot express. This toy had been set up on a stand near the window of my brother's room for more than two months, but I wasn't even allowed to touch it or inspect it closely. Now, I held it tightly in my arms; it was all red with sparkling dark and silver spots on it. When I fired it, it gave out a loud sound, and a small green bullet came out very straight and flew a short distance in the air. But I was very disappointed. I remembered that when my father gave this present to my brother, everyone in this house rushed to his room and looked at it; it was joyful to have so many people gathered in a room. But when I had it, the situation was completely different. Nobody did the same thing and I was still alone in the room; no one came and asked me how did I get the gun or say how beautiful it was.

Another thing surprised me was that I didn't touch it again after I put it down, because I was extremely despondent. My maid gave it back to my brother the next day after she asked me if I was sure that I didn't want it anymore. I said immediately, "No, I don't want it, I don't like it. It's a boy's toy, not for a girl." My maid was so honest that she told my father exactly what I said in the morning, and my papa wanted to see me again at night. He asked me why, if I didn't like this, why had I asked him to give it to me as a present. I didn't know how to answer him, and looked at the floor silently. My mother was in the room too. She said that I was not a good girl because I had asked something from them which was my brother's favorite toy and then I didn't like it. What she said made me feel that I just wanted to fool them and make my brother unhappy. I started to hate my mother, because she always said something bad about her daughters to my father. I thought that she was foolish. She always thought that her daughters got her husband's love away from her. But this was nonsense. If a man loves his children, he more or less loves his wife too. Otherwise he will dislike his children because they have some part of blood and bones that came from a body whom he dislikes. Once I heard what she said, I replied to my papa at once the reason I chose the gun: "I wanted somebody to like me, to pay more attention to me. When you brought the toy gun to my brother, everyone in this family rushed to his room and saw it. I wanted the same thing to happen to me. I wanted people to love me, to visit me, and to talk and listen to me, to care about me. So, I took this gun as my present. But when I had it, everything was different. Nobody came to me. That wasn't what I needed, so I would rather give it back to my brother." My parents said nothing and just asked me leave their room.

Later on, I found out that my father paid more attention to me. Sometimes he even stopped in the front of my bed to watch me sleeping or to put a blanket on my body to make sure I was warm enough. My mother started to eat breakfast with us. Oh! That was so lovely. But this phenomenon continued for only few days, and then everything became the same.

Anyhow, I wasn't mad any longer because I found out later, happiness and kindness are inside your own heart and your body. Nobody can make you happy or satisfy everything in your life. Only you can do it. From then on, I started to find out what my own interests were, such as starting to study hard, to learn to take responsibility, to draw and dance.

Saying Goodbye to Motor Racing
KURT HAMILTON

This was just about the hardest thing I had ever done in my life. The thought of not being able to drive a race car for a very long time or maybe for the rest of my life had never crossed my mind. It was four years ago, and the idea still haunts me to this day. With my luck it occurred on the biggest but hardest day of my life, the very day I had the opportunity to win a sponsorship that would have stuck with me for a lifetime. This would have meant a professional career as a motor racer.

There were about five of us that needed and wanted to win this particular race. The reason was it meant that one of us would not have to maintain himself in such an expensive hobby. For me it meant a little more. Motor racing was not just a hobby of mine. I thought of it as my future life and a great relationship between myself and my father. He is also a professional driver. I had a good start and a great future ahead of me. It was all I knew how to do; I loved it and I did it well. At least, the public, my dad, and I thought so. At the bottom of all this I had one small problem. My mother. She hated it. It was all I needed. This never helped at all.

My dad's and my relationship with my mother always went the wrong way. Our values differed a great deal. She would think of me as a lawyer or doctor or maybe even a pilot like I now plan to become. On the other hand dad thought of the world driving championship. I was on my dad's side of course. As a matter of fact I was always on his side whenever it came to my career as a motor racer. I have always respected him as an adult and as a motor racer. He did the same when it came to motor racing. Even when I screw up he has respected my judgement as one professional to another. This is what I really needed. He went as far as jeopardizing his marriage with my mother. Dad stuck with me through thick and thin. He built my first racing machine and bought the rest from then on. He has spent no end of money just to watch my mother dump it all away. She did this when she refused to sign the contract that would have closed the deal for my sponsorship.

This was something that both myself and Dad had always hoped for. Again he supported me all the way. He tried unsuccessfully to settle the whole thing in court. He was always there for me. I did the same for him. Ever since I can remember I have never missed any of his races. I always admired him and was proud to have him as my father. He would make anybody proud to be his son. I spoke of him all the time to my friends. Even if he was in a slump or on a winning streak, I spoke whole-heartedly of him as the greatest driver in

Europe. He felt and spoke the same way of me. I think and hope I made him proud to be my father. I tried my best to be just like him. Dreams, determination to be like him, and lots of support from him had brought me this far. However, all this came to an end.

I distinctly remembered that day which I loved at first and hated by that night. I arrived at the track two hours before race time. People were everywhere, sun shining, and the entire place was bright and colorful. The smell of petrol and humming of engines hit me immediately. The race began at 11:00 a.m. with a field of 42 drivers. Five hours later it boiled down to eleven potential and two laps to go. I was in fourth position. I then moved to third in the first turn. I had driven a hard race all the way and finally got a break. The guy in front of me had shot a loose plug through his hood and had to pull out. Now I pulled into second position and gained on the leader. I hung there and tried to make my move in the last turn before the finish. That's where everything went wrong. It was too fast to realize what happened.

I woke up in Birmingham General with two broken wrists, two broken ribs, a punctured lung and a dislocated ankle. This was the first time I felt any type of fear for motor racing. This was also the first time I ever thought of quitting. Dad was on my left hand supporting me all the way. He had dragged the fear out before I really knew I was scared. I needed that. He knew what to say and what to do, to keep my spirits up. Not one person in my room knew what I wanted to hear except Dad. They all spoke against my racing. Dad knew how to relate to me at this stage, and we spoke of my next race before I dozed off again.

I woke up early the next morning, and he was still there. This time he had bad news. My mother had refused to sign the contract and renew my license. This meant no more racing until I was able to sign my own papers. Dad was really upset, and so was I. I begged mercilessly and pleaded with my mother, but it never worked. She didn't even listen to me.

I remember until this day what Dad said before he walked out of the room. He said, "Son, don't give up. As a matter of fact don't you ever give up on anything you believe in." I promised him that I wouldn't and he said, "That's my boy." I knew it bugged him. It also had a lot to do with the way the relationship between himself and my mother turned out. Since then he has just raced for the hell of it and to support himself. He has not driven an inspiring race since then.

I guess in a way he hoped for me to take his place. It was just what I wanted, and he has wished for me to get what I wanted.

Autobiography: Phase

Tell what you did or what happened to you during a certain period of your life covering months or a year or so— some "phase." Allow plenty of wordage to do justice to both what happened and what made it a phase, that is, a period having its own beginning, development, and end. This could become an installment in a full-dress autobiography comprising all the phases up to now, or it could be offered separately.

Wintering in Manhattan
CINDY STRAND

When I was about nineteen, I moved into New York City with a friend from high school. I had just gotten back from Florida and had no car, no money, and no job. This friend, who was already living in Manhattan, persuaded me that it would be a lot easier for me to "make it" in the city than on Long Island. Part of me wanted to go, but another part of me was afraid to make such a big move. After a great deal of struggling within myself, I decided to push aside all my fears and reservations, and just *do it*.

Although this conquest over my fears had its merits as far as my self-image was concerned, my decision to move to Manhattan acted as a bomb being dropped in my parents' laps. This was because my friend was a guy. No matter how hard I tried, I could not convince them that our relationship was platonic. So I moved to the city without my parents' consent and did not communicate with them in any way for the entire time I lived there. This was quite a burden for me, emotionally, and consequently contributed a great deal to my unhappiness those six months.

Concerning the details of my stay there, it is difficult to know where to begin. Those things that had such an impact on me may seem obscure, even trivial, to an outsider. Ironically, everyone in that entire city was an outsider to me. That's one of the miserable facts about being alone and lonely in such an ominous place as New York. My relationship with my room mate slowly deteriorated for reasons too difficult and numerous to explain here. What matters is that it didn't make much difference to me, emotionally, that I was living with someone. He was out when I was in, and after a while, neither of us cared to see one another anyway. As far as I was concerned, I lived alone.

As a result of my experiences in Manhattan. I've been given a new understanding of the word "lonely." I realized then that I had never *really* known what it was like to be alone. Living with my family in Suburbia all my life sheltered me from things that I never even knew existed. I experienced feelings that I never had before, some worse than others. I lived there in the middle of winter, which seemed to add to my bleak state of mind and to the misery which I perceived all around me. There was not a day that went by when I didn't see someone lying on the sidewalk, their clothes, what was left of them, filthy and torn; their faces, dirty and full of sores. The worst place to see them lying was in the subway corridors. The corridors were damp and dark and stunk of urine, whiskey, and vomit. I hated walking through them. I hated seeing people who were part of the same "system" as I was, existing on a level far beneath that of any animal. Strangely at times I felt a certain kinship with their suffering. But even then, I knew it was still *their* city—a claim that I could never make.

Every day I rode the subway to and from work. I had to give myself extra time in the morning for walking on sidewalks that were always full and to wait for enough trains to go by until one was empty enough to get on. The ride to work wasn't that bad. It was the ride home that I dreaded. The trains were always crowded around the time I left work. People would literally push and squeeze their way into the train. Bodies were pressed tightly against one another, and often it was nearly impossible for me to see the street numbers on the subway walls, to know when to get off. At times I would feel myself beginning to panic when I was in a train that was very crowded. There was always at least one guy giving me the "eye" as opposed to fifty or so other people who looked wherever they could to avoid making eye contact with anyone. It was hard sometimes to know which was worse.

The subway itself revealed so much to me about the city, and the people, and the lives they were leading. In the morning, herded into the trains like cattle; in the evening, herded back again. I was part of it. Though I despised it on every conceivable level, I was part of it. And I hated it. It wasn't just the subway though, it was everything. And it seemed that everything that was true of the city above-ground, was true of it below. But what was true below stirred in me more than just anger. At times, the crowded, stifling atmosphere of the subway was unbearable. I remember one day in particular. I had been miserable that entire day. I wanted to leave the city and move back home. But I didn't have a home to go back to. I no longer wanted to live in a place I had to fear, a place that did not care whether I lived or died. I remember I had been crying on and off at work for most of the day, so by the time I reached the subway, I was feeling exhausted and in no mood for crowds. But, as usual, the trains were packed. After a long wait, I finally got into a car that was fairly comfortable. However, as I had learned soon enough while riding the subways, that situation did not last for long. The train filled up quickly at the next two stops, pinning me in a crowd of people. I was just *not* prepared for it. I felt my eyes slowly filling with tears. A huge lump formed in my throat, making it hurt to swallow. I knew my stop was coming up, so I started moving, as much as I could, toward the door. I said "excuse me" to the person in front of me, barely getting the words out. I tried again. My throat felt thick and swollen, and my voice was so frail that it didn't even sound like mine. "Excuse me," I said, trying harder, tears beginning to roll down my cheeks. Someone *did* hear me, but not the person I had been talking to. I heard a man's voice behind me saying "excuse me," "excuse me," in a weak, pathetic voice, meant to be my own. I turned around slowly and saw who it was. At that moment, I was too drained and miserable to be embarrassed. It bothered me a little, though, that he did not stop mimicking me, even after I turned around. We looked at each other for a few seconds, then I turned around again, and faced forward. My stop finally came; the doors opened, and I rushed out.

Though it may be obvious, I need to say that my loneliness in Manhattan was continuous. Although I wasn't always miserable, like that time in the subway, I was always lonely. My moods would change from not wanting to go out at all to taking long walks into parts of the city I didn't know. I remember a poetry reading that took me about an hour to get to, because I got onto the wrong bus. Once I arrived, though, it acted as a temporary neutral ground—a resting place for me. I needed that. Though much of the poetry being read was somewhat inaccessible to me, the atmosphere alone was very calming.

Besides searching out poetry readings, I spent a lot of time in Central Park. Sometimes I went and walked aimlessly about, not noticing very much at all. Other times, when I had nothing but time, I would sit and watch the people. I would look in their eyes and create stories for some of them. Such good writing material—park people. So many faces and tears, inside and out. Old men that sit for hours, maybe days, I don't know. Some with curled-in fingers, peeling and red. Others with eyes watery and clear and blue, always blue. These people, whom I envied and wondered about, always, when I was there; whom I watched, cautiously, quietly—those tempered time pieces— how much of what they were was already me?

I tried very hard to share in the comfort and familiarity which I knew many people felt in Central Park. And I did, but only to a point. Then it always seemed to creep up on me how truly unhappy I was in

Manhattan. Then I would always be reminded that this was not my park, nor was it my city. Towards the end, before I left, I was feeling more and more a oneness with those people lying in the subways. It was then that my existence there began to make sense. It was then that I knew I had to leave.

Unwanted ·Houseguest

BRIAN FLYNN

I remember the intial shock slowly turning into dismay and my thoughts of how things would be different around the house once he moved in. I thought about coming home from school and not being able to blast my stereo or have the guys over because he would be there. He would always be there. My greatest joy had been those hours in the afternoon when the house was mine alone. That time was gone now. All because of him.

"He" was my grandfather, a frail old man who formerly lived in a tall building with many other frail old people and many doctors and nurses. When I was younger I used to visit him with my family every Sunday. My folks still visited him regularly, but I had cut my visit down to about once a month. Don't get me wrong, I liked the man, but I was sixteen and a very busy person. Besides, old people really got me down.

But now there was going to be an old person living in my very own house. All I could think about was that melancholy, defeated atmosphere that surrounded the hospital being brought into my home.

What brought all this about was the discovery of a tumor in my grandfather's stomach during a routine examination at the rest home. Somehow, the supposedly skillful and caring doctors on the staff had managed to overlook the tumor for the better part of a year. Now it was too big and too late to remove it. And my grandfather was going to die.

When all was explained to me I became furious. How could they have made such an incredible oversight? The people responsible for this should be shot. My father shared this opinion completely and told me he understood my feelings. But he really didn't. He was upset and angry about the fact that his father, whom he loved, was neglected and was now going to pay the ultimate price for that neglect. I was simply mad because their incompetence was the direct cause of this old man invading my space. I am ashamed now of having had those feelings, but they were, in truth, the main cause of my bitterness.

I was helpless to change the situation, though, and the day came when my folks brought him home so he could spend his last few months among his "loved ones." My initial reaction to having him around the house was totally irrational. I resented him for being there and showed him very little attention, almost to the point of rudeness. Here he was, a sick old man who deserved nothing but kindness and sympathy and did not even ask for those small courtesies, and I treated him like he had deliberately come into the house to spite me. I am sure he noticed my behavior, but he never mentioned it.

I decided that I would not let him take over my domain, and so when I came home from school I started playing the stereo louder than before. This was my grand gesture of defiance.

One day I had just returned from school and ritualistically set the stereo at the usual window-shaking volume when my grandfather asked me to come into the kitchen. I figured he was finally going to complain about the music, and I had firmly resolved in my head not to give in. Every bit of control of this house that I gave up to him, he was going to have to fight for. What he really had to say took me by surprise.

He told me he was aware of the fact that I resented him for coming into the house. He even said he understood my reasons. He then told me he had tried not to interfere in my life at all (which he really hadn't) and went on to ask if there was anything he did that infringed on my privacy or hampered me in any way. I couldn't think of anything to tell him then, but I did gain a lot of respect for him at that moment. I was still not happy about him living there, but I realized that he could have gotten me to bow to his wishes or give into any demands he might make simply by telling my father what those demands were. My father, at this point, would do anything for him.

He then asked me to try and understand that when a man has just a short time left on the earth, he needs to be around the people that mean the most to him. If he were to spend this time in the hospital, then he wouldn't care if he died tomorrow. By living with us, though, he had something to look forward to when he got up in the morning and was truly thankful for each new day he got through.

I thought about what he said for a long time after that talk. I realized that my life was no worse, and was actually even a little better since he had come to live with us. A lot of chores that I used to have to do when I got home from school were already done by the time I got home. This really hit me when I thought about it. Between the pain of the cancer and the natural hardship of old age, this man went through a constant struggle just to get through the day, and for him to assume my chores so that my pitifully easy life could be even easier was hard for me to understand. This type of behavior pointed out to me, better than anything else could have, how incredibly selfish I was acting. I decided from then on to try and make his life a little more enjoyable.

I figured that since his greatest pleasure, according to him, was being around us, that I would give him something I had plenty of...my time.

And so it began. Instead of turning on the stereo when I got home, I would go in and sit down to talk or play cards with him. This soon became a ritual with us, spending hours every afternoon talking and him telling me stories of his life. I had begun this routine with his happiness in mind and thought of it as a sacrifice on my part. I soon realized, however, that I was looking forward to our talks as much as he was.

He told me things about himself that made me see him as someone who was not always an old man. He was young like me once and had very similar aspirations and ideas. And the obstacles that he had overcome and the things that he had accomplished in his life made my admiration for him grow in leaps and bounds.

I soon began to take him on outings to local parks or local beaches or little league games, anywhere that there were a lot of people, young people. He was always happiest when he was around kids running and playing. He loved to sit and watch them and tell me about when he used to play stickball and soccer when he was a kid. He never failed to tell me that he hit more homeruns than any other kid on the block.

As time went on, I began to realize just how hard it must have been for him at this point in his life. He was an intelligent man with an active brain trapped inside an old and sickly body. He was starting to become noticeably weaker, and I began really worrying about him. I began cutting out of school a lot just so I could spend time with him and help him do what used to be for him menial tasks but were now becoming major undertakings. My grades dropped, and I began spending less time with my friends and more and more time with him. He used to joke that my grades were directly related to his health and that if he didn't die soon I would never get into college. He made jokes about his death more now to try and keep it from getting everyone down, but I could tell he was getting pretty scared himself. This was a hard time for everyone in my family. For me it was hell. And, ironically, the person it should have been hardest for was the one who kept our spirits up the most.

I remember him calling me into his room one morning to talk before I left for school. He told me that when he was living in the rest home, he was surrounded by people who had given up the will to live and were just waiting to die. He said he had started to become one of these people before he had moved back in with us. Since that time he had enjoyed his life totally and that I was one of the biggest reasons for that. He told me that one of the greatest gifts in life was for a man to die when he was still not tired of living. I didn't fully understand this at the time.

When I returned home from school that day I went into his bedroom. He was lying in bed just as I had left him, and although he had a peaceful, rested look on his face, I knew that he was not just sleeping. I had dreaded this day for a long time and had had all sorts of macabre fantasies about how it would occur. But it turned out to be a lot easier to handle than I had pictured. I think it was the fact that he looked so peaceful. It still hurt me to know that I would not ever be able to talk to him again, but the knowledge that I had personally contributed to his contentment and happiness prior to his death was a great solace.

I called my father to tell him what had happened, and as I sat in my grandfather's room waiting for him to arrive, I thought about what we had shared in the past few months. All his stories and advice came back to me then and I realized that although my grades for this spring would not reflect it, I had learned more in this short time than I could ever have done in a classroom.

Study of a Fallen Glass Sphere
KATHLEEN CONDON

Her father died November 29, 1979....

It was an unbelievably confusing time—a glass sphere falling from an elevated and seemingly secure place and shattering into hundreds of slivers and tiny, jagged-edged pieces, so little hope of ever putting them together again. After a time she discovered that some of the pieces could be fitted together, while at the same time she was forced to accept the fact that the globe would never be as it was.

...It was completely unexpected. One day he was there, returning from work, carrying on lively, evening banter with the family, the next day he was gone....

As the devastation remaining at the end of a war brings about change, so does the devastation after a life crisis. Her life in every aspect changed, if not in actuality, certainly in her eyes. Defeatedly she asked, "What is important in life?" It occurred to her that, like most people, she had been caught up in petty arguments and trivial worries such as grades, clothes, and appearance. After he died, however, much like the person who cleans a large smudge off his glasses and discovers that it is not actually a cloudy day, she realized that her perspective had been hazy and rather distorted. Wiping away the smudge she was able to see the truth in the proverb, "I shall pass through this world but once. Any good therefore that I can do or any kindness that I can show to any human being, let me do it now. Let me not defer or neglect it. For I shall not pass this way again." People matter. In the same way, each moment of every day is valuable. She pondered the ease of sliding through life in innocent ignorance, not seeing the good in anything and taking everything for granted. It's sobering to think that it takes a tragedy to change a person's ways.

...Startled from deep morning sleep by her mother's urgent whisper, she discovered him lying on the plush, green carpet of her parents' bedroom. His face had a horrible bluish tint, but his expression was peaceful. More than once she's been thankful his eyes were closed....

She realizes that death, although unpleasant, is generally accepted as an everyday occurrence; people die, those left behind grieve, then, picking up the pieces, go on with their lives. However, she was irritated by people comparing their own losses to hers, "I know how you feel...." No, she thought, you don't know how I feel. How could you?

...Deliriously she performed CPR. With her first breath the stilled lungs filled with air. She thought he was breathing....

Her father used to say that if you were going to ask someone, "How are you?" you should really want to know.

...In tauntingly cruel disappointment she realized it was only the sound of her air filling his lungs and automatically being released. It sounded so real, so alive....

She remembers one Sunday after 11 o'clock mass. They made their usual stop at Albertson's to pick up oatmeal-raisin cookies and various odds and ends. Her father, a tall, well-built, rather distinguished-looking man, was feeling particularly silly and, knowing that at fourteen she'd "die" of embarrassment, decided to skip down the frozen foods aisle saying in a sing-song manner, "I'm Kathleen's father."

...Waiting for the ambulance, she continued artificial respiration and chest compressions, hopelessness and panic rising every second. "Dad?!...Dad?!...."

Sometimes she catches a reflection from a fragment of that broken glass globe and wonders why this happened to her family or why people have to die at all. There is no justification. Then the light changes and in the altered reflection off that shard of glass she notices that there are some positive aspects of her father's death. Her family pulled together and is now closer than it's ever been. She and her mother, in relying on each other for various needs, were drawn together; but it took time. After he died the two went through at least a year of painful, heated conflicts—inflamed mother-teenage daughter friction.

Her parents had a good marriage and were extremely close, so when she lost her father, in a sense she also lost her mother, who became markedly different. She felt that she no longer knew her mom. Like the little kid who looks at his parents and assumes they're infallible, she clung to an idealistic view of her supposedly flawless parents. Dying's a pretty mortal and imperfect thing to do. It was shattering for her to see her mother lay her head down in utter defeat and cry. An awful time—she couldn't believe what was happening. She stood barefoot among the chaotically scattered splinters of that once-stable glass orb.

...An air of futility settled in a heavy haze over all her efforts to breathe life into the quieted lungs. She crouched over the cool, limp figure, frantically thumping the broad chest as if to shock him from too deep a sleep....

He used to pick her up from her ballet class on Saturday mornings. Once after he died, she saw the familiar car approaching, her father at the wheel. She thought nothing of it until she realized that the person driving was actually her mother.

...They took him to the hospital. The family waited. The ring of the telephone sliced the bleary silence; she looked questioningly at her mother. Pain gripping her face, her mother shook her head....

She used to dream about that morning—the deathly, sour smell of his breath, the lifeless coolness of his skin, the sounds of artificial breathing and aimless, lost footsteps. In her dreams, he lived.

Despite changes in perspective and values, in the day to day routines of school or the working world it's easy to unknowingly slip back into focusing on trivialities. Five weeks into her first quarter of college, for example, she was failing chemistry and getting C's in calculus and sociology. She had chosen UCSD with the intention of preparing for med school and eventually a career as a pediatrician. Her father had wanted to be a doctor but due to circumstances beyond his control, was unable to do so. It seems that while he was still alive she adopted his dream and shaped it into her own. He believed in her, making her lack of success in science-related courses at this decidedly pre-med-oriented school doubly disheartening. She had lost her perspective, and her thoughts were muddled. Somehow she ended up on the beach talking about life with a newly found friend. The conversation drifted and, looking out at the peacefully droning ocean and feeling the crisp saltwater slap her legs, she talked about her father. Something in the calm steady permanence of the mass of midnight blue and in the sincerity of her consort eased her foundering mind. Haltingly she glanced at the transformed ball. In the complex merging of bits of broken glass, it is almost more beautiful now than it was before.

Memoir of Another Person

Tell someone else's story as you witnessed it. This may be an incident that occurred on one occasion or what someone you knew or observed did over a longer period of time amounting to a "phase" in that person's life. Tell about yourself only enough to recount how you came by the knowledge and how you reacted to it. You might place this in a collection of your other memoirs or, if it makes a certain general point, consider how you might get it to an audience that would appreciate that point.

On Safari with Uncle Phillip

LYNDON CHARLOT

I can remember the summer of seventy-six when my mother sent me to San Francisco to visit my Uncle Phillip. I was excited because I had never been to San Francisco before, and Mom was sending me on the train all alone. I was only twelve years old and had just completed the sixth grade.

I left home on the nine o'clock train one Sunday morning in June, and arrived in San Francisco later that afternoon. The train ride was very long and I was very happy to see the Transamerica Building as we entered the city (I'd seen the building in a magazine before). As I walked through the station with my suitcase in my hand, I could see a distinguished-looking man facing me, dressed in a black pinstriped suit. I said to myself, "That must be Uncle Phil," and it was! Mom said he always dressed well.

As I met up with Uncle Phil, I greeted him and shook his hand. His hand was so soft that I thought I was shaking my mother's hand. He showed me to his car, which was a red, two-door, convertible Mercedes. We put my suitcase into the trunk and left the station for his apartment.

Uncle Phillip lived in a large three-bedroom apartment that was on the top floor of one of the tallest buildings in San Francisco. The house had a swimming pool, sauna, weight room, and a terrific game room. I knew I was going to have fun here. That evening I unpacked my clothes and made myself feel at home by playing in the game room and watching a little television.

When ten o'clock came around that night Uncle Phil explained that he had to go to work. He works nights and doesn't get home until six in the morning. When I asked him what kind of work he does, he told me, "I'm an entertainer." and wouldn't tell me any more.

Uncle Phil left for work, wearing a long trench coat and a pair of boots. I couldn't see what he had on under the coat. Maybe if I did, I could tell what kind of work he actually does. But in thirty minutes I forgot about my uncle and concentrated on exploring the apartment.

That night I did a lot of snooping around the apartment. It was fascinating. There were so many plants and animal-skin furniture that I thought I was in a jungle. For example, my uncle had a leopard-skin blanket on his heart-shaped water-bed. In another room the floor was covered with a zebra-striped shag rug, and there was a couch covered with bear fur. I felt as if I were on a safari expedition. But before I could complete my journey, the phone rang.

I answer the telephone, and the caller asks to speak to a Phyllis. I tell him that there is no Phyllis living here, but he insists that there is and even repeats the phone number to assure us both that he doesn't have a wrong number. So I tell him, "Well, I'm sorry, sir, but I'm the only one home, and you will have to call back when my uncle gets home." That caller was mighty strange because he had me convinced that there was a Phyllis living here. But I wasn't going to concern myself over the matter and went to my room and to bed.

When I woke up the next morning, I crawled out of bed and went into the kitchen, where the smell of bacon and eggs grabbed me by the nose. As I entered the kitchen I could see my uncle facing the stove. He had on a silk robe and furry slippers.

I said, "Good morning, Uncle Phil," and when he turned around to greet me his face looked as if there was a different coloration to it, just like my mother's face when she tries to look pretty. But my uncle was an entertainer, so, I thought to myself, maybe he has a costume at work or something, and whatever he actually did I didn't give a second thought until I got back home.

During the rest of the week, I managed to see practically all of San Francisco and had a great time. Uncle Phil would go to work at night, come home in the morning, sleep for a few hours, then spend the rest of the day with me. I admired the resemblance between him and my mother. The only difference between the two was that mother had long dark hair and Uncle Phil had very short hair. Other than that, they could have been twins for all I knew.

That week, when Uncle Phil went to work I continued to snoop around and found all sorts of objects. Uncle Phil left the closet in his room unlocked, and I happened to notice it. When he went to work, I found a lot of woman's stuff like shoes, dresses, purses and even that make-up stuff. Maybe Phyllis did live here, but I never saw her. And that man who called for Phyllis the first night I was here continued to call. But I never asked my uncle about any of it.

I took the train home at the end of the week and when I got home I told mom all about my fun and I also asked her about Uncle Phillip and what does he really do when he goes to work. She simply replied, "He's an entertainer."

Max Delivers

XOCHITL MYLES

"Station 3" the call came over the radio. "We have an altercation over here at 483 Brady Ave. Could you please send us an ambulance right away?" Max glanced over at me, and I quickly jumped to my feet. I knew Max didn't like half-steppin! I loaded the equipment into the ambulance and sat in the back. Max switched the siren on as always, and headed down the highway as expertly and as fast as a race car driver. I braced myself and prayed a lot. Anyone else would have treated this like a routine run, but not Max. Everything was treated like a life-and-death matter. He took on a new aliveness behind the wheel. He would be totally immersed in a minute and be yelling out things we shouldn't forget. There would be a wide confident grin on his face as he cursed traffic.

Max Greyson was a large man about 35 years old. He always had his uniform in immaculate condition. His shoes could be spit-shined, and his hair very short. He was a no-nonsense kind of guy. He spent most of his adult life in the military and was attached to a medical outfit during the Vietnam war. He'd told me many stories about those days because I was the only one who would listen to them. He would go on and on relating one heroic act after another. All his stories ended on a basic theme—"those were the good old days"—the days where a man lived on courage, honor and comaraderie. Max had many medals for bravery, but he never bragged about them. He said it didn't seem right to be awarded a special ribbon for a normal humane deed.

The ambulance screeched to a stop in front of a well-kept lawn. We arrived to see two policemen leaving. "OK, you're here. I don't think anything is wrong, but you can check it out." Max looked at me and rolled his eyes. "What do you think?" I knew he wanted to leave, but I said, "I think we should check it out." Max went in and began asking the woman where she hurt. Her husband was sitting on the couch, crying and kept repeating how sorry he was. Once satisfied that no major physical damage was done, we left and said goodbye. We drove back in complete silence. As we neared the station, I said, "Nothing like those good ole days." Max looked at me, thankful that I understood.

As we entered the station someone called out, "Hey, Max, where's your P.E.?" "Max don't bring back P.E.s" cried out another. "Man, he's like a doctor, didn't you know that? He can fix them on the spot, isn't that right, Max?" Max ignored them and went out to clean his truck.

"Hey, Xochitl, is it true that Max broke a man's arm because he didn't want to come in?" The whole station roared with laughter. I could usually be counted on for a smart retort, but when it was directed towards Max, I always declined. Somehow it was always more cruel then funny when it was about Max.

The question was in reference to an incident in which Max had been called out to the scene of a suspected drug overdose victim. When Max arrived at the scene, the guy insisted it was all a hoax and refused to go with Max. Max's intuition told him the boy was lying, so he became more persistent. The boy got violent and they fought. Accidentally, the boy's shoulder was dislocated in the struggle. Back at the hospital, doctors were unable to find any evidence of drugs. After this the story got turned into a joke about his bedside manner. This along with his militarized mannerisms and etiquette won him about as much popularity as homework assignments in college. Someone was always trying to make him the butt of a joke.

While Max was out cleaning the ambulance a call came over the radio. "I not speak good. I need help." The dispatcher copied the address as best he could. "Hey, anyone want this call? This woman sounds real flaky. " "Then gave it to Max." The dispatcher radio'd out to Max: "F-32, we have an unknown injury which could be serious and possibly dangerous."

Everyone in the stationhouse was laughing. I got up and got my equipment, and Max replied on the radio "Roger, Station 3, I copy and I'm on my way." I met him at the station entrance and got in. Max had that familiar zest in his manner as he spoke on the art of being calm when going on a run like this. We got to the address and ran up two flights of stairs to the apartment number. Max knocked on the door...but there was no answer. He pushed the door open and called out, "Anyone need a paramedic?" We passed the bathroon. There was a woman on the floor. Max turned her over on her back, she was unconscious. There was blood on the floor where she lay. Max slapped her gently, but she would not come to. Max checked her stomach for contractions, then he checked the baby's heartrate. He looked at me and told me not to be nervous. He said in a very calm manner, "we are about to deliver this baby." He slapped the woman harder this time. She roused....she started talking very desperately and quickly in a foreign language. Max began speaking with the woman in a quiet, mild tone. He reached out and placed his hand on her cheek. The woman immediately calmed down. He looked over and told me that the baby was on its way and that there was nothing for us to do but to let nature take its course. He smiled sincerely at the woman and caressed her forehead. She didn't seem frightened anymore and looked relieved to find someone there who could speak her native tongue. I realized the woman was speaking in Vietnamese.

The woman yelled out in pain, and Max gave her a command in Vietnamese. I saw a round bloody form emerging from between the mother's legs. She panted for a while and then Max repeated the command. She pushed with all her might, and out slipped the figure into Max's waiting hands. The mother gave out a cry of relief. Tears of joy were streaming down Max's cheeks. Max nudged the baby under the chin and he gave out a loud cry. The mother cried out loud too....she managed a thank-you doc-tor. Max was holding the baby up to the mother and saying something in Vietnamese. He then turned to me and said "Isn't she beautiful?" and I said, "Yes." I said, "Yes, Max, you are beautiful."

Memoir of a Group or Place

Tell what you remember that a group did one time or that happened at a particular place on some occasion. You were there but not central. Whatever feeling or idea makes this memory stand out now may provide the mood or angle to give it in telling others about it. Could this be a feature piece for some newspaper or magazine? Or include it with your other memoirs of people and places.

We Tried to Tell Them

FLOYD JACK

The Vietnam war was funny. Oh, not "ho-ho" funny—"strange" is probably a better word. It was fought in a strange land, it was either raining in great torrents or it was bone dry. Wet or dry it was always hot, usually muggy. It had an abundance of creepy, crawly things which infested your clothing, your hootch—you didn't live in a room in Vietnam, you lived in a hootch. They crawled into and onto everything. Those not crawling were flying. All sorts of flying things. Some tiny, some not so tiny, and one beetle, which was eaten by the Vietnamese, was huge.

There was also an abundance of prostitutes, which isn't strange in the Orient or in war, but they all appeared strange. It is rather hard to say how old they were as the Vietnamese people seem to look younger than we. They were all about five feet tall, if that, skinny, and not very well padded. They always reminded me of a skinny, twelve-year-old boy. As I have no interest in young boys they just weren't for me, and besides, being married I like to think of myself as something of a "straight arrow."

There was also strange food, not all of it served in the military mess either. Aside from the flying bugs which I mentioned, the Vietnamese tend to eat things most westerners consider repulsive. So repulsive in fact I won't go too deeply into it. I'll just mention a fish sauce which they make. It is pronounced "nook-mom"—how you would spell it I don't know.

Once I was on the Ile de Phu Quac, which lies off the southwest coast of Vietnam. Actually, it is directly south of Cambodia. Unwilling guests of the Saigon government were kept there. I imagine they still are, though Saigon is now Ho Chi Minh City, and the hosts are now probably the guests. Not far from the dirt strip on which we had landed was a nook-mom factory. The basic ingredient for this sauce is fish. Dead, rotten fish.

Various forms of marine life go into the making of nook-mom, and these are dumped into a large, elevated concrete tank. Boards, weighted by rocks, old tires—just about anything heavy will do—are placed on top of the fish. As the fish rot they liquify and that liquid runs into a smaller tank at a lower level. In the second tank hot red peppers and parts of the large flying bugs are added to the liquid. It then steeps for some time before being bottled. No one told me how they keep from bottling it before its time.

Of course these strange things, and there are more, could be tolerated, even enjoyed by some, if it weren't for Charley. Charley is what we called the communists. Charley was either doing something

quite nasty and unpleasant to us, or we to him, and it tended to take
the joy out of life. I won't dwell on that either. We did have our
moments though, and that brings us to the point of the story.

We were sitting in the DOOM Pussy bar one afternoon—that
isn't as sinister as it sounds—it is the Da Nang Officers Open Mess
bar, and the pussy part came from the wildcat insignia of one of the
Air Force's fighter wings which was stationed there. We were talking
to some civilian scientists from NASA. They had just arrived and,
despite their long flight from The World, still had that wonderfully
clean smell of home and another sort of life. For some reason, probably
the tax break for serving in the combat zone, these gentlemen from
the National Aeronautic and Space Administration had arrived to
study a natural phenomenon. As you fly over the Vietnam coastline
from seaward there is a decided "thump" as your aircraft drops about
200 feet in altitude. The opposite occurs as you depart the coast
towards open water; the aircraft just blops up about 200 feet.

The civilians that afternoon were telling us some extremely
interesting, although idiotic, theories they had brought from Washington concerning this phenomenon. Washington abounds in such theories,
and those who live there have an almost lemming-like compulsion to
go forth from time to time to impress others with their theories.

We heard about air currents, anomalies in the earth's magnetic
field, even some ridiculous talk of solar flare predominance. We tried
to tell the scientists why it occurred, but they didn't seem to care
about our theories—we were, obviously, pretty well sotted down with
booze, raunchy of appearance. We also reeked of the stink of jungle
and death, and they just didn't care to hear us. I don't think they really
liked sitting with us at all.

Well, they flew their fancy C-141 about the country for some
weeks. They would cross the coast out-bound, then recross it in-
bound. First at high altitude and then low, sometimes even at a
middling sort of altitude. They had all kinds of gadgets aboard for
measuring and determining things, and then, finally, they went away.

Just before I left for The World on one of the big Freedom Birds
from Ton Son Nhut—that's the air field just outside Saigon—I met a
couple of the scientists in the bar. They didn't seem to remember me—
combat soldiers all look alike to outsiders—but I sat down anyway and
asked about the study. They didn't want to say too much about it.
They seemed to indicate it was classified and of such scientific mag-
nitude that I could probably not understand the results of their
scholarly probings.

Booze has a way of easing tensions and tongues, and pretty soon
they were talking about the project. They had flown a lot. They had
collected reams of data, mostly worthless, and yes, we had really pin-

pointed the difficulty for them that first afternoon there in the DOOM Pussy bar.

The aberrant flight pattern we had observed, and they had studied, was due to the one thing which we had told them that first afternoon. It alone caused the drop and rise in aircraft altitude crossing the Vietnam coast line. Simply put, the placed sucked.

1336 Higuera Street

KENDRA FRENCH

Saturday morning had finally arrived; the weekend was here, which meant the traditional trip to Grandmother's. This summer Saturday morning was no different than the previous ones; the car was to be loaded—bicycles, travel bags, cameras and other useless paraphernalia. It appeared as though the family was embarking upon a trip across the United States, yet in actuality we were only going across town. These weekend visits were looked upon with sincere welcome. Having spent the majority of my early childhood with my grandparents, I believe they thought of my sister and me more as their children than their grandchildren. They played a major role in raising us, as my parents pursued their educational careers. My grandparents desired to remain active in our lives, and these weekend trips fulfilled their need.

The red station wagon pulled into the driveway, rolling over the shuffle-board court and hop-scotch. Today would be exceptionally exciting, for my Uncle John had invited several of his friends over to dinner. I desired to get out of the over-packed car, to enter the lovely old Victorian style home on 1336 Higuera Street. Actually my attention went beyond the large off-white house; my thoughts were focused on the swimming pool in the front yard. The pool, its warm water rippling from the hot Santa Ana wind tossing the magnolia leaves around.

My thoughts were broken by Uncle John and his friends crashing out the door, ready to tackle Dad. In an assembly line the necessary (or should I say unnecessary) equipment was piled into its respective place—bikes in the garage, travel bags and toys tossed into the house. Our neighbors and those living next to my grandmother must have wondered about our elaborate packing for a two-day trip. My sister and I would evade the job of unpacking due to our size. While all the commotion was going on we decided to make a break for the bath-house.

The bathhouse was the beginning of our aquatic adventure. This small wooden structure contained a bathroom and a changing room; our swim suits rested upon their designated pegs year around. It was located on the side of the house. In order to get to the pool, one took the treacherous path of sharp piercing pine needles and a jagged rock walkway through a creaking gate which needed oiling, and then at last relief for the feet was felt on the soft moist grass.

Anxiously Kristy and I sat on the edge of the pool, our feet dangling in the cool refreshing water. My sister and I hollered at the tops of our lungs, hoping someone would hear our pleas to come and play. Suddenly, my uncle and his friends came flying out the door screaming and then doing belly-flops into the pool. My squeals of laughter must have been heard by the entire neighborhood.

Sitting in my inflatable swan, I drifted casually in the shallow end, watching the diving board exhibition—cannon-balls, swan dives and various types of flips—some planned and others just happening. The performance was excellent. I am sure that I provided them with entertainment also, for my appearance was very funny, black and white ruffled bathing suit and a multi-colored swim cap covered with plastic flowers.

The best part of these afternoons was that age played only a small role. My uncle and his friends answered to my every call for zealous piggy-back rides and swimming pool volleyball, a constant watchful eye making sure no casualties occurred. While we were frolicking in the pool, a faint call could be heard. I was so involved in play that I did not notice the girls entering the yard with my grandmother. As soon as the guys caught sight of them there was a definite decline in their enthusiasm for my sister and me. Our "special playmates" climbed out of the pool to engage in another type of fun. Floating alone lacked the earlier excitement.

With a deserted feeling and chlorine-burnt eyes, I crawled out of the pool onto the hot cement. The sun's toasting rays had consumed all my energy. After the drops of water were soaked from my body, I creeped into an inviting cushioned lawn chair, covered myself with a towel, and drifted off to sleep, slowly rebuilding my energy.

The crisp sharp scent of burning charcoal could be smelt as I awoke from my nap. We always had a bar-b-que on especially warm days. Casually sauntering over to the picnic table my eyes engulfed many tantalizing delicacies. Glancing around to make sure no one was looking I grabbed a few olives, some strawberries, and a handful of chips.

The guys were setting up the croquet course for a traditional before-dinner game. Being certain that I would not be invited to play, I chose a spot for observation on the steps and sat with a mopey look on my face. Much to my amazement, my uncle asked if I wanted to be a "junior partner" with him. I was a little hesitant at first, yet with the others' encouragement I was quickly involved in the game. In croquet, relatives are not allies; strategy is the key even if it is illegal, like hitting the balls into the pool. Looking back on the game, my family may have felt like professionals, yet their skills scarcely showed it; wickets were always bent out of shape and a ball hit through the gate went into the street. Throughout the game the sound of sizzling fat could be heard. Everyone's mouth would water. We would try to pass it off as concentration, not letting onto the fact that the tempting scents had reached our tastebuds.

The croquet game came to an immediate halt when Grandmother placed the final salad on the serving table. Tonight my sister and I were fortunate to have fallen into the care of two older girls. Usually my family is ruthless at the picnic table, everyone must fend for themselves. The girls maintained a steady pace at placing food on our plates. Succulent juicy steaks, browned on the edges yet pale pink in the center, crisp, crunchy salad, zesty salsa and the dark, moist chocolate cake were part of the feast. A cooling breeze signaled that evening was here. The sky projected hues of red and orange. I was full and tired from a fulfilling day. When it became apparent that my uncle and his friends would be heading out for a night on the town, my heart grew gloomy. They were such wonderful playmates; they were unaffected by the thought that Kristy and I were mere children. It was quite clear that they too received genuine pleasure in being with us. School was out for a while. Its strains and tensions vanished, allowing my uncle and his friends the chance to act as children themselves, without fear of teasing.

This summer day, like so many others, contained the special feeling of family unity. The warmth and relaxation associated with summer stimulated sentiments of pleasure. As a child the emotions which stemmed from days like this particular Saturday became embedded within me and return every summer.

Memoir of an Eyewitness Incident

Tell anything you saw happen once that was a brief incident you merely witnessed as a spectator, something of some significance to you but not necessarily very unusual or dramatic. Would this go well with some of your other writing? Or would it fit into the theme or subject characterizing some publication or audience you know of?

Cycles

PABLO O'BRIEN

It was a beautiful, clear day at the summit of Mount Diablo; the entire bay area was visible, from the spectacular Marin Headlands to the endless monotony of the broad, flat inland valley. Enjoying a rare moment of solitude, I sat on the cliff's edge and tried hard to forget my responsibilities and pressures. I was doing fairly well when several voices intruded on my silence. Slightly irritated, I turned to see who was speaking.

A young, average-looking woman was standing a few yards away from me with two small children—a toddler of about three or four years old and an infant in a stroller. The lady's face hovered on the brink of being pretty, but a harassed look and deep worry lines made her seem faded. The toddler must have taken after her father; there was almost no detectable resemblance between her and her mother.

"Why isn't Daddy with us, Mommy?"

"Daddy gets to have you next weekend, honey. This weekend, you're staying with me."

Mommy started walking towards the cliff's edge to get a better view, pushing the stroller with one hand and holding the toddler with the other. About five feet from the edge, the toddler dug her heels in and refused to go any further.

"Come on, honey, you can see a lot better from the edge. Look how pretty it is."

"I'm scared, Mommy. Daddy always says, 'Don't go near the edge.'"

"Well, Daddy isn't here right now, so come with Mommy. Don't be scared, I'll hold you."

"No, Mommy!"

Personally, I agreed with the kid; I wouldn't have been too thrilled about going to the edge of a cliff at the age either. But if I was surprised at the mother's persistent efforts, I was shocked at her reaction to the child's final definite refusal.

Letting go of the stroller, she tightened her grip on the toddler and violently dragged her to the edge. Shaking her roughly, she tried to get her to look down.

"Look down, dammit. You're not Daddy's little girl any more. You're going to have to grow up a little bit, because I will *not* put up with your tricks like he does!"

She hit her a few times and then dropped her. The little girl ran a few steps, tripped, and lay on the ground sobbing. The woman looked off the cliff for a few minutes and then turned and walked to the child.

"Look, baby, I'm sorry. I shouldn't have hit you, but Mommy has a lot of problems right now and she loses her temper sometimes. Yes, we'll go right back down. You don't have to go to the edge again."

She held her for a few moments and then took her hand and walked her to the stroller. The woman turned once more and stared at the view. Still crying, the toddler checked to see that her mother wasn't looking, and then reached into the stroller.

As she withdrew her hand and the infant screamed, a familiar look passed over her face; I finally noticed the resemblance to her mother.

The Scene of a Bad Accident

CHRIS GORDON

The accident occurred on a brisk autumn evening five years ago next to the East Pond in Eastport. When my brother and I got there we found the scene lit up from the flashing lights of fire engines, patrol cars, and an ambulance. Numerous volunteer firemen, including my father, were standing about. The skid marks on the road showed the vehicle's path where it veered out of control. A section of a once straight guardrail was now contorted. The telephone pole, which stood behind it, was snapped in half as the result of a high-speed impact. Although it could not be seen we heard that a car had gone into the water. It was evident that this is what must have happened. Numerous questions were tossed about the group my brother and I were now standing with. "Who reported it?" "Is it a car?" "Did they get out?" "Why is everyone just standing around, why isn't someone doing something?" But nothing could be done. The water was so very cold and the vehicle had been submerged for quite some time now. The fire department launched a small rescue boat which several firemen got into. They then began to search the calm, dark water for the wreckage while a crowd of onlookers, including myself, watched. It was soon found. "It's a car," one man yelled.

As we stood and watched, a man approached my brother and me and asked for details. The man was middle-aged and sloppy in appearance. His half-unbuttoned flannel shirt hung partially out of his trousers, and the shaving cream which he had obviously applied to his face earlier had now dried and hardened. I didn't know this fellow, but it sure seemed like he left someplace in a hurry. Little expression was on his face, but I distinctly remember his eyes, how worried and scared they seemed. He appeared to be quite nervous and was anxious to find out what color the car was. Numerous times he asked, "Is it a tan car?" He explained that his reason for concern was that his wife had left for work earlier, but she was upset and angry, for the two had quarreled. It's five years later and I can still hear in my mind the man saying, "I sure hope that isn't my wife because she just left the house." The man then walked away.

Although the firemen must have known, or at least hoped they did, my brother and I wondered if someone was still inside the car and if there was any hope. The firemen had a problem, for they did not have the equipment or trained personnel to dive down to the car. One fireman tried, but he exited the water almost as quickly as he entered it. A scuba team was called in, but in the meantime a local resident donned his wetsuit and scuba gear and entered the water. Numerous times he dove, then resurfaced. One time he came up to get a crowbar.

A tow truck soon arrived and a cable was attached to the submerged vehicle. The gears strained when the winch was activated. I remember how quiet it became as the car was slowly pulled out. My brother and I stood in silence as the red and white lights of the fire engines periodically danced across us. As the water rippled, pockets of escaping air bubbled up to the surface. The roof of the car could be seen slowly rising out of the water. When fully out of the water and now resting on the bank the car looked like an oversized, twisted or mangled colander as the water streamed out.

From our viewpoint we could see no occupant. Incidentally, the car happened to be tan. One fireman stood ready with a yellow plastic blanket, the kind that a body is usually covered up with. After a few minutes two men got out of the car and then the man with the yellow blanket covered up whoever was inside. One body was finally removed and placed in the ambulance. That poor unfortunate individual, I thought. As others watched and wondered I sadly enough found answers to many of my questions. As I walked around to better my view I saw the man to whom my brother and I had spoken earlier. He was now being helped, more like carried, away from the scene by two police officers. Those worried and scared eyes I had seen earlier were now flowing with tears. Numbness set in as I now realized that the wrecked vehicle was his own and the victim of this tragic accident was his wife. How that poor man must have felt, for the last time he had seen his dear wife alive the two had been angry at each other. Unfortunately, it was too late to say "I'm sorry."

Memoir of Nature

Give an account of some action you witnessed in which people played little or no part, such as some animal behavior or weather that particularly impressed you. Give your own thoughts and feelings, however. You may include this in a collection of your memoirs, to diversify them, or make it part of a booklet of nature memoirs by you and others.

Spider

TY SHIMOGUCHI

I first saw the garden spider while I was watering the plants. Indeed, I almost ended its short life as the mild stream of water from the hose nearly washed the spider away, in, for it, a torrent of water. Luckily, I had missed the small creature whom I had first not seen. It was sitting on a leaf at the time, hiding from the heat of the sun. Although the stream of water had missed directly hitting the spider, it was alarmed. The frightened insect drew it's long legs into its body as it huddled in a ball-shaped mass.

Now, I have always been fascinated with insects and have never been one to purposely harm them. Spiders are an essential part of the environment, and they aid the garden by eliminating garden pests. Also, spiders are an integral part of the whole food chain. I was worried that I had injured the spider, and who was I to end one of God's creations' life?

I stooped, hoping to get a closer look, but the spider quickly dashed away down into the dim denseness of the bush. I was relieved that it was uninjured but slightly disappointed that I didn't get to see the spider more closely. I finished watering the plants, this time keeping a close eye out for any water-endangered insects.

The next morning I awoke early to go to school. I stumbled outside to get the morning newspaper and saw that it had been thrown near the garden. As I retrieved the paper, I noticed the same garden spider I had seen the day before. The garden spider was up and about at dawn. He appeared to be doing some task, so I went for a closer look. The sun glinted on something, exposing two glistening strands of webbing. The spider web, or the start of the spider web, was almost invisible unless the sun reflected off of it. I was amazed to see the little creature working so diligently on his web. The long-legged insect climbed to a high leaf where it plunged itself down to another, lower leaf while trailing its rope behind him. The spider worked carefully, seemingly measuring the specifications of its web. After it did this it paused a moment, as if reflecting, and then it scurried off, up the bush to another high leaf where the process again was repeated. I longed to stay and watch the spider, fascinated with the little architect, but school called. I glanced back as I opened the house door and I saw the spider once again parachute down.

I returned from school in the late afternoon, and I was delighted to see the spider out. He was still working on his web as hard as he was in the morning. Surprisingly the web was not yet near completion. I wondered why the web was not finished because the spider worked at a pace that would surely have entailed its completion if it had worked the entire day on it. It then dawned on me that the spider probably did nothing but seek shelter during the heat of the day. I remembered that when I first saw the spider it had been in the shade away from the direct rays of the sun. Anyway, the web's outline was complete. It was hexagon-shaped and amazingly symmetrical. Obviously this spider was a master web-builder. I watched the busy spider until the sun went down.

The next morning I awoke early and with sleepy eyes I went out to check on the spider. The web was now complete. It was a superb web made very precisely. The web also was ideally located in a spot where insects often traveled through. Either the spider had been lucky in choosing the location, or its minute brain had worked efficiently. Or, maybe evolution had a hand in the placing of the web by the spider. Whatever the reason, the spider sat in the middle of its web, and for the first time I got a careful look at it. The spider was round through its bi-segmented body and it had eight long legs protruding from it. On closer inspection, I found the spider wasn't small at all. It was about one-half inch in length. The spider's body was jet black with yellow dots splashed on it. Its long legs were all black. The legs were interesting, as they were long and thin, yet they could move with deft quickness. Its skin was neither hairy nor shiny but of a rough texture. The spider's head was tiny and its beady eyes showed no emotion. And yet even though spiders are synonymously thought of as evil or sinister, I got much the opposite feeling. I do not believe the spider had emotions; therefore it could not be mean. I believe the creature only wished to survive.

Just as I was looking deeply at the spider an unsuspecting fly flew into the web, fooled by its perfection. Little did the fly do but try to unloosen itself from the cement-like grasp of the web when the spider pounced upon it. Here was survival for the spider. The hours of work spent on the web were paying off. It stung the fly with poison, slowing the fly's frantic thrusts for escape. While the fly was losing its struggle for life the spider was quickly weaving an iron casket of webbing around it. Soon, the fly was enclosed entirely by webbing although it was still alive. The spider carried his paralyzed morsel to the middle of its web, where, like all spiders, it began to drain every bit of moisture out of the fly. The feeding wasn't cruel though, only survival. The fly had to be sacrificed for the spider to live. I marveled at the spider, who wasn't mean, vicious, or sinister but just an efficient integral of nature. I left understanding nature a bit more than before.

During the night a storm unexpectedly arose. The wind blew and rain poured out of the sky. By morning, though, Mother Nature had calmed herself, and I ventured out to see if the spider and its web had survived. To my disappointment the web was destroyed. I eyed the bush closely, hoping to see the spider. At first he was nowhere to be seen. Then I spotted him sitting on a leaf. He had survived. I watched the spider joyfully, but then out of the sky a bird swooped down on the spider snagging it in its beak as it flew off. The Victor had become the Victim. Again I more clearly understood nature, but I was a bit angry at the loss of the spider I had so carefully watched. But then on the bush nearest my door I saw a little creature parachute down trailing a silky web. The process was about to begin once again.

Memoir Profile

Show what someone was like or is like by telling typical things about their behavior that you know from knowing him or her. Use their actions and habits and words to sketch the main lines of their character or their relationship to you.

Archie Williams
KURT BELL

"Hey Arch', what's happenin'?" was a familiar phrase in the corridors of Drake High. Archie Williams always had a nice response and would often stop and "rap" with one student or another.

He was a black man, probably in his mid-sixties. He walked with a slight limp and was usually shabbily dressed in baggy polyester pants with a clashing shirt that had gone out of style in the early '70s. The palms of his hands were usually white with chalk from not using the blackboard eraser; as well as a spot on his pants where he had obviously wiped his hand. An old green visor hung across his forehead, parting his long, thin, grey, afro-ed hair, and a pair of silver-rimmed glasses, that he was always pushing up, covered the rest of the upper portion of his face. A grey mustache wrapped around the sides of his mouth and met the unkept goatee that covered his chin.

Archie was a man with two identities, the present and the past: he was the kind-hearted old computer teacher and also a gold medalist at the 1948 Olympics. I don't know by which I was most attracted to him. When I first learned he was a gold medalist—before I knew him personally—I was in total awe of him. I couldn't even imagine the work and dedication it took him to be the fastest 200-meter runner in the world. On the surface he hardly looked Olympic caliber or that he ever could have been; his body seemed tired and worn, drained by years of strenuous exertion.

I had known who he was since my freshman year—everyone knew who he was—but didn't really meet him until the final semester of my junior year, at which time I enrolled in his computer class.

I remember the first day of class. He put a number problem on the blackboard and said the first one to answer it would get a buck. I answered it first but got the wrong answer. He said he guessed that really didn't matter because all I had to do was answer it first; he gave me the buck. He continued, "OK, the first one to answer it correctly gets another buck." I walked out of computers that day with two dollars, a new friend, and the nickname "Taco Bell." I still don't know why the name.

Although he never had much money, Archie was a generous man. He had purchased four of the school's ten computers and started the program, despite the fact that he had to teach night school to adults to earn enough cash. Often when I was down at school working on the school paper at night I would bring him a beer or tell him the latest dirty jokes. He loved dirty jokes, especially black racial jokes, which I thought was odd, he being black himself.

Passing by his room one evening, I recall him yelling across a crowded room, "Hey, Taco Bell! You hear about the latest video game? It's called blackman; it has big lips and eats watermelon. You can only play the home version on a stolen TV." I can still picture the astonished adult faces in the room. They had never seen that side of him, the only side I had ever known. As far as teaching is concerned he is a far cry from the best—at teaching computers, that is; I learned very little about the computer in there. I did learn a lot about playing craps and 21 and a number of other computer games. I did, however, learn enough about the programming to be able to alter programs just enough to edge most students at almost any game; I won a good deal of lunch money in that room. I was also able to make computer-printed report cards in there, custom-made for any student. Arch thought they were funny and even showed me how to make them look more realistic. He never seemed to care much what we did in there. After all, he was just a couple years from retirement.

As I got to know him more, the great Olympian that I once imagined he was no longer seemed a dominant part of him. He appeared to have nothing special, no particular drive, no fire in his eye, nothing extraordinary that would seem necessary to mold a man into the world's greatest. It was like he'd accomplished what he'd set out to do and now seemed carefree and worriless. Maybe nothing could compare to the moment the tape struck his chest in London. It's a saddening thought but could there be nothing left in life for him? Was that the reason for the alcohol on his breath at 10:00 a.m.?

I don't know why I think of him now negatively; he was always my favorite teacher. I'd go in his class when I cut others. We'd joke and laugh. Maybe I'm afraid that I see too much of myself in him.

Last I saw him was the last day of school. I asked him what I'd gotten in the class. "You got a lousy A," he answered. "Why?" I asked. "I don't know, you sure didn't earn it." "Thanks, Arch', take care of yourself," I said as I left.

"Hey, Taco Bell! A giraffe walked into Perry's bar and said the highballs are on me," he yelled out the door, then added, "Good luck in life, kid, and don't you dare turn out like me."

I often ponder the thought and wonder where my road leads.

Dead Issue

BRUCE CORNISH

"Bullshit that's pure bullshit."

I knew before the words were even out of my mouth that what he was saying was true. He took a hard line on it, but....

"Would you calm down. God, you're all red in the face."

Mitch was right about that too. I could feel the heat radiating from my by now crimson ears. My heart was pounding so hard that each beat jogged my vision. Why did he have to do this? All I wanted to do was to look at our parents' wedding pictures, but he had to turn it into some kind of fact-finding mission. Dad had died only a couple of years ago, and I saw no reason for Mitch to slander his name.

I enjoyed looking at his picture in the wedding album. He looked too young to have ever been my father. His smooth, angular face seemed very white compared to his curly, black hair slicked almost straight with more than a dab of Brylcreem. I looked at the photos for a long time thinking that he was drunk until I realized that he didn't have his glasses on. His poor tired eyes had given up squinting, and their weak gaze gave his face a placid, helpless look. He was only a boy of twenty who in four short years would have a family of five to support. He could hardly have known himself, much less a new wife and three little boys. There were no self-help books for him, no articles on how to be a better husband or father. These were reserved for a future, supposedly more "self-realized" age. How could we judge him?

My father was more of a legend than a man in the earliest times. He was in the Navy and spent four of the first five years of my life on aircraft carriers. Often we would not see him for nine months at a time. We would plan and prepare for his homecoming for weeks, and when his ship came in Mom would drive us hundreds of miles to the port where he was due. We would stand at the dock watching the thick, oily, green-black water surge against the huge wooden ties. We would stand for hours waiting for the massive steel structure to round the point and come into view. Slowly it would move into port, steam billowing from unseen vents on the giant, vertical gray walls of its hull. On the deck there would be hundreds of men dressed in the same white sailor uniforms with black neckerchiefs. All with those white cloth sailor hats that invariably one of us would get to wear before the day was out. All of us would strain our eyes trying to be the first to see Dad. Finally, Mom would point us to his tall, lean frame, and we would scream and wave, jumping up and down to get his attention. When at last he got to us, he was instantly besieged by Mom and three wild crazy things squeezing his legs and wiggling and jumping madly. This was no ordinary man.

I spent many of my childhood years never considering the possibility that my father could be wrong. That was like God making a mistake, ridiculous. Once when I was in the 3rd grade, my father lined us all up for interrogation. He said that one of us had been playing with his shaving cream, and he wanted to know who. No one confessed, so he let us off with a warning not to mess with it again. The next day, however, the same thing happened, but this time he said in a very stern voice, "If this happens again, I'm going to find out who did it if I have to beat all three of you."

The following day he lined us up and said that somebody was still playing with his can of shaving cream. He was going to ask us again who it was, and if nobody confessed, he would hit each of us once with the belt then ask again. Well, we got about three licks each before Shaun confessed to something he never did. In fact, none of us had done it. It was not until years later that I realized the can of foam was defective and oozed cream, leaving the impression that it had been tampered with. At the time, however, the thought that Dad was mistaken never entered my mind.

That realization of error, as I said, came late in my childhood, and the memory of it is far from dim. My father often took his vacations in the summer and we would visit relatives across the country. We were visiting his parents' house in Chicago one year and we were having one of Grandma's big "family" dinners.

Everything in the whole world was there on the table. I can still see that fat, honey-brushed ham glistening in the late afternoon sun as it shone through the kitchen window. Those soft, yellow rays of the late summer sun turned to solid beams as they hit the rising steam from the hot mashed potatoes, buttery acorn squash and other greens and vegetables.

"Boy, do I love liver," declared Grandpa, as he smacked his lips above the clatter and clanging of the silverware. As he spoke, he reached over and stabbed a few lightly browned chicken livers. It was well known in my family how much I hated liver. It was so well known, in fact, that I never had to eat the stuff at all. (I would actually gag.) "But that was cow's liver," I thought to myself. Mom always burned it the way Dad liked it, but these were chicken livers and they looked so soft and tasty. Dad would be so proud to see me eat liver. "Please pass the liver," I said confidently.

Dad immediately stopped what he was doing and looked at me.

"You little pig. You hate that stuff and won't eat it at home, but as soon as you know somebody likes it you want to eat it all."

"I didn't think tha—."

"Shut up and eat, and when you're done go sit by yourself in the family room."

I knew I was not being a pig, but there was nothing I could say. Talking back was out of the question, but I knew he was wrong.

It was hard being a kid. I was sort of half-human. Nobody really considered what I wanted. It must have been just as hard for Dad to see his kids grow older, knowing that we would not have that bigger-than-life image of him forever. All too soon we would begin to see him as the fallible human being that he was.

Dad tried to keep that bigger-than-life image, and for me at least, it never failed him. I can only think of one time that I ever saw him at a loss. He had recently retired from the Navy, and he and Mom bought a house in suburban San Diego. I remember one night that I was visiting he and I talked late into the night. He didn't like the house that they had bought. It was dirty and ugly and it made him feel cheap. He had been in the Navy for twenty-six years and much of that time held a good deal of authority. Now he was retired, had no job and no direction. He felt he was nobody. I don't think I had ever seen my father afraid before, but that night his despair was overwhelming. He longed for the days when we traveled across the country singing romantic Western ballads and tried to catch glimpses of deer in the night. He started telling a story about those days, and we laughed and then we cried.

That was in the summer of '63. We were on our way to the east coast, and we were taking the longest route possible. The old '58 Volvo had made this trip before, but not with two adults, three kids (ages 5,6,7) and a 120-pound German shepherd. In the daytime the sun was blistering, we kids were arguing and the dog was slobbering; we drove mostly at night.

Our best times were had at night when we would sing, play word games, and stop at coffee shops. When we stopped at these places each of the three of us would get hot cocoa. Invariably, every time we stopped one of the three of us would spill our cocoa. This went on for some time until finally Dad, having lost all patience, told us that if we spilled cocoa this time we were all going to have to wait in the car. It was about two in the morning, and the place was empty. We got a corner booth, and we all sat down on the padded red vinyl seats.

I was in the corner kicking my feet, playing with the revolving song selector for the jukebox and watching the moths flip around the lamp in the graveled parking lot, when my elbow hit the cup of hot chocolate. I looked up at Dad as the thick, brown liquid spread slowly and evenly across the table.

"That's it," he cried. "Back in the car." As he spoke he was picking up the empty cups and stacking them so he could take them to the trash can. As he put the last cup on the stack, he gave it a decisive smack for good measure. The cup beneath it was not quite empty, however, and as the top cup hit cocoa, it sprayed all over the restaurant. On the table, the chairs, the walls and the ceiling, but mostly all over Dad. For a second, it was deadly silent; even the crickets seemed to stop. Dad started laughing; he laughed so hard he could hardly catch his breath, and then everybody was laughing. He put his big arms around the three of us and said, "Let's clean this mess up and get back on the road, gang."

> "We beat the drum slowly and played the fife lowly, and bitterly wept as we bore him along. For we all loved our comrade, so brave, young and handsome; we all loved our comrade although he done wrong."
>
> "The Streets of Loredo"
> author unknown

Investigation
(Looking Into)

Reportage

Visit

Go somewhere that you would like to report on as for a journalistic feature—a locale that's colorful or significant, a place where things important or amusing or typical take place. Observe, move around and take notes until you feel you have enough material to do justice to whatever drew you to the spot. Use your notes now to render the place according to what it most seems to have to say. You might submit this to a local newspaper or magazine.

The Road Test

JHOJANS RAMIREZ

On the way to school I used to walk by a park where people take the road test. This little park is between two streets that meet at one end. It's shaped like a triangle and it's very congested. I don't know why the people from the motor vehicle bureau decided to pick this spot for the test.

One day coming home from school I decided to sit down and watch the people take their road test. There were four cars in line waiting to take the test. The first person was an old happy man between fifty and sixty years old who looked like he still partied, by the way he was dressed—baggy pants, white shoes and a very colorful tie. He was with a pretty young lady who drove him to take the test. He handed the registration and rest of the papers to the instructor,

69

who proceeded to test the old man and told him to get in the car. The old man got all excited and started walking to the car. He tripped on his way and the instructor helped him get up.

By this time the instructor appeared to be panicking and praying. The old man tried five different keys to open the door. On one key chain he had fifteen different keys. He told the instructor to be patient with him, that he only had to try ten more keys to find the right one. After the eighth key he started to force the door open. The instructor went around to his side and told the old man there was no need for the key, that the door was already unlocked. Both men got in the car. The instructor didn't want to go through the same thing with the key, so he found the right key for the old man, who started the car pretty well. The instructor was telling him to go slowly, but the old man shifted into drive and stepped on the gas so hard that he left a cloud of smoke and burnt rubber behind. I was wondering if this old man was going to pass the test.

The second person to take the test that day was a young lady. She looked very nervous and scared to go into the car. She handed the papers to her instructor, and they got in the car. Everything seemed to be normal except she was sitting in the car for more than fifteen minutes. She tried to pull out of the parking spot, but other people wouldn't let her go. Finally she pulled out but very fast, burning wheels, and almost hit the car in front of her.

The third person was a big fat woman. She was so big she could barely fit in her 1972 Volkswagen. I don't think she knew how to drive a standard shift. She kept shifting into the wrong gear and the car kept stalling. After she tried several times the instructor asked her to let him out.

The fourth person was a man around thirty-three years old. He seemed to know what he was doing. He handed his papers to the instructor, and they got in the car. Everything was just fine until he pulled out and hit the car next to him. I guess he failed the test, but I don't know about the other people.

I started walking home laughing but watching every step for crazy drivers.

Torrey Pines Hangglider Port

CHRIS STIRRAT

A beach can be seen far below the sheer face of the bluff with crystal blue water crashing and flowing up the beach, only to return white and foamy moments later. The sky is a deep blue color, disturbed only by occasional white billowing clouds, and a foggy haze on the horizon. The view from up here, some three hundred feet above the beach, is spectacular. I notice some people to the left, enjoying the view, and I am startled to see an older man, in his seventies at least, making his way down the treacherous cliff. He stops about thirty feet down, promptly takes hold of the binoculars from around his neck, and enjoys the view. The view, that is, of Blacks Beach (the nudist beach) that is just below. To the right, the people are using this cliff for its designated purpose, a place to launch and land hanggliders.

I look just in time to see a man wearing a bright orange helmet, and a padded nylon harness around his trunk which in turn hooks on to an oversized kite, to hold him suspended beneath it. He is about to step off of this cliff into nothing but air. Two assistants, a young blond girl in her twenties, and a rugged, middle aged man, who sounds official as he barks at some spectators to stand back, help to steady the kite as the pilot mentally prepares himself for flight. The assistants nod to each other and simultaneously release the glider. The pilot takes two steps forward, steps that appear to be his last, and continues gracefully off the earth. Immediately, the whole apparatus rises sharply and continues to rise up as if some force were pulling it up in the sky. After ascending high enough to be comfortably clear of any earthly obstructions, the pilot raises his feet behind him and inserts them into his harness and now lies on his stomach comfortably suspended below his glider. As he secures his feet, the glider turns instantly to the left and accelerates away from the launching area. This is the Torrey Pines Hangglider Port.

After watching contentedly as the hangglider launches, an older man exclaims, "Like I told him, the wind conditions are ideal today. After watching the winds here for seventeen years, I ought to know when they are good." This man works at the hangglider port and wears a shiny black jacket with a large Hanggliding Association patch on the back. He is a balding man of about fifty years, ruggedly clothed with cowboy boots, jeans, his black jacket, and an old baseball cap. He is a relative expert on the sport of hanggliding and loves to talk about it. The ideal wind conditions according to the expert are fifteen to twenty knot winds. They should be steady but not gusty, blowing from the ocean directly inland and perpendicular to the shoreline. "A steady strong wind makes for a smooth and safe ride. Gusty winds cause the ride to be bumpy and more tiring," he states. "Could use a little stronger wind today, but ya can't complain too much." We watch another hangglider move into launch position, go through the pre-flight ritual of steadying the glider inches away from the cliff's edge. It launches and immediately climbs to a comfortable altitude before making its turn. "See what I mean?" asks the expert contentedly. By now, there were several gliders in the air. I notice two of them floating almost motionless, and point this out to my expert. They are riding warm air columns called "thermal lifts."

A thermal lift is caused by warm air patches rising from a source on the ground such as a large rock formation that has been warmed by the sun's rays. The air rises in a column and naturally causes the hangglider to rise along with it. A small white billowy cloud usually forms at the top of thermal lifts and makes them easier to identify. These columns of warm air are important to hanggliders because they are a way of gaining altitude, which is important because they must land at the same place they took off and so sometime during their flight must gain some altitude. It takes experience and a sixth sense to find thermals, but there are two clues to look for—small white clouds and certain earth formations known to store and release heat, such as rock. When a pilot flies through a thermal an instant lift can be felt on the glider, so an experienced pilot can find them by feel. To efficiently use a thermal lift, the pilot must maneuver the glider with slight adjustments to stay in the lift for as long as possible. This causes the glider to appear as if it is suspended, motionless in the air.

Hanggliding is an expensive sport to pick up. "It is something that you should look into throughly before becoming actively involved," warns my new-found expert in the sport. The gliders range in price from $400, for something that is barely safe enough to attempt to fly, to $2600 for the brand new top-of-the-line model. Experienced hang-glider pilots usually only keep one glider for about a year, then buy a new one to keep up with the latest technological advances in the sport. There are enough people just beginning in the sport to provide an adequate market for used gliders.

The gliders themselves look like large triangular kites, with metal-lic tubing supporting them. A small triangle formed by the tubing hangs below the kite and looks like a built-in stand for the glider when it is on the ground. The tubing is reinforced aluminum tubing, which is both light and sturdy. Stainless steel cables help hold the tubing rigid and in place. This makes a strong but light frame. The wing is constructed of sailcloth and is usually brightly colored. There are long, thin pockets that extend from the leading edge of the wing to the back of the wing, every two feet across it. From above, they look like pin strips going down the wing. These pockets hold battens, which are rigid, thin aluminum slats that are inserted into these pockets to keep the cloth more rigid, and to help it maintain its winglike shape. My friend, the expert, sees his own hangglider, worth $2600, approaching for landing, piloted by his son, and leaves me to go meet him in the landing area. The bright orange and white glider circles inland, turns to face directly into the wind, the same direction as when it launched, and then descends quickly towards the raw earth below. Just before crashing into the brown dirt, he pulls up, floats for a second, then kisses the ground gently with his feet and keeps walking as if nothing special has happened.

As I look around, I notice how large the hangglider port is. It is a large open lot of land located on the cliff overlooking Blacks Beach, just north of the Salk Institute. It is owned by the city of San Diego. A small boxlike office maintains and regulates the hangglider port. The office is located between the large, open parking lot and the restricted take-off-and-land area. It serves as a sort of boundary between spectators and participants, so that the participants can have complete freedom to launch and land in the designated area without distractions or obstructions. This area is restricted by orange construction cones and is large enough to insure safety for both take-offs and landings. This area is located on the north side of the office because the face of the cliff is steeper there. It is easier to launch off of a sheer cliff because the hangglider becomes airborne immediately. On the south side of the office is the spectator place. All along the edge of the treacherous cliff-edge are danger signs warning of the edge. The area around the cliff is just brown, dusty, raw earth. Little vegetation grows there, and the whole area has a desertlike appearance. In this hard-packed earth are troughs and shallow canals scarred into the earth by drainage water flowing. They are deep enough to hinder you as you walk across them in pursuit of the cliff edge. There are two park benches placed near the edge of the bluff for people to sit and enjoy the spectacular view. The parking lot is located directly inland. It is a large, flat, dirt lot and caters mostly to vans which are used by most hangglider pilots to transport their equipment. There aren't any marked spaces for parking, the drivers just park anywhere.

The office is called Flight Realities and offers lessons, gliders, and accessories. It also is responsible for maintaining and regulating the rules and conduct of the hanggliding port. Lessons range in price according to amount of lessons and extra benefits such as a flight manual. The lesson package that covers most of the essentials, and actually teaches you to fly and turn, costs $325. This port is for advanced-to-expert pilots, and all pilots must present proof of hanggliding proficiency (rating of at least 4) and proof of proper insurance. It takes about a year to attain the experience and proficiency needed to launch from this port. On top of those qualifications, there are strict flying rules which must be obeyed. Helmets and proper harnesses must be worn, and whistles must be carried at all times. The whistles are used to signal to other hangglider pilots when a person is either launching or landing or when a glider passes through the "window."

The window is the area of space just in front of the take-off area. It is entered every time a glider launches, and lands, and sometimes when a glider is in flight it gets too low and must pass through. The window is the most congested piece of air space, and the whistles are used to warn others when a glider is in the window area.

As I, along with a few others, watch more hanggliders move into position and launch, we suddenly hear a loud booming voice. "Does anyone want to go for a ride? Twenty bucks will get you a half-hour ride with me." The guy was friendly looking, but from the way he was talking, I didn't think I'd trust him with my life. He had grey curly, wild hair but wasn't older than forty. He wore large mirror sunglasses and talked like he was on drugs. He was serious about riding people tandem with him, and a brave person volunteered to try. First Milt, the pilot who gives tandem rides, got a harness for this poor, brave person. The harness is worn on the trunk and up over the shoulders with straps that hook around each knee. The two straps from the knees come up and join the straps from the back of the harness, and all of the straps join onto a metal ring. With this ring hooked to the glider, the harness holds the person in a horizontal position on his/her stomach. This poor guy realizes too late that maybe it wasn't such a good idea to trust this guy with his life. He starts asking about the safety of hanggliding. Milt assures him, "It's just like driving a car down the freeway, or riding a bike. The glider will practically fly itself." He explains how each harness has a parachute in it for emergencies, such as the wing collapsing or breaking. "It is extremely safe if you don't push your glider too hard," he explains, but I get the feeling that Milt has pushed gliders to their limit many times and wouldn't hesitate to do it again. The guy asks Milt what happens and what he should do if they get into trouble in the air. Milt says calmly that if they get into a dive or out of control, they should just relax and the glider will fly itself.

As they continue to prepare for flight, I notice another pilot packing up his glider to transport home. The glider is fully collapsable and can be assembled or disassembled in about fifteen minutes. The cables unclip, and the wing folds in together around the middle tube. The sailcloth wing is rolled up carefully from each side to make the complete wing in one long thin bundle. The triangular rack comes apart and packs in along with the long thin bundle into a nylon bag. Now the whole glider is about fifteen feet long and about a foot wide, neatly packed and ready for transport. Most pilots drive vans and have racks on top of their vans to hold their gliders.

The wind has died down and Milt can't take his passenger for a ride. The guy is disappointed but a little relieved, I'm sure. The sun starts to set as the final gliders approach to land. Some of them have been up for over an hour. It doesn't get tiring when the wind is steady and some pilots have stayed airborne for up to twelve hours. The sunset is incredible from this perch above the ocean. As the last glider approaches, and gently lands, the sun slips out of sight. The pilots are all excited because of the ideal hanggliding day at the Torrey Pines Hanggliding Port. As I leave, I wonder if I would ever have the courage or stupidity to step off a cliff with only a kite strapped to my back.

Interview

Choose some person you'd like to interview for his or her special knowledge. Tape-record or take notes. Plan some questions according to what you want to know, but be prepared to follow up the responses with new questions you hadn't planned. Write up the interview by summarizing it to convey the main things you learned from the interview. Use direct quotes; they'll add flavor and precision. Perhaps show a draft to the interviewee to check for accuracy and emphasis.

You may want to specialize this assignment by choosing a person in a career you want to know more about. Direct your questions toward what the career requires and what it's like to follow. With other interviewers plan to put out a booklet that would be of use to people not yet committed who are seeking information about the right career for them.

Behind the Microphone with Bobby Rich

STEVEN OTT

Recently I had the privilege of interviewing one of San Diego's leading radio personalities. The man, the incredible Bobby Rich, is program manager of the popular radio station, B-100, which is a station that the radio industry calls Adult Contemporary. In other words, it is a top-40 station geared for 21- to 45-year-olds. I think Bobby Rich summed up best what B-100 is really all about. "My philosophy is that you can be all things to all people, or at least a vast majority of them... I program less to the age group than I do to a type of person, and that is somebody who has a good sense of humor, is fun loving, is an up kind of person. I like to play music that is basically up tempo."

Bobby Rich's ability to make a radio station appeal to so many people has skyrocketed his station towards the pinnacle of success. Not only does his job title, program manager, mean he is responsible for making sure the station gets good ratings, but it also makes him the first man to get any credit or blame for the ratings the station gets. Said Bobby Rich, "We live and die by ratings." Along with carrying the heavy load of running a radio station, Bobby Rich also does a weekday morning broadcast which is advertised as the B-morning zoo with the Rich Brothers. The Rich Brothers, actually four non-related disc jockeys, base their 6:00 to 10:00 A.M. show on a mixture of comedy and music for an overall unusual and zany radio broadcast.

My intent for the interview was to find out exactly what his job as program manager means, and to find out what I could about what it took to get where he is today.

The first time I saw Bobby Rich was when we met at his radio station the day of the interview. He was fairly tall, at least 6'2", had a solid kind of build and a beard and for some reason struck me as being a funny guy. He was pleasant and cooperative as he gave me an informal tour of the radio station that included the broadcast booth and allowed me to meet the disc jockey on duty. Whether he was giving instructions to radio personnel or simply walking down the corridor, there always seemed to be a friendly "Hi Bobby!" to greet him. Bobby Rich was well-liked by everyone around him.

I immediately felt important to be able to walk with Bobby Rich through the station, and often I would get a bewildered look from employees to whom I would be unfamiliar. It was a hard-to-grasp fact that soon I would be interviewing somebody with the influence over what so many people hear on the radio. We then went into Bobby Rich's office to begin the interview. He closed the door, and as he took a minute to look through a pile of papers, I took a minute to observe the room. His office consisted of two plants, a stereo, a couple of chairs, a typewriter, B-100 signs and stickers, even a B-100 license plate, yellow walls, and blue carpet, all squeezed into about a ten-by-ten-foot room. However, it did seem unexpectedly well-organized, considering everything crammed in there. I began the interview by asking him about his job.

"One description of my job is someone who is in a position to be able to direct the personality of the entire radio station. In addition to selecting and hiring and firing the personalities who perform on the radio station, I'm responsible as program manager for deciding on basically everything that goes out over the air, and, as a result, I can vary it so the sound and personality of the radio station reflects my own personality." Bobby Rich spoke with the clarity and confidence one might expect from a disc jockey. Suddenly I noticed how his voice projection commanded my attention. It wasn't that he spoke loudly, but his deep, rich voice carried so well that when I spoke again, my voice sounded feeble in comparison.

"Do you think that the success of the radio station is due to the fact that you have so much control over what goes out?" I asked.

"The most successful radio programmers are those who find a way to have the station be a mirror of their own personality." he answered.

I realized that I needed more information about Bobby Rich's actual job, so I pursued, "In general, what does the title 'program manager' mean?"

"The program director's job description can vary slightly. At other stations all the program director does is just pick the music and decide what contests are going to be run. My title is program manager. I answer to the general manager of the radio station. He's my boss, but he gives me all program-related assignments to oversee."

Often Bobby Rich would speak for minutes at a time, but that was a blessing for me. He always looked at me when he spoke, and I remember thinking that he would have made a good politician. His poise and voice projection, symbols of his occupation, are the necessary ingredients of a good speaker. After a short pause he continued speaking.

"So I hire and fire the disc jockeys and everybody else heard on the air. I decide on the contests and the music, and everything else that goes on the air."

I remarked, "Isn't that an awful lot for one person to do?"

"But then I have a lot of people working for me who do a lot of preliminary [things]....I have to explain to somebody what I want the station to sound like...and then leave it up to that person to do all the research and do all the listening and figure out what they think is right and then submit it to me. So then I approve it (or disapprove it)."

"Your radio listeners don't normally think of you as program manager. To them you're Bobby Rich, one of the Rich Brothers on the B-morning zoo," I said. "How do you run the morning zoo?" Calmly and patiently he answered my questions, and gave me no sign that he wanted to finish the interview.

"My major philosophy in programming is that it should be fun. I have this belief that if it's fun to work here then it will also be fun to listen to. I like the disc jockeys to basically be up, positive, happy, forward-moving, active-sounding people, young but mature-sounding. My instructions to the on-air personalities always include the line, 'Have fun, and sound like it.'"

Bobby Rich said that he didn't actually originate the zoo concept, but what is different is that none of the four disc jockeys stand out above another. In other words, everyone supports each other equally. "It's important to me because even though I'm the boss and even though I'm the manager of the radio station and maybe the director of the morning show, in my way of thinking, I'm asking the other participants in the show for their support, because I don't want it to be that I have to carry the show or that if I'm not here the show doesn't work anymore."

Considering the fact that I perceived him to be such a busy man, he sure didn't seem to be in any hurry to get rid of me. I attributed this action to one of two possibilities. Either the impression I got of him, a busy man, was wrong, or he was too nice to say "get out."

I asked Bobby Rich to tell me briefly how he got where he is today, and what got him into the radio industry to begin with.

"I wish I had one of those great stories most people do, you know, about how they were inspired at age six when they woke up in the middle of the night and the radio was playing in the background. I did know by the time I was in the fifth grade that I was destined to perform on the radio. I told my fifth grade teacher when he asked us all what we were going to be when we grew up and everybody else was saying fireman and cowboy and I said I was going to be a radio announcer. I just knew that that's what I wanted to do and I was lucky to grow up in a real small town where there was one small local radio station....I was just a kid, and when I was ten years old I started going in and hanging around the radio station and sitting in the control room and talking to the disc jockey and doing odd jobs. By the time I was a junior in high school I started talking on the radio. They gave me a job first doing high school news, which I read out of the high school newspaper once a week, and later doing newscasts and disc jockey shows. So I basically worked all the way through my junior and senior year in high school and then went on and pursued my career, which has taken me all over the country from Washington State to Oregon to Ohio, Iowa, Florida, New York, Los Angeles, Philadelphia, San Diego, Michigan, New Haven, Connecticut." He laughed, "A few others. A lot."

His story seemed fantastic to me even though he admitted that it wasn't. I remember suggesting to Bobby Rich that he hire a professional to write a book on his life. He said that he might consider that possibility someday. He also admitted to me that one of the reasons he has worked at so many different stations was because he enjoys a challenge. But if a station doesn't give him enough freedom to shape it the way he sees best, he moves on. Bobby Rich is a man who is always striving to be number one. When I asked him what his favorite radio station to work at had been, he simply said, "this is the best place to be."

Oral History

Interview an older person who lived through some history of your locality or remembers lore about how things were done or made in the past. Take notes or tape-record and put this together later in your own words. Photos might also be helpful. Try to recapitulate accurately in a readable continuity what you learned from your oldtimer.

Collections of these by a team of interviewers can reconstruct vanishing practices or a bygone era and may make a valuable publication if well-edited and introduced. These collections could be mixed or specialized by history, crafts, health care, and so on. By interviewing older relatives, you may write a family history and genealogy to share with family and friends.

The Man Behind the Smile

ELISE DeCARLO

Al Keith, my father, was born prior to the Depression in Kansas. He grew up with windmills and farm animals. Al was one of seven children, five boys and two girls. Pride in his family and country was instilled in him with over two hundred years of heritage and family lines dating back to the Revolution.

Al was brought up knowing how to work. He spent his summer vacations when he was young plowing fields, milking cows, fixing windmills and digging out storm cellars. Grit was always in his mouth because of the Dust Bowl.

Al met his wife when he was nine and she was only four and very ill. Instead of playing ball or fishing on his free time, he read her stories. If any other boys laughed at him he would beat them up and then make them read to her. His motto has always been "let the punishment fit the crime."

Growing up in the Depression wasn't easy, but living on a farm had its advantages; the cows, goats, chickens, wheat and vegetables supplied their food. Their clothes were made out of grain sacks; it was itchy, but it kept them warm. The children walked five miles to and from school everyday. Al was an excellent student; he skipped two grades. But he was not past trying to close school by putting a skunk under the schoolhouse or stealing the school bell.

In January of 1942, one day after he graduated from high school, he enlisted in the Navy. Like several generations before him, America needed him to protect her. Love and honor for his country stopped him from even questioning or feeling any bitterness about what he was doing in the following years. A sixteen-year-old boy joined the navy because he never saw the ocean and loved his country.

In the navy he was put into Naval Intelligence and made a warrant officer. His job was to learn a language in a short time, blend into the community, and go back with news about the enemy.

He went through living hell in the following three and half years. He was almost caught in Northern Italy in civilian clothes by the Germans. That one fact could have ended his life, so he played a deaf mute. He somehow made himself a deaf mute so well that even their tortures of pins and needles didn't make him cry out. Loud noises didn't make him jump. Luckily, he found his way back to his ship, three months later and twenty pounds lighter.

Al was captured in the Black Forest with eleven other men. They were putting down black transmitting boxes. All twelve men were put into a POW camp. They were starved and then fed dirt: he ate it. Al and his friend Bill James escaped one night before the rest of his men were executed. They had figured that they really had nothing to lose.

After a ship went down Al, with shrapnel in his chest and the captain's brass clock, floated in the Atlantic for a week. The clock gave him something to focus on as he slipped in and out of consciousness.

Three years after he left the United States he returned, but it wasn't a permanent stay. He looked up his soon-to-be wife Sylvia; he hadn't seen her in eleven years. After a month's romance, he kept his promise that he had made eleven years earlier. They were married in New Jersey by a judge that he bribed. Sylvia was only fifteen and Al was nineteen. They lived as man and wife in New York for three months with daily visits to the VA hospital.

He was shipped back out to North Africa as soon as the doctors said he was ready. Sylvia was going to have his child, and he left her not knowing if he'd ever see her or his child again.

The day the war was officially over, he was back but waiting to die from new wounds in a VA hospital in Providence, Rhode Island. After six months he went home with Sylvia and his baby daughter, Lorraine.

With all of the men home from the war, jobs and living quarters were scarce. Al worked as a welder and lived in the Quonset huts in the Bronx. But his Kansas upbringing got the better of him and he felt closed in.

They moved to Illinois and lived in a trailer. Al had a job as a brakeman on the Santa Fe railroad. His second child, Georgia, died when she was three days old, and his third child, David, died in the trailer within two hours of his birth. It was no one's fault that there was a snow storm when he came into the world.

Al decided finally to go home to Kansas with Sylvia and his daughter. His father and brothers built them a brick house to live in on the farm. After a year of farming he had to accept the fact that his war wounds would never allow him to be a farmer.

He decided to return to Italy to apprentice as a jeweler for two years. Sylvia and Lorraine stayed with her parents in New York. He saw them three times in two years. When he returned he had a marketable trade; he was considered an artist in jewelry.

After returning to New York he worked in various fashionable jewelry stores. His son Michael was born premature and ill, he was only two and one half pounds. Due to the neighbors complaining about Michael's crying, Al and Sylvia bought a house in the suburbs of Long Island. They moved to Mineola, and Al opened a jewelry store on Willis Avenue, a few blocks away from his home.

I was born during this time of their lives, a year after my brother Mark died at three days old. Against doctor's orders I was conceived. My mother used the drug DES, so I was two months premature but strong.

Al and Sylvia adopted ten children along with raising three of their own. It didn't matter what race, color, or culture the children were. If they needed love and security Al and Sylvia provided it and much more. I was still the youngest. Al loved practical jokes, and with thirteen children he certainly had a lot of them played on him, but he got each one of us back with his own, no matter how long he had to wait.

The hardest thing Al found he had to do in his life was to realize that all of his children are grown up. But he's satisfied and fullfilled knowing that all thirteen children grew up with morals and manners and the ability to stand on their own two feet. That is his reason for saying that he is successful.

Family History

Put together some kind of story of your family by combining what you find out from talking with older relatives with what you learn from doing some book research on genealogy or regional history. Fuse this material together into a narrative that brings out something interesting to you about your background.

You can make this family history part of your autobiography, include it with others' genealogies in a collection, pass it around among family members near and far, or, if it is of general interest, submit it to an appropriate publication as a regional feature or bit of sociology.

My Blond Roots

KERRIA DeLUCIA

I've always wondered why, being Italian, I have fair skin, blond hair, and blue eyes. With ancestors originating from Sicily, southern Italy, and Naples in central Italy, I'd expect to have darker features. Many have mistaken me to be Irish. For my own interest, I have collected data from both books and family to find my origin. I now have a clearer picture as to where my ancestors have come from and about the lives they have lived.

I have found the history of Sicily to be very interesting. Sicily was originally in the hands of the Greeks. It was then seized by the Romans to be later controlled by the Barbarians and then the Saracens. By the eleventh and twelfth centuries the Normans controlled the Mediterranean island of Sicily. They in turn were overruled by descendants of Frederick Barbarossa, who was a Holy Roman Emperor. In 1943 Germany had attempted to conquer Sicily but did not succeed. In the summer of 1943 the separatist movement rose. The fall of the Fascist government and the Allied occupation in World War II gave a sense of neglect. Sicily was given a degree of self-government when they were granted the constitutional statute of February 26, 1948.[1]

Naples was originally a Greek colony. In the fourth century B. C. it was conquered by the Romans. The French Revolution of 1789 brought in French troops, and in 1800-1815 a French kingdom was set up. Joseph Bonaparte, Napoleon's brother, and after him, Joachim Murat, Napoleon's brother-in-law, ruled the kingdom.[2]

I also found that Sicilian people still show the Arab physical type with occasional Norman blue eyes. Neapolitans on the other hand have small and dark, almost Grecian, profiles.

In researching, I found my last name, DeLucia, spelled DeLuca in the dictionary, to be defined as "the son of Luca, Italian form of Luke (light)."[3] Words meaning pale or white, in a person's last name, are found to symbolize light complexions. My mother's maiden name, De Pasquale, was originally spelled Di Pasquale. Its spelling had changed when her family came to America. This often occurred as families migrated to America. Both forms of the name are "descendants of Pasquale, Italian form of Pascal (sufferings; child born during Jewish passover or Christian Easter)."[1]

By speaking to my grandparents, I now have an idea of how my ancestors had lived. My grandfather, my father's father, had a very good memory and was able to tell me a great deal. His family originated in Naples, and each member had a dark complexion, brown eyes, and brown hair. His parents, Andrew DeLucia and Mary Conte, were both born in Naples. After hearing of the fortune in America they left for the new country. Living in Ohio, Andrew worked as a coal miner till the day he found himself lost in a dark mine shaft. Finding a flint in his pocket, he carefully lit the wick of his lantern. Despite the broken nose he had acquired during a fall in the shaft, he found his way out. The Pittsburgh Lake Erie Railroad became his next place of employment. Not having much luck on the job, he got hit by a motor-running hand car. Andrew then sued the railroad and received two thousand dollars. He had then worked at a steel mill for a while until he bought land in Ohio. The land served as the family's food source. They had various crops which produced just enough to feed Josephine, Patrick, Sam, and Sue, their children. Any excess was sold.

When the children were still young, their mother had developed dropsy. Dropsy is "an abnormal accumulation of fluid in body tissues."[5] Mary eventually died from the condition. Not being able to raise the children on his own, Andrew placed his children in the care of a children's home. He did, of course, provide the home with funds to help raise his children. When they had grown older, Andrew took responsibility of his children once again. Wanting also to marry again, Andrew sent money to a woman in Italy he had previously known. After having enough money to make the trip, she joined Andrew in America. They wed and had six children.

Patrick, at age 23 in 1927, moved to New Jersey. A friend of his, Joe, owned a company manufacturing Daisy, a cleaning product. Patrick was given the position of general manager. The company was being financed by an outsider, a businessman who owned a vast amount of stock. The Great Depression hit in 1929. The funds were no longer supplied, and the company folded. Like other companies, it had felt the pain caused by the Depression.

Patrick then became an employee for a drug store in Union City, New Jersey. One evening a friend, while visiting the store, introduced Pat to a young lady. Her name was Maria Maiorana and in time she became Patrick's wife. Soon after, Pat got very ill. By the time he was cured, his position at the store was filled. Being the time of Depression, it was very hard to get a job. Turning to a friend for assistance, Pat was given a position with the Pennsylvania Railroad. The job only required his services three times a week, but he was still thankful he had some type of income.

The couple then had a child, naming him Patrick Jr. While leaving the hospital with the new born, they found a dollar bill on the ground. They hoped that their findings suggested that Patrick Jr. would later become a millionaire. Unfortunately, he never did become a millionaire, but he did indeed become my father.

Both Salvatore Maiorana and Josephine Franco, Maria's parents, were born in Sicily. Salvatore was a sea captain in the European Marines and also an importer. Sal and Josephine went to America on their honeymoon and never returned to their homeland. In America, Sal became wealthy, owning many apartment buildings. During the Depression, he let many people occupy the premises without charge. Eventually, he over-extended the credit given to his tenants. In no time, he went bankrupt.

Maria's maiden name, Maiorana, was changed to Mayo by her two brothers. Both, planning to be successful businessmen, thought Mayo was more appropriate for business purposes. They did indeed become successful, but I believe they would have even without the name change.

Like my grandfather, my mother's mother gave me much information. She spoke of the lives my mother's side of the family led. Fidel and Rosalie Bauccio were my grandmother's parents. Both, having brown hair, blue eyes and fair skin, were born in Palermo, Sicily. In Italy, Fidel built furniture, mostly for newlyweds. One day, while delivering furniture to a customer, Fidel met Rosalie. At the ages of nineteen and seventeen, they wed.

Rosalie's parents, Paul and DeGuvani Manno, were living in America and wanted their daughter to join them. The family, already containing three children, moved on to America. During their taxing trip, Frances, the youngest child, got a terrible fever and as a result nearly died. When landing in America, Frances was confined to an infirmary. By morning she was well enough to join her family. Fidel became a building contractor in America. In time, his family increased as three additions joined.

Fair-skinned, blue-eyed, Frances had attended a party her brothers were having. One of their guests brought along a gentleman named Joseph De Pasquale. Frances and Joseph met and eventually became husband and wife.

Joseph came from Sicily and, like everyone else in his family, he had brown eyes and brown hair. His parents, Anthony and Dominica De Pasquale, lived in Newark, New Jersey. Anthony worked with the railroad. When the Great Depression came Anthony and Dominica took their family to Italy, hoping Anthony could find a better job. The trip took a toll on the family as it took the life of one son.

While they were living in Italy, war broke out. At age eighteen, Joseph made his way back to America. His father later joined Joseph, planning to call for his family once he was settled. At the time, America had limited its intake of immigrants. As a result, the remainder of the De Pasquale family had to stay in Italy to dwell.

In America, Joseph first worked as an apprentice to a carpenter, while his father acted as a bailiff in the court system. Joseph then moved on to work for the Brooklyn Navy Yard, where he constructed parts for shipping vessels. By this time, Joseph had met Frances Bauccio. He was next an employee of E.W. Bliss, working as a machinist. When the company moved to Chicago, he joined the Ford Motor Company. Joseph also worked part time at a bus terminal repairing buses. In the blizzard of 1948, while working at the bus terminal, he had a stroke which kept him from working again.

Joseph and Frances had four daughters, one of which, Rosalie, later became my mother. Rosalie's older sister, Dolores, at age eighteen, dated a young gentleman. When visiting Dolores one afternoon, the young gentleman was accompanied by Patrick DeLucia Jr. Rosalie and Patrick found each other attractive and, in time, wed. The couple later had three children, the second of the three being myself.

From my research I found my fair skin, blue eyes, and blond hair not to be much of a trait in my family but indeed common in Sicily. At least now I can answer for my traits when someone is telling me I'm not Italian, but Irish. I also found out about the hardships my ancestors experienced throughout their lives. I now feel closer to them and to the family name.

Notes

1 Michelin Tourist Division, *Italy* (Jarrold and Sons Ltd. of Norwich, Great Britain, 1974), p. 254.
2 Michelin Tourist Division, p. 151.
3 Elsbon C. Smith, *New Dictionary of American Family Names* (Harper and Brothers Publishing Company, New York, 1956), p. 113.
4 Elsbon C. Smith, p. 115.

5 G. & C. Merriam Co., The *New Merriam-Webster Pocket Dictionary* (Pocket Books Publishing, New York, 1971), p. 152.

Bibliography

Michelin Tourist Division. *Italy.* Norwich, Great Britain: Jarrold and Sons Ltd., 1974.
Smith, Elsbon C. *New Dictionary of American Family Names.* New York: Harper and Brothers Publishing, Company 1956.
The New Merriam-Webster Pocket Dictionary. New York: Pocket Book Publishing, 1971.
note: My grandfather and grandmother supplied me with the information about my ancestors' lives.

Visit Plus Interview

Choose a person and place that go together, like some local character in his or her natural habitat or someone holding a key position in some operation. Arrange to interview the person in these habitual surroundings and to look around while you talk. Record or take notes and also jot down anything about setting or behavior that suits your reason for choosing the subject in the first place. Write an article based on your notes. Weave together the relevant details of setting and action with things the person said. Consider when to quote directly and when to summarize or paraphrase. This could become a character sketch, an atmosphere piece, or a short factual article—some kind of journalistic feature.

The La Paloma

MARIANNE BINKIN

The bright light of the marquee is reflected on the dark, wet pavement of downtown Encinitas. Tonight there are two Woody Allen movies playing and a line of people standing patiently along the sidewalk. Two bums sit on a bench nearby, clutching brown wrinkled bags in their wrinkled, aged hands. They sit quietly in their rags with far-away looks in their eyes. A girl sits in the wooden ticket booth warming her hands over an electric heater.

At 7:15 the doors are opened. The chilled voyeurs hastily present their tickets to the bearded ogre at the door. They look with anticipation as the ticket is torn. Having entered into the lobby, most head immediately towards the snackbar. Awaiting them is a multitude of sugary delights arranged attractively in a brightly lit glass case. The smell of fresh popcorn permeates the air, and the symmetrical mountains of soft-drink cups are slowly disappearing. Suddenly the lobby is filled with people standing, smoking, and talking. Groups of two's and three's linger near the ashtrays set against opposite walls. The din of conversation increases as friends are greeted and acquaintances are made.

The theater is beginning to fill up as the voyeurs take their seats. On the screen flash slides of local scenery taken by local photographers. A medley of Beatle songs is played out over the speakers. At 7:30 the lights dim and the curtains close. The movie is to begin and the voyeurs, armed with their softdrinks, popcorn, and candy, fall silent, waiting for the escape to begin. A voice comes over the loudspeaker and says, "Welcome to the La Paloma. Tonight we have two great films for all you Woody Allen fans out there. The first, *Take the Money and Run*, was put out a few years ago and is a personal favorite of mine. Enjoy the film." The voice belongs to Joe, the projectionist.

Climbing carefully over a chain stretched across the foot of the stairs, on which an "employees only" sign is suspended, I ascend the steep, plushly carpeted stairs. I can see the silhouette of Joe in the door of the projection booth. He is on the phone and motions to me to come in.

The projection booth is a long thin rectangle measuring 7 ft. by 24 ft. Over half of the room is dominated by the three blue Xenolite machines, one of them flickering with light. The remaining space is occupied by Joe's desk and a table with a rewinding machine built into it. Above the desk is a bulletin board covered with flyers, surf pictures, strips of film, and newspaper articles. Along another wall hangs a framed blueprint of the theater, the way it looked before it was remodeled a few years ago. Underneath the blueprint is a chair piled with blankets. A door at the end of the booth leads to a small apartment complete with a shower (and a large, smart rat).

Joe, having finished with his phone call, is perched on a stool beside his desk, and looks rather elfish. He props a leg up on his desk and tells me the history of the La Paloma.

The La Paloma Theater, located at First and D Streets in Encinitas, with its white stucco walls and high-beamed ceilings was built in 1928 by Aubrey Austin ("a weird little guy"). A. Austin, a banking tycoon, had bought much of Encinitas in hopes of developing it into another Palm Springs. Legend is that Austin made his fortune not in banking but in illegal rumrunning. One of his main purchases, Moonlight Beach, is said to have been the rendezvous point for liquor-laden boats from Mexico.

The theater was designed by architects from Hollywood and was the first equipped to show sound films. All films prior to then had been silent. The architects, not knowing of the vocal future of films, built the theater as they had many others. Because of this, the theater has problems with acoustics. It was fine for an organ accompanist, but the soundtracks to modern movies tend to get distorted. Looking through the window, out over the audience Joe says, "Today we have bi-amp Dolby sound, which is one of the best systems out of the theaters around here. The only way we could get rid of the acoustics problem would be to tear down the theater and re-build it."

During the war, the theater remained open for a while, but the income was meager and the theater was finally forced to close. While out of use as a theater, the space was used for various odd purposes, mainly for church services and recitals until it was bought in the late 1950's by a surfboard manufacturer. The theater retains this legacy even today. "We're the largest grossing surf-theater in the States," he explains as he jumps up to change the reels on the machine. It is intermission, and he is setting up the next film. "Yeah, we're second only to a theater in Sidney, Australia. But it's a different story over there. Surfing is considered a national sport in Australia, and here it is barely recognized."

With the second machine set up and ready to go, the lights are dimmed, and once again the theater fills up. "Welcome to the La Paloma. Our feature film tonight is Woody Allen's Zelig." Turning off the P.A. Joe turns on the machine and continues telling me the history of the La Paloma.

After the surfing boom of the early sixties, the surfboard manu-facturer went out of business. In the late sixties, the space was often rented out by Timothy Leary for use as a meeting place for his LSD followers. Joe recalls an incident that occurred during a speech that Leary gave at the theater once. "He gave a speech here about seven years ago. That guy's a genius. He knows exactly what is going down. He had a slide presentation to accompany his speech, and a few times he flashed to slides showing a tableful of drugs. He said that they were aphrodisiacs and they hadn't been made illegal yet. Sure enough," Joe says shaking his head, "a few weeks later he was arrested for those drugs."

In the seventies the La Paloma, once again a theater, became known for its concerts and special events. Among the performers were members of the Greatful Dead, Ritchie Havens, and Jane Fonda. Referring to the Jane Fonda event, Joe says proudly gesturing to himself, "I was the one who made all the phone calls for that show. It was my show, and it was a success." His enthusiasm is what has made him invaluable to the theater.

Joe's first job with the La Paloma came in 1978. He was working for a tree surgeon (hence his nickname "Doc"), and was hired to trim the trees in front of the theater. From there, he began cleaning the parking lot and was soon asked to work as an usher. When the opportunity to become a projectionist presented itself, he accepted. "I had to learn a lot of shit real fast," he recalls. "I was lucky though. At the time they were remodeling, and I got to re-do the projection booth. Everything you see here is my creation."

During college, he had worked as a film critic for a magazine called *Techniculture*. "I just like movies, I guess. When I was a kid I used to go into the projection booth at our neighborhood theater. Once, the projectionist gave me a piece of film from the movie *Ben Hur*. I still have it."

Besides being the projectionist, he is also the theater's film booker. He is the person responsible for the theater's wide variety of films. Since the La Paloma is independently owned, they are rarely able to rent first run films. "The big theaters are like McDonald's. They're huge corporations that do their best to eliminate the indies." Instead, the La Paloma relies on movies that the chain theaters won't show. It features adventure films, foreign films, surf films, and old films, and they even showed a fishing film (*Salmon Spectacular*) last year.

Joe's favorites are the old Hollywood movies. When asked why, he laughs and explains, "I like the American crap, not the European crap. The filmmakers in Hollywood were the craftsmen of the time. The techniques were handed down father to son. It was real quality back then. The foreign films just couldn't cut it." Our interview is ended on that quote as Joe leaps up to turn off the machine. The movies are over for another evening. The reels are rewound and put back into their cans, the lights are turned off, and the doors are locked.

The voyeurs, returned once again to their ordinary selves, file out of the theater laughing and talking. They leave behind the used utensils of a good time. Candy wrappers, popcorn tubs, and soft-drink cups are strewn throughout the theater and will be left until morning to be cleaned up.

As the door is locked behind me, Joe calls out "Hey, you should come next week and check out the Laurel and Hardy films with a live organist doing the music. Its going to be great!" Life at the La Paloma goes on.

Friday Night Shift

STEPHEN BEESON

The Pomerado Emergency Room, adjacent to Pomerado Hospital, serves the mild communities of Poway and Rancho Bernardo in North San Diego County. The lightly browned five-story hospital sets atop grassy hills off the main drag, with chaparral mountains standing abrasive in the background.

The emergency room is located at the far north end of the hospital. Ambulance and out-patient access to the ER is facilitated by a single mechanized door that opens laterally by electronic eye well before your entrance, in the case of a genuine emergency. The dull yellow L-shaped room contains nine beds, one through four lining the south wall (the "critical beds"), and beds five through nine lie against the west wall for lacerations and other less serious ailments. On each wall, above the beds are rows of cabinets containing a wide assortment of remedies—epinephrine, sodium bi-carb, atropine sulfate, calcium chloride, eg tubes, catheters, i.v. lines, splints, ace bandages, betadine scrubs.

The critical beds are the heaviest equipped. The most crucial of this equipment is the M/J2 Datascope Defibrillator, a device made to stop pathological defibrillations of the heart by using electrical countershocks to the heart through electrodes placed on the chest wall. It is hoped that this countershock will allow the heart's normal pacemaker to take over.

From behind a counter at the opposite end of the room, nurses and doctors keep a watchful eye on those with cardiac ailments through a complex system of monitors. By simply strapping small electrodes to a person's chest, independent electrical conduction of each of the four ventricles can be observed. They refer to this display as the "QRS Complex," each letter signifying separate portions of the heart's electrical function. "If the 'Q' is off, then we've got a problem in the left ventricle, if the 'R' is off it's the right atrium, and different combinations of each represent different problems which require different techniques in their treatment. It can get kind of tricky, that's why I make a lot of money," explains Dr. Blake.

Dr. Blake, part-time triathalon athlete and full-time doctor, is a 1975 graduate from the UC Irvine School of Medicine and is head of the ER department at Pomerado. Over the past five years he has spent over 7,000 hours in the ER, fulfilling the criterion for the speciality. Over the course of a month Dr. Blake works eight 24-hour shifts, giving him plenty of free time. "When I'm not working, I'm out riding my bike. Sometimes I'll ride to San Clemente and back, that's a good workout. The rigorous exercise provides an outlet to my stressful days," explains Blake.

He enjoys his work, most of the time. "When I've got three guys with ab pains, a couple of old ladies that are dizzy and have been for the past fifteen years, and basically just a bunch of bellyachers, I wonder, why the hell I went to all that work just to do this."

To the outside observer, it is obvious why Dr. Blake became a doctor. He's working eight days a month and making well into the six figures for it. "I originally went into medicine to avoid getting drafted and going to Viet Nam. First, I wanted to go to regular grad school, but at the time PhDs weren't getting jobs and if they were, they didn't get much for it, so I decided to go to Med School. I always loved the sciences. Getting A's in chem and physics was a real challenge and kept me motivated throughout my undergraduate days at UCSD."

Although he is now thirty-four, he sometimes has a problem convincing patients that he is old enough to be a "real doctor." "Ya, it really bugs me when people say I don't look old enough to be a doctor and mistake me for a nurse or something." One might guess him to be a surfer or lifeguard with his blond-tipped, brown wavy hair and brown eyes, but certainly not an M.D. On the whole, he is not what you would consider a stereotypical doctor.

Dr. Blake had always dreaded Friday nights. "Fridays are always a mess. On a real busy one we'll probably save two and lose one." At approximately 5:30 p.m. a family of four had been driving highway 67 from Poway to Ramona when they had collided head-on with another vehicle. They occupied beds 5-9 on the west wall. Dr. Blake approached the most serious patient first, the wife and mother of the family. She lay there, flat on her back with hands tightly grasped around the rails of the bed. Her head nodded back and forth with mouth gaping open and closed in a silent expression of pain. She had suffered a massive laceration on her knee and was losing blood at a rapid rate. Dr. Blake slapped surgical gloves in place and slowly began to probe the perimeter of the wound with his forefinger. "4-0 nylon and 1% plain xylocaine." The nurse quickly responded. The injection of xylocaine acted as a membrane stabilizer to nerve cells, thus preventing nerve impulses from passing from the wound to the brain. "If the wound can't tell the brain it hurts, it won't hurt."

Dr. Blake entered the needle through the open gash to avoid making additional punctures. As the fluid entered, the surrounding areas ballooned out and caused spillage of a less viscous mixture of clear xylocaine and blood onto the once clean white sheets. Dr. Blake again used his forefinger, but this time stuck it knuckle deep, directly into the wound to check the numbing effect of the medicine, "Yep, that's a deep one all right." His face, only inches above the knee, wrinkled as his concentration increased. The focal beam of a surgical light explicitly revealed the bone-deep gash. A curved suture needle pierced one side of the laceration, forming a small ring of blood around its entrance, then again, but this time from below, the needle emerged, spurting droplets of red blood onto Blake's greens. Dr. Blake tied the ends together, bringing the wound to a partial close. The suture nylon was cut and the procedure was repeated eight times. With that, Blake's work was done. The EMT (Emergency Medical Technician) then oozed a hazy, colorless ointment and wrapped the wound in a white cloth bandage, instantly relieving the woman's agony as the laceration was covered, out of sight.

The EMTs play a major role in the efficiency of the ER. Their responsibilities are vast: they wrap wounds; clean sheets; take temperatures, blood pressures, respiration rates, and pulse rates; give boosters; take histories; and are responsible for maintaining emotional stability among traumatized patients. EMTs are also often dispatched in ambulance units, where they are trained to stabilize patients before transport through i.v.'s, oxygen, and an assortment of other means. Their training is intense—144 hours in all, six hours in lecture and application for one full semester. Then shifts must be taken on in each of the hospital segments—the emergency room, cardiac care unit, intensive care unit, respiratory intensive care unit, and OB-GYN, and after all a final exam is taken and, if passed, certification is awarded. The EMTs are faced with constant trauma: "It's like we're all addicted to adrenaline."

It was 6:13 and Dr. Blake was still busy sewing up the car accident victims. "Don't do that, don't give that to me!" screamed an eight-year-old child in response to the xylocaine injection. A fruitless attempt was made by Dr. Blake to comfort the child in the presence of the syringe. "Come on now, it feels just like a little bee sting." The screams continued. The young boy had also suffered a deep laceration, only this one was located just above his left eye. Dr. Blake called for the assistance of two nurses, "Do not let his head move." His reasons for concern were well-justified, the needle being so close to the eye. Muscles from head to toe winced and quivered as the needle entered the wound.

Dr. Blake and his staff dealt with the influx of patients with amazing efficiency. From one patient to the next: sew this one, wrap that one. Most weren't in for over an hour. Almost all patients admitted are sent home, with a rare one being admitted to the hospital for further treatment.

At about 7:33 p.m. Medavac One had arrived, pulling behind them in a stretcher an old man about seventy years old. "We've got a possible MI here (heart attack)," informed one of the paramedics. "He's complaining of severe chest pain and shortness of breath and has a heart rate of 152." Dr. Blake stood idled in contemplation of the situation. "OK, let's run a CBC, chest x-ray and EKG." Dr. Blake begins his "head-to-toe" physical examination. First checking blood flow to the brain by placing his two forefingers on the basilar artery of the neck, then moving to the chest and abdomen, rubbing the fingertips in a circular motion, searching for a cause. Finally, checking the arterial flow in the feet, a sure indicator to the heart's efficiency.

The old man, white-knuckled as he grasped the railing of the stretcher, exerted periodic spastic expulsions of air. Eyes closed and head tilted he seemed to wince in pain. Dr. Blake unbuttoned his shirt, revealing a tired, sagging chest, and checked respiration, which surely must have been in better condition than his heart.

It was 8:00 o'clock and thus far it had been a busy but tolerable evening for the ER staff, but the worst was yet to come. The mechanized doors pulled open and a family had rushed in, led by the father, who held in his arms his 5-year-old son, who had been kicked in the back of the head by a horse.

"Bed one," ordered Dr. Blake as he and RN Tom Banazack began to take vitals. "Heart rate twenty-five, blood pressure sixty-two over thirty," a sense of urgency was forming over the child's bed. "He's bleeding bad somewhere with that blood pressure." The parents and two sisters, nine and three, stood waiting, watching in the hall, unaware of the seriousness of the injury.

A CAT scan of the boy's head confirmed a massive hemorrhage in the occipital region. "Give me 20 epinephrine." Epinephrine is a synthesized hormone more commonly known as adrenaline which is used as a vasoconstrictor and cardiac stimulant to help the body in cases like these.

"This boy needs to go to OR now!" Minutes after the orders were given orderlies rushed him to the third floor, where Dr. Obenchain, a neurosurgeon, would attempt to stop the bleeding. "Each drop of blood that isn't properly delivered to the brain will take a small portion of that boy's ability to live."

Although he had responded well to the heart stimulant drugs, his prognosis was not good. The hemorrhage in the brain would inevitably cause brain damage, probably severe. After the boy had gone to OR, Dr. Blake left to inform the parents of the situation.

An hour and a half after the operation had begun, the ER phone rang. "We've got a code in ICU." The boy's pulse could not be found. Dr. Blake ran in hopes of getting there before it was too late, only to return ten minutes later having failed.

The family had gone to the Poway Stables to look for a horse for their eldest daughter when the boy had walked behind the horse, a fatal mistake. The daughter's cries could be heard from the hallways, "It's my fault, it's my fault." The family huddled together in shock and dismay. The father knelt on one knee in an attempt to explain to the youngest daughter that she would never see her brother again.

Dr. Blake had just returned from the ICU after consulting with Dr. Obenchain and officially declaring the boy dead. He gently sat himself down in the cushioned armchair behind the administrative counter. He sat slouched and rubbed his forefinger slowly against his chin, which had become abrasive through the long shift. Eyebrows propped and eyes aglaze he fixed on an imaginary spot in space. "Bad technique, bad technique," he softly whispered to himself, bringing to bear the responsibility of the loss upon himself. A nurse, overhearing the doctor's whisper, approached him, reassuring him that nothing could have been done and his death must be part of some master plan by God. No relief was to be had. It had been another working day in the Pomerado ER...lives saved, lives lost.

Biography and Chronicle

Biography: Incident

Tell what someone did on one occasion and whose story came to you secondhand from other people or from records of some kind. The person could be alive or long dead, and the incident could have general human interest or historical value. By informal reference within the text or by footnotes and bibliography, indicate your sources—interviews, diaries, letters, autobiography, memoirs, histories, or public records. (How you indicate this will depend on your general manner of presentation.) What group, organization, or publication might want to know of this incident?

The Reunion

LISA SCHROEDER

Despite the humidity of a typical summer day in Vancouver, Wulf Krüse wore a three-piece suit. He was a withered old man, but he was carefully groomed. Every hair was in place, and his teeth, although false, gleamed. The only thing that marred his appearance was the jagged scar that ran across his cheek and throat. He seemed eager, yet apprehensive, as he sat in the restaurant with his daughter. He sat rigidly, his body betraying the tension he tried to conceal.

His daughter, Anna, did not even attempt to hide her nervousness. After forty years she was finally getting to know her father. It was exciting, and yet frightening for her. Anna had grown up believing her father had been killed in World War II, after he had been taken prisoner by the Russians. It was not until 1974 that she found out he was alive, and then it took five long years before Anna was able to facilitate his release. After that there were further delays, as Wulf, originally a German soldier, had to be debriefed in Germany. Now he had come to Canada, and at any moment his ex-wife, Anna's mother, would see him for the first time in four decades.

Anna had had to persuade her mother to meet with Wulf. Hilda had been devastated at first, when Wulf was reported missing in action, but forty years is a long time. Hilda had had to survive, and to support Anna. They immigrated to Canada after Hilda had been told Wulf was probably dead. Eventually Hilda fell in love and remarried. She had made her choices, and she did not want to have to account for them now that the circumstances had changed. Hilda had honestly believed she was a widow when she remarried. Now she found out she was, in essence, a bigamist. Hilda felt that meeting with Wulf would be betraying her second husband. However she finally agreed to see him, if only to pacify her conscience. Now she was late.

Anna knew that her mother's tardiness was a subtle form of protest. She wondered if she had been right in trying to pressure her mother into the reunion. Anna tried to pass the time by talking with Wulf, but conversation had to be held through an interpreter, so she found it very awkward.

Wulf excused himself and headed for the restroom for the fourth time since he had arrived, twenty minutes before. Anna watched him slowly walk away, his movements careful but steady. After all he had been through he still carried himself proudly. She smiled at the thought of how indignant he had been when he arrived at the restaurant. He was appalled at the plasticness, the fake decor. The restaurant was a mistake. Anna realized that as soon as she arrived. She had chosen it because it specialized in German food. Unfortunately it was heavy, starchy food, unappealing for such a hot day. It was a dark, depressing atmosphere, setting the tone for disaster. Anna hoped that the tone would not prove prophetic.

Hilda arrived then. The look on her face suggested that she was not pleased to be there but since she was she would put on a good show. Hilda seemed pleased that Wulf was not at the table. It was a last-minute reprieve for her. She sat, shifting several times to get comfortable. Her massive body dwarfed the chair. Although she looked old, she was obviously well cared for. Anna thought about what a direct contrast she made to Wulf's emaciated body.

There was little conversation between the two women. Hilda was immersed in her thoughts, torn between guilt and resentment about the reunion. Anna was nursing her shattered dream that the three of them could become a family. Wulf returned to the table. He formally took Hilda's hand and greeted her politely. The look in his eyes betrayed his shock that this was his lithe, beautiful Hildegarde. Forty years had changed her. Wulf sat. He stared at Hilda for a few minutes. No one spoke. As the silence became oppressive they all spoke at once. After the initial outburst all were silent again. What is there to say after forty years?

Wulf spoke then, and in measured sentences he told Hilda how much she had meant to him. He spoke of the years of prayers that she and Anna were safe. He described memories he had treasured of her, and the times they spent together. He thanked her for raising his child, and for surviving. He said she had been right to remarry, and although it hurt his pride, he knew it had been the right decision. He took her hands in his and thanked her for the love she had once given him. Then he was silent.

Hilda cried for a time. Her pain was audible when she whispered "I love you still." Wulf smiled; that statement meant so much to him. He knew that he and Hilda could never be husband and wife again, but at least they could be friends.

Conversation came easily now. They spoke of old friends, and memories. There was laughter, and tears, and happiness as the time wore on. The afternoon melted away too quickly.

It was getting late, and everyone had commitments. Anna slipped away, giving her parents a chance to say goodbye. The interpreter had left long before; Hilda easily translated. Hilda left reluctantly, and then Wulf sat alone, a withered old man, but carefully groomed. Every hair was in place, and his teeth, although false, gleamed. The only thing that marred his appearance were the tears that fell on his cheek.

Note: Information from multiple interviews with participants.

Biography: Phase

Narrate some experience another person went through during several months or years that amounted to a phase of that person's life having something of a beginning, middle, and end of its own. The person may be from the past or the present. When possible, draw from fresh sources such as interviews with the person or diaries or memoirs and indicate in some way appropriate to your presentation what these sources are. Or, if necessary, draw from what a number of other people have said and written about the person. Bring out the nature of the experience that makes for the phase, and keep in mind an audience that might be interested in that person or that experience.

Pleasure Turned Job

EUGENE WU

To the tennis world the loss of the great Bjorn Borg has been heartbreaking. His retirement at the early age of twenty-six was a shock to many. However, those closest to him realized he had lost the competitive edge that kept him at the top. What factors caused him to give up everything he had worked so hard for? Was he afraid of losing the number one position? Will he ever return?

The phase in Borg's life from late 1981 up to retirement day on January 23, 1983 was full of turmoil and deep thought for the great champion. The significant change during that phase was his dethroning as the Wimbledon king by John McEnroe. This upset ended Borg's record string of five straight Wimbledons. Then the loss to McEnroe again during the final at the U.S. Open confirmed the worst fears. This was not the Borg of the years past. The disappointing match marked the downfall of a legend's dream, the dream shared by all touring pros. This dream of being number one abruptly and surely ended in the next months.

Lennart Bergelin, Borg's mentor since the ninth grade, said it well many years ago. "The day that Bjorn says he is going to practice only two hours instead of four, then I will know it is finished." A main factor in the different Borg was the lack of concentration. After his defeat at the U.S. Open, he stormed off the court and refused to speak to anyone. Borg, the usually extremely gracious loser, was not himself as he avoided all. He had always been known to have the emotional stability of a Mr. Spock on the court. This immense concentration may have been the key to Borg's success. This high level of concentration is so mentally rigorous it would be rare for one to maintain it over five years on the tour. But to maintain his suppressed emotion for eleven years is unheard of. Borg did retire at an early age, but many don't realize he began touring as a pro at the early age of fifteen. Physically, Borg was still among the best; but he had lost the ability to concentrate.

Borg understood this and believed a complete layoff from the sport would be the remedy. After the U.S. Open, he announced he would "vacation" for three months and begin practice two months before touring in April of 1982. During the rest he spent precious time with his wife, Marianne. The fifty million plus dollars in endorsements and prize money was used extravagantly during his rare free time. In the next three months, Borg did not touch a racquet. He traveled around the world and even spent time with his parents. There were some rumors of his riding elephants in his backyard at one of his four homes, the one in Nepal.

After such fun, Borg returned to practice for two months. He claimed he was anxious to return to tournament play; the itch stayed with him throughout his lay-off. But just as he was to return, many problems occurred. The ATP, Association of Tennis Professionals, forced Borg to qualify for the seven tournaments he scheduled to play in 1982. An old rule stated that any player not scheduled for at least ten tournaments in a year would be forced to qualify for those tournaments. This rule would force Borg to play as many as three extra matches per tournament. He requested that an exception be granted because he was away from the tour completely for three months of the year. Furthermore, he argued, the rule was intended to sift out the lower-quality players. Thus, such a rule would be inappropriate for a player the caliber of Borg. Many officials sided with the champion and agreed the rule was unfair, but such an exception might be looked upon as favoritism towards a highly respected champion. What they did not realize, however, was that if an exception were not granted for such a man, the embarrassment would be even more horrendous. A high majority of the players didn't understand the purpose of the rule and sided with Borg. They declared he was a great athlete and deserved an exception. The poetic Guillermo Vilas of Argentina argued for him in his usual fashion. "The rules were not thinking about this guy, this great champion. Life rules itself; there is balance in life. But this.... We are so sick about this."

The ATP called Borg's play and stood steadfast. Borg reluctantly conceded and began qualifying for each tournament. He took all matches very lightly. Even defeats came as no problem. His nonchalant attitude was also noticed by the players. Dick Stockton, after defeating him in Las Vegas during the qualifying rounds, said, "Half the time, he is serving with two balls in his hand. How can a guy with a two-handed backhand play with a ball in his hand?"

Borg also wondered. He then decided to cancel the rest of the year. He again needed time off. He felt there would be a new start for 1983. He scheduled himself for twelve events for that year. This led many to believe Borg was back, ready to start afresh. The exhibition matches he limited himself to in 1982 showed he still had the magic. Interviews from established magazines reflected a Borg with a new fire in his eyes. His words sounded reassuring and full of confidence.

But suddenly, without warning, he announced his retirement just as the 1983 season was to start. Perhaps Borg himself couldn't explain the sudden change of heart. It is certain it had much to do with his marriage. He tasted the freedom from the sport, the sport that soon became a job. He realized during his furlow exactly how pleasant life could be without tennis, without the long hours, and without the pressure. With rest came contentment and commitment to his other love, Marianne. Borg summed it up. "We were able to go out together without thinking about training or a match the next day. It's a nice feeling."

Biography: Life

Recount the central story of another person's whole life in a way that brings out the main features or significance of it. This could be a summary of a person's life to date, an obituary for a newspaper, or a "life" of a person who lived long ago. Use fresh sources as much as possible that you draw together in your own way—interviews, diaries, letters, autobiography, and memoirs of the person or of those who knew him or her, as well as public records. Or if necessary pull together what a number of other people have said and written about the person. Indicate sources in a way appropriate to your general presentation, if such indications themselves are appropriate. Local or Regional historical societies might appreciate the result and have a journal to publish it in.

And More
SEAN LIBBERTON

Howard Hughes is an Ameican legend. He was an aviator, a film producer, a captain of industry, a billionaire. He was also a recluse and an eccentric. Some thought that he was insane. In actuality, Howard

Hughes was probably all of these and more. He will always be remembered as America's first and last great eccentric, a title that he deservedly earned. Yet Hughes was also a pioneer in the fields of business, aviation, and engineering. To remember Hughes only for his idosyncracies does him much injustice.

Yet that is exactly what has happened. Books with titles like *His Weird and Wanton Ways; The Secret Life of Howard Hughes* and *Howard, the Amazing Mr. Hughes* portray an image of reckless spending and haphazard investment. The fact remains, however, that Hughes parlayed a 600,000 dollar enterprise into a 2.5 billion dollar empire.

Born on Christmas Eve, 1905, Howard Hughes was an offspring of the Texas oil boom. His father, an underachieving Harvard Law School graduate, was the inventor of a much sought after drilling bit that could penetrate solid rock and granite. The discovery launched the elder Hughes into the world of high finance and corporate investment, a path that young Howard at first disdained. Instead, he went to Hollywood, determined to make a name for himself as a film maker. He had no experience, no idea how to gain it, and little respect for the business' institutions and traditions. But he had the drive, spirit, and the financial backing of somebody genuinely bent on revolutionizing, for better or for worse, this potentially glamorous and profitable industry.

And perhaps herein lies the key to Hughes great success. For how else can we explain his technical ingenuity and business acumen? Hughes attended seven different schools during his childhood, graduating from none of them. He had little formal engineering training, and yet he helped to design and build a number of different types of aircraft, not only for his own personal use but for several major commercial airlines *and* the U.S. government. With the help of his accountant, primary confidante and perennial sidekick, Noah Dietrich, Hughes amassed a fortune through his father's Hughes Tool Company. In his biography of Hughes, Dietrich explains that "Howard charged everything to the company. All his major expenses—planes, automobiles, houses, etc.—were paid for by Hughes Tool Company. Naturally the Internal Revenue Service went over his return with a fine tooth comb....but it was hard to prove which were business expenses and which were personal." In this way Hughes avoided literally hundreds of millions of dollars in taxes, and this enabled him to buy controlling interests in Trans World Airlines, RKO Pictures Corporation, Hughes Aircraft, and a number of real estate ventures. In short, Howard Hughes was a gambler, a businessman who was unafraid to take chances (he personally lost millions of dollars in the stock market during the 1930's and, by some accounts, lost upwards of 100,000,000 dollars of his, tax payers', and stockholders' money between 1930 and

1960), and a man who thrived in situations where others predicted failure.

In the meantime, Hughes pursued film making, air racing, and a number of other hobbies. His short-lived career as a movie producer-director was at one time the joke of the industry, but by the early 1930's Hughes had made a number of well received films, including *Hell's Angels* (1930) and *Scarface* (1932). It was his integration into the Hollywood social circles which helped earn Hughes a reputation as a ladies' man; in reality, Hughes held a more or less Svengali type relationship with a number of untalented but beautiful starlets. Few of these actresses ever made it "big," but the careers of such notable celebrities as Jane Russell and Ava Gardner can be attributed, at least in some part, to the financial backing, packaging, and selling of Howard Hughes.

Still, Hughes' first love was flying, and the contributions he made to the fields of aviation and aeronautical development are significant. In 1938 Hughes set a world speed record by flying around the world in just over three days. During the next ten years, he spent over 50,000,000 dollars on the "Spruce Goose," an eight-engined airplane made largely out of plywood. Critics swore the plane would never fly, but Hughes proved them wrong when, on November 1, 1947, he piloted the plane for a one-mile flight over Long Beach harbor. The plane was terribly impractical amidst the advent of the jet age, but the affair of the Goose for which Hughes claimed to have "designed every nut and bolt....to a greater degree than any one man has ever designed," has left its mark in aviation history.

It, too, might have signalled the beginning of the end for Howard Hughes. The Goose was a tremendous financial drain, especially considering the plane's commercial uselessness. Even after its maiden flight, over 3,000,000 dollars a year was spent on its upkeep. He began to make some very reckless investments. He lost 24 million dollars of stockholders' money with RKO. He set up, at great personal expense, 7000 Romaine, a message center created to satisfy his desires at any time of the night or day. He wasted millions on Las Vegas land which he never developed. He seemed to lose perspective on the importance and value of his wealth. And all the while, Hughes Tool Company, the source of his income, was having a difficult time earning enough to support Hughes' mad spending habits.

It was about this time, the early 1950's, that Hughes began to withdraw from the real world. He developed a phobia of germs and disease and fought a constant battle against sickness, a battle that only served to perpetuate his uncontrollable alienation from the outside world. He avoided contact with all but his most trusted friends and associates. He demanded that his room and personal belongings be sterilized at all times. He refused to shake hands or open door knobs. His life, which had always been secretive, was becoming the subject of gossip and fascination. And no one, not even Hughes himself, seemed able to understand the problems he had created.

Howard Hughes dropped completely out of the public eye in 1956. What transpired between then and his death in 1975 is purely speculation. It is believed that he lived, for the most part, in the Nevada desert, surrounded by his bodyguards and doctors. Few people saw him during this time. Whether or not Hughes, through his self-imposed isolation, believed he was achieving a higher spiritual understanding, as some have argued, or whether he spent the last years of his life hopelessly addicted to drugs is unknown. What is known, however, is that Hughes had little contact with his business advisors, and he gradually lost control, if not interest, in the huge financial empire that he created. He died far from penniless, yet, with the access to most of his wealth cut off by the litigation which Hughes had miraculously avoided for most of his life, his once enormous assets were but a fraction of what they once were.

Though he died over ten years ago, the legend of Howard Hughes lives on. He represented the Horatio Alger myth turned on itself, a victim of the multi-billion dollar empire which he almost single-handedly created. We will always be fascinated with Howard Hughes, just as we will always be fascinated by celebrities, heroes, the wealthy, and the sick. For Howard Hughes was all of these. And more.

Chronicle

Tell the story of what some group did far enough in the past that you must rely on documents such as first-person accounts from the time and public records. Weight the reliability of these and piece them together to fashion a narrative doing as much justice as possible to the combination of all sources. Submit to a historical periodical.

History of Fire Island
KAREN DEMMERS

Fire Island is a special place. Many people find it offers an escape from the busy world they live in. It is a small island, 32 miles long and about a half mile wide. It is a barrier beach, with the Atlantic Ocean on the south shore and the Great South Bay to the north. Long Island is on the other side of the bay. Because of the constant winds, the plant life doesn't grow very tall. The ocean and weather conditions insure constant changes in the island's physical features.

Fire Island is not the island's original name. If you ask people on the beach how the island got it's name you'll get many different replies. I shall relate some of these stories, saving the official version for last.

Before the Dutch claimed Long Island and Fire Island in 1614 the only inhabitants were the local Indians, known as the Unquachogs. They were famous for their fine wampum made from shells. They called the island, appropriately, Sechochaka, Island of Shells. They also used Fire Island as a base for whaling expeditions.

For years the island was referred to as Great South Beach by many, and some old timers still use that name. The name Fire Island wasn't really popular until 1920. Many of the stories about the origin of the name Fire Island are based on fire. Some cite Indian fires as the source. Others say that the fires that prompted the island's name were those made by land pirates who would light fires and lure ships toward the sand bars. The ships would be wrecked, the goods they contained stolen, and the people aboard murdered. One famous land pirate who was known for doing this was Jeremiah Smith, who is said to be the first inhabitant of Fire Island. He lived there in the 1760's in what is now the community of Point O' Woods. It is not known how many people were victims of this man.

Still other stories are told about fires on the island. Fires from whaling stations have been cited as the source of the name and also fires that lifesaving stations kept lit. Also poison ivy, which abounds on the island was said to set fire to people's skin.

The official version of the origin of the name Fire Island was related to me in an interview with Isabelle Adler on April 22, 1984. Isabelle's family has been on the island since the early 1920's. She is active in the Ocean Beach Historical Society. When the area was surveyed for the first time in 1688 the island was divided into five parts by inlets which have since disappeared. When the next surveyor came the island was one again and perhaps he misread it or else he decided that five was a misprint and that fire was the correct word. After all, fires did appear. Whatever the origin it is a wonderful name.

The early settlement of Fire Island began with the arrival of the Dutch in New York. An article by Patrick Harris appeared in the *Fire Island Tide* in July 1978. It states that:

Dutch Traders on Long Island first made contact with the Indians in 1614. The Dutch, too, were very interested in the

Unquachog wampum and purchased it in increasing volume
as its value to other Indians became apparent to the Euro-
peans. Eventually, the early European settlers began to
make their own wampum and used it as a medium of
exchange among themselves, as well as with the Indians. In
1638, English colonists from Massachusetts had moved to
Long Island and settled in South Hampton. This heralded
the eventual demise of the Dutch in New (Amsterdam)
York. In 1653, Isaac Stratford of Babylon (Long Island)
established a whaling station on Fire Island opposite present
day Bellport. It was named Whalehouse Point and it is
known by that name to this day. Brookhaven Town was
chartered in 1655 and its bounds included the length of Fire
Island.[1]

Private ownership of land on Fire Island brings us to 1693, when
all of Fire Island was owned by an Englishman, William Tangier Smith.
In a wonderful book by Madeleine C. Jonson titled *Fire Island 1650's-
1980's* this story is related. I will paraphrase: Smith grew up in the
court of King Charles II of England. He eventually became Chief
Justice of the Supreme Court of New York and died in 1705. He left
his lands to his sons. The eastern half was left to two of his younger
sons. His oldest son Henry inherited the western part, which in turn
was left to his great grandson, who sold the land for 200 pounds to
"twenty yeomen of Brookhaven," who owned it in common, each
holding an equal and undivided share. They used it to graze cattle, so
still there were no human inhabitants. This common ownership led to
much confusion in the future as to who owned what land. By the
middle of the nineteenth century Fire Island was becoming a resort
area. Sailing parties were being brought from the mainland (Long
Island). In 1856 David Sammis, one of the owners of the common land,
constructed the Surf Hotel in what is now Kismet. It could hold 1500
guests and was a very popular resort. The Great Partition of 1878
resulted from a lawsuit against Sammis in 1871. The result was a clear
set of boundaries for private property.[2]

The Surf Hotel played an important part in the island's history
when in 1892 the state purchased it for cholera quarantine. The many
shiploads of immigrants coming to America had to be quarantined and
checked for cholera, and the facilities in New York City were filled. An
article in the *Fire Island Tide* of July 2, 1982 tells the story. The
following is a summary of that piece. The local residents of Long
Island reacted strongly against the use of the Fire Island hotel as a
place for quarantined immigrants. The Town of Islip Board of Health
had a judge draw up an injunction against the landings. The first ship
to be assigned to the Surf Hotel was named the Normannia and it

came from Hamburg, Germany. The 500 men, women, and children on board were transferred to a ferry boat, the Cepheus, which could come closer to shore. One hundred and fifty angry baymen and a lawyer came to resist any attempt to land the Cepheus, and they would use force if necessary. By the time the Cepheus came to land there were 400 protestors dead set against them. They tried to land but the protestors aggressively prevented them from doing so. The passengers were forced to remain on board 100 yards away from the dock. These poor people were dealing with conditions that were overcrowded and lacking in sanitary facilities and food. It was a miserable night for those on board the Cepheus. The next day Federal troops and the National Guard arrived to contain the uprising. The passengers were finally allowed to land. After being given a clean bill of health they got back on board the Cepheus to continue their journey to New York City, ready to start new lives in America.[3] The Surf Hotel returned to private ownership in 1893 and burned down in 1918. In 1868 a marine observatory and a Western Union telegraph station were built next to the hotel. But still there were no communities on Fire Island until 1898.

The development of communities on Fire Island began in Point O' Woods. "It was begun in 1894 by the Long Island Chautauqua Assembly—a cultural, educational, and Methodist religious organization with chapters throughout the northeast—as a beach community offering cultural and educational advantages. Four years later the Assembly was supplanted by the Point O' Woods Association, which began the history of the village as it is today."[4]

Next in chronological order is the little town of Oakleyville with its ten houses. There are no stores, ferries, or services there. It lies between Point O' Woods and Sunken Forest. In 1905 Lonelyville was started by the South Shore Realty Company. As in Oakleyville there are no stores or ferries.

Ocean Beach (founded in 1908) is the town that I am most familiar with. I lived there from November 1975 till October 1983. It is a year-round community and the largest on Fire Island. The Ocean Beach Association was formed in 1912 to maintain order and property. It became an incorporated village in 1921. Isabelle Adler (already mentioned) gave me a tape of a man named Gordon Roberts from November 29, 1983 telling about life in Ocean Beach in 1910. The following are his descriptions. There were few boardwalks then and in 1910 the Ocean Beach Association had a clambake to raise money for new boardwalks. The water supply consisted of two handpumps, one near the bay and one near the ocean. There was no running water in homes. There was a windmill for lights, and sewers appeared before 1920. People buried their own garbage, although there was a man who collected garbage and composted it. Buckets of sand were people's protection against fire. There was no police protection until 1927, when a jail was built. In 1910 there were only three houses and a larger number of shacks. People ate what the bay and the ocean provided, along with local plant foods. Groceries were brought over once a week by boat. In 1918 the first school on Fire Island was created in Ocean Beach. It was a one-room schoolhouse with ten pupils. Today the population and number of houses has increased dramatically. The summer brings thousands of people. "Ocean Beach is the core community on Fire Island upon which all other communities depend. It is noisy, sophisticated, and crowded. Its achievement in creating a family community with numerous planned activities for children is overshadowed by its reputation as a 'swinging singles' playground."[5]

Saltaire was settled in 1911. In 1939 the Fire Island School was moved to Saltaire but moved back to Ocean Beach in 1943. It is basically a middle-class family community. Cherry Grove is not what you would call a family community. It has been gay since the 1920's and has quite a reputation. Water Island started to develop around 1912. During Prohibition liquor could be gotten in the White House Hotel there along with gambling. Although it is close to Cherry Grove, it is quite different—more low key. They have no stores or restaurants or services.

> As is becoming obvious, the origins of Fire Island's communities are quite diverse, as are their present "personalities." Point O' Woods grew from an educational and religious assembly. Oakleyville sprouted alongside as a labor pool. Ocean Beach and Saltaire grew out of real estate promotion. Water Island and Cherry Grove expanded gradually around hotels. Seaview developed from Gil Smith's fish factory. The first house in Seaview was built in 1895 for workmen at the factory. When Smith got out of the fish business he started gradually selling lots to summer vacationers...In the 1960's came a boom in construction of large houses of modern design attractively landscaped....[6]

Fair Harbor was founded in 1923, and in 1925 Ocean Bay Park was established. Kismet also came about in the 1920's. The Fire Island Guide describes Kismet this way. It is the community that is the farthest west. Its beginnings can be traced to the Surf Hotel and David Sammis. The hurricane of 1938 which caused much destruction all over the island destroyed most of the houses there, "even lifting the ground cover, leaving Kismet like a desert." It was slow to rebuild, but by the 1950's it became a community of mostly renters—singles in particular who engaged in group rentals.[7]

Later starting communities are Davis Park, which began as a public park and town marina in 1945 and Dunewood, started in 1958.

No work on the history of Fire Island would be complete without mentioning the life saving stations and lighthouses. A booklet called *The Story of the Fire Island Light* gives us information on this.

> In March 1847 Congress had appropriated an additional $5,000 with an additional $10,000 the following year, to establish voluntary lifesaving patrols on Long Island and New Jersey beaches.
>
> These volunteer crews were supposed to keep vigil along the shore at night, ready to spring into action to aid ships in distress.... This voluntary life saving service actually formalized a voluntary "spy glass patrol" that had existed for years. Men and women who lived by the sea were always ready to help, and at the signal...would bring the volunteers from their fields or roust them from their beds to do what they could to help a vessel in trouble.
>
> One of the early lifesaving stations was set up adjacent to the Fire Island lighthouse.... In time the voluntary surfmen evolved into a paid organization known as the U.S. Life-Saving Service. In 1915, it was merged with the U.S. Coast Guard.[8]

The first Fire Island lighthouse was established in 1826. It was equipped with 18 lamps and burnished reflectors and was visible for 27 nautical miles. The kerosene lamps made a complete revolution in one and one half minutes.[9]

In 1858 the second lighthouse was completed, which still stands today just west of Kismet. It is 168 feet high but no longer flashes once a minute as it did till 1974. Now there is a third lighthouse at the end of the Robert Moses Causeway just west of the second lighthouse. That one is quite modern.

Although it is still quite removed from the busy mainland, Fire Island is now filled with too many houses and too many people. The wildlife of the island has suffered due to the overdevelopment of the land, and it is still continuing. The National Seashore is trying to do something about this, but they can't do very much about it. However, for me it is still a place of peace where I can retreat from everyday activities. I hope that its special atmosphere can be preserved and that future generations will be able to enjoy this special place as I have.

Notes

1   "Fire Island: The Lonely History of a Barrier Beach," *Fire Island Tide*, July 1978 issue, page 16.
2   Madeleine C. Johnson, *Fire Island 1650's-1980's*, pp. 91-97.

3 "Trials of the Cepheus," *Fire Island Tide*, July 2, 1982 issue.
4 *Fire Island Recollections*, published by the Fire Island Association, page 25.
5 Madeleine C. Johnson, *Fire Island 1650's-1980's*, page 126.
6 Madeleine C. Johnson, *Fire Island 1650's-1980's*, pp. 132-133.
7 Bee Garfield, *The Fire Island Guide*, 1980, page 68.
8 Henry Bang, *The Story of the Fire Island Light*, page 12.
9 Ibid.

Bibliography

Books:

Johnson, Madeleine C., *Fire Island 1650's-1980's*. (Shoreland Press, Mountainside, N.J.) 1983.

Pamphlets:

Bang, Henry R., *The Story of the Fire Island Light*, 1981.
Fire Island Association, *Fire Island Recollections*, 1983.
Garfield, Bee, *The Fire Island Guide* (Trigar Publishing Company, Ocean Beach, N.Y.) 1980.

Newspaper Articles:

Bullington, Neal, "Trials of the Cepheus," published in the *Fire Island Tide* July 2, 1982.
Harris, Patrick, "Fire Island: the Lonely History of a Barrier Beach," published in the *Fire Island Tide* July 14, 1978.

Case and Profile

Case: Individual

Choose some person whose story typifies the experience of some other individuals, such as a runaway teenager or a middle-class person reduced to welfare, and tell what that person did or underwent. A case may present an instance of a current social phenomenon, a kind of personal behavior, or a feature of history. If the person is alive, you might interview him or her and others involved as well as seek out letters, journals, newspaper accounts, records of public agencies, and other documents that would have to be consulted to deal with someone from the past. Though basically a narrative, your case might include background information about whatever the case exemplifies. Think of your audience as people concerned with this subject. You might make a case book with others who are writing cases.

Gina and Bulimarexia

MARGARET COFFEY

[based on interviews]

Gina kept thinking to herself, "God, I'm five pounds overweight, I feel so pudgy and fat. I definitely need to go on a diet!" Unfortunately though, her parents didn't like the idea of her dieting. Her mother would say, "You don't need to diet, you're 5'5" and you weigh 118 pounds, that's a good weight for you." When Gina would fix her own low-calorie dinner her mother would say, "I've been working on this meal a long time for you and the rest of the family and you're not going to eat it?" After taking this guilt trip every time she would try and fix her own meal, Gina decided to make it easy on herself and started eating what had been prepared.

A few days later while she was at school a friend of hers, Kari, said "Yeah Gina, I've lost 10 pounds already. It's great, I eat when I have to in front of my parents, but then as soon as the meal is over I just go to the bathroom and throw it up. No one has any idea of what I'm doing, and I'm getting tons of compliments on how I look too." This idea stuck in Gina's mind, though at the time the thought of it was not too pleasant.

About one month passed since she had had that conversation with her friend. She tried to make herself vomit but was too disgusted with the idea to be able to. However, one night after her parents made her eat dinner she felt very full and extremely fat. Gina proceeded to the bathroom and was able to make herself throw up for the first time. She was still revolted by the idea but had a greater desire to lose the weight. Gina became bulimarexic during her junior and part of her senior year in high school.

Gina said to me, "My counselor told me that 1 out of 30 teenage girls are bulimarexic, I just happened to be one of them." A bulimarexic is a person who gorges food to deal with emotional problems and then uses diuretics, laxatives, or vomiting as a way to expel the food from the system.[1] Gina never would gorge food, as the majority of bulimarexics do. She would eat a normal meal and then simply throw it up.

Gina had several contributing factors to her becoming bulimarexic. Things weren't going too well at home. There was a distance between Gina and her parents that upset her. She also didn't like being the middle child: she was constantly being compared to her little sister and her older sister. "I felt lost between the two."

Gina also told me, "I would begin to feel depressed after a while so I'd eat to get rid of the depression." This was never a good idea because when the food hit her stomach she'd begin to feel fat again. Depression would hit once again and she'd be off to the bathroom to throw up.

Her main motivation for throwing up was her quest for attention. She was constantly striving for her parents to take notice of her. First she tried positive means of drawing attention. She achieved and maintained excellent grades all through high school. These grades would please her mother for a short time while her father remarked only once on a "C" that she received. Gina tried once more by running for class offices and being elected. Her school involvement had no effect on her parents, however.

Her frustration led her to rebel against her parents. She resorted to purging her meals. "This was my way of dealing with my feelings at the time. I couldn't talk to my parents, they wouldn't have understood me. Besides I wanted to lose weight, and my mother was being such a rag about not eating the same thing as everyone else."

Gina began receiving compliments on her figure from friends and classmates. Her parents finally began to take notice. They'd make comments such as, "You've lost weight, Gina," "You're getting too skinny" or "You should eat more."

"I received more attention from my parents than I ever had before. I didn't like the attention I got though; this fact surprised me. They began to pester me a great deal more than usual and that began to bother me. However, it was attention so I kept up my 'learned habit.'" That she did too, for a year in fact. She lost a total of 10 pounds, she didn't look too thin or emaciated; actually, she looked exceptionally well.

Gina would never make herself throw up more than four times a day, but then she could go a week, two weeks, or even a month without vomiting. Her sister, Mary, began to suspect Gina and her actions. Mary told me, "I knew a few of her friends were bulimic and anorexic, so when she started heading off to the bathroom after dinners I had an idea what she was up to." It was Gina's sister who caught her and told their parents.

"I got so much attention at that time and during my recovery that it made up for the lack of attention three times over," Gina said.

Gina's mother took her to the doctor the day after her discovery for a check-up. Everything was fine, Gina seemed to be in extremely good health. She was even still within the safe weight for her age and size.

Gina was referred to a counselor, Liz, who gave her helpful advice on how to avoid vomiting. Liz warned her that it would be difficult at times not to throw up, that it would take a little time to have full control over it.

One thing that made it easier was her realization that the more she accepted herself for what and who she was, the less likely she would be to hurt herself.

Notes

1 "Eating their cake and heaving it too." *Macleans*, November 3, 1980, volume 56, p. 51.

Bibliography

"Bingeing and Purging the Pain, the Hope: When There Is Never Enough," *Glamour*, May 1983, p. 258.
Paula Dranov, "When Eating—Or Not Eating—Is a Sickness," *Cosmopolitan*, January 1984, p. 190.
Arlene Fischer, "Do You Stuff Yourself One Moment and Starve Yourself the Next?" *Cosmopolitan*, January 1984, p. 190.

Finding a Way Out

RON NEPOMUCENO

Slap! She felt her mother's cold fingers swipe across her left cheek. It stung and made her cry—but she didn't. She wouldn't give her mother the satisfaction of knowing the slap had hurt. Sharon just stared at the center of the lace tablecloth underneath the quarter-inch slab of glass. Her eyes followed the intricate pattern of the cloth while her ears heard her mother's now-hoarse voice yelling at her. Sharon heard but didn't listen. After all, they were the same words yelled at her before, but now in an all new, revised edition.

"What's wrong with you? You have no respect for me, no respect for your father.... You lie to us all the time. Lie, lie, lie. Then I catch you. What do you do? You lie some more. We don't need this shit from you! Who do you think you are?"

Slap! Still no reaction from Sharon. No tears, no emotion. Just a constant stare at the tablecloth. She knew that her mother was becoming infuriated that the slapping and yelling were not generating the desired reaction. Sharon smiled to herself.

"...you're doing it with him, we find out, you lie to us, and you're just 'sorry'? What if you got pregnant? You wouldn't be able to finish your last year of high school, going to college would be screwed up, you couldn't get a job...and who would have to take care of the baby? Us. Well no way! I'm not going to have a teenage mother in my house."

That part of the speech made Sharon laugh to herself. Twenty years ago, her brother, Robin, was born to a seventeen-year-old girl. Hypocrite.

Throughout her mother's ravings, Sharon's father sat silently at the head of the table, skimming the *Evening Tribune*. He never said much during these speeches, only a glance up from the paper whenever there was another slap.

The shouting continued. "If you don't like it here, you can get the hell out! Just get out!"

One time, Sharon got up and walked to the door. Her mother grabbed her arm, shoved her back into the chair, and locked the door. Then the obvious question—"Where the hell do you think you're going?" Slap! Ridiculous. Sharon figured that she should just ride out this attack as she usually did. Just wait until Mom got off the warpath and cooled down.

A while back, during one of these same speeches, Sharon believed she knew the reason why her mother always got so mad. Whenever one of her children screwed up, they were a reminder of what a failure she had been as a parent. Sharon knew her mom would never admit to that. Never. But Sharon had her all figured out. She remembers when her brother, Robin, was put on probation at school. Their mother had a great day of "verbal expressions." She put so much pressure on Robin that he said screw it, quit school, and joined the Navy. Their mom was unusually quiet when she found out. Sharon guessed that it was too late to "correct" that failure, so her mom saved her breath about that. But now she wanted to "correct" Sharon before it was too late. "Keep the leash tight before the kid feels freedom," Sharon thought. "Just get off my back and leave me alone. You say you don't need this shit from me, well I don't need this shit from you. Just let me be who I am and not who you want me to be." These thoughts flowed through her mind yet remained unspoken. No excuses here. No understanding. No pity. No listening. Just yelling.

Why had the yelling started this time? Cheryl. Miss Purity. Miss I-Can't-Lie-to-Mom-and-Dad. "Sharon hasn't called in...She told me that she would be home by now...I saw her car at her boyfriend's house...."

Sharon wondered how such a little girl with little eyes, little ears, and a little mouth could see, hear, and report so much to their mother. It was just Sharon's luck to have an enemy spy for a sister.

After about half an hour of yelling, Sharon was left alone, to let her mother's words sink in. They never got past her ears. It was all the same. All she could think about now was her boyfriend, or ex-boyfriend, Ray. "How could he do this to me?" she thought. "Bastard." She remembered seeing Ray, by accident of course, with another girl. Sure he had to go with his parents to L.A. Two-timing jerk. But she still loved him. Her anger wouldn't let her admit that, but she loved him. Pretty soon, that anger turned into pain. Pain of losing the only person she has ever truly loved. Pain of losing the man she wanted to spend the rest of her life with. Pain of being betrayed by that man.

Sharon wanted to cry again, but she stopped her tears. She didn't want to cry in front of her mother. It would give the impression that the yelling and the slapping were the cause. So she built up the courage to move. Her mom and dad were in the room behind her, looking at the television, but thinking about their daughter. Sharon scooted her chair from the table, the seat's wooden legs noisily vibrating against the tiled floor. She didn't have to turn around to know that her parents were watching her. She could already feel their eyes following her movements. Not wanting to make eye contact, Sharon looked at the floor as she hurried to her room. She quietly closed the door and then flopped on her bed. Her tears finally began to flow as she buried her face in her pillow. Sharon cried until she fell asleep, wondering what she was going to do.

When she awoke, she found herself in a pitch-black room. She glanced at the clock, its glowing red digital numbers the only light in the room. 8:38, the numbers displayed. They hadn't called her to dinner as they usually did. It didn't matter. She wasn't able to eat anyway. All she could do was think.

For a long while, Sharon lay on her back, staring into the deep blackness of her room, thinking. She began to evaluate her life. She thought about school. What a joke. She was failing two of her classes and getting C's and D's in the other ones. What did it matter anyway? She had no plans for college. She just wanted to get married to Ray. The tears began again.

"How could he do this to me? What did I do to make him do this to me? I loved him. Now he's gone. Why me? Why?"

Sharon's tears began to grow and her nose started running. She then heard her own voice letting out little whines and whimpers.

"I need him so much. I can't handle my life without him. I just can't take my mom any more. I can't. I'm trapped in this prison and there's no way to escape. What am I going to do? I can't stand this any more!"

Sharon's eyes were now flooding with tears. Her fingers began to ache from clutching her pillow so tightly. She curled up into a little ball around her pillow. She wanted to make herself so small, she would just disappear. She already felt that insignificant. Sharon drew her knees up to her chin and hugged them tightly.

"There's only one way to escape—to end it all." This thought scared her when it first crossed her mind. But then she began to feel that it wasn't such a bad idea after all. She could get back at Ray for betraying her. She could hurt her family like they had hurt her. Most of all, she believed that she would be so much better off. No problems, no worries, no pain. Sharon would just be gone. Poof!

But how could she do it? Easy. She remembered her mom's sleeping pills in the medicine chest. All she had to do was take the whole bottle of pills and go to sleep. Clean, simple, and painless. In the morning, they'll try to wake her, but it will be too late. Sharon will be free.

10:30, the clock glowed. Everyone should be asleep by now. She poked her head out of the room. No one in sight. She crept into the kitchen, grabbed a glass, and crept into the bathroom. The bright light of the small room stung her eyes. She saw that they were bloodshot when she looked in the mirror. Too much crying.

Sharon opened the medicine chest and surveyed its contents. There was the bottle, wedged on the third shelf, between the can of band-aids and the dark bottle of hydrogen peroxide. She reached a trembling hand for the pills. "Do not drive, operate dangerous machinery, or consume alcoholic beverages when taking this medication," the fluorescent red sticker warned. Perfect.

Sharon filled the glass with water and opened the bottle. About a dozen or so pills spilled out when she dropped the bottle into the sink. They rattled around in the basin, like marbles falling from a bag. Each pill was a small, gelatin time capsule, half blue, half black. The label said to take only one, so she knew that they were strong. She picked up one and looked at it. Her hand holding the water began to shake. Then her whole body started to tremble. The tears once again flowed as Sharon remembered all of her problems again. It was her way of building up enough courage to take the pills. Then she remembered seeing Ray kissing that other girl. That did it. Before she knew it, she popped the pill into her mouth and took a sip of water. Then she swallowed another one. Then another. She kept going until she felt that she had taken enough to kill her.

Kill her. The idea of that phrase began to sink into her. She was going to die! DIE! Her tears stopped. She began to panic. "No! This is wrong. I don't want to die. He's not worth dying for. My God, I'm going to die!"

"I have to stop this," she uttered as she lifted the toilet seat and plunged her fingers into her mouth. The feeling of her fingers groping around the back of her throat instantly triggered her digestive system to reverse direction, and Sharon began to vomit.

"I have to get all of these pills out!" she thought, as she forced the convulsions again. Her sides began to ache as she continued to gag. "Stupid, stupid, stupid!"

Sharon never told anyone in her family about the suicide attempt. She just became one of the estimated 500,000 young adults who fail at suicide each year. This figure remains an estimate because of the number of attempts, like Sharon's, which go unreported. Luckily she didn't become one of the 5,000 teenagers who succeed. (Hutchings, 1985) More specifically, she was one of the more than 300,000 girls who unsuccessfully commit suicide—three times the number of boys. Yet despite that statistic, boys account for more than sixty percent of all teenage suicide successes, due to the more lethal methods they use such as shooting or hanging. Sharon, like many of the other at-tempters who fail, took pills or other "passive," "half-hearted methods of destruction." (O'Roark, 1982)

For the 15-to-24-year-old age group, the suicide rate has in-creased 300 percent in the past two decades, while the adult rate has remained constant. (Thornton, 1983) One reason for this has to do with the increase in pressures on teenagers these days. These include broken homes, drug and alcohol abuse, the peer conformity of adole-scence (including sexual activity), the influence of movies and tele-vision, and the lack of family ties. These pressures have increased the number of teenagers susceptible to suicide, when combined with insufficient and inadequate family support. (Gorman, 1984; O'Roark, 1982)

The last is something Sharon suffered from. She felt that her mother was constantly against her, her sister was an enemy, and her father was nonexistent. She had all of her problems and pressures building up within her and no way to deal with them. She was one of the many teenagers who have trouble coping and see suicide as the only way out. "As the pressures of life build, so does the urgency for quick solutions—such as suicide." (O'Roark, 1982)

Most adults know that certain disappointments and setbacks can be handled and dealt with, that they won't affect the rest of their lives. But young people like Sharon think, "My parents are on my case again," or, "I'm breaking up with my boyfriend, "and they don't see past that. (O'Roark, 1982) Sharon only saw her problems and not any solutions to them. She did not understand her mother's lectures, nor did she listen to them. She looked at them as just words to make her feel bad, and not as a mother's concern for the welfare of her child. Also, Sharon thought only of the loss of her boyfriend, and not of the possibility of finding another.

Interestingly, suicide in all young adults can be tied to some sense of loss. The loss can be that of a friend, a member of the family through death or divorce, a pet, a job, or even a sense of control over their lives. (Thornton, 1983) Sharon had the loss of her boyfriend as her main problem and concern. Such losses can usually develop into depression in teenagers, according to one source. Until recently, depression was thought to be primarily an adult problem. Yet unlike adults, teens don't tell when they are depressed, like Sharon. (Gardner, 1981) She did not vent her depression to anyone. Instead, she let it develop within her until it became despair, and finally, the quick solution, suicide.

One thing saved her from this solution, her feelings towards dying. Ambivalent feelings towards suicide have almost everything to do with the success or failure of an attempt. Someone who tries suicide is usually very determined to die, but once they feel the poison in their body or have that moment of realization about what they have done, the other side of their ambivalence takes over, and they don't want to go through with it. (Hutchings, 1985) This is exactly what Sharon felt when she realized what she was doing and desperately tried to save herself. Deep down, she didn't want to kill herself, she just wanted to find a way out of her problems and thought that suicide was the solution. Fortunately, she realized in time that she was wrong.

Bibliography

Gardner, Sandra. "Suicidal Behavior," Senior Scholastic, Jan. 9, 1981, pp. 9-11.
Gorman, Michael. "The Increase in Teenage Suicide," Ladies Home Journal, June, 1984, p. 57.
Hutchings, David. "Teen Suicide," People, Feb. 18, 1985, pp. 76-89.
O'Roark, Mary Ann. "The Alarming Rise in Teenage Suicide," McCall's, Jan. 1982, pp. 14-16, 22.
Thornton, Jeannye. "Behind a Surge in Suicides of Young People," U.S. News & World Report, June 20, 1983, p. 66.

Case: Group

Tell what some group did or underwent that represents other collective experiences, such as the founding of an enterprise together or the combining of two families through re-

marriage. Consider all possible sources of information, given your distance from the group in time and space, and combine what you learn from your sources to show its significance as you tell the story. Feed in whatever background information is needed to fit your instance into the phenomenon it illustrates. Perhaps you should put your case together with other reportage and research done by you or others on the same subject.

The Burden of the Grandparents on the Family

JEFFREY MILLER

While talking with my mother recently about my grandmother (her mother) many memories about her came to the surface.

As my grandmother grew older she began to suffer from a thyroid condition, diabetes, hypertension (high blood pressure) and a little senility. "The thyroid is a gland whose functioning affects you both physically and mentally. The result of improper functioning is depression."[1] Depression is strong; it can kill you. An example of the power of depression is suicide. My grandmother suffered from severe depression.

In an interview with my mother given earlier this month my mother says that one time my grandmother picked up a knife in the kitchen and threatened to kill herself. My younger sister Cindy witnessed the incident. She was about sixteen in 1980 when the incident occurred. She was the only one home at the time because everyone else was working. My father leases a golf business where all family members contribute. At the time it was summer, which is the busiest time of year for golf. My grandmother kept saying she "was better off dead." She also used to threaten to throw herself in the pool. Cindy got so upset and scared she called my mother at work, and my mother sent my older brother Michael (then twenty-six) home with herself directly behind him. My mother told Cindy to get help from one of the neighbors, but my grandmother put the knife down of her own free will. Michael arrived home and talked with her. She was acting hysterical. She "wished God would let her die." She didn't want to feel sick. She felt like she was a burden on the family. My mother arrived home and took her to the doctor, who prescribed her different medication.

The news of my grandmother was very depressing to me.

"She was given medication which controlled the depression and she had periods of good health but it was always only temporary." When she was feeling well she would always say, "I hope I never get sick again." It was something that was beyond her control." "The reason may be that she eventually became immune to the drugs she was taking." "She was suffering from something known as hypothyroidism." She went through various forms of medication. Two were "iodine and cortisone."

My grandmother was most helpful to others. When she was well she would always help with the housework and bake us grandchildren cookies, cupcakes, and my favorite, rice crispies marshmallow treats.

When my grandmother was sick I was in my early teens. I remember one incident where I was walking down the hall past the laundry room and saw my grandmother and mother through the open door. They did not hear me arriving because the washing machine was running. My grandmother was speaking in a sorrowful tone saying, "I don't want to get any older" to my mother. They both looked up with the unhappiest faces I have ever seen when they noticed me in front of the doorway. I felt sorry for my grandmother. I wanted to help, but what could I do?

My grandmother throughout her life was a "shy and insecure person." When she got sick she would always "revert back to her childhood." One day when I was going out to play my grandmother grabbed me by the arm and asked me not to leave (there was nobody else home). There are seven of us children and so there is usually at least one of us home. She asked me to stay and talk with her, but by the way she was talking she made no sense. She was in great despair at that moment. I left her at this time, not because I didn't want her company but rather I was scared at her childishness and gibberish. My grandmother would always ask us, "What am I going to do?" She never knew what to do with her time. She was looking to my mother and us children as "authority figures." It is ironic that though she would constantly ask us what she could do it was nearly impossible to get her to do anything when she was sick. "This can be attributed to her senility." My mother was told by my grandmother's family doctor that she should get "involved." My mother was supposed to "keep after her so she would not get so depressed that she would withdraw all together and end up in a mental hospital."

However, this was difficult for my mother. She was working as a cashier for my father, who leases a golf driving range in a Nassau County park. My father is dependent on his family and is constantly calling us when the machinery for the tractor breaks or if he is overly busy and he needs help, or maybe someone he hired didn't show up for work, or if he is running low on golf balls and he needs us to bring some from home because the tractor broke down. Such are the disadvantages of owning your own business.

My mother in an interview says she tried to get my grandmother involved by taking her out to the stores when she went and giving her chores to do before she went to work such as pressing clothes and cooking. When she was leaving for work her famous words to us children were, "Check on grandma, talk to grandma." Grandma, however, had no interest. She was too tired. She was constantly going to bed to go to sleep. This is a form of hiding or escape from reality in the same sense that others may use drugs or drink. My mother was forced to scold her like a child so she would stay out of bed. My mother told Doctor Becker that she could not "keep yelling at my mother this way." The doctor replied, "You love her don't you? That is why you are doing this." Incidently, according to Alexander Lowen, "depression is marked by a loss of energy."[2]

I used to become angry at my mother for scolding my grand-mother. My mother could see this (she is a very understanding woman) and she attempted to explain her reasons for doing this. However, her attempts were unsuccessful. I don't believe it was because she wasn't clear, I believe I was too young to understand. Whatever the reason or reasons, I was continually saying, "Leave her alone." Never did I say it in front of my grandmother, and I wasn't yelling at my mother, but it was an annoyed tone of voice.

My father felt neglected by my mother, and it was at a bad time since he was having trouble at work. My mother felt she had neglected us children, although I don't feel that way. My mother spent a lot of time working, visiting with my grandmother when she was in the hospital, taking her to the doctor, and trying to keep a watch over her. She often said, "the doctor was expensive and I was trying to put you kids through school." I felt pity for my mother. Doctor Stanley J. Brody says that, "Recent studies show that twenty percent of families caring for an older person experience stress severe enough to lead to the seeking of professional help or to a breakdown of the family unit."[3] My grandmother regretted having no money and living with her daughter and not independently.

My grandmother has been in and out of the hospital: She had a stay in the hospital for three weeks and another time, which was her last, for three months consisting of the entire summer. My mother felt bad that she was well the entire winter, when there was nothing to do, and had to spend the entire summer in the hospital, where she died September 7, 1980. She was eighty-four years old. My mother would never want her to die in the summer, when there was so much to do. She died of stomach cancer. My mother and I feel my grandmother never deserved the suffering she had to bear. Her senility had reached the point where she did not recognize my mother when she went to visit her in the hospital.

Maybe it was better that my grandmother died at that time. Had she lived my mother would have been forced to put her in a nursing home. She couldn't stay in the hospital forever. And there wasn't enough time for my mother to give my grandmother the care she needed. It is a difficult decision for a parent to make.

Notes

1 Except as otherwise cited, all quotations are from interviews with my mother.
2 Alexander Lowen, *Depression and the Body*, p. 91.
3 Adrian Perocchio, "When Health, and Wealth, Fade," *Newsday*, p. 26.

Bibliography

Lowen, Alexander, *Depression and the Body* (Coward, McConan and Geoghegan, New York) 1972.
Mace, Nancy, *The Thirty-Six Hour Day* (The Johns Hopkins University Press, London) 1981.
Perrochio, Adrian, "When Health, and Wealth, Fade, *Newsday*, May 1, 1984, p. 26.
Weber, Sidney, *The Thyroid* (Harper and Row, New York) 1962.

Profile

Like a sketch, a profile shows outlines. It answers the question, "What is this person or this enterprise like?" If your subject is a person, get information from as many sources as possible. Visit and interview the person. Interview others who know the person. Read any diaries, letters, memoirs, articles, etc. written by or about him or her. If you choose an enterprise, such as a factory, office, laboratory, farm, or project, visit it perhaps several times, take notes on what you observe, talk with people there, read whatever brochures might be available, research any possible sources outside the site, and assemble the information so that a reader learns what habitually goes on there. What are the traits of this person or place? Organize your profile by these traits, illustrating each by anecdotes, quotations, observations, or factual information.

Consider this as one kind of feature article for a newspaper or magazine of general interest or for one specializing in a subject your profile fits into. Or include it in a collection of other articles treating the subject that your person or enterprise relates to.

Video Mates
JACK BOLADO

Would an ad like this attract you? Would you think, like the majority of people, that this service is only for "losers"—those who could not find dates, who stay home and watch TV for hours at a time, are unattractive, boring, shy, and just outright "goons"? Well, apparently the members of Great Expectations, a video dating service in San Diego, are not so, according to Bob, the owner of this "relationship shop."

"In fact, the service is the opposite. We cater to the busy professional who has no time to come into contact with the quantity and quality of people they would like to."

What they do here is provide the busy, active, single person a modern way to meet people—an alternative to the uncomfortable bar scene. "It cuts through the baloney" so you know beforehand what you are up against. Great Expectations is a video-dating service which is unlike some computer services where you are matched by your age, backgrounds, job, income, likes, and dislikes.

"That is what makes Great Expectations unique," Bob said. "Our philosophy is based on mutual consent, where you do the choosing yourself—you yourself are in control."

Their office is located in the heart of Mission Valley right above Radio Shack. The stairs to the office are painted a dark brown with a handsome clear varnished hand-rail. At the top of the stairs, the first door on the left, stands their office. It is only marked by the room number 352, but hanging on the bottom corner of the clear glass window pane is a stylish red-oak carved sign with the words "Great Expectations" on it.

If you are a prospective member, you are greeted by two very lovely and cheerful receptionists, Katie and Judy. Once you begin to feel comfortable in the cozy office, with plants growing in each corner, a leather sofa with fat pillows, and an oil painting of a beach house on the edge of a point with waves breaking on the shore, one of the receptionists will take you to either Beth's or Donna's office. They are agents and will do the screening of a prospective member. Donna, who has brownish-blond hair which falls to her shoulders, conducts most of the interviews, since Beth usually handles the P. R. Her office has an oak desk with a matching swivel chair, one large hanging plant, and a cushioned love-seat which was placed so you would be able to talk to Donna while she was sitting in her desk and not feel uncomfortable.

In the interview, Donna looks for attractive qualities in a person. She sees if you are successful and happy with your life, if you will have success in their service, if your attractive qualities are worth being pursued, and also if you have an outgoing personality. They only want people who will be chosen by other members. Donna said, in a somewhat reserved voice, "I don't intend to sound too blunt, but obese people don't do well here and usually don't pass the screening. They usually end up feeling worse off than before they came here. I try to be realistic to them and say that they probably would not get picked. It hurts, but it's the truth, and I don't want them to waste their money."

If you are selected after the screening, you must do a writing assignment. You will be taken to the quiet room where there is nothing but desks so you can concentrate on a short autobiography which will be put on your personality profile. A wallet-sized picture will be taken then (compliments of Polaroid) to be placed on the back of your profile, so the opposite sex will be able to see what is in store for them. The last step of the procedure is the video-taping of a five-to-eight-minute casual conversation, where Donna will try to bring out your true personality on film, so you could be placed in the video library next to Albert 5471 or Diane 1213. Now you are all set: your personality profile is on the middle shelf of the wall unit in the library, either in the brown binders if you are a male or the orange binders if you are a female, and your video-tape-to-romance is right on the next shelf, right above the profiles, in easy access for any prospective mate.

Now that you are a full-fledged member, you do not have to wait for phone calls in this game of love. You can be assertive and take the first initiative...start looking at them videos! But before you view the videos, you should relax in the library and flip through the profile sheets, while enjoying a glass of wine. The library is equipped to serve several purposes, either to look through the profiles, to party, or to party while looking through the profiles. In the library is a refrigerator, which holds a few bottles of wine and beer, a coffee and tea maker sharing the same corner of the room as the refrigerator, several lounging chairs, and a couch. After looking through the profiles, you can view the short video of someone that attracted you—it might have been the short essay on "What I Like To Do" or "What I'm Looking For." After viewing the video in one of the four viewing rooms adjacent to the library, and you've gotten real excited by his or her vulnerable and sexy voice, you can tell Donna that you're interested in, let's say, Mary 3121. She will then call Mary up and have her come down to the office to view your video. If she likes what she sees, by "mutual consent" phone numbers are exchanged. The next step is yours now; you can arrange a secret rendezvous at a small intimate restaurant or have a casual meeting at your house. If this love-connection does not work out, you can always go back to the library any time and look through the files for another video mate.

Great Expectations is a nation-wide franchise, which makes it the most prominent of all video dating services. Right now in San Diego, there are 700 "hunters" searching via TV monitor for sizzling passion ... and this number is growing. "You see," Donna explained, "people are becoming busier and busier and have less time to intermingle with the opposite sex. These men and women, mind you, are just ordinary people whose ages range anywhere from 21 years old to about 55 years old and whose occupations range from doctors to chefs to janitors." Donna was right. Hanging on the walls of the library are collages made of pictures of the members—a handsome, clean-cut man, with well-groomed brownish hair, dressed in a navy blue blazer and khaki pants, enjoying one of the many cocktail parties the Great Expectations office gives in bars around the Valley, a fairly short woman with rosy cheeks, covered with an aqua ski jacket atop a run at Park City, Utah, and a group of people, everyone smiling (probably because they were drunk) and having a good time enjoying a lobster dinner at Puerto Nuevo, Mexico. In one of these pictures was a blond-haired, blue-eyed beauty who would have caught anyone's attention. Her name is Ms. S.

Ms. S. is a very attractive woman with blond wavy hair who stands about 5'4" and whose skin is tanned perfectly. It would seem odd that a lady like this should belong to a dating service, considering how pretty she was and how many men would be knocking at her door. But at thirty-two, she was ready for something more substantial than hit-and-run seduction games at Friday night happy hours: she wanted an established and secure man who shared her interests. Through video dating, she had actually found some men seeking serious relationships, men bold enough to admit their need and advertise themselves in a costly marketplace.

"My dates ranged from mechanics and mail carriers to attorneys and architects. During a very socially active year, I also sampled countless new restaurants, gained ten pounds, became more assertive, took the controls of a twin-engine plane, sipped wine with the author of a best-seller, and fortunately shed those same ten pounds."

At first she was skeptical about entering the video circle. "I imagined that only the most desperate sorts would resort to a dating service, but after reassurance from Donna, I'd decided to give it a try. I asked myself, 'why not?,' and the newspaper ad had strong cerebral appeal to a woman pushing thirty-three: 'Finally an intelligent way to meet people.'"

After she got over the hurdles of writing her profile sheet, taping her video debut, and, yes, the five-hundred dollar membership fee, she was allowed to start her shopping spree. "I began with Abe, Al, Art, Barry, Ben, and Bill. I was astounded at their unabashedly honest pitches. Only a couple of men stipulated that their dates be slender or nonsmokers or childless. Everyone, it seemed, was casting a big net.

"With so many men available to me, I started to resort to my usual appraising techniques and glanced quickly at physical appearance, age, and occupation. David captivated me. He had curly suntanned hair, bewitching green eyes, a strong jawline and a Kirk Douglas chin. He was even more gorgeous in person, but witty he wasn't. All he did was talk about a book that he wrote while I attended to—cheese, crackers, wine, questions, more questions...it was getting quite boring. As I recall, he asked me only one question, and that was 'where's the bathroom?' He left soon after and never did call me back. I'll always remember him because he was my first date through the service."

Ms. S. just kept talking. She had a wonderful personality, so full of energy that it wasn't surprising that after only her third week of membership, ten men had requested her. Of these ten men, she had said yes to every one of them. On one day she would be eating breakfast by the beach with a mailman, the next day she would be going to a drive-in movie on a Saturday night with an accountant. She was seeing quite a bit of men before she thought she found her "video dream mate." His name was John, and they dated seriously for about a month or so. "We eventually developed a strong friendship, which I almost missed out on because I was programmed only for romance—a friendship had not even occurred to me.

"I had found a friendship but I wondered where the sizzling passion I sought for was." After a couple of months enters Jim 1522. In an excited voice, Ms. S described Jim. "He was a handsome airline pilot who was as charming as he was attractive, and I soon became involved. He flew us to Colorado to ski and to Las Vegas to gamble—it was a whirl-wind romance. I found that I was falling in love with Jim, so I went on hold at the library." She was becoming deeply involved with him, but when Ms. S began to make demands on him, he started to pull away. "I realized that there wasn't enough commitment on his part to keep the relationship going, so I went back on the active list and started to hit the shelves regularly."

Ms. S. loves the idea of Great Expectations, and she recommends it for everyone. "The best part of it is that it does all the labor for you. The first half-hour of a date is answered before you meet the person, so both of you are comfortable with each other." Another thing that Ms. S. is impressed by is the staff of Great Expectations. "The people that work there are very friendly, and they care about you...unlike some of the other services that I looked into where the workers only had dollar-signs flashing in their eyes."

"That's a common misconception about dating services," Donna said. "The public usually sees us as trying to take advantage of all the lonely hearts out there, but we aren't. It's just a business that happens to bring people together, and right now it is very successful." Successful it is, having doubled the amount of members in the past year. Most of these new members joined the video circle for the same reasons as Ms. S. did: "...a better, nicer, cleaner way to meet people," "(you are) exposed to hundreds of people," "you know who is in the back of someone...their personality," "the single bar scene was getting old," etc.

Being such a growing company, it would seem likely that there would be members who were left disappointed. "Actually," Donna explained, "I have only heard from one person that complained about our service in my five years working here, and it was our mistake, he shouldn't have been allowed to be a member in the first place." (He was an old college professor at a local college who lived in the country growing avocados, and all he really wanted was a live-in maid to do all his cooking and cleaning.) "I am happy with what I am doing, and I know that people are happy with our service." To prove her point, on top of her desk was a letter. It read:

Dear Donna,

Mike and I are now married and very grateful to your service. I guess that you can put us on your success list!!

Love,
Mrs. Ann Davey

The Business of Death
ANGELA LU

The couple got out of their car and made their way very slowly to the door on a cold, clear evening. The man appeared to be in his 70's and moved solemnly in a long, black wool coat with his sagging eyes fixed on his black patent leather shoes. A luxurious black mink coat wrapped the thin body of the woman, who stumbled with her little head buried in his arm. The tall sign "Clairmont Mortuary" lit their path as I follwed their shadows. They huddled together in grief and uncertainty.

"This business is either feast or famine," said Wanda, the receptionist, rocking in her chair while staring at the busy streets outside her window. Her green polyester pantsuit reminded me of the retired school teacher next door. The mortuary looked like a church with rust roof and lime-green tiles; an oasis in the busy city streets. The bright red doormat inharmoniously placed among the earth-tone funitures stood out unyieldingly. The entrance that leads to the chapel resembles an old hotel lobby with polished brick floor. The smell of gummy bears and cherry air freshener filled the entire building. No ticking sound was made by the antique clock standing still against the wall. The dark brown reproduced antique Victorian chaise, tables, and lamps gave the place solemnity while giving the illusion that the ceiling was coming down to crush the life out of you.

"Remember the PSA crash? Oh, we were so busy! All 144 bodies were embalmed here. I worked 60 hours per week for three straight weeks because the phones would not stop ringing. Imagine 144 death certificates, families, insurance companies to deal with, services, flowers, billing notices... Oh, the list can go on forever!" Her salt and pepper hair gleamed in the afternoon sunshine as she spoke professionally without much feeling about the tragedy itself. "I never thought I would be into this type of business. It's simply depressing, you know. But here I am, 20 years later, working at a mortuary. How did I ever get into this mess? Well, the employment agency offered me a receptionist position, and I took it without knowing the type of business I was leaping into. If it had indicated 'mortuary', FORGET IT!" Pausing for a sip of coffee, "I guess I am the uncompromising type of person. Really, I am here to take care of the paper work. No bodies. I don't comfort people either." She looked directly into my eyes, "You probably think that I am cruel, but death is a reality. Everyone needs to learn how to face it on his own. We see deaths between the age of 18 and 45 all the time. Car wreck, alcohol abuse, drug abuse, homicides, suicides, accidents.... Our fate is not in our hands, you must understand." Although she tried to sound impersonal, I could see her getting emotional about the issue. Her eyes blinked compulsively as she tried to squeeze a stiff smile on her wrinkled face.

"Hey, how's our UCSD journalist doing?" Elmer squeezed my shoulder as he entered the office. He is a tall, jovial, and fatherly man, unlike the other director, John. Having been at this business for the past 35 years, not only death doesn't bother him any more, but he has become "attached," according to his own words, to this place. At the age of 62, his blue eyes still sparkled with enthusiasm and his voice full of life.

"You don't want to hear about this mortuary...." Covering my ears with his big, hairy hands, "Let's go see some bodies." He joked and pushed me out of Wanda's office. Walking towards his office, he began bragging about his experiences. "I've been at this long enough to know that death is simply a reality. People die at your age, and people die at my age. Body is only an empty cavity, and your soul goes to Heaven. Don't you believe that? Everybody believes that." He said sarcastically, waving his arms in the air as if he were preaching. "Funerals are for the living to come and say, 'Hey, buddy, I did this and that to you 30 years ago, please forgive me.' The PSA crash brought mangled bodies. Heads, arms, legs, feet! All were closed caskets. Can you imagine a head and a leg in a 200-lb casket? We might have put one person's head with another person's foot in the same casket. Who knows? Who can distinguish what belongs to who?" He talked as if totally untouched by the loss of those lives. "This business has dulled my feelings. All I'm concerned now is my paycheck. My family comes first and everything else last." I called the day with a somewhat negative feeling about Elmer.

I met the cleaning lady Louise at 8:00 one morning. She had been working there for the past 12 years. "Since 1972," she proudly stated. Her grey, frizzy hair covered half of her face like a lousy wig. "I used to be afraid of the embalming room. It was a zone where I would not clean. Although I'll never get used to this chilling fact (death), at least I don't pay attention to it anymore. I'm here at 6:00 every morning sterilizing the embalming room. Sometimes there's just me and some dead bodies here. Do I get scared? Well, they're just dead. Dead people can't hurt you. They can make you hurt yourself if you're scared. When I first started working here, I felt eyes looking at me, forces resisting me. Now I'm used to it. I can even talk about it." Under the yellow gloves, her hands busied wiping the black fluid from the walls of the huge sink in the embalming room.

I was surprised to find that the two embalmers had been truck drivers previously. To me, embalming is such a delicate process that it was amazing how their not-so-delicate hands could manage to do such a good job. Inside the embalming room, Steve and Barry were both wearing their blue uniforms and were working on two men while chattering with me. "I like embalming," declared Barry, a stocky, witty-looking guy, "It's not as sickening as you people envision it. It takes five to seven hours to make a body look perfect. I'm picky, so I always re-do things if I'm not completely satisfied. My main concern is to make the deceased viewable," he said, pumping pressure into one of the corpse's abdomen through a transparent tube connected to a machine. Embalming is the process of the chemical replacement of fluids, mainly for preservation and sanitation. "We force the fluids out by using this pressure pump, along with blood in the arteries. Then we make a Y incision like such,"—he drew a Y on the man's white chest with his index finger—"remove the internals, embalm, and put them back." I stood frigidly watching the black fluids flowing through the transparent tube as the body turned whiter and whiter. I had to take a walk outside.

The guys were putting makeup on the two men when I returned. "We covered them up so that you won't be scared." They smiled as I stared at the two pairs of white feet extending beyond the white sheets. "Do you think about death?" It suddenly occurred to me that the employees at the mortuary have a mysterious attitude towards death. They do have their fears of the fact, and yet they try to disguise the fact by telling an outsider that they are "experienced enough" to be casual about it. Steve looked around and then at the floor. "Well, it does get to you. You begin thinking seriously about life and death. Sometimes I tell myself that I never want to come back again. No I don't think about my own. I realize the mortal end, but I don't think about my own." Steve has a well-built lank stature, not so typical of a truck driver.

"Sometimes after doing six bodies," Barry took over, "you just want to see a living human being to assure yourself of your own state. In this room you can usually expect lots of joking and laughing. But that's to keep sanity; if we don't do that, if we don't loosen up, we'd crack up. This job can get to you." He stopped rolling the stick foundation on the man's face as if he thought of something funny, putting his left index finger that was on the man's chest on his thick mustache. "Steve, tell her what happened that time when you called the paramedics."

Steve raised his head and smiled coyly, "Oh, I called the paramedics once because I thought that the poor woman was still alive. She had a slight pulse on her neck and her wrist. She gripped onto the table so tight that I couldn't even move her. I didn't want to embalm her because if the blood squirts...that'd be the end of my career."

"Decomposition takes place right after death, so a dead person's blood will not squirt," Barry added authoritatively. "What color eyeshadow shall we use on his lids, young lady?" Barry asked me with an array of crayon-like eyeshadow sticks on a tray.

"Well, I don't want to decide for him, what if he doesn't like the color I pick?" They laughed and thought I was funny. But it wasn't meant to be humorous, I was really frightened. "We're going to make two incisions in his pelvic area to pump out the blood in his lower body. Would you want to watch?"

I thanked him for his warning and was ready to leave when Elmer's voice came suddenly from the silent hallway, "What do you people want for lunch? Hamburgers, tacos, or burritos?" "I'll take a burger." Steve shouted excitedly into the empty hallway. "Two soft tacos sounds yummy," Barry followed. Jokingly Elmer suggested that we could all have lunch together in there since Steve and Barry weren't finished. I looked around at the immaculate white tile, white sheet, white bodies, and felt myself turning green.

The lobby was brightly lit, but the hallway leading to the viewing rooms was shadowy and empty. "It Is Well with My Soul" effused from the walls as I searched for the ever-present organ. The "director," as John called himself, of the mortuary appeared from one of the closed doors and greeted the mourners hospitably. In deep sorrow, the old couple didn't reciprocate his "good evening" nor his warm smile. The ease and the phony smile he wore disgusted me when I remembered how rudely he refused my interview. I followed the old couple silently into the viewing room, where a faint sobbing was coming from. There were three services in progress that evening, and one was a rosary service.

The first man's solitary visitors stood motionless for a few minutes in front of his body, staring at the casket, not looking at him. The woman buried her entire face in the arm of her husband and leaned against him. In their 70's, they probably realized the fear of death, the creak of age, the destiny they faced. Two elderly women in the same room busied themselves fixing the flowers that encompassed the casket, expressionless, hands trembling.

Entering the second viewing room with no one around but the deceased black gentleman was frightening. It was dim and cool in the room, contrary to the warm and sun-lit room I entered four days ago. There was a crucifix in one corner of the room, behind the open casket. The same red vinyl, sponge-padded kneeling bench I saw during my first visit still sat silently in front of the pedestal under the casket. Two red candles on either side of the casket glowed in the corner. A large box of over-stuffed Kleenex atop a coffee table in the deadly silent room seemed useless. The gentleman appeared to be peacefully sleeping, wrinkled hands folded over his chest. Gazing at the dark waxen fact, I expected the maroon-shadowed eyelids to open, but they were glued shut. Staring at the peaceful face, I could imagine him moving. It was too difficult to imagine not. No one was in sight, so I reached out and felt the foundation-covered hand with my index finger. I was instantly filled with uneasy terror. My arm extended over the casket. He felt like wax—neither hot nor cold. He looked like a mannequin or a plastic dummy. There was a nothingness about him; the absence of life brought goose bumps all over me. Stumbling, I exited the room.

Wandering into the chapel, I saw a few rows of people sitting quietly with their heads down. The open casket in front of them did not seem to stir any emotions. A young man in a black pinstripe suit lit the candles behind the casket. Unmoved by the occasion, he walked towards me as I observed the people in the chapel.

"Hi! You must be the girl from UCSD," he whispered as I followed him into the hallway. "My name is Jack, by the way." He shook my hand vigorously. His voice was full of energy, and he bent forward slightly when he spoke. "Yeah, I heard about you from our receptionist. Let's go into the office and talk. You'll get too depressed from being around these people." He squinted mischievously. He appeared to be in his early 20's with a thin mustache and blond hair.

"What type of work do you do here?" His age, the way he was dressed and his attitude presented a mysterious contradiction. "Good question!" he laughed, resting his feet on the desk, "Can I say I don't know?" I found his humor rather annoying before I caught myself being overly serious about all the sorrowful scenes. "I do all kinds of miscellaneous chores the bosses don't want to do. This job's great. I mean it. It affords great study time while I attend the Chiropractic

College. Working here made me realize how fragile life really is although we think we're so smart that we have control over our lives."

He suddenly became serious as he plunged into some past cases which involved tragic deaths. "Half of the cases we handle involve individuals under 45. We had a rosary for a five-year-old girl Tracey last week. She fell down on a playground and hit her head against a pole. That was the end to her budding life. She was only five! Life is fragile." He sighed. "I haven't been in this business long enough to be unsympathetic; unhuman. I don't know if my attitude is good or bad." He shrugged.

"What are your personal feelings?" It seemed that he didn't want to reveal too much of his own feelings. I questioned if working at a mortuary had changed his perspective on life. "This job reaffirms my belief in life. Bodies are shells...." After a long pause, "There's no magic left once the last breath is gone. Same as rocks and fallen trees." He spoke with confusion written across his young face. I wondered what they do with the embalmed bodies after each service, flashing back on the black gentleman. "Oh, we usually leave them out embalmed. A lot of people ask that question. We lock up and leave, once services are over. They are dead. What harm can dead people do? Like I said, there's no magic left. I think people should be fearful of the living rather than the dead. This might all be difficult for you to understand, but this is my job and I've seen enough of it that it has become a routine to me. Perhaps I'm a little weird. Weird, not insane." He got up abruptly as if I had offended him. "Sorry, I need to go out there to see if everything is OK." He left the room swiftly as if running from a threat.

The priest arrived in a rush, nodded at me and at those who were standing emotionlessly. Half of the people kept changing seats to console each other, the other half simply stared at the floor and appeared to be in deep thought. A few latecomers shuffled in and were escorted into the chapel. They smiled cheerfully at some of the people sitting in the back as if they had come to a reunion of some sort. The door finally shut behind them.

"There's always a wide range of mourners." Jack suddenly reappeared behind me outside of the shut door. "Some scream and cry as if they had gone insane. Some just cry constantly as if they were hired to do so. Some come in with bright smiles as if they had come to a party." Jack spoke enthusiastically, "There was a lady who was dragged constantly to see the corpse. She fainted every time she was dragged to the casket, but her protests were not enough for the grieving family. Then there are those who don't really know what to do. They'd ask ME my feelings and views on death so as to measure their own feelings." Chuckling, he waited for my response, but I was too upset by what I saw that evening to say anything.

He believed in an all-accepting God who sees the positive of man's ills and is pleased when we please ourselves. His is a belief in the best of all religions. To stay in this business, he stated, one has to believe in good. One has to be an energetic, eternal optimist. To emphasize his point, he told me that both directors are members of the Optimist Club.

John, the rude director, emerged behind us, "Is it over yet?" he asked impatiently, peeking into the crack on the door, which at the same time was opened by mourners. Slowly they came out of the chapel, weeping into handkerchiefs, their shoes clinking on the brick floor.

The organ music effused from the walls again, "It Is Well with My Soul" continued where it had left off. Broken people emerged, hanging on each other and supporting each other. A young mother fixed her little girl's dress and combed her hair as they exited the chapel. "Are we going home now?" The sweet and innocent voice sounded impatient as her mother picked her up. They would all leave after the service—all except the three. The three would remain where they were, and they would be okay. For them, nothing mattered any more.

Factual Articles

Directions for How to Do or Make Something

Explain step by step how to do some activity such as operate certain equipment, practice certain health exercises, influence other people, or care and feed certain plants or animals. Or explain step by step how to make something, so that your reader can make the item by following these directions. Insert strategically into the directions whatever background information may be required for a full understanding of the directions. Have in mind a certain audience for whom these instructions will make sense.

How to Make an Easter Egg

MICHELLE SEIM

Are you one of those people who experiences genuine heartfelt sadness when you hear the dull thud of an Easter egg shell being rapped against the edge of the coffeetable? Can you bear to think of someone peeling off its shell, flaking it away and discarding it as though the egg were merely any hard boiled one and not the work of art that you've so meticulously dipped in vinegar tainted bowls of blue, red, and yellow water?

Blown eggs are an Easter novelty that eliminate edible artwork while enabling you to make truly exquisite works of colored calcium by using felt tip markers.

Before you begin you should take preparatory measures to gather all the tools that you need. Scrounge around the house. You need an implement which is sharp enough to puncture the surface of the egg yet small enough not to crack the surrounding shell when the tool is inserted. You must surely have a pin of some sort. A safety pin, straight pin, or needle will work just perfectly. You will also need a large spool or an empty toilet paper roll, salad oil, clear nail polish, paper towels—lots if you're messy—and as many different colored pens as you can find.

Now you're ready to blow the egg. First, shake the egg vigorously like a can of spray paint. You are trying to rupture the membrane that separates the yolk from the white so that you have scrambled eggs inside the shell. If you do not heed this tip and don't shake your egg you will only have to do so at a later date, probably when your blowing has been thwarted by a yolk blocking the pinhole. It is impossible to blow an egg with the force of lung power alone unless the egg has been scrambled. So, please, just shake your egg or you will blow out your cheeks in an attempt to blow out your egg.

Next, pierce the egg at the ends of an imaginary axis that runs the length of the egg. These are the strongest points of the shell and will best withstand the piercing. And besides, it's the most aesthetically pleasing place to poke a hole. I mean, think about it, because an egg is elliptical it will rest on its side, and no one wants to look at a hole in the side of an Easter egg, O.K.? So, puncture the egg on the ends, it's less noticeable. Don't just poke the pin in once and think that you'll be able to blow the egg out that tiny hole. Poke about five holes in close proximity and break the shell away so that the resulting hole is the diameter of a pencil lead. Break away too much shell and the egg will crack.

After you've made the holes, blow! Blow! BLOW! Puff out your cheeks like you're blowing up a balloon. And don't breath in. And DON'T lick your lips. Blow until there's nothing left in the egg. I'm telling you, leave the littlest bit and it'll rot! Ever smell rotten eggs? Whooo-ee!! You'll be glad to put in the extra effort.

After you've blown the egg you prepare it for the coloring. First, to assure that any residual egg is eliminated, rinse the inside with water and blow this out. Wash the outside of the shell as well to assure the pens of a clean surface to adhere to. Allow the egg to dry THOROUGHLY! It is extremely important that you stifle your eagerness and exercise patience in allowing the egg to dry; water may get trapped inside of the egg and then leak out, and any wetness will cause your ink to run.

Once you are absolutely sure that the egg is dry, then you can color it. Gather up your many colors and exercise that creative flair. Colored ink pens not only offer a more extensive range of colors but are also easier to draw delicate and intricate patterns with when compared to common dyes and food colors. You may want to use indelible markers to safeguard against running or bleeding of colors. Or you might purposefully choose to use pens that will run; this causes a tie-dyed effect when the egg encounters water. But be careful not to get the egg too wet or all the colors will wash off and you'll be left with an elliptical muddle of hues.

While you are coloring, it will be helpful to use the spool or the toilet paper roll to stand the egg upon so that you will have less surface contact with the egg and will, hopefully, have less chance of smearing it.

After you've added your last squiggle, dot, or geometric pattern, let the egg dry once again.

The egg is completely dry and you're ready for the finishing touches. This is where your common, chicken-laid egg becomes an exquisite work of art—with a coat of shine and lustre. Shellac is what hobbyist and artsy-craftsy people have in their storage cabinets. You and I have probably never used shellac. Besides, I never told you to get any. So, we'll improvise. With the salad oil and the paper towels that you should have gathered (all right, go and get some more paper towels!) you can put a beautiful gleam on your egg. Just dab the paper towel in the oil and polish the egg. Yes, polish it like a car and then buff it with a clean towel. Next, for the shine, paint the egg with nail polish. Clear or opaque colors are best, but it is also quite neat to use opalescent colors as long as the shade is light enough that your designs aren't hidden. And your egg is ready for display, a veritable work of art, more than just a hollowed shell.

How to Catch and Prepare California Spiny Lobster

LISA OBERMEYER

Open season for California spiny lobster is from January 14 to March 14. During these months lobster-loving divers everywhere are in hungry pursuit of these delicious crustaceans. Armed with a fishing license (available from drugstores and dive shops for $5 a year), a large mesh "goody bag," scuba gear (don't forget your gloves), and a measuring device, Joe (in this case Jane) Diver is ready for the hunt. During the closed season immature lobsters are left in peace to grow, moult, and grow some more. California state law prohibits the taking of lobster measuring less than 3¼" along the length of the carapace.

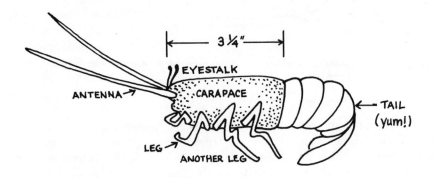

Here is an absolutely terrible drawing of a lobster, but the point is that the carapace is the largest, most anterior section of shell which cloaks the entire front half of the body. The first time you see a lobster you'll know which part I mean. The question of how you measure the critter is trickier, as it involves catching the thing first.

Lobsters are algae eaters as well as scavengers of fish and other dead animals. Spiny lobsters are clawless, unlike the big Maine lobsters (fortunately for us), but they are protected by hard spines, which is why gloves are essential. They feed at night, so many divers prefer to go "bugging" after dark (don't forget your light). During the day the bugs—called bugs because they look exceedingly like large insects—sit as far back under or between rocks as they can get, which is often annoyingly far. Their long antennas (10-12 inches) wave back and forth out of the hole opening, detecting movement and approaching predators.

Since the antenna is the only accessible part of the body, it is often successful to approach the hole quietly, trying not to let off too many noisy bubbles, and seize both antennas. At this point the bug, taking a dim view of the situation, will start to buck violently with his extremely powerful tail (see diagram), trying to move backwards into the safety of his hole. Quick as you can, work your fingers down to the base of the antenna for a firmer grip, pull, and hang on to the struggling thing around the carapace.

With one hand hold it—they generally sit still at this point—with the other hand get your measuring thing (caliper) and place it along the top of the carapace. The caliper should fit well down over the shell.

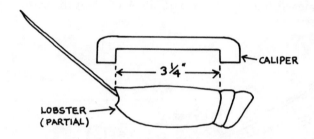

If it's longer than the shell, your bug is too young, and you'd better part with it or get hit with a fine from a Fish & Game warden. The main problem with this method I've found is that the antennas snap off quite easily, which is why it's essential to get your hands down at their base quickly, so they can't break off.

Oh yes, well now that you've got this kicking, uncooperative insect-thing in your hand, simply open your bag, which is clipped to your weight belt, and stuff it in. They usually settle down after a while.

Getting them at night is easier, as I said, because they've come out from their nooks and crannies to get some dinner and are freely roaming around. The first thing you see are little eyes reflecting back at you in the flashlight beam, like a cat caught in headlight glare. Well, when you see this, just get over to where he (or she) is and go for it. Experience is the best teacher. They are sometimes dazed by the bright lights, and this gives you a momentary advantage. They're still not cooperative though, and if one gets away from you don't bother chasing it, as they're powerful swimmers.

Anyway, after a successful evening of bug collecting, you're sure to have an appetite. The most appropriate recipe on this occasion is the Basic Boiled Bug. Quick and great tasting.

Boil a big pot of water, and drop 'em in. Don't try to listen for high-pitched screams, or meditate on their death too much—although these days it's an unusual experience, killing your own food. They're ready in about fifteen to twenty minutes, depending on their size, usually about two to four pounds. When cooked, they should be a bright red color, instead of the darker reddish brown they were before. During this time you should have melted some butter with a bit of lemon juice in it, in which to dip the tasty morsels, and maybe even have made a salad if you're not too tired. When done, pull the bugs out, place on a cutting board legs down and cleave lengthwise with a big knife. (Watch out, it's hot.) You'll find the tail to be the meatiest part, easily pulling out with fork or fingers. Above the tail it's slim pickings—but don't hesitate to chew on anything that looks edible. You'll learn!

State-of-Knowlege Article
Lay out the known facts on some topic about which knowledge is constantly accumulating or changing, such as certain social, technological, and scientific developments. Draw your information from interviews with specialists in the field, from recent articles in periodicals, and perhaps from background books as well. Consider as you write this up how general or specialized an audience you want to read this.

Do You Love Your Ozone Layer?
PETER ABACI

Imagine living in a world where radiation from the sun is so powerful that skin cancer is as common as the flu. Lakes dry up, once gushing rivers now trickle, and deserts lie where ski resorts once flourished. This dramatization is not from a science fiction novel; instead, it is a theoretical possibility of the future of our planet, earth. Research has revealed that the ozone layer is changing in such a way that the earth can become significantly warmer. These are changes that affect everyone, and the results could be disastrous.

In 1974, scientists discovered that fluorocarbons posed a threat to the ozone layer in the earth's atmosphere. Until then, the ozone layer was of little significance in the scientific world. The results of the fluorocarbon experiments aroused concern over the ozone layer and fostered intensive research. Initially, scientists panicked that the ozone layer was facing destruction, and in 1978, they persuaded Congress to ban the use of most fluorocarbons. This panic brought forth more discoveries and the realization that industrialization on earth was affecting the ozone layer in a negative way.

Before the causes of ozone destruction can be properly understood, it is necessary to analyze and define the ozone layer. The second layer of the earth's atmosphere is called the stratosphere, and it is in the stratosphere that ozone is most prevalent. Ultraviolet photons (hv) emitted by the sun dissociate oxygen gas (O_2) in the stratosphere The dissociated oxygen (O) reacts with more oxygen gas to form ozone (O_3).

$$O_2 + hv \rightarrow O + O$$
$$O + O^2 \rightarrow O^3$$

Oxygen exists in abundance in the atmosphere because of biological activity on earth. Stratospheric ozone is, therefore, a product of biological activity, and it also protects that activity by absorbing most of the sun's ultraviolet radiation.[1] The system is a lovely wheel—life leads to ozone, ozone leads to life—and perhaps a fragile one.[2] Because of this chemical process, there is always a layer of ozone in the stratosphere. The ozone layer is not very concentrated, but it shields the earth from essentially all ultraviolet radiation that would be biologically harmful. In effect, without ozone, we'd be cooked.[3] Apparently, the protective umbrella effect of the ozone layer is not appreciably altered as long as a certain ozone concentration range is maintained.[4] Manmade disturbances can disrupt such a concentration range and damage the environment.

Over the last ten years, scientists have discovered causes of concentration changes in the ozone layer. Fluorocarbons were the first cause to be discovered. Fluorocarbons are unreactive until they reach the stratosphere where the unfiltered sunlight is able to break them up into several chemicals, some of which destroy ozone. According to present atmospheric theory, one fluorocarbon molecule can destroy 100,000 molecules of ozone.[5] This is not an amount to be taken lightly, considering fluorocarbons (aerosol spray-cans, etc.) were widely used by the industrialized world in the seventies. In addition, ozone is already sparsely dispersed throughout the stratosphere.

Dangerous fluorocarbons, however, are still being dumped in the atmosphere, mainly by industries. The National Oceanic and Atmospheric Administration has confirmed their presence in the stratosphere. According to the National Academy of Science, European countries are only using eight per cent less aerosol propellents than they did in 1976, which is twenty-four per cent more than the amount recommended by the NAS.

Carbon dioxide (CO^2), in excess, may be the most damaging of substances to the ozone layer. Measurements have shown that carbon dioxide in the atmosphere has increased by six per cent over the last twenty-four years, and there are estimates that it has risen by twenty per cent since the industrial revolution. The major cause of this increase is the mining and burning of buried carbon, which is fossil fuel. If this increase persists, the effects could be disastrous. Like the glass in a greenhouse, carbon dioxide lets solar radiation pass but inhibits the passage of infrared radiation, which is heat.[6] Carbon dioxide in the air lets the sun heat the earth, but it keeps some of that heat from traveling away from the earth and into space.[7] As the amount of carbon dioxide in the atmosphere increases, the earth's temperature rises. This is known as the "greenhouse effect."

Many scientific theories exist over what the greenhouse effect would do to the earth. No important depletion of ozone has occurred so far, but that fact does not invalidate the theories, since they predict no measurable depletion yet.[8] Some scientists believe the West Antarctic Sheet will slide into the sea within two hundred years, causing the water levels to rise above coastal cities. Large increases in skin cancer would also occur, and some even believe bees would no longer be able to pollinate in the unfamiliar light. According to Dominick A. Labianca, Professor of Chemistry at New York University, there would be "biochemical alterations resulting from animal exposure to ozone: structural changes in lung tissue; low resistance to respiratory bacterial infection; reduction of pulmonary function and disruption of cellular biochemistry."

Nitrous oxide (laughing gas) also affects the ozone layer. Like fluorocarbons, nitrous oxide does not react until it diffuses to the stratosphere, where it is transformed to nitric oxide, which destroys ozone. Nitrous oxide is released into the atmosphere by bacterial action in soils.[9] The amount released is increasing due to the expanded use of nitrogen fertilizers. Surprisingly, nitric oxide is emitted by airplanes, which leads to an increase of ozone in the stratosphere. Nitric oxide can either produce or destroy ozone, depending on the altitude at which it is injected.

In the face of these scientific calculations and hypotheses, one ponders the question of what can be done to curb this young but potentially dangerous trend towards damaging the ozone layer. Michael McElroy, a theoretical chemist at Harvard and one of the leaders in ozone research, believes this can be done by controlling carbon dioxide. He sees carbon dioxide as the major problem facing the ozone layer,

140ACTIVE VOICES IV

and by regulating it, he feels the climate can be controlled. What he suggests is combatting the release of fossil fuels with a delicate global system. For example, a calculation would be done to find out how many more trees would be needed to help bind up the released carbon and bring it back down from the stratosphere.

I believe that there is an alternate solution in the making that hasn't yet reached the press. Hans Oesterreicher, Professor of Chemistry at UCSD, heads a research program that is studying utilizing hydrogen as a fuel. This notion really isn't as far-fetched as it may seem. According to Oesterreicher, hydrogen-powered cars exist but are quite expensive. Work is still being done to improve them, and studies are under way to determine the safety of hydrogen-powered cars. Its potential effects on the ozone layer seem positive. According to Kurt Marti, a cosmo-chemist also at UCSD, "No, the hydrogen fuel would not be dangerous to the ozone layer." The popularity hydrogen fuel could attain cannot be overlooked because it would mean less dependence on imported oil and would therefore be economically advantageous.

Another point that cannot be overlooked is that a fluorocarbon molecule remains in the ozone layer for an estimated fifty years. Scientific results show that fluorocarbons intensify the greenhouse effect. This means that the large amounts of fluorocarbons emitted in the seventies will still be eating away at the ozone layer well into the next century. The problem won't end there, either, because fluorocarbons are still being emitted into the atmosphere daily.

However mankind decides to resolve the problem of stratospheric ozone depletion, one point is quite clear—the fate of the ozone layer is in his hands. Industrialization in our world has created the trend, and if ozone depletion is allowed to get severe, future generations may find themselves living in a distorted world of science fiction. The best thing we can do now is weigh the facts and possible alternatives and start making decisions. We know what is happening to the ozone layer and why. It is time to come up with a solution before it's too late.

Footnotes

[1] Kidder, T., "Trouble in the Stratosphere," *Atlantic*, Nov. 1982, p. 34.
[2] *Ibid*, p. 34.
[3] Labianca, D.A., "Ozone: Menacing Pollutant and Solar Umbrella," *USA Today*, May 1982, p. 49.
[4] Kidder, T., "Trouble in the Stratosphere," *Atlantic*, Nov. 1982, p. 36.
[5] Schiff, H., "Report on Reports: Stratospheric Ozone Depletion," *Environment*, Sept. 1982, p. 26.
[6] Labianca, D.A., "Ozone: Menacing Pollutant and Solar Umbrella," *USA Today*, May 1982, p. 50.

7   *Ibid*, p. 50.
8   Kidder, T., "Trouble in the Stratosphere," *Atlantic*, Nov. 1982, p. 42.
9   *Ibid*, p. 42.

Delayed Stress of Vietnam Veterans

JEAN McIVER

Dan Spranger still dreams of Vietnam, 1969 again. He is with his buddies bombing villages. But the villages are filled with American women and children. He sees his wife and baby trapped.[1]

There is a mixture of fantasy and reality.

Psychologists call this type of behavior Post-Traumatic Stress Disorder (P-TSD). P-TSD is defined by the time lag from when the veteran returned home to the point where he started to experience the most severe of symptoms—to his inability to easily accept civilian life as well as the military training that didn't permit periods of reflection while he was involved in warfare.[2]

An estimation of up to 700,000 of the nation's nearly 3 million Vietnam vets suffer from delayed stress.[3] Why are Vietnam veterans suffering from P-TSD in higher percentages than other vets? They are suffering delayed stress more because a different type of war was fought in Vietnam. To begin with, the average age of the soldier, nineteen and a half,[4] made him more vulnerable to mental stress. At this age, people are just starting to find out who they are and what their morals and values are.

The Vietnam War was a harsher war, and the reason for fighting was unknown or not clear to the soldiers. Their main reason for fighting was for survival. Winning wasn't as important. They were put together in groups and sent off to fight a war without battle lines. Without battle lines, the men weren't able to distinguish who the enemy was; therefore, there were times when American soldiers fell into their own traps and were killed. The Vietnam War was the first war America ever lost.

On the other hand, America won all the other wars that we were involved in. The average age of the soldier in other wars was twenty-six to twenty-seven years old.[5] Age didn't have such an impact on the vets. When the soldiers joined, or were drafted, they were trained in advance, before being sent away. The units or troops were raised and trained together and then sent out into the battle field together. There were definite battle lines, and the reason for fighting was absolutely clear to the soldiers. These factors made the veterans of other wars more stable mentally.

The symptoms of P-TSD of Vietnam veterans often appear ten to fifteen years after the war.[6] The level of stress is directly related to the level of exposure to combat fighting. An eight-year, $2 million study by a New York based research team for the Veterans Administration showed that delayed stress is more prevalent among vets who were exposed to heavy combat.[7]

The Vietnam War left many scars on the soldiers. The organization of the troops is a major factor. Psychiatrists feel that the vets suffer delayed stress because of the rotation system used to assign the troops. They were sent for fixed tours of duty in the combat zone. The setup of the troops was always changing, not letting the men develop close relationships with buddies. The vets tried not to get too close to each other. A close relationship was hard on the vets because friends were always getting killed. It was also hard not to develop a close relationship. Too many things were shared, such as food, shelter, wants, and fears.[8]

When going into combat, there was a lot of pressure put on the soldiers. It was their job to kill and to count bodies. Body count was important to their superiors. One vet said that when he went into villages, to search the houses, he was taught to shoot at anything that moved. Once when he was searching a house in a village, he saw a movement out of the corner of his eye. He turned and shot a row of bullets into the object. When he was through shooting, and thought it was safe, he went over to see what it was. He had shot through a basket which held three babies in it, all dead. He had to include them in his body count.[9]

All or most of the assignments that were given to the soldiers were very risky. Going through a village was scary. Women and even children would offer the American soldiers candy or food, but it would turn out to be a grenade. There were times when a woman would be pushing a baby carriage through the street in a village and leave it near some American soldiers, but it would have a bomb in it instead of a baby. The soldiers weren't really able to distinguish who the enemy was.

They joined the service and sacrificed their lives for different reasons. Some went because others had gone, whether they were friends, relatives, or even older generations that served in other wars. Some thought it was tough and romantic to join, and it was a macho thing to do. Others went to be loyal and patriotic to their country. Others went because it was something you just had to do. It was their duty. Although there were 2.8 million men who served in Vietnam, many others did not.[10]

An estimated 16 million men did not serve in Vietnam,[11] most of whom made up excuses not to serve. Many others left the country and went to Canada or Europe. Others simply got married and had children earlier than they wanted in order not to be drafted.

When the men who served in Vietnam came home they had to face a nation full of hostility. They weren't welcomed home in the least bit for fighting for their country. There were no parades, no banners, or homecomings for them, as there were for veterans who served in other wars. A Mexican Vietnam veteran once said, "Others got invited to parties, I got invited to fights."[12] In 1978, when the hostages came home, all around the country, people had put out yellow ribbons in honor of them. This caused the Vietnam veterans to be more full of rage.

During the Vietnam War, some vets were sent home immediately after their tour of duty was up, with their uniforms on, and were expected to carry on with life as if there never was a war. Upon arrival, they were spit at, kicked, and called all sorts of names. They would call the vets "beasts," "baby killers," and "murderers." People would ask the vets, "How many babies did you kill?" The public blamed the vets for losing the war. This caused a tremendous increase in cases of delayed stress among Vietnam veterans.

Many vets were unable to complete their education when they came home from the war. There was a lot of pressure on them. Their peers who hadn't gone to war had finished school already and had steady jobs. Their age, not completing school, and pressure are some factors that contribute to the veterans' inability to hold jobs. Another factor is that they were discriminated against for being veterans of the Vietnam War. Employers would hire other people and other vets with the same qualities over Vietnam vets. All these factors contribute to building Post-Traumatic Stress Disorder.

What is the effect of P-TSD on the Vietnam vets? The Vietnam veterans were marked by the public as being junkies, alcoholics, murderers, and psychopaths.[14] Not all but a good portion of the vets later showed signs of delayed stress.

Exposure to heavy combat is indirectly related to the increase of alcohol and drug dependence, arrests, medical problems, and other long-term emotional problems.[15] The General Accounting Office made an estimation that of the nation's 29.5 million vets, 3 million were alcoholics.[16] One vet, an alcoholic, was found in weeds under a bridge. He said he was more comfortable there. "In his mind, he never left Vietnam," said Arlene Tuffetts, an ex-marine counselor.[17]

Many times the Vietnam veterans are unable to separate family life from memories of the Vietnam War. At times a vet goes into a trance and relives parts of the war. One man, without realizing it at the time, shot and killed his brother-in-law, because he thought he was the enemy.[18] Such cases lead to arrests, and court hearings. When a vet goes into a trance and does commit a crime, the crime is from reliving combat, and therefore the vet is unable to tell right from wrong.[19] In many cases the jury does not accuse the vet of being guilty but makes sure he receives psychiatric help.

Committing a crime may not just occur by reliving the past but by having a feeling of guilt. This sort of guilt is called "survivors guilt." Psychiatrist Harold Jordan says that Lewis Lowe III, a Vietnam vet, has committed many felonies because he feels guilty that he survived the war and his buddies didn't. Therefore the crimes that he commits put him in a position to be caught or shot, just like his buddies.[20]

Most Vietnam veterans don't commit crimes but show other symptoms of delayed stress. Many vets experience heavy depression, recurring dreams, and nightmares about the war. Some feel isolated or different from other people and are unable to express their feelings because they feel that their family will not understand them. This leads to many family problems. In order for a family to survive, they must be able to communicate with each other. When a vet is unable to communicate his feelings to his family, he often becomes full of rage and frustration because he is not understood. How do the Vietnam vets overcome the stress that they face after coming home from the war?

"There is no comfort to those who've been able to overcome physical or psychic problems of war. The nation has not done enough to respect, to honor, to recognize, and reward the special heroism that those vets have shown," President Carter said in 1979.[21] 1979 was the year when organizations first opened up. One organization was called Operation Out Reach. It has 91 counseling centers dispersed throughout the nation,[22] run by psychiatrists, psychologists, and Vietnam vets. These centers were set up so that a vet with psychic problems can go there to talk about his problems and let out his feeling. This is helpful to the vets because the staff at the center understands how the vets feel. By 1981 an estimated 67,000 vets were helped since the centers opened.[23]

Another organization which helps Vietnam vets is the Disabled American Veterans (DAV). This organization has 67 pilot "storefront" centers.[24] These centers are similar to Operation Out Reach centers. The Operation Out Reach, DAV, and another organization called Vietnam Veterans of America (VVA) were set up to allow the vets to sit and talk to each other about their common experiences.

The VVA is run by Robert Muller. There are 55 chapters set up nationwide.[25] Muller in 1980 was proposing a $250 million deal for Congress to give more help to the centers.[26] He wants more staff people for the centers, more time for the G.I. Bill, now limited to 10 years after discharge. He wants to help vets get jobs and get help from the Veterans Administration (VA) for Vietnam veterans with physical problems.

In 1979 Congress put out $20 million to set up the centers.[27] The Vietnam Affairs Committee in Congress wanted to build up the funds again in 1981. In 1981 the House extended the G.I. program three more years on vocational and on-the-job training. It is also letting the vets get treatment at the VA hospitals and allowing Vietnam era vets to take out small business loans.[28] Also in 1981, though, Ronald Reagan put funds for the counseling centers on a hit list for a budget cut.[29]

How are Vietnam veterans going to cope with life if the budgets are cut from the centers? The veterans' only hope of recognition and understanding may soon terminate and they will be back where they started from.

Footnotes

1   T. Morganthau, et al. "Troubled Vietnam Vet," *Newsweek*, vol. 97. (March 30, 1981), p. 24.
2   Marlene Cimons. "'Delayed Stress' The Anguish of Vietnam Plagues Veterans," *L.A. Times-Washington Post Service*,   reprinted by *The Courier-Journal* (August 19, 1979), from *Social Issues Resource Series*, vol. II. "Mental Health," article #12, p. G1.
3   T. Morganthau, et al. "Troubled Vietnam Vet," p. 24.
4   "What Vietnam Did to Us," *Newsweek*, vol. 98. (December 28, 1981), p. 46.
5   "Advise and Dissent," *Time*, vol. 118. (July 13, 1981), p.22.
6   T. Morganthau, et al. "Troubled Vietnam Vet," p. 24.
7   "Viet Combat Linked to Postwar Stress," *Facts on File* (March 23, 1981), p. 257.
8   M. Norman, "Wounds That Will Not Heal: Vietnam Veterans," *N.Y. Times Magazine* (November 11, 1979), p. 134.
9   "War Comes Home," *Time*, vol. 117. (April 6, 1981), p. 17.
10 "Viet Study Reveals Problems," *Facts on File* (September 25, 1979), p. 725.
11 M. Norman. "Wounds That Will Not Heal; Vietnam Veterans," p. 134.
12 "Advise and Dissent," p. 18.
13 *Ibid*, p. 18.
14 J. Seligman, "A Good Year for Vietnam Vets," *Newsweek*, vol. 99. (May 17, 1982), p. 16.
15 "Viet Combat Linked to Postwar Stress," p. 257.
16 "Alcoholism Reported Up," *Facts on File* (June 7, 1977), p. 472.
17 T. Morganthau, et al. "Troubled Vietnam Vet," p. 24.
18 A. Press, et al. "War Echoes in the Courts," *Newsweek*, vol. 98. (November 23, 1981), p. 103.
19 *Ibid*, p. 103.
20 *Ibid*, p. 103.
21 Marc Leepson, "Vietnam War Legacy," *Editorial Research Reports*, vol. II. (July 6, 1979), p. 496.

22 T. Morganthau, et al. "Troubled Vietnam Vet," p. 24.
23 "Advise and Dissent," p. 21.
24 Marc Leepson, "Vietnam War Legacy," p. 494.
25 J. Seligman, "A Good Year for Vietnam Vets," p. 16.
26 "Pleading P-TSD," *Time*, vol. 115. (May 26, 1980), p. 59.
27 T. Morganthau, et al. "Troubled Vietnam Vet," p. 24.
28 "Advise and Dissent," p. 21.
29 "Pleading P-TSD," p. 21.

Bibliography

"Advise and Dissent," *Time* (July 13, 1981), vol. 118. p. 23.

"Alcoholism Reported Up," *Facts on File*, (June 7, 1977), p. 472.

Buchbinder, Jacob T. and Shranger, J. Sixney. "What Post-Vietnam Syndrome?," *Science News* (September 29, 1979), vol. 116. p. 213.

Cimons, Marlene. "'Delayed Stress' The Anguish of Vietnam Plagues Veterans," (August 19, 1979), pp. G1. and G6., from *Social Issues Resources Series*, vol. II; Mental Health, Article #12.

Cimons, Marlene. "Did Vietnam Experience Lead Veteran to Suicide?" *L.A. Times-Washington Post Service*, reprinted by *The Courier-Journal* (August 19, 1979), pp. G1 and G6, from *Social Issues Resource Series*, vol. II: Mental Health, Article #12

"Heroes Without Honor Face the Battle at Home; Vietnam Veterans," *Time*, (April 23, 1979), vol. 113. p. 31.

Leepson, Marc. "Vietnam Veterans: Continuing Readjustment," from *Editorial Research Reports*, vol. II. Edited by Gimlin, Hoyt. Washington: Congressional Quarterly, Inc. (October 21, 1977), pp. 707-792, 802-803.

Leepson, Marc. "Vietnam War Legacy," from *Editorial Research Reports*; vol. II. Edited by Gimlin, Hoyt. Washington: Congressional Quarterly Inc., (July 6, 1979), pp. 483-497.

Marvin, P. "Living in Moral Pain," *Psychology Today* (November, 1981), vol. 15. pp. 68-9.

McFadden, Robert D. "U.S. Study of Veterans Ties Combat Strain to Several Impairments," *N.Y. Times Index* (March 23, 1981), pp. 1, B12.

Morganthau, T. et al. "Troubled Vietnam Vet," *Newsweek* (March 30, 1981), vol. 97. p. 24.

Norman, M. "Wounds That Will Not Heal; Vietnam Veterans," *N.Y. Time Magazine* (November 11, 1979), pp. 134-141.

"Pleading P-TSD," *Time* (May 26, 1979), vol. 115. p. 59.

Press, A., et al. "War Echoes in the Courts," *Newsweek* (November 23, 1981), vol. 98 p. 103.

Reinhold, Robert. "Mentally Wounded Are Rare, But Not Nearly Rare Enough," *N.Y. Times Index* (April 15, 1979), vol. LXXVIII. p. 18E.

Seligman, J. "A Good Year for Vietnam Vets," *Newsweek* (May 17, 1982), vol. 98. p. 16.

"Viet Combat Linked to Postwar Stress," *Facts on File* (March 23, 1981), p. 257.

"War Comes Home," *Time* (April 6, 1981), vol. 117. p. 17.

"What Vietnam Did to Us," *Newsweek* (December 14, 1981), vol. 98. pp. 3, 46-87.

Survey and Research

Explore a subject by combining information from a survey of your own with information from books or articles. Make up a questionnaire that asks what you want to know and get appropriate people to answer it. Put the results together with what you learn from reading on the subject and develop a conclusion, citing all sources.

The Pleasures and Pitfalls of the Non-Traditional Student

SHARON C. KORNREICH

It rained the first day I came to Dowling. I still remember the queasy feeling of anticipation and trepidation I had in the pit of my stomach. I had already quit my part-time job and, after twenty-two years, had committed myself, once again, to being a full-time student.

After the interminable interview and registration process was over, I wandered, quite by accident, into Fortunoff Hall. The dark, curving stairway, framed by stained glass, was an imposing sight. It was very quiet and peaceful and, as I gazed admiringly at the random pattern in the windows, the sun broke through for just a moment, turning the somber colors brilliant. I remember smiling to myself and thinking, maybe it's a sign.

There have been many "signs" since that January day—small victories (over algebra and fear of tests) and flashes of insight but also, doubts and questions. I wondered if other women students were going through the same role-juggling act and were as plagued by scheduling conflicts and the same constant need to prioritize as I was.

I am one of a group of women described by Stephanie M. Bennett as "re-entry," "high-risk," "mature," "working mothers," "students older than average," and "non-traditional."[1] What non-traditional women students have in common physically is obvious. We are older than the student who comes to college directly from high school. We arrive at school after having spent time in the paid work force or raising a family. What we have in common emotionally and intellectually is not always so apparent at first sight. Though our numbers are growing, we are still a distinct minority on campus and are not readily accepted as more than just classmates by the younger students. Because of our hectic schedules, time is not always available for extra-curricular activities during which friendships commonly develop. In the "OPEN" office, a campus haven for non-traditional students, small clusters of us gather for coffee and hurried conversations between classes. We all cherish these moments of companionship and communication, support and reassurance. As natural as it is to breathe, we all long to know how we are doing compared to others like ourselves, and to reach out to them and say, "I understand what you're going through." To this end, the idea for the following questionnaire was born.

April 5, 1984

Dear Fellow Student:

Like Mayor Koch, we all want to know "How'm I doin?" One way to find out is to compare ourselves with others doing the same thing. Accordingly, I am collecting data from the point of view of the non-traditional student. Won't you please take a few minutes to share your thoughts? All answers will be kept confidential; you may sign it or not, as you choose. When you're finished with the questionnaire, please fold, seal, and mail it. A stamp and my address are on the back. A copy of my paper will be available in the Writing Center after May 1. Thanks so much

Sharon Kornreich

USE BACK OF THIS PAGE FOR ADDITIONAL SPACE TO
ANSWER

Freshman_____ Sophomore_____ Junior_____ Senior_____ Major_____
I attend school (full-time) (part-time). Age _____. I am (single (married) (separated) (divorced). Children (sex and ages) _____
I am employed outside home: P/T_____ F/T_____ Not_____
I originally atteneded college in 19_____. I have wanted to attend college since 19_____ and decided to do so now because _____

I chose Dowling because _____

Attending college (is) (is not) what I expected it to be because _____

My main satisfactions have arisen from _____

My main dissatisfactions are a result of _____

The problems I've encountered are _____

I resolved them by _____

Still unresolved are _____

I'm proudest of _____

The biggest pitfall for the non-traditional student is _____

Since beginning college, I've changed my feelings about _____

I've (not changed) (changed) as a person since attending college.
(Explain) _____

My relationships with other students are (satisfying) (not satisfying)
(other). (Explain) _____

My family is (supportive) (not supportive) (other) of my efforts.
(Explain) _____

I (would) (would not) consent to be interviewed in person. (If you
would, please note phone number and convenient time to be called)
ADDITIONAL COMMENTS: _____

OPTIONAL Name and address _____

According to Mike Secko, Registrar and Director of Institutional
Research for Dowling College, figures compiled for last year's "Middle
States Report" indicated that "twenty-three percent of Dowling's
1,849 undergraduates are over 25 years old." Since approximately fifty
percent of that figure are females, there are about 425 non-traditional
women undergraduates presently attending Dowling.[2] The fact that
our numbers are sizeable is reflected by the following:

> More than one-third of the students on college campuses
> these days are over the age of 25. In fact, of the 2.9 million
> student increase in college enrollment from 1972-1979, one-
> half of the new students were part-timers 25 years of age
> and older.
> The influx of women reentry students is especially dra-
> matic. Among students age 35 and older, women outnum-
> bered men nearly 2 to 1. Between 1975 and 1978 the
> number of female students between the ages of 24 and 34

rose 187 percent. Women who have never worked outside their homes, women who have been happily or unhappily employed for years, and women who have contributed tremendous amounts of energy to volunteer work are all returning to school.[3]

I encountered difficulties in locating enough participants for my study on the pleasures and pitfalls of the non-traditional student due to the lack of time many re-entry women have to participate in campus activities. Though there are one or two re-entry women in each of my classes, they tend to disappear quickly after class due to their hectic schedules. Nevertheless, from the responses I received, I hoped to get a picture of the average non-traditional student and compare her pleasant discoveries and proudest academic moments to my own experience. Because the rose that is our educational experience is not without thorns, I added questions dealing with some of the pitfalls and negative experiences she'd encountered, as well. I eventually received thirty responses. Though the sample is not nearly large enough to provide conclusive judgments, it nevertheless does present a random sampling of non-traditional women's views.

The composite woman who emerged from the responses in 35.9 years old, married (with 1.8 children), and not working in the paid work force. I qualify "work force" because the demanding role a wife, mother, and full-time student fills would fetch a top salary and fancy title in most companies if her true value were assessed. Returning after an average of 8.7 years, the great majority—sixty-six percent— found college to be what they expected, frequently mentioned that the work was easier than they thought it would be or that they underestimated the amount of time studying would take. Most women, however, anticipated it would require a lot of juggling of schedules and roles and found that, in fact, it did.

One of the expectations that many returning women share is that of obtaining a better job or a higher salary. That was one of my primary expectations in going back to college on a part-time basis. When I found that going to school part-time and working part-time created twice as many scheduling difficulties at home and at school, I reluctantly quit my part-time job. I found that the added flexibility I had gained in scheduling classes more than made up for the small salary I was losing. However, giving up a part-time job or full-time job to concentrate solely on getting one's degree is a little scary. Depending on one's age and career plans, it may not even be wise.

Consider, for example, the case of a fifty-four-year-old former dean of women at the University of Tulsa who gave up her job in order to upgrade herself professionally. She entered a Ph.D. program, and five years and several thousand dollars later she was awarded a doctorate in educational administration. She has been unable in the three years since then to find employment; with her Ph.D. she is overqualified for the jobs that are available, and she is beginning to wonder whether she will ever find the kind of position for which she has been trained.[4]

Despite the fact that more than half of the women who responded found college to be what they expected, "time"—the management of it, lack of it and scheduling of it—ranked number one on fifty-five percent of the questionnaires under "problems" or "pitfalls." If I ever had any doubts as to how typical I am, they vanished as I read the story of my life in those questionnaires. A sample of some responses to the question "My main dissatisfactions are a result of...:"

"Inadequate time to do the things I would like both as concerns my family and course work."

"Lack of time to attend more classes."

"Teachers' lack of understanding about having a life besides 'the' class he or she teaches."

Other problems, pitfalls and dissatisfactions included: Lack of confidence, course selection and scheduling problems, stress and lack of a "responsive administration." One student cited as her main dissatisfaction, "Administrative inefficiency and lack of interest in the students on the part of administration." Her complaints were echoed by others, especially evening students. One respondent noted, "I believe that when I began at Dowling there were far more course offerings available. The evening student brings no hardships to the campus in the way of additional expenses due to vandalism as evidenced from time to time in the student newspaper. However, we seem to be unfavored in respect to adequate course offerings, work-study groups, student association activities."

Many problems that non-traditional women students at Dowling face have been solved by other colleges using innovative programs. Details are provided in an enlightening paper developed by the Department of Education. Some suggested solutions involve: The establishment of "an advisory board composed of re-entry students to provide input on campus government decisions that might have particular impact on the part-time re-entry population" and "the development of a part-time adult student association." Additional ideas include "reduced student activity fee" and "special social events such as an annual dance or dinner for part-time re-entry students."[5] It seems to me that in neglecting to solicit the potential input of a group of intelligent and dedicated students, Dowling is depriving itself of a valuable asset. I hope that dialogue will be established to address and solve these problems that other educational facilities have dealt with successfully.

Because of the fact that the non-traditional student is usually involved in numerous family and social relationships, the home support system is a critical factor for most returning women in their successful adjustment to school. No other answer in the questionnaire was as indicative to me of the sources of strength and the personal struggles of the participating students. Sixty-six percent of the responses indicated that the families were enthusiastic and supportive. One woman said, "Managing a household and scheduling my time for studies without my family it couldn't be done [sic]."

The other thirty-four percent shared varying degrees of frustration with the reluctance of spouses and/or children to adjust and grow in new roles. One response struck a familiar chord: "My children were always supportive. My husband at the beginning was verbally supportive, but as I progressed, he has increased his help by assisting me at home. His helping me has helped him to be more self sufficient...."

Having fought my own battles in this arena, I am on intimate terms with the guilt trip that begins, "When are you going to cook a real dinner again?" In self-defense, I've encouraged my sons to utilize my neglected cookbook, reminding them it's just like chemistry lab at school. I console myself with the fact that someday their liberated wives will bless me.

According to Miriam Hecht and Lillian Traub, in *Dropping Back In*, returning to school presents both parents and children in the family with mutual opportunities for growth. Children may "take their own studies more seriously when they observe the importance" parents attach to theirs. In addition, communication in general may be enhanced, due to shared concerns and challenges.[6]

Though participants in the questionnaire did not specify difficulties with childcare as being a pitfall, I feel that this issue was one of the major considerations to be faced and dealt with before they even attempted to return to school. Dowling College, in choosing to ignore this potential obstacle to some women's pursuit of an education, is failing to attract a potential pool of education consumers. They are also missing a valuable public relations opportunity to express their commitment to making education available to all sectors of society.

The fact that a majority of the women responding listed "getting good grades" as one of their main satisfactions or proudest accomplishments came as no surprise to me. Though I was an average student in college at eighteen, I'm an "A" student now, and extremely conscientious. Perhaps the reason is one a fellow student advanced to me some time ago: "When we graduate, we'll need everything we can going for us." This may prove to be a true observation. However, equally true for many of us, myself included, is the need to prove to

ourselves as much as anyone else that we can do it. Caryl Chudwin
and Rita Durrant addressed this drive to succeed in *College After 30:*

> What I often see in adult students is the feeling of anxiety
> about their performance. They have great expectations to
> do well. They will say, "Now don't expect me to do as well
> as some of the younger students. After all, I've been busy
> earning the bread or doing the bacon at home." Yet they
> feel they should do better because they are older and more
> mature. There are great expectations on their parts. They
> are anxious about failure. Yet, in terms of basic skills, they
> are better at reading and writing and they think more
> clearly. They are typically bright or they wouldn't want to
> be in school.[7]

Pam Mendelsohn, in citing a research project that correlated
women's age and grades in college, pointed out that "women 40 years
old and over did an average of 10 percentile points better than their
classmates between 18 and 25. They earned more A's, an equal
number of B's and C's and fewer D's and F's than the younger
women."[8] Pam Mendelsohn offers several explanations for the results
of this and other studies she cites. Two possible reasons are returning
students are so "thoroughly goal oriented" and another involves the
myriad of other responsibilities returning students often have that
make measuring one's progress as a student and "immediate feedback"
a "relief" after dealing with harder-to-measure jobs.[9]

Naturally, all this emphasis on reaching goals and achieving good
grades is bound to have its effect on professors. Wilber Cross and
Carol Florio quote Dr. Aaron Warner, dean of the School of Continuing Education at Columbia University, as saying, "Older people are
good people to teach. We find them very highly motivated, very
thoughtful people, and usually highly intelligent. Their life experience
is rich."[10]

Dr. Tony Giordano, of Dowling's Art Department, offered still
another view of the returning student. In describing his pleasure at
having them for students, he noted that they returned to school with
tremendous energy to work towards goals and often regretted the
length of time it took for them to reach this point. He explained that
the period of time before their arrival at school is "far from idle"
despite their commonly held view to the contrary. "Unconsciously
cultivating insights" and storing experiences, they arrive at school
with great "stored energy" and are much more productive than many
would have been starting younger.[11]

Initially, I began this project to learn more about my fellow non-
traditional student; however, I ended up learning just as much about
myself.

Though I usually participate actively in class and appear self-confident, shyness inhibits me from reaching out and getting to know many people I come in contact with. During the entire process of designing the questionnaire and circulating it on campus, I spoke intimately, for the first time, with other students about pleasurable experiences we've had and pitfalls we've encountered. In gaining their input, I also gained their reassurance and friendship. In discovering a group of women with struggles remarkably similar to my own, who get "high" on accomplishing goals and have a wealth of both good and bad experiences to share, I discovered a wonderful new bonus in attending school.

Edward Gibbon, as quoted in *The Lifelong Learner,* wrote: "Every man who rises above the common level has received two educations: the first from his teachers; the second, more personal and important, from himself."

With this study, my second education at Dowling has begun.

Notes

1 Stephanie M. Bennett, Dean, Westhampton College, University of Richmond, "The Re-entry Woman," *Vital Speeches of the Day,* p. 502.
2 Mike Secko, Registrar and Director of Institutional Research for Dowling College, Interview, April 11, 1984.
3 Pam Mendelsohn, "College Campuses See Influx of Women Re-entry Students," *The Christian Science Monitor,* Aug. 13, 1981, p. 15.
4 Elinor Lenz and Marjorie Shaevitz, *So You Want to Go Back to School* (New York, 1977), p. 210.
5 Roberta M. Hall, "Re-entry Women: Part-Time Enrollment, Full-Time Commitment," *Field Evaluation Draft*: A paper developed under Grant #G0079-01070 from the Women's Educational Equity Act Program of the Department of Education (Washington, D.C., 1980), pp. 4-5.
6 Miriam Hecht and Lillian Traub, *Dropping Back In* (New York, 1982), p. 172.
7 Caryl Chudwin and Rita Durrant, *College After 30* (Chicago, 1981), p. 136.
8 Pam Mendelsohn, *Happier by Degrees* (New York, 1980), p. 24.
9 Pam Mendelsohn, *Happier by Degrees* (New York, 1980), p. 24.
10 Wilber Cross and Carol Florio, *You Are Never Too Old to Learn* (New York, 1978), pp. 17-18.
11 Dr. Tony Giordano, Dowling College Art Department, Interview, April 12, 1984.
12 Ronald Gross, *The Lifelong Learner* (New York, 1977), p. 15.

Bibliography

Bennett, Stephanie M. "The Re-entry Woman," *Vital Speeches of the Day,* vol. 40, (June 1, 1980), p. 502.
Chudwin, Caryl and Rita Durrant. *College After 30* (Chicago, Illinois: Contemporary Books, Inc., 1981), p. 136.

Cross, Wilber and Carol Florio. *You Are Never Too Old to Learn* (New York: Academy for Educational Development, Inc., 1978), pp. 17-18.

Giordano, Dr. Tony, Art Department of Dowling College, personal interview, (April 12, 1984).

Gross, Ronald. *The Lifelong Learner* (New York: Simon and Schuster, 1977), p. 15.

Hall, Roberta M. "Re-entry Women: Part-Time Enrollment, Full-Time Commitment," *Field Evaluation Draft:* A paper developed under Grant #G0079-01070 from the Women's Educational Equity Act Program of the Department of Education (Washington, D.C., 1980), pp. 4-5.

Hecht, Miriam and Lillian Traub. *Dropping Back In* (New York: E. P. Dutton, Inc., 1982), p. 172.

Lenz, Elinor and Marjorie Shaevitz. *So You Want to Go Back to School* (New York: McGraw-Hill Book Company, 1977), p. 210.

Mendelsohn, Pam. "College Campuses See Influx of Women Re-entry Students," *The Christian Science Monitor* August 13, 1981, p. 15.

Secko, Mike, Registrar and Director of Institutional Research for Dowling College, personal interview, April 11, 1984.

Research Generalization

Examine some set of documents, literary works, or other texts that constitute the evidence by which some question may be answered or explored. Citing the content of these texts for support and illustration, argue a thesis that does the most justice to the evidence these texts afford. Submit for a reading course or to a publication specializing in the subject. Or present to a club or society that meets to treat this subject.

Theories on Aging

CHRISTINE C. BROWN

Introduction

Old age is the leading cause of death today. If all of the major diseases were cured the average life span would only increase by about fifteen years (Bjorksten, 1963). Many theories have been offered to explain the occurrence of death, far too many to even list here. There has not been enough conclusive research done to single out any one in particular, although some are surely more complete than others. This paper will focus on two of these theories, somatic mutation and cross-linkage.

Somatic Mutations

Somatic mutations have long been thought to be among the primary aging mechanisms (Curtis, 1958). Senescence, then, would result from the accumulation of cellular mutations, leading to eventual cell death. Orgel (1963) proposed the "error catastrophe" theory to account for the occurrence of death after a certain level of mutational build-up. According to this theory abnormal proteins accumulate in the cell, causing it to become less and less viable. This accumulation results from the degeneration, on subsequent cell divisions, of those enzymes involved in sustaining DNA integrity and in preserving the accuracy of the transcriptional level in protein synthesis. The final result is a wide range of useless enzymes, at which pont there is an "error catastrophe" leading to the complete breakdown of the cell.

This "error catastrophe" level is consistent with the Hayflick phenomenon (1961) in which normal diploid cells appear to have a limited capacity to divide. Hayflick took cells from donors of various ages and cultured them in vitro until they could no longer sustain normal growth and division. He found that as the age of the donor increased, the number of times the cells divided before they died decreased. The limits varied from one species to the next in direct relation to their life spans.

The cells that play the most important role in aging are those that divide slowly or not at all. In fact, the organs which deteriorate with age are made up of cells which do just that. Mutations which occur in rapidly dividing cells tend to be disposed of quickly and are thus less prone to aging. The slower a cell divides, the less chance it will have to eliminate resulting mutations.

Research by Stevenson and Curtis (1961) on rat liver cells showed a definite accumulation of mutations with age. Both this and research done by Williamson and Askonas (1972) lend direct support to the somatic mutation theory. Williamson and Askonas did an experiment with lymphocyte cells in which they succeeded in isolating a single clone of cells. They traced the development of these cells in living mice by a series of transfers; it was found that always in the eighth transfer the cells died. Appropriate calculations were made and it was shown that this time of death corresponded to the Hayflick phenomenon.

Even those cells that function properly might not survive. Although the DNA that controls cell function may be intact, if the non-essential DNA is damaged the cell will not be able to divide (Curtis, 1963). Due to the research supporting Orgel and Hayflick, somatic mutations remain a major issue among gerontologists.

Cross-linkage

Some researchers believe that somatic mutations are merely a result of cross-linking between two macromolecules. This theory was first introduced by Bjorksten (1942). The cross-linkage between two molecules, generally proteins and nucleic acids, causes drastic changes in their characteristics. They have altered diffusion and solubility characteristics in addition to reduced motility and increased fragility (Bjorksten 1963, 1968). Accumulation of immobilized material and loss of elasticity are therefore also secondary to cross-linkage.

Cross-linking agents include those that are fast-acting such as aldehydes, lipid oxidation products, sulfur, alkylating agents, quinones, and free radicals formed by ionizing radiation; and those that are slow-acting, such as antibodies, poly-basic acids, polyhale derivitives and polyvalent metals. These agents react randomly with macromolecules, binding them together. Cells in the process of division are highly susceptible, for their chromosomes are lined up in parallel and may be easily bound together by any cross-linking agent that happens along. This damage to the chromosome could lead to somatic mutations and even cell death. Many of these joined molecules are removed in normal metabolic processes. However, this is not one hundred percent efficient and there will be a gradual accumulation since these molecules can not be broken down.

This theory is very appealing because there are so many cross-linking agents known to be in the body that cross-linkage is inevitable. Research on the aging of collagen (Verzár, 1958) showed conclusively that cross-linkage was responsible, thus proving loss of elasticity to be secondary to cross-linkage. Tyler (1953, 1965) has shown that the life of a spermatozoan can be significantly increased by the removal of polyvalent metals, a known slow-acting cross-linking agent.

Further evidence in support of this theory is presented in the fact that ionizing radiation has a life-shortening effect and also produces free radicals, a highly effective cross-linking agent. Overeating, also linked to a shorter life span, causes increased cross-linkage. The intermediate products of digestion are known to contain cross-linking agents which, when an over abundance of food is taken in, tend to accumulate.

In view of all the evidence the cross-linkage theory seems to be very plausible. This is especially true when compared to somatic mutations as this theory indirectly proves that these mutations are secondary to cross-linkage. Also, cross-linkage can account for these environmental stresses that are known to shorten life and cause age related changes.

Conclusions

The changes that occur during the aging process are many and complex. While somatic mutations may account for some of these changes, they cannot account for all. Cross-linkages also account for some of these changes, many more than somatic mutations can. These mutations are shown to be one of the secondary results of cross-linkage (Bjorksten, 1963). For these reasons it is felt that the cross-linkage theory is the better of the two. However, until a great deal more research is done, somatic mutations will remain in the running along with the many other theories.

References

Bjorksten, J., and Champion, W.J., 1942. Mechanical influences upon tanning. *J. A. Chem, Soc.* 64: pp. 868-869. Cited from Bjorksten, J., 1963 Aging, Primary Mechanism, *Gerontologia,* 8: pp. 179-192.

Bjorksten, J., 1963. Aging, Primary Mechanism. *Gerontologia,* 8: pp. 179-192.

Bjorksten, J., 1968. The cross-linkage theory of aging. *J. Am. Geriatrics Soc.* 16(4): pp. 408-427.

Burnett, M., 1974. *Intrinsic Mutagensis: A Genetic Approach to Aging.* John Wiley and Sons, Inc., New York.

Curtis, H.J., 1958. Rad, Res. 9: p. 104 Cited from Curtis, H.J., 1963. Biological mechanisms underlying the aging process. *Science, 141:* pp. 686-694.

Hayflick, L., and Moorhead, P.S., 1961. The serial cultivation of human diploid cell strains. Exp. Cell Res. 25: pp. 585-621. Cited from Burnett, M., 1974. *Intrinsic Mutagenesis: A Genetic Approach to Aging.* John Wiley and Sons, Inc., New York.

Hayflick, L., 1975. Current theories of biological aging. Federation Proc. *34*(1): pp. 9-13.

Orgel, L.E., 1963. The maintenance of the accuracy of protein synthesis and its relevance to aging. Proc. Natn. Acad. Sci. USA 49: pp. 517-521. Cited from Burnett, M., 1974. *Intrinsic Mutagenesis: A Genetic Approach to Aging.* John Wiley and Sons, Inc. New York.

Stevenson, K.G., and Curtis, H.J., 1961. Chromosome abberations in irradiated and nitrogen mustard treated mice. Rad. Res. 15. pp. 744. Cited from Burnett, M., 1974. *Intrinsic Mutagenesis: A Genetic Approach to Aging.* John Wiley and Sons, Inc., New York.

Tyler, A., 1953. Prolongation of life span of sea-urchin spermatazoa, and improvement of the fertilization-reaction, by treatment of spermatozoa and eggs with metal chelating agents. Biol. Bull. 104: pp. 224-239. Cited from Bjorksten, J., 1968 The cross-linkage theory of aging. *J. Am. Geriatrics Soc. 16*(4): pp. 408-427.

Tyler, A., 1965. Longevity of gametes; histocompatability-Gene loss and neoplasia, in aging and levels of biological organization. ed. by A.M. Brues and G.A. Sacher, Chicago. Univ. of Chicago Press, Sect II (Genetics and Environment). Part II pp. 50-86 Cited from Bjorksten, J., 1968 The cross-linkage theory of aging. *J. Am. Geriatrics Soc. 16*(4): pp. 408-427.

Verzár, F., and Huber, K., 1958. Thermic-contraction of single tendon fibers from animals of different age after treatment with formaldehyde, urethane, glycerol, acetic acid and other substances. *Gerontologia* 2: pp. 81-103. Cited from Bjorksten, J., 1963 Aging, Primary Mechanism. *Gerontologia 8:* pp. 179-192.

Williamson, A.R., and Askonas, B.A., 1972. *Nature,238.* pp. 337. Cited from Burnett, M., 1974. *Intrinsic Mutagenesis: A Genetic Approach to Aging.* John Wiley and Sons, Inc., New York.

Imagination
(Thinking Up)

Dreams

Jot down a dream soon afterwards so you'll remember it better, or keep a notebook of dreams regularly. Tell the dream to a partner or group until you have it well in mind, listen to what they have to say about it, then write it as a story and perhaps as a poem. If it didn't end, or ended in a way you don't like, add an ending or change the original one. Read it to a group and talk about whether others have had similar dreams. Include it in a booklet of stories or poems by you or others. If the dream features dialog, script it and give it to others to perform.

Journal Extract
Thomas DeMaggio

3/7/83 Monday
I had a weird dream last night. Me and Dean were in the cafeteria and Lisa walked in and this big Black guy was following her. He was really starting to bother her when I stepped in. I hit him and we got into a big brawl. It ended and Lisa wouldn't talk to me. Everywhere I went I ran into this guy and got in another fight. Well anyway it started to be a real pain. No one would take my side. Everyone was convinced it was me starting the fights and I was alone with no one to talk to.

Black Giants in Viking Hats

Dean and I were sitting in the cafeteria talking. Lisa (girl I just started seeing at the time) walked in and headed towards the counter. Now, behind her comes this big giant black guy with a Viking hat on. He starts bothering her and you could see she's getting upset. Right away I get up and go after him, mad as hell. I remember he was in front of the soda machine. I hit him with a chair and when he went down I pushed the soda machine over on top of him. This took care of him for a while.

Now, you would think after I did this Lisa would be grateful. You know, because I was defending her. Wrong. She was super mad. She said I was violent, rude, and where did I get off thinking it was my job to defend her. Then she stormed off. Just when I was going to go after her to explain why I did it and how I felt about her, who grabs me but my friend with the Viking hat. We really went at it, busting tables, windows, chairs, everything.

Somehow the fight ended and I got away, but whenever I saw Lisa and tried to explain, this guy would jump out of nowhere and we would start going at it all over again. Lisa was even madder now. Every time she saw me I was in a fight, and she really didn't want anything to do with me. The way it ended was this guy had me covered with a gun and he was just about to blow my brains out and I woke up.

Now, the reason this dream is so vivid in my mind is that the day after I had it I called Lisa and told her about (believe it or not) it. I was surprised to see her reaction. I figured she'd think I was a weirdo or something, but she was flattered that I was thinking about her so much that she was in my dreams. She also said a few other mushy things that I don't want to go into, but now whenever we're together and some big black guy goes by we either both start laughing or she asks me if I see any Viking hats.

The other reason I remember the dream so well is that I couldn't figure out why I had it or what it meant. When I first took Lisa out, its a long story but one of my friends liked her and I kind of stabbed him in the back. So everyone told me the guilt was getting to me. Also when you first start seeing a girl you're not really sure about how you feel about each other, and everyone was telling me this dream meant she didn't like me. This is why she was ignoring me in the dream. Well anyway, now the dream just serves to give us a few laughs, and I must say I really don't believe that dreams have a hidden meaning or that they're going to come true. It was just something I had on my mind at that moment. She said she was flattered that she was in my dreams, but I bet if she ever saw some of the other dreams I had about her she wouldn't be so flattered. (Ha, Ha, just a little humor to brighten your day. You don't really think I have dreams like that, do you?)

Chocolate

TRACY McNAMARA

During my dream I had just come from my best friend Janet's house. Janet is a very pretty small girl with big brown eyes. One of the things that Janet and I share in common happens to be our love for chocolate. While I was there I had told Janet that my fiancé Kenny and I were going to the circus. I asked Janet if she wanted to come. She said she had some things to do, but she would probably meet us there later.

When we arrived at the circus I remember being very pleased with Kenny as we walked through the parking lot, because Kenny finally parked my car in a spot which I approved of without me saying a word. Normally he would park my car in a place which was very dark, where it could easily be broken into.

When we went inside, we bought pink cotton candy and all the other novelties which are sold at the circus. We were there a while before I began wondering when Janet would arrive. There was a small elephant doing tricks in the ring when we decided to leave our seats and take a walk around. We kicked the straw on the ground with our feet. There was plenty going on that night and the excitement was in the air. As we walked around the coliseum I kept noticing that the baby elephant which was doing tricks in the ring when we left our seats was following us. We walked a little more, absorbing all the sights. The elephant kept appearing wherever we went. Finally the elephant was close enough that we could pet it. I touched its hard wrinkled skin, which looked worse than it felt. As I was petting the animal, I noticed a familiar scent and looked around. It was the perfume Janet always wore. I knew what it was because I gave it to her for her birthday. As I looked down to see the animal's face its deep brown eyes seemed to recognize me. It began wrapping its trunk around me and making all sorts of noises. I got scared and backed away from the elephant. Kenny and I stood there trying to figure out why the animal acted that way. The elephant just stood in front of us staring at our faces.

A few minutes later, one of the concession sellers walked by us carrying a tray of chocolate pudding. The elephant leaped and knocked the man over and began eating the pudding. It was then that I realized that Janet had indeed met us at the circus. She had been turned into an elephant. I was the only one who suspected this. Kenny would never believe it! I whispered in the elephant's ear, "Janet, is that you?" The animal nodded slowly. Now what do I do?

Dream Textures

MAUREEN CRONIN

The dream transpired
in art book illustrations
and post card portraits of tropical forests.

My feet fell on cool Venetian marble
and thick Oriental carpets
walled in by steaming jungles.

At the stark center
of the dream
pure white stone balls
fell
into red stone cups.

The stone—smooth and cool.
The red—crusted, sticky.

There was heat
and the smell
of people
pressing.

The forests dissolved
and the light of a winter dusk
enclosed me
in a mahogany-paneled room
hung with paintings,

swirling textures.

I admired
while my feet sank in rancid mud.

Plays

Duolog

Invent a conversation between two people by writing down just what each speaker says in turn. Place the name of a speaker just above his or her speech or in the left margin and followed by a colon. Don't use quotation marks for these speeches. Indicate action and setting by stage directions placed in parentheses. The time, place, and circumstances have to be clear from the words and actions of the characters or from what else can be seen or heard. This is a script for a single scene that should run for a playing time of 4-8 minutes. It will be given to others to act out and may be included in a printed collection of scripts. A script for radio or audiotape should of course include nothing that can be seen but only directions for sound effects.

Two Over One

HARRY ESCALERA

LISA: Have you seen Gus today?

JO: No, I wasn't looking for him, I'm mad at him.

LISA: (*sarcastically*) I can't imagine why.

JO: Don't get smart with me. You know why I'm mad. I don't want you going out with him again!

LISA: How did you find out about us?

JO: I have my ways. Besides, you make it so obvious telling all the girls in class.

LISA: I didn't know you two had something going.

JO: Well, you know now, so keep away.

LISA: Are you telling me or asking?

JO: I'm telling you this time. Let's hope there IS no next time.

LISA: (*very casual*) That almost sounds like a threat.

JO: Look, I'm telling you for the last time. Gus is my boyfriend and I don't want to see you two together again.

LISA: I think you should know something. I've been dating Gus for longer than you think. And I don't think he's very serious about you. Think about it. He tells me everything that goes on with you two, but he never told you about me. Doesn't that tell you something?

JO: (*thinking about what was just said*) Well, I'm supposed to see him tonight and we'll see who Gus wants to be with.

LISA: Can't you get it through your head? I know he wants me. He just doesn't want to hurt your feelings. He said he was waiting for the right time to tell you. Since you asked I thought I would let you know what was going on.

JO: I suppose you knew he was coming to see me tonight.

LISA: I knew. I'm going to be waiting for him. After he sees you tonight he said he would come by my house.

JO: We'll see if he wants to leave tonight. I'm not going to let him leave.

LISA: I'll make you a deal. If he doesn't come by to see me tonight I'll give him up for good. But you've got to tell him that you know about me.

JO: How are you going to know I've told him that I know about you?

LISA: I'll just ask Gus next time I see him. I've got to go—see you in class.

Father

PETER BELLI

Characters
DEAN
FATHER WILLIAMS

Scene

A dimly lit confessional. Dean enters and kneels as the small black door slides open.

DEAN: (*squinting, searching before him until the priest's profile clears from the dark*) Bless me, Father, for I have sinned. It has been seventeen years since my last confession.

FATHER WILLIAMS (*repeats the ceremonial rites in a monotone voice. His chin moves slightly towards Dean*): Seventeen years? What has kept you from the Church all these years? Have you lost your faith?

DEAN: Father, to tell you the truth, I never had much faith. It kind of wore off over the years. You know, with the bogeyman and all.

FATHER WILLIAMS: Please! Sarcasm is unnecessary. Tell me, after seventeen years, what brings you here?

DEAN: Well...I guess you could describe it as some sort of...ah...of a calling. You know, sometimes we're just driven.

FATHER WILLIAMS: Driven? What exactly do you mean by driven?

DEAN: It's difficult to describe, Father...I suppose you'd be better at understanding it than I would. I mean...it is your business and all.

FATHER WILLIAMS (*perturbed at Dean's thoughtless statement*): My dear boy...(*He pauses to take a deep breath.*) The Church is not involved in the business of anything. We are here on God's behalf. So please!...refrain from that type of thinking. We all work according to His wishes and are not a profit-seeking organization.

DEAN (*smugly*): Well you'll have to excuse me, Father. After so many years I've developed a different view of things. By the way...why did you call me your dear boy. Have you....

FATHER WILLIAMS: Well....

DEAN: It is appropriate, though.

FATHER WILLIAMS (*ignoring Dean's question*): Would you like to begin?

DEAN: Begin?

FATHER WILLIAMS (*becoming hostile*): Yes...begin! Your confession. Remember. That's what we're here for.

DEAN (*mockingly*): Oh yeah, right! Well...where do I start. You know it has been a while. I've got plenty of sins. This could take hours!

FATHER WILLIAMS (*ignoring Dean's disrespectful attitude*): Listen!...If you don't mind, I have others waiting. Begin with your last confession. And if it will make things easier, you may leave out financial matters; tax evasion and business transactions, I mean. They do not concern us here.

DEAN (*hesitates for a moment*): Yea...sure. Well...since my last confession, which was when I was about nine or ten, I'm not really sure, a lot has happened. Oh, by the way...I haven't any financial sins to speak of. Money was never our thing while I was growing up. My mother was poor. We invested what we had in breakfast and dinner and stayed away from that over-the-counter-shit. We....

FATHER WILLIAMS (*turning his head away*): If you would like to continue, please do not use that sort of language here. Otherwise I will....

DEAN: Oh!..you'll have to excuse me Father. It just comes natural when you've spent your childhood in the streets. It's rough, you know!

FATHER WILLIAMS (*in a condescending tone*): The streets have nothing to do with your attitude. Rich or poor, we are all His children.

DEAN: Sure. That's easy for you to say.

FATHER WILLIAMS (*brings his face closer to the screen*): Listen you! I've dealt with your type before. Don't think I won't hesitate to have you dragged out of here and locked up. You punks think you know everything. Let me tell you.... I spent eight years in Bedford Stuyvesant working with those...those people. So if you think you've had it bad, just try living there for a while.

DEAN: (contemptuously): Well...what a coincidence. That's my old neighborhood. You mean to tell me...I mean...is it possible that you served at St. Joseph's The Divine? You know...the one with the statue of Christ with the missing right arm. It sits right in the front. You can't miss it.

FATHER WILLIAMS (becoming perplexed. He takes on a reticent tone): Why ...ah...why yes. That is my old parish....

DEAN (chuckling): Well, well. It really is a small world, isn't it? Say Father, do you know how that statue lost its arm? Have you ever heard the story? Let me tell you. It's really interesting.

FATHER WILLIAMS (agitated): This is not....

DEAN: Oh yes it is! This is just the place for it. Now you listen....

FATHER WILLIAMS: I do not....

DEAN: You...SHUT...UP! (Father Williams jerks his hands feebly in an attempt to say something, then looks down, openly grieved.) That's better.

FATHER WILLIAMS (head in hands): Who are you? What do you want?

DEAN: Ohhhh...come on Father. Let's not spoil the story....

FATHER WILLIAMS: I beg you—.

DEAN: You...ha! You beg nothing. Now just sit and relax like a good, God-fearing priest while I fill you in on all that happened. (Father Williams reaches for the small door.) You touch that and after I break your fucking arm, I'll go to the newspapers.... You know, I know some close friends there. We spent a lot of time together taking a lot of crap just to get through college. I've got favors coming (Father Williams places his hands on his lap.) Well anyway...once upon a time.... Hey! Ain't it nice having an ed-uuu-cated son. Sorry the color won't wash off. Anyway...once upon a time, there was this cleaning lady at this church who busted a statue of Jesus cause some horny priest had to get his rocks off and.... Oh, by the way...you don't have to listen all that carefully cause I'll be back real regular to see you. Anyway this priest gets her knocked-up and soon he's gone, good-bye....

Triolog

Set down in script form what three characters say to each other during one continuous scene running for 6-20 minutes and developing to some sort of climax. It's better to try this after doing Duolog at least once. If your script is for film, look at a film script for terms and directions indicating camera angles and actions. If for radio or audiotape, where visuals are missing, you might use "stage directions" to indicate how lines should be read. But rely for this mainly on the way lines are written and punctuated. If possible, have your script performed, filmed, or taped. A Readers' Theater presentation is often a simple and appropriate way to perform a script essentially depending on voice, since it requires no memorization, costumes, or staging.

The Girls

MARGARETE MILLER

Scene

A fairly large office area with three desks. One door is marked Private. Each desk has a typewriter. Time: 9:00 a.m.

Sitting at each desk, behind a typewriter, are three women:

KATHY:

She is approximately 26-28 years old, fairly attractive, dressed fashionably. Her appearance is spoiled by a slightly sullen expression which appears to be pasted on her face. Even when she laughs or smiles, her features revert to a bored, sullen look. She is daintily chewing on a bun and sipping coffee from a container.

LORRAINE:

She is approximately 30-32 years old, also fairly attractive. She is slightly heavyset. She is sitting dejectedly at her desk, looking decidedly unhappy. Her eyes look swollen, as if she has been crying. She is also sipping from a container of coffee.

ROSE:

She is also in her early thirties. Something about her appearance suggests that she is the leader of the group. There is an authoritative air about her. She is not as attractive as the other two girls. She wears enormous amounts of jewelry and smokes incessantly. She has just finished reading a newspaper and folds it carefully, putting it in a desk drawer as the curtain opens.

ROSE: Well, Lorraine, did he come home last night? (*looking sympathetic*) Oh, sweetheart, I can tell from your face, something's wrong. Ohhh, that bastard! Not again!

LORRAINE: (*looking weepy*) Please, girls, don't get me started.... I just don't know what to do anymore. He came home around 3:00 in the morning, and I pretended to be sleeping. This morning, he told me he has a very important meeting to go to after work that will be very late. How many meetings can he go to? I just know he has someone else.... I just want to die!

ROSE: I can't stand to hear any more.... I feel so bad for you....You deserve so much better than him, Lorraine. I could just take him by the throat and strangle him. You're such a sweetheart, with so much to offer, how could he do this to you?

(*There is silence while the girls nod sympathetically.*)

KATHY: Personally, Lorraine, you're a fool to put up with his nonsense. I'd be damned if I would. I'd have him out the door so fast his head would spin. And I'd take him for all he's worth, too. You're too easygoing. You're acting like a door mat, for God's sake!

LORRAINE: But I still *love* him! I don't want to throw him out...Without him, I'd be nothing.

KATHY: (*defiantly*) Love, shit! You've spoiled him rotten, letting him come and go as he pleases! That husband of yours is nothing but a woman chaser, and he knows you let him get away with it. (*She sees that Lorraine is starting to cry.*) Oh Lorraine, come on. You have a lot on the ball yourself. All you have to do is lose ten pounds or so, and you'd be an absolute knockout. You can get something better any day of the week. Come on, buckle up. Hey, I have an idea! Let's all go out tonight and get ourselves bombed! Call up Scotty and let him know that *you'll* be out too!

LORRAINE: Oh, I don't know....

ROSE: Yeah, let's do that.... I know a great singles bar in West Babylon. We could have a ball. In fact, Friday nights are free drinks until 9:00.... Let's go.

LORRAINE: I'm not any fun. I'd be a drag. (*gets up to leave the room*) I'm going to the ladies' room for a minute. (*picks up her purse and prepares to leave*) Listen, I know I've said this before, but I really appreciate you two. I don't know what I'd do without you guys.... All these weeks of crying on your shoulder. I know I've been a crybaby, but you have been just great to me. Every time I get down on myself, I think of you two and I feel better.

(*The girls gather together and hug briefly. Lorraine, blowing her nose, leaves the room.*)

ROSE: Listen, if we can't stick together, who can?

KATHY: Yeah. Oh nuts, I have to get this contract out today and I didn't even start on it. (*puts paper in typewriter*) There has to be a better way to make a living than this. (*turns to Rose*) You know, that girl is something else. I love her dearly, but I'm losing patience with her. She's such a mealy mouth. Sometimes, I can't help it, I'm on Scotty's side, the way she carries on. Imagine the tears at home, the way she is in here. I hate self-pity. Lorraine is getting to be a drag, and if she don't watch it, she's going to end up behind the eightball for sure. She's making her own problems as far as I'm concerned.

ROSE: Well, he is a son of a gun. He must have had at least four affairs since last year. I think there's something wrong with a guy like that. And he's breaking her heart, the bastard.

KATHY: I'm not sure if he's the bastard that Lorraine makes him. (*She sniffs a little haughtily.*) I hate to sound like a goody-goody, but *usually*, when a man fools around like that, it's because he's missing something at home, if you know what I mean....

ROSE: Yeah.

KATHY: And I'll tell you something—but don't you dare mention this to Lorraine! I've talked with Scotty, and he has his side to the story, you know. He's called me a few times, and we've met over a few friendly drinks, and I don't think he's such a woman chaser, at all. Lorraine doesn't understand him, or appreciate him. And she's letting herself go too. No, Scotty is really a pretty decent guy, once you get to know him....

ROSE: I didn't know you were friendly with Scotty. You always act as if you hate him.

KATHY: Oh no, I don't hate him at all. I'm just saying that I can see the other side. Scotty is looking for a woman who is warm and sympathetic. If he found someone like that, he'd be home every night, I bet. (*She takes out her compact and looks in the mirror, pleased with what she sees.*) Of course, I am not getting too involved right now, and I told him that. After all, Lorraine is one of my best friends. I would feel like a heel. Of course, when two people are wrong for each other....

ROSE: I didn't know that you were dating him, Kathy.

KATHY: I'm not dating him, I'm being a friend, that's all. I like him, and he is a sexy bastard, you have to admit. He has a way of looking at you that.... I would be willing to give the poor guy half a chance to prove himself, that's all. Lorraine isn't doing that. All she does is cry and whine and gain weight. Listen, Rose, don't you dare tell Lorraine any of this! There's no need to get her upset any more than she is now.

ROSE: You're absolutely right. I wouldn't breathe a word...I swear. To be honest, you have a point. Lorraine is getting on my nerves, too. I try to change the subject, but all she can talk about is her problems with Scotty. She is a pain in the neck. Maybe Scotty is just running away from her and her tears, who knows?

KATHY: And she's not doing her share of the work around here any more. We all have problems, but we don't carry them around with us 24 hours a day....

ROSE: Speaking of 24 hours a day, we better get some work done. Mr. Brewster should be in any minute. It's 10:30 already. Where does the day go to? (*She puts paper in her typewriter and they both type for a few minutes.*)
(*Lorraine returns. She is obviously making an effort to look cheerful.*)

LORRAINE: Hi, girls. I feel much better. And thanks for the offer to go out tonight, I think I'll take you up on it.

KATHY & ROSE: Great!!

ROSE: And let's all have lunch together tomorrow, even if it is a Saturday. I miss you guys on weekends, we should get together more often.

LORRAINE: But we see each other almost every Saturday and last Sunday, we....

KATHY: Look, all I can say is that we are very very lucky that we're such good friends. Imagine if we weren't compatible and had to work together all day long. Some offices, they have all kinds of friction between them. We're best friends, and it makes things so much nicer.

(*They all nod in agreement.*)

ROSE: I just know that it will be me that gets the dictation today. It seems that Mr. Brewster is using me as his private secretary and forgetting you two. I wouldn't mind, but we all get the same pay.

KATHY: Yeah, peanuts! (*They all laugh and prepare to work. A buzzer is heard. Rose picks up the telephone.*)

ROSE: Mr. Brewster's office. Oh, hello there. Yes sir, I'll be right in. (*She picks up her pad and pencil and gets up from her desk.*) See what, did I tell you? He wants ME again! (*She leaves the room, entering door marked "Private."*)

KATHY: (*mimicking Rose*) He wants me again!! She loves it!

LORRAINE: I'm glad you noticed too. Between you and me, she is hankering after a raise for herself. She's always buttering up to him. I think we'd better stick together, or we'll be left behind.

LORRAINE: I'm a better typist than she is, anyway. All she does is yak all day and pump me about what Scotty does. But I suppose she means well.

KATHY: Oh, she probably does mean well. She can't help it if she has to lean on your problems in order to get her jollies. What else does she have?

LORRAINE: (*laughing*) Oh, Kathy, you are terrible. She can't help the way she looks. (*She takes out her mirror and looks.*) After all, we can't all be beautiful!

(*They both laugh at this.*)

KATHY: Seriously, though, you should start thinking a little more positively and get rid of the lying two-faced excuse for a man you have. You can do much better. You have a lot on the ball.

LORRAINE: Well, without your encouragement, I don't know. Sometimes, I feel like such a nothing. And Rose has a way of talking down to me that makes me feel so inferior, especially about my work. I know it's just the way she is but she acts like she's the only one who does anything around here. Do you think she acts so superior because she knows she's not as attractive as we are? She is a dog, even if she is nice.

KATHY: Probably. I think she needs a man, that's what. She's frustrated. Hey, do you think she's making it with the boss?

LORRAINE: Oh, no! Not Rose! He is a flirt, though. He can't keep his hands to himself sometimes. If I gave him half the chance, you know....

KATHY: Well, honey, that's the best way to get a raise.

(*They are both giggling when Rose returns to the room. She is smiling.*)

ROSE: (*looking almost coy*) That Mr. Brewster! What a character! The things he says.... Well, it's nice to know your boss appreciates you. He always says the nicest things.... You know, what do you think of this idea? Don't you think we should have an office manager around here? Someone to assign the work and all. Someone really should be in charge, even though we all cooperate so well. I mentioned it to Mr. Brewster just now, and he agrees.

LORRAINE: And who would it be? You?

ROSE: That decision would be up to Mr. Brewster. I did mention that right now, Lorraine, you have a lot of personal problems and they get in the way of your work. I hope you don't mind. We all know that it's only temporary. You're going through a crisis just now. And you, Kathy, you usually come in late, after staying up all night and going God knows where all the time with God knows who....

KATHY: (*to herself*) Oh shit. (*sarcastically*) Would you be getting a little raise for this, Rose?

ROSE: Well, he mentioned something about a raise, but of course, it's all tentative right now.... The job would involve more responsibility and it should pay more, don't you think?

(Kathy and Lorraine exchange knowing glances.)

KATHY: *(gets up from her seat, yawning.)* Almost lunchtime, girls! Where shall we go? Rose, you decide—you make all the other decisions around here. I'm going to the ladies' room for a breath of air.... *(She leaves the room)*

ROSE: *(after Kathy leaves)* Was she being sarcastic?

LORRAINE: Kathy is always sarcastic, you know that. She's jealous.

ROSE: Jealous? Lorraine, I have to tell you something very very personal. I better wait and talk to you later after work, she might come back. It's about Kathy though, and about her being jealous. Lorraine, she is not the friend you think she is. She twists things you say....

LORRAINE: Oh, I'm not surprised. I wasn't born yesterday. Tell me now, Rose. What?

ROSE: No, later. Just remember, I am your true friend. I care about you very much.

LORRAINE: And I feel very close to you, too. You always give me your shoulder to cry on. Somehow, I just don't feel as close to Kathy.

ROSE: There's a reason for that, believe me.... I'll tell you all about it later.... That Mr. Brewster, I think he likes me too much, if you know what I mean....

LORRAINE: Sure do. You're an attractive woman, Rose. Why shouldn't he?

ROSE: That Kathy thinks she's the most gorgeous thing in the world. How many times do you have to go to the bathroom, anyway? She just wants to look at herself again, to see if she's still there, I guess.

LORRAINE: She is conceited. Oops, here she comes....

KATHY: *(returning to the room)* Well, where shall we go for lunch, girls? Let's really treat ourselves for a change, to celebrate Rose's upcoming promotion and Lorraine's liberation.

(They all laugh.)

ROSE: Should we ask the new girl in the next office?

KATHY: Hell, no—just the three of us—she looks like a snob, anyway....

LORRAINE: And that hair of hers....

(Giggling and talking, they all leave for lunch.)

Exterior Monolog

Make up a character whose way of speaking you feel confident you can imitate. Imagine him or her telling something to another person in a certain place. Write down exactly what she or he says and nothing more except minimal stage directions to indicate setting and action. It should have a playing time of

2-5 minutes. Such a monolog calls for a situation in which one person is realistically holding forth while the other or others merely listen and react without words. What you want to accomplish by this depends on how you see such a situation being used. Consider different media too. For a more challenging version of this task, write your script for pure voice—no visuals, no sound effects.

Only a Passport

PAMELA SCHURE

Where am I from? Good question. Actually, I'm open to suggestions. Why don't you just name a country and I'll tell if I'm from there.... Where was I born? That won't help you any. Why don't you just listen to the spiel, okay? Do you want the 50-second version or the 5-minute version? I've got them both down pat. You see, my passport says I'm an American, but that has nothing to do with me.

I was born in New York City, and nine months later we left and moved to Lagos, Nigeria, by way of London, England, where I learned to walk. I barely missed learning to walk at my Oma's. My Dutch grandmother's house. Got that? Right.

Anyway, my brother was born in Nigeria by a midwife. Nigeria is so messed up. The doctor never even made it to the hospital until it was too late. Next stop was Rhodesia. In 1965, Ian Smith declared unilateral independence from Britain and IBM pulled everyone out. Next stop was Vienna, Austria. There my parents' marriage fell apart, and in 1968 we found ourselves on a freighter bound for "America."

My brother and I had a tough time figuring out where we were. We kept saying, "When are we getting to America?" while we were driving to Texas! We ended up at my other grandmother's, Nana in Sicilian dialect, house in Monterey, California, where my mom had grown up. My mom went back to school and got her AA degree at the Monterey Peninsula College.

Then we moved north to Santa Cruz, and two years later, further north to Santa Clara, where she got her master's in Psychology. We then moved back to Monterey.

Hey, I told you you were in for it! Anyway, every summer we were flying back to Europe to visit our father and our Dutch family. We were really poor for nine months and then, miraculously, got rich during the summer and flew off to Europe.

After one year in Monterey, I was not happy, so when my aunt got a divorce and needed someone to babysit her kids while she worked at night, I volunteered. Well, that lasted four months. When I wasn't babysitting, I was being babysat.

So I moved back to my mom's, who by now had foster kids. Can you imagine six teenagers in one house? Well, after six months I left to go to Paris. You see, the summer before I'd promised my father to go live with him, but only if I was accepted at a special French high school called, get this, the "Lycée International de St. Germain-en-Laye." Well, I was accepted and I went, even though I didn't want to go. After two weeks of school, I realized that I'd have to stay to finish high school since the French and American systems didn't mesh at all. I ended up having the two best years of my life there. I had good friends and my place in this weird international world. I had found other people who were like me. No one had a country either and so we could just be who we were with each other.

After two years, my dad had to go back to the United States. He moved to Alabama for, get this, the weather! They had a hurricane the week after he got there! Can you imagine Alabama after Paris! My mom ordered me back home, and so I went, but on the condition that I would not live at home.

I rented a room from this lady named Naeda, who was a really neat lady. I mean, she opened the door and I just knew that this was it. I stayed there for a year, but I knew that I had to move out. You see, I couldn't have friends over, and so I moved into this apartment with an Army lieutenant. Which was great. He worked at Fort Hunter Ligget, a military base two hours south of Monterey. So he only came home on weekends. Besides, he made great ice-cream. I love guys who can cook.

After three months I found myself spending all of my time with some friends at their house. We were *bon'g da Lejje*, which means "God bless you" in Swahili, but really means nothing. It's actually a song that some of us made up. Well, I lived there for two months and then I moved across the street with my Dutch boyfriend, Hank. Then I moved to Holland with him, but it didn't work out, and after two months we broke up and I came to the states after visiting my Dutch family.

Do you see this scarf I'm wearing? Well, my favorite aunt gave it to me. She sent it over from Holland with my brother last summer. But that is beside the point.

Anyway, I moved back to the states and lived with my mom for three months until I came down here to UCSD. I love it here. It's great can you imagine San Diego after Monterey? Monterey is soooo boring. So, the answer to your original question "where am I from?" is ????? Decide for yourself, one place is as strange as any other.

Corsages for Joni
FREDERICK COLWELL

Three, two, one, green.... Damn, these lights never listen to me. Now turn left at the next one and you'll be on El Camino Real. Wasn't that movie great? The sound was too loud though. I loved the part at the party where he walks into the bathroom and those two are in the bathtub: "Have you seen...?" What was the guy's name? Then he walks out and leaves the door open. Oh, and he shreds the lawn just as the parents are getting home. That was so funny. Go Kevin, it's green. Look out! That ass-hole—he did that on purpose. You should have honked.... Not now.

Of course he just happens to have a key to fit Sting's bike. Oh, and you know that if Sting is there the police aren't far behind. That girl in the movie reminds me of Joni.... OK. OK. So every girl in the movies reminds me of Joni. But I can't understand it. What is going on in that girl's mind? She says she wants friends, but I want to be her friend and does she want to be friends with me? No!... What do you mean, I don't love her anymore? I'm even trying to avoid her! It wouldn't be so hard to avoid her if she didn't make it so easy. You know what I mean?.... A little time? A little time? When was the last time we did anything together?.... Well, yeah, Valentine's day, but come on. I call her up and warn her not to eat anything because I was going to take her to dinner.... OK, OK, so I told her roommate to warn her. But what's she doing when I get there? Eating fudge. And even then, when we still go out she wants her roommate to go along. This light is too long. There's nobody coming the other way. Did I tell you the one about the two psychics and the rabbit from Wyoming?.... Oh. Right.

Joni says she wants to have fun and go out with her friends, but whenever I ask her if she wants to do anything she's got homework, she's tired, she's already eaten, it's too late. And when she does do something, she acts like it's a big favor. Like when we went to Disneyland. She didn't really want to go on any of the rides we wanted to go on, but she wouldn't tell us what *she* wanted to do. "Oh, what ever you want. I don't care...." No I'm not just mad because she went on all the rides with Zach. Not to say that I wasn't a little annoyed, but that wasn't the only reason.

Three, two, one, green. Damn. These lights don't work right. In Carlsbad they all turn green for me. Hey! Check out that truck. That's the last year they made them like that. It's just a little larger than the one I wanted Joni to buy. She could have had a classic: a '38 panel truck is not a common thing any more. And the guy was only asking $200.... She wouldn't have had to. I could have loaned her the money.... But she wouldn't have had to pay me back right away and then she'd have her own transportation. . . . A little paint and that dent pulled out and it would look great. . . . Yeah, but I could help her rebuild the engine. It wouldn't be too hard. And a new radiator shouldn't be too hard to find. But she says she'll think about it. And while she's thinking the guy sells it to someone else. What a shame. Don't hit the rabbit! Hey, how many Dutchmen does it take to eat rabbit stew? . . . . Two; one to eat and one to watch for cars. . . . But I didn't tell it to Joni, I told her the other one about the abortion. . . . But what does being Catholic have to do with liking a joke? It was a funny joke. Hey, the Translators! Turn the radio up? . . . . "You're in New York, but I'm not. You're in Afghanistan, but I'm not. You're insane, but I'm not. . . ."

I'm trying to be her friend. She needs somebody to talk to. I just want to be friends now. . . . But how long does it take for somebody to forget. I did that three years ago, and besides everybody was giving everybody else corsages on Valentine's day. . . . Well I had to give her six: I wrote a long note and I couldn't fit it on just one. Besides I'm trying to set an example for bringing the flower business back. If everybody sends corsages, we won't go out of business.

If you turn left here you'll get to the place where we pack our bulbs. No, don't do it, I said, "If you turn left." When I took Joni there she acted like such a bitch. . . . I did not threaten marriage! I was only joking: all I said was, "Someday all this could be yours," and she acted like I was laying this big guilt trip on her. . . . But it was only a joke.

Even Eric thinks there's something wrong, and he ought to know. . . . Well, he said he'd have a talk with her, but he sounded like he was trying to convince me to give up. Oh, well. Let's drop Fred off first. Three, two, one, green. See? What did I tell you? It always works in Carlsbad. Well, this has been a fun evening, but let's not do it again soon. Maybe tomorrow we can invite some people over to watch MTV and get drunk or something. . . . Well, you guys, Erin and Jim and maybe George, Dave and Dave, Eric and Zach, and Joni. . . . Of course, if everybody else is invited we'd have to ask her. Besides, I wouldn't invite her, you would.

Interior Monolog

Make up a character whose way of thinking and speaking you feel confident about imitating. Imagine him or her somewhere in particular doing something in particular. Write down what this person is thinking and feeling during this time in the exacts words the person would think this in. Use interior

*monolog for what you think it can do best. Playing time should
be 3-5 minutes. What medium would be best for your script?
Write the directions accordingly. Or write the script totally
without any directions at all.*

Study Break

TERESA WHALEN

I've already put a total of five hours into studying for this speech
exam. It's just not sticking. One night left to.... I'm so nervous....
Study, yeah, better get on it. Can I remember all this by tomorrow
morning? I doubt it. Sure wish I could be watching the game tonight
instead of studying. I got it—I'll skip class, then I'll have the weekend to
study and I can watch the game tonight! Math test. Monday...oh...
need all the time I can get to study for that test...worth half my grade.
There's no way around it. I have to do it so I best stop thinking of ways
out. Get the notes...eh...first question, perception three stages, ISO-
PPG. Interpretation, organization,...eh...oh yeah, selection, and
under organization is patterns, proximity, and good form. OK, that's
good. Next...so far so boring.

Number two, four facts involved in perception. FEEL...I feel
terrible, I bet $15 on the Islander game and now I can't watch it. Now
that's the pits! FEEL F, what does F stand for?...eh...familiarity, and
E, expectation, second E...eh...what is.... It's probably going to be
the best game of the season...eh, second E...but can I watch it? Of
course not. Seems I always have a test to study for the night of a good
game. L. L is limiting of the senses...eh, oh yeah, second E...eh...oh I
don't know! That's it, I'm going to watch the game. I can't remember
this stuff anyway. Oh, knock it off. You know the importance of this
exam, since you sunk the last one because you watched a game instead
of studying. OK, stop thinking about the game and just study. Stop
wasting time! Next question: What are three functions of self-
concept...? Pb, FS, IWT...eh...Pb, what is Pb?..FS is filter of
statements and IWT is ...eh...influence of word...eh, word selection
and...and...oh yeah, tone of voice. Now what is Pb? Oh, I can't
remember. Come on, what is Pb? I don't remember, I'll check it and
come back to it. Next question: list ten...Oh no, last time I could only
recall six...eh...SKOR...eh, 2 IGA. So far so good. One A is age, 2 g's
uniqueness. 2I, eh...2I...eh...I have no idea...alright, SKOR...O.
O is occupation. S...eh...K...eh...R...R...eh, I can't remember. I
didn't even match last time's results. At least last time I recalled six. This
is so depressing....

Look, it's already 15 minutes into the game—with these results I'd
rather just pack it in and watch the game. I can't do that...can't afford
to fail this one. Well, maybe if I take a ten minute coffee break I can clear
my mind while I catch ten minutes of the game. Yeah, that sounds
great. Oh no, it doesn't. That's exactly what I did last time. Ten minutes
ran through the game and into the line interviews broadcast right after
the game. I know if I stop now that will be the end of studying for this
test. I best get back to studying. Next question: How is self-concept
formed? S, 2R, R...What a crazy way to study. I wonder how many
other people study like this. S is self-appraisal, 2R...eh, R something
and something...eh I don't know. Next R...eh...come on, what does
this R stand for? You make up these silly codes to help you remember, a
lot of good they do when you can't decode them. 2R, what's 2R?
Rejection...no, no that's not...re-...reactions and...and...27 questions. I'll never get through this without a cup of coffee. OK, for sure
only ten minutes this time!

Ode to Pac Man

DANTE JAMES MANFREDI

This martini definitely tastes like unleaded gas. Well Dante—just
hold your breathe and swallow...after the first one, the next six should
be no problem! I bet that I'm the only person in the world who makes
getting drunk a chore....

"Another martini—yeah, sure, why not." Maybe the noise of the
ice melting will drown out that damn wak-a-wak-a from that *Pac Man
game*! I hate video games, but this one tops 'em!

It's been five years since I've seen these characters, five long years;
I'm not into talking about the past. Reminiscing just isn't what it's
cracked up to be. Guy Lombardo had the right idea—dropping dead and
becoming the past.

Ya know, people in bars even sound like Pac Man. All of their
superficial bullshit has the same sound... "Hey, what's your sign?"...
Wak-a-wak-a... "Can I buy you a drink?" ...Wak-a-wak-a..." "Can I
have your number?"...Wak-a-wak-a..."Do you have herpes?"
...Wak-a-wak-a! Come to think of it, I'd rather talk to Pac Man!

Oh God! I think I just swallowed the olive. Now, do I act cool and
quietly choke or act uncool and go with my instincts and spit it out? I
hate trying to be cool in uncool situations!

I wonder what would happen if Pac Man choked on those damn
dots.... How the hell could you apply the Heimlich Maneuver to
something without an abdominal region? Great! Knowing my luck I'd
have to give mouth-to-mouth to that damn yellow smiley face! Well, it's

the best offer I've had all night. I'd probably end up with a hickey the size of New Jersey.... God, I must be wasted, I don't even like the color yellow!

Speaking of hickeys, if this guy kisses her one more time, I'm going to puke.

I don't think that their kissing is bothering me as much as my loneliness, jealousy, and pangs of envy. I guess I'm kinda like good ol' Pac Man—swallowing relationships, like dots, but I just keep spitting them out. I know it's not the relationships that have caused this distaste in me, it's my own bitterness and hurt. The bitterness of this vermouth is nothing compared to what I feel inside.

I've never seen anyone so pregnant...she looks as though she should have given birth last week. I hope that this place is equipped with enough pots for boiling water.... Maybe she's a Pac Man in disguise who ate one too many dots. Nah! I think I just drank over my limit—I'm never gonna make it through this night!

I can't believe that there is actually life inside of that big belly—a life created out of love—especially since life died a long time ago in my chest, a death caused by my own loving. A death/abortion that has turned me into a devastated Pac Man—devouring everything in my path—running from my own past. At least Pac Man can energize himself by swallowing those big dots and destroy his monsters. I can't find an energizer. When will love find me! I don't even know what to be hopeful about.

I can't wait to leave—I can stop at 7-11 and pick up a "six pac"...Wak-a-wak-a.

Bars make me crazy...Nah...Life makes me crazy!!

Easter Litany

DELESIE MORRISON

"Dear Heavenly Father, I thank you for all that you have done for me. Lord, I thank you for my health and strength; for my family and friends; for my trials and tribulations because you said in your word, 'In everything give thanks: for this is the will of God in Christ Jesus concerning you' (Thessalonians 5:18). Lord, I pray that you forgive me for every misdeed: intentional and unintentional. Help me to grow strong in your word so that I may not yield unto temptation and not do the things that aren't pleasing in your sight. And then Lord, I pray that you heal those who are sick all over the world and bless those who have experienced the death of a loved one. Let them know that you are God and besides you there is none other, and all power in Heaven and on

Earth is in your hands. Answer my prayer, Lord, according to your will. Amen."

It sure feels good to be back home. It looks like we've got a full house at Sunday morning worship today. But then, we always have a large crowd on Easter. It's either Easter or Christmas when everybody comes to church. You look around and wonder, "Where in God's name did so many people come from?" Huh! This Easter has even brought the winos out of the garbage cans. God does work miracles, doesn't He? Look at those kids over there talking out loud and acting wild! No respect in the Lord's House, whatsoever! I'd say about half of the kids in this sanctuary aren't disciplined the way that they should be. And probably sixty-five percent of the people here today won't be back until Christmas or next Easter.

Well, well, well, it looks like a lot of eggs are gonna be hatching soon and I don't mean chicken eggs either. I'll tell you, more women in this church get pregnant than you can imagine! Sister Bass is pregnant. Sister Price is pregnant again. Barbara just had her baby. And I'll bet so-and-so will be the next victim. Is that Robbies Spears? I haven't seen her for a while. Her baby sure hasn't grown any. Could this be another one? Naw. Another baby? The girl has been a member of this church since we both were knee high, and now she's had two kids and is still not married? That's a doggone shame. Isn't that...What's her name? Tonya's sister!?! What? She's pregnant too? And she's not even out of high school yet! I just bet it was by a jarhead. Yeah, yeah, I've heard the nightmare a thousand-and-one times. Young high school girl falls for marine. Marine uses his charm techniques to get girl in bed. Naturally he succeeds because she is too young and naive to know better. Before she realizes it, she's pregnant. And where in the hell is he? Transferred. Now he is stationed somewhere on the east coast so that he can be closer to his wife. That's the price you pay for being young, in love, and living next to one of the world's largest marine bases.

Good! The choir is going to sing. I hope like crazy that Danny has taught the choir some new songs. Don't tell me that Charity is going to direct this song. Surely they could have chosen a more experienced person for such a complicated song. Oh, I can just hear my mother at the dinner table tonight: "Did you see Charity up there trying to direct that song? Her and Barbara need to lose some of that weight. They look as though they could burst any minute." My darling mother. She always has something good to say.

Is that Greg Holmes in the choir? It is! And who are those two strange women wearing those giant afro wigs? Don't tell me that he's rejoined the "street-life scene" and those are his two...no, couldn't be. I wonder where his wife is. I haven't seen either one of them since they both got thrown in the Tijuana jail for possession of drugs. They ought to be shot! Lord help! I can't believe that people would actually come to church with Bacardi breath. My God! They call themselves Christians, but their actions sort of scream out at you. I know I'm not perfect, but at least I don't claim to be Diana Ross and sing like Olivia Newton-John.

It's time for offering. I wonder where the Dandridges are today. There's Darlene...and there's Sheila and John. Sheila's had a baby? The last time I heard from her, she had a miscarriage. Boy, people don't waste no time around here! I can't wait until I receive my degree and get a good job. I'm going to settle down with the perfect gentleman. (If there's any left without herpes.) My husband is gonna be six feet tall and have dark, smooth skin. Of course he's got to have a build and especially a nice behind. He's got to be open-minded and honest, compassionate and loving, giving and forgiving. He's got to love and respect me for who I am. I wonder how Daryl is? He had almost all of those qualities. But then he had to go off to South Carolina. What a drag! I never understood why he stopped writing. Perhaps it's not for me to know. Perhaps, in time God will allow our paths to cross again.

I wish Reverend New would stop making googley eyes at me. And look at the other ministers on the rostrum. When they aren't trying to look under the ladies' dresses in the front row, they're practically asleep. Honestly, if the ushers got paid for their services...never mind. I hate it when it's prayer time and Deacon Gibbons has his eyes wide open checking out everybody's expressions on their faces. And look at Danny over there. He's a homosexual if I ever saw one. And to ice his cake, he had to go and marry a female homosexual for convenience. Lord, what is this world coming to? What ever happened to principles and morals? Times are changing but I can't accept that as a justification for immoral behavior. It's time to pray once again.

What Grandpa Sees

KIM HANSEN

Who are all these people?
What are they doing here?
What am I doing here?
I want to go home,
But they won't let me go.
They say I live here,
But I don't.
I know that is my name
On the front door,
But they just put it there

To keep me here.
If this is my house,
Where is my mother?
So many strangers in this house,
This just can't be my house.
Who are all these girls
Kissing me?
There are so many,
Why do they kiss *me*?
They tell me they love me,
I answer them, "You do?"
Who are these people?
Please tell me who.

One-Act Play

Write a script of several scenes that would take 20-30 minutes to perform and that would place several characters in different combinations. If this is to be a theater or film script, keep the number of scenes and characters low and the staging feasible so that it might actually be performed or filmed locally. Imagine some characters and events at least somewhat like the kind you have observed in real life. This might be an occasion to combine **Duolog, Exterior Monolog,** and **Interior Monolog** with the dynamics of more crowded scenes. For fantasy you might try a radio play or an animation film script.

The Reunion
SUSAN M. PERINO

Scene:

Stage is set up for a high school gymnasium party. There is a basketball hoop upstage, streamers are hanging, and cafeteria-type tables are decorated with "worn" daisies. There is a basketball on the floor, upstage right.

Characters

MARIE WILSON—*A very attractive, upper-middle-class woman of twenty-eight who looks more like twenty-four. Marie gives the impression that she is a confident, mature woman.*
DAVID YAEGER—*An average looking middle-class man of twenty-eight, 5'10" tall and 160 pounds.*
FATHER—*A strong, well-built man of fifty-three. He is 6' tall and about 200 pounds. He is a man who started out as a carpenter, but through perseverance and hard work, has made his fortune.*
JASON WILSON—*An active, easygoing ten-year-old with an air of excitement about him. He is a handsome boy with bright brown eyes that seem like windows to his soul.*

Setting

The play takes place at a ten-year high school reunion in the school gym. The school is Deerfield High School in Florida. It is the end of the reunion and most of the alumni have left.

(David and Marie enter from stage right and proceed to a table center stage.)

DAVID: It looks like everyone has left in here. I think there are still a few stragglers in some of the classrooms and the cafeteria. *(They sit down.)*
MARIE: I still can't believe you came! *(Pauses, sighs)* It *was* a nice evening though, wasn't it?
DAVID: Yeah, it was...*(Quietly)* Except for all those Cubans who showed up. *(Normal voice)* I was so glad to see you again. You know, I've never forgotten you. You'd be surprised how many times I wanted to call you, but I was afraid you wouldn't talk to me.
MARIE: *(Surprised)* Now, why would I not talk to you?!
DAVID: Well, I was afraid you would still be upset about my family moving away. You were so angry and upset at the time that you wouldn't even return my letters.
MARIE: *(Slowly)* David, we were very close, if you remember. We had plans to be together, not apart. Then you inform me that you're leaving...never saying a word about our plans. I didn't know if you still meant all those things you told me. Besides, all that you spoke of in those few letters was all the new friends you met. You became very distant, and that hurt me very much.
DAVID: I was hurt too. After all, my mom told me about the move only a month before we were to leave. And I didn't want to leave you or all our friends. How do you think I felt!...My senior year and I had to leave and start a new life in a new school in the middle of the term. When I did leave, and I wrote you, you never answered me!

MARIE: (*Trying to change the subject*) Oh, ah...What made you change your mind about coming tonight? Joe Reams said that at first you weren't going to come.

DAVID: I wasn't going to, but I really wanted to see the old gang. After all, they did invite me even though I didn't graduate from here. What about you? Everyone I spoke to tonight said they were surprised to see you. They said you haven't been with the old gang since I left. No one that I spoke to knows anything about your life since graduation.

MARIE: Well, that's a long story.

DAVID: I've got time. (*Stands*) Would you like to go out for coffee? Everyone else seems to have left, and we have a lot to catch up on.

MARIE: I'd like to but I really can't leave. My father is picking me up later. I didn't think the reunion would end so quickly. He's coming from a dinner, so I can't even call him.

DAVID: I guess I'll stick around then. (*He sits on a table next to the one Marie is at and puts his feet on his chair.*)

MARIE: Good! So, tell me...what *has* been going on with you? Are you married?

DAVID: No. I came close, but I couldn't go through with it. She just wasn't my type, I guess. (*He stands and turns averting his eyes from Marie.*) Rita and I went so far as to order invitations, but then that bunch of guineas that she calls her family got to be too much for me. They had the nerve to say I wasn't good enough for her! They thought she should marry some nice Italian boy! Well...I couldn't take *that* anymore, so I just left.

MARIE: You just left?! Didn't you talk to Rita first?

DAVID: (*Turning quickly to face Marie*) No!! Why should I? (*Pacing*) She never stopped them from putting me down. She would just sit there...not say a word...no defense, nothing. (*Pause*) I don't think I really loved her anyway. I just felt that it was time I settled down and had some kids. (*He sits.*) For some reason, I feel that I need children to...Oh, I don't know...make me feel like a man. Macho, Huh? It was for the best, I suppose. I could not have put up with her family, anyway. I would never have been able to please them.

MARIE: That's a shame. (*Pause. David sees a basketball and goes to pick it up.*)

DAVID: I was never any good at this game. Maybe you're never too old to learn. (*He starts to bounce the ball, but it bounces too high and knocks over a centerpiece as it hits the table*)...What about you? What have you been up to? Are you married? (*He picks up the ball and carries it back to the table where Marie is sitting.*)

MARIE: Oh...Um...I was.

DAVID: What do you mean—was? You're divorced.

MARIE: No...widowed. (*Silence. Marie stands and takes the ball from David and just looks at it and turns it.*)

DAVID: Oh, I'm sorry...what happened?

MARIE: (*Marie places the ball on the table and tries to spin it.*) It was an accident. Kevin fell four stories from a building he was working on.

DAVID: He was a builder? Oh, that's right, your father owns a construction company. Did you meet him through your father?

MARIE: Actually, I met him when you were still living here. He was in my Accounting class. We used to talk about our homework. He was very bright, and so easy to talk to. (*Marie starts to bounce the ball and she does it well.*)

DAVID: What was his last name?

MARIE: Wilson. You might have known him...he was captain of the football team. (*Marie stands holding the ball.*)

DAVID: No. You know how I felt about sports. If you're not black or a brown-noser to the coach, you sit on the bench. (*Pause*) Did he know someone?...Friends of the coach or someone...?

MARIE: (*Slowly*) No....

DAVID: Well, maybe he was an exception. (*David takes the ball and steps back.*) Here, catch. (*He throws the ball to Marie, and she catches it and bounces it back to David. They continue to bounce it back and forth while talking.*) You seem OK now...how long ago did your husband die?

MARIE: It will be seven years this summer.

DAVID: (*Surprised*) That long ago?! You must not have been married long.

MARIE: Three years...We were married in June, a month after graduation. You see...I was pregnant.

DAVID: (*Shocked*) You're kidding!! (*He stops throwing the ball.*) You have children?! (*He sits on the edge of the table, stunned.*)

MARIE: Not children...child. I have a son.

DAVID: (*Confused*) A month after graduation?...But that must mean....

MARIE: (*Marie starts getting nervous, begins to fidget during this monologue.*) What it means is that Kevin was there to comfort me when you walked out....

DAVID: Walked out...?

MARIE: Yes...anyway, he helped me through a very emotional time. I was hurt and confused. Well, we didn't want anyone to know because we didn't want any nasty cracks. Everyone knew me as YOUR girl...You know they would never have accepted an outsider into the gang...And when I found out I was pregnant, we decided to skip college and get married right after graduation. Kevin agreed to work for my father's company. My parents made a nursery out of the guest room, and Kevin moved in with us. (*David does not seem to be listening.*)

DAVID: That means you have a son in school already.

MARIE: In school! Jason is almost ten years old. He is a little man. Since Kevin's accident, I have been a bit overprotective of him. As a matter of fact, since then, my father has been very protective of me too. He worries too much.... He didn't even want me to come here tonight.

DAVID: Why not?

MARIE: I don't know. He never likes me to go out. He only agreed to let me come here if he could drop me off and pick me up.

DAVID: I can't believe it...Marie is a mother of a ten year old boy. (*Pause*) I'll bet you're a wonderful mom.

MARIE: I think so...but most importantly, Jason thinks so.

DAVID: I'd love to meet him. Maybe now that I've transferred to Pompano, we could get together sometime.

MARIE: You can meet Jason tonight. My father is bringing him when he picks me up. I've always wondered how the two of you would get along. Let's try a little basketball while we wait. (*She gets up and takes the ball and bounces it.*)

DAVID: I'm not very good. Let's just see who can get the most shots into the hoop. You go first. (*Marie shoots.*)

MARIE: Your turn. (*They continue to take turns taking shots.*)

DAVID: Why don't we have the loser buy the winner a dinner. (*David is not having much luck with his shots.*)

MARIE: We'll see.

DAVID: I just don't understand how these blacks play this so well! ...So, what do you say...dinner this weekend on the loser? You can bring Jason.

MARIE: (*Unsure*) I don't know. There is something that I haven't told you.

DAVID: We'll talk at dinner.

MARIE: I want to tell you something before Jason gets here.

DAVID: What about?

MARIE: It's about Jason...and...uh...his father.

DAVID: Just let me get this shot. (*Pause...David is concentrating on trying to make a shot and does not seem to be aware of a door slamming offstage. While David is engrossed in his playing a young black boy enters from stage left. He meets Marie in center stage.*)

JASON: Hi Mommy. Granpa is waiting in the car. He said I could come in to get you.

MARIE: OK, Honey. David, I'd like you to meet my son.... Jason, this is the man Mommy was telling you about, his name is David.

JASON: (*Jason puts out his hand as if to shake hands.*) HI! (*David turns around and upon seeing Jason drops the basketball out of his hands. He just stands, with his mouth opened. Jason looks at him curiously and then at his mother. Jason puts his hand down.*)

DAVID: Oh..ah...um....Hi. Ah, so...ah, you're Jason. It's ...ah ...nice to meet you.

MARIE: (*To Jason*) All right, Honey. You go wait in the car and tell Grandpa that I will be there in a little while. (*Jason looks at David curiously again and walks slowly offstage while glancing back to David.*)

MARIE: (*Matter of factly*) So, what do you think?

DAVID: I don't believe it. HE is your son? Your husband was *black*?

MARIE: That's right. My husband was black!

DAVID: But how *could* you?!

MARIE: How could I what?! Marry a black man?

DAVID: How could you let him touch you?! I just don't believe it! You—

MARIE: David, stop it? I've had enough! (*Marie turns to leave.*)

DAVID: Wait! (*David goes to Marie and grabs her by the arm turning her to face him.*) Just tell me why! Why?! You said you loved me and the minute I leave, you jump into bed with someone like *that*!

MARIE: Let me go! You're hurting me! (*Marie yanks her arm free.*) I have to go, Dad and Jason are waiting in the car.

DAVID: (*David grabs Marie's arm again but lets go when she turns back around.*) You're not leaving until I get an answer.

MARIE: (*Marie starts to pace the floor, flinging her arms in anger almost to the point of hysteria.*) You want an answer...FINE! It's all your fault!!

DAVID: My fault?! But... (*The father walks onstage but Marie and David are unaware of his presence.*)

MARIE: Yes, your fault. If you hadn't left me, my life would've been perfect. (*Marie stops pacing and sits...exhausted. She has a dazed look.*) You know, I still have that first note you wrote me in class. It's so worn by now, what with me taking it out all the time to look at it.... Everything was going so well until you said you were leaving. I felt as though my life was over. I needed someone to comfort me.

DAVID: But why *him*?

MARIE: Well, Kevin always *did* like me, and I felt like an outsider around our old friends without you.

DAVID: I don't understand....

MARIE: Kevin knew how hurt I was over you, and he just tried to help me through a tough time. I don't think either of us realized it would go so far.

DAVID: Why *sleep* with him?

MARIE: Well....(*Marie stands and faces away from David.*)

DAVID: Answer me! Why?

MARIE: Neither of us planned it. I was so confused. Kevin was such a wonderful friend through all of it. He knew how depressed I was. One night it just went too far. About a month later, I found out I was pregnant. (*Marie faces David*) I thought it was *your* baby!! Don't you understand?!

DAVID: Why didn't you tell me?

MARIE: I don't know...I guess I was afraid you wouldn't care, since you already left. (*Pause*) Anyway, Kevin found out and insisted we get married.

DAVID: But, you said you thought it was mine?

MARIE: I did...but I wanted the baby to have a father and...Kevin was so insistent. I did care about him in my own way. So, we got married. I thought that maybe after the baby was born, I would write you and tell you about the baby and see how you reacted.

DAVID: And Kevin?

MARIE: He didn't know that I thought the baby was yours. He was so busy trying to protect me.... (*There is a pause as Marie begins to cry softly.*)

MARIE: (*Between sobs*) When I saw that baby...a black baby...Kevin's baby, I just could not believe it. At first, I didn't even want to hold him because I was in shock. The nurses just thought I was too tired. (*Pause*) But then I realized that no matter what, he was still my baby too. (*Pause*) Kevin was so good with him. Kevin even picked out his name...Jason...he said Jason was a strong name. He said he would need to be strong to fight all the prejudice of living in an all-white environment. Ha! If Kevin only knew!....If he only knew.... (*At this point Marie's father walks up to David and Marie.*)

FATHER: Ahem...Marie. I think we'd better go...Jason is waiting in the car. (*In the distance we hear a car horn.*) That must be him. We really should get him home to bed. (*Marie turns toward her father, wipes away some tears and starts to leave.*)

FATHER: (*To Marie*) You go on...I'll be right out.

MARIE: Why?

FATHER: Just go on. (*Marie walks offstage.*) (*To David*) What did you do to make her upset? She's been crying. (*Pause*) That girl is my life and if you've done anything to hurt her I'll—.

DAVID: You'll what?! If you're so protective of Marie, how could you let her get mixed up with someone like Kevin?

FATHER: For your information...Kevin treated Marie better than you ever did. He idolized that girl.... (*Quietly*) I only wish I had treated him better.

DAVID: How could you possibly have treated him any better? You let him live in your house. You gave him a job. You....

FATHER: All I did was for Marie. The problem was that I never let Kevin forget it. I never let him feel like he belonged. I should have left him alone.

DAVID: How can you feel sorry for him? He was just a nigger. (*Marie enters from SL unnoticed.*)

FATHER: (*Father grabs David by the collar.*) That nigger, as you call him, was the father of my grandson...my daughter's husband ...and I won't stand for talk like that.

DAVID: And just what are you going to do about it?

FATHER: I'll show you. (*As the Father raises his fist, Marie runs to stop him.*)

MARIE: Wait! Please...don't do this. (*To David*) David, why do you keep calling Kevin a nigger?! What did he ever do to you?!

DAVID: Kevin may not have done anything but those "soul brothers" of his did.

MARIE: What are you talking about?

DAVID: Remember those two troublemakers, Magee and Parnell? Well, just before I moved, they mugged me! They beat me up and stole about fifty bucks from me!

MARIE: I don't remember that.

DAVID: I was too embarrassed to tell anyone.... Niggers... That's what they *all* are. (*Father starts to go towards David again but Marie stops him.*)

MARIE: David, I want you to know that Kevin called those two thieves niggers too.

DAVID: Oh...ah.

FATHER: Marie, let's get out of here! You don't have to explain anything to him.

MARIE: Dad, will you just *stop* telling me what to do!!

FATHER: I'm only trying to protect you.

MARIE: Well. *Don't!* You've protected me long enough. I'm so tired of being protected. For seven years...not being able to leave the house without you monitoring me every minute. I'm *sick* of it! You're just so worried that I'll slip and tell someone....

DAVID: Tell someone what?

FATHER: Never mind...we have to leave. (*Father takes Marie's hand and starts to lead her SL but she yanks her hand free.*)

MARIE: Stop it! Just stop it! I can't take it anymore! (*To David*) You wanted to know what a wonderful mother I am? Well, David, I'll tell you. I am such a wonderful mother that I killed my son's father!

DAVID: Wha....

FATHER: Marie don't. Please!

MARIE: That's right...I killed Kevin. I pushed him off that building.

DAVID: Why? I don't believe...

FATHER: Please...Marie.

MARIE: That's right...he wanted to leave me. (*Almost childlike*) Just like you did...only he was leaving me with a three-year-old boy. (*Angry*) How could I find someone to raise a black man's child as his own. Oh, sure...Kevin said he would always be there for us. He just wanted to find a job on his own and then he was going to send for Jason and me. He said we would be our own family. (*Father sits down and buries his head in his arms. David collapses in a chair stunned. Marie rambles on as if in her own little world.*)

MARIE: He said we could be so happy if we were on our own. Kevin was going to go to Texas, find a job and then send for us. Ha! Sure! (*As if speaking to Kevin—she is reliving a scene from her past. We hear a wisp of eerie music.*) Listen, buddy, I fell for that once, but no more. Kevin, how could you leave us? How could you leave Jason? He is your son! (*Pause as if listening to someone answering.*) Yeah, that's what you *say* but I know better. (*Pause*) No, you won't be back. I know it. (*Pause*) That's just what David said before he left, but he never came back (*As if walking to this imaginary person.*) I can't let you do this to me, Kevin. I just can't. (*Pause*) I can't go on anymore, I'm going to jump! (*As if struggling with someone.*) Get away, Kevin! You can't stop me. No, Kevin...leave me alone...Let go of me! Oh, WATCH OUT!! OH MY GOD...KEVIN!! (*Marie begins to waver and the Father jumps to catch her before she slumps on the floor. He tries to snap Marie out of her trance.*)
father jumps to catch her before she slumps on the floor. He tries to snap Marie out of her trance.)

DAVID: My God! You mean Kevin died while trying to keep her from jumping? He saved her life?

FATHER: Yes, he did. It was an accident, but she blames herself. He saved my daughter's life and kept her from suicide. I'll never forget that. I blame myself...if I had only treated him better, he never would've tried to leave.

DAVID: (*Shaking his head*) He must have loved her an awful lot. (*Marie begins to come around.*)

FATHER: Come...Let's get you home.

(*As Marie and her Father slowly walk offstage, David, who is sitting, gets up, and picks up the basketball and cradles it in his arms. From offstage, we hear the sound of a car engine. David drops the ball, and starts offstage.*)

DAVID: Marie...WAIT!!

(*With that, we hear the sound of the car driving away.*)

(*Darkness*)

Mixing Techniques

In order to achieve a certain effect in conveying a story idea, theme, or relationship, combine interior monolog with exterior monolog or with some other technique such as narration, dialog, or correspondence. That is, use juxtaposition of two or more of these to contrast different points of view.

The Letter
VALERIE ROMERO

Dear Chuck,

DEAR?? How about DROP DEAD! If there were anything I
would not call that jerk it is DEAR!!

Hi! Guess who? I know it's been a while,

A WHILE?!? Try six months! And I wrote the last letter,
too! Jesus! You'd think it would kill him to pick up a
pencil...they don't weigh that much!

But I guess we've both been pretty busy.

Yeah, sure. I know how busy you are. I mean, we all know
how much time picking your nose takes!

I'm doing OK, how are you?

I really don't give a damn how you are, and just to set the
record straight, I'm doing real crappy. Not that I'd get any
sympathy from you.

*Let's see, what's new that I haven't told you? Gosh, It's been so long, and I
can't think of a single thing to tell you!*

I can think of plenty of things to say to you, but none of
them are nice. Besides all my good news and nice comments
I save for my FRIENDS!

*Mom came out to visit me last weekend. She says she hasn't heard from you in
ages.*

Jerk! Not writing to your sister is one thing, but you ought
to write to your own mother!

*She was saying that she wants to try and go visit you out in No. Dakota this
summer. She hasn't seen your kids in ages, and wants to see her grand-kids.*

I thought I'd come right out and tell you this so you'd have
time to start cleaning that pigpen that you so ignorantly call a
house! I also hope you can retrain those little animals into
decent children by the time she goes out there. I'd hate to
shatter her image of her good little grandchildren.

*How old are Brian and Stacey now? Gosh! Can Brian be starting junior high
next year?*

Oh great! Now that little brat is turning into a teenager! I
hope he is going to give you three times the trouble that
you gave Mom. If I remember that little creature correctly,
I'll be guaranteed that little bit of satisfaction!

Oh! How time flies!

But believe me, I'm not having fun! I wish that this letter
would fly...out the window! I'm running out of crap to
write. Ha! I wish you would fly too...*Away!*

I'm doing O.K., surviving at least!

Ha! I wish I was doing O.K. Scholastic Probation kind of has

a way to get people down...and as far as surviving goes, if homework were water, I'd be drowning! I really can't complain though, at least I'm in college, that's more than you ever tried for!
Busy at work still! (When do things ever calm down?)
Let's see...I've covered Mom, his kids, school and work.... what's left? Oh! His wife! Can't forget her! She'd bitch about it forever!
Is Liticia still working at Sears? Does she like it any better now?
I'd be surprised if she liked anything! Well, I've covered everything, so now I can end this torture!
Well, I've gotta run! Give my love to Liticia and the kids!
I've not really got anything else to do, but I don't feel like writing to YOU any longer than I have to! As for the love, I LOVE ENDING THIS LETTER!

Your Little Sister
Though I'd never admit it in public.
Vicky

What Should I Wear?

DORIE OLSON

This is tragic! I simply have nothing to wear tonight. Should I wear pants—or how about a skirt? Then again, I could wear pants. After all, it still is fairly cold at night.

Which pants? Jeans? Cords? I'll wear my burgundy Espirit ones. On second thought, he's already seen those. I could wear these khaki ones. No, I want to wear something special. I'll wear my new white pants. Here they are. I'm glad I ironed them yesterday.

Now, should I wear a sweater or blouse? I better hurry up and get dressed. I want to be ready when he gets here. Damn, I can't decide. Let me see. Either this red one, or I know, I'll wear this powder blue sweater.

I hate this song! I gotta change the station.

Phone? For me? Okay Mom, I'll get it in here. Hello. Oh Cin, it's just you. I'm sorry, I'm a little jumpy. I decided on those white pants I got two weeks ago and my furry powder blue sweater. Yeah, the Sassons. Either heels or espadrilles. Heels are a little more dressy. Ya think so? Okay, I'll wear the heels. Wait a sec, I gotta change the station again. *(Pause)* Okay, I'm back.

He was over here yesterday. We just talked mainly about school and both of our families. He seems to really have his act together. Pre-med....

Six-thirty. Dinner and movies. I don't know. Uh-huh. they said he is handsome and nice. I tried to explain what GQ meant to my mom but she couldn't really catch on. Yeah, I told her that. You know my mom—a little out of it....

A black Mustang GT. No. 1982. I love the t-top because you can see the stars at night. He is so lucky to have that car.

How's Don? He still won't quit? Hang in there. I know, but he's been smoking for seven years. Is he working tonight? Too bad.

Well Cin, I really should go and finish getting dressed. Okay, okay, I'll call you tomorrow and tell you everything. See ya later, bye.

Now let me see. what? No, Mom, you can use the phone now. Well, if you got me my own number then it wouldn't be tied up so much. My phone bill wouldn't be *that* huge, most of my calls are local. Whatever....

Geez, now I can't decide which earrings to wear. I could wear these white spirals or these blue hoops. Oh I know, I'll wear my sapphires.

Why didn't I change this nail polish? It's so chipped and old-looking. I think I'll redo them before he gets here.

Which color? Um, platinum lamé. I'll put a top-coat of gold on to make them shimmery.

I can't Mom, I just put a coat of nail polish on. Oh no, Shadow, stay—STAY! Damn, who let the dog in? I just ruined the polish on my entire right hand. Rich, get the dog outta here, please. Now I really have to speed things up.

Finally, they're dry. Mom, where's the lint brush? Shadow shed all over my white pants.... You don't know where it is? Mom, I can't go out of the house with Shadow's hair stuck all over me. Where? I'll check.... Yeah, I found it. It's a good thing that this brush actually works. There, that's much better.

Why should I turn down my stereo? It's not *that* loud. Oh, all right. Just when a good song finally came on.

Now where did I put that white purse? Think, think, think. Mom, have you seen my white purse? You know, the one I got when we went shopping the other day. I've looked there. That's a good idea. Yeah, here it is. Can I borrow your small comb? Mine is too big for this purse. Thanks....

The thin gold one? Sure, I'd love to wear that ring. I promise I'll take good care of it....

I know it's cold, Mom. I was planning on wearing my light spring jacket. You know, the white one that'll match these pants. I better check it to make sure it's not wrinkled.

Oh no?! It's got a spot on it. I bet it's from when Pam borrowed it. That's just great. I'll never lend anything to her again. This better wash out.

What? Yeah, it's coming out. I'll use my blow dryer. Sure, it'll dry in time. Now, what else could go wrong?

I better check my make-up and hair before he gets here. (*pause*) Everything seems to be fine.

Huh? He's here? Okay, I'll be there in a sec. Calm down and pull yourself together. (*big sigh*) Well, here goes nothing.

Fiction

Fictional Correspondence

Write a short story told by one or more of the characters in the form of a correspondence, that is, a series of letters from one only or an exchange among two or several.

Buyer Beware

BOB KUBICA

Department of Consumer Affairs
1900 Pennsylvania Avenue
Washington, D.C. 20050

Dear Sir:

While browsing through the June 1983 issue of *Model Aviation* magazine, one article ("Just For the Joy of It," by Mr. Bill Summer) awoke a long forgotten memory which I had hoped was firmly embedded beneath a solid mental block of granite. Portions of the article expound on the accomplishments of young Mike Summer, the author's son, who supposedly developed a successful electric-powered "Leisure Playboy" radio-controlled model airplane. You see, sir, I have personally experienced the raptures of electronic flight with the Playboy so aptly portrayed firmly in the embrace of young Mike "Midspectrum" Summer. As a matter of fact, sir, this particular Playboy, which still exhibits vice-like traces of young spring's grasp, has afforded me countless hours of amusement, excitement and enlightenment.

It all began on a grim, overcast day in February. Young Mike had completed preliminary construction on the Playboy and proposed that I "finish off the electronics and cosmetics." Being an ardent novice tinged with a touch of naivete, I tackled the job with a fervor the "Duke" would appreciate. Besides, I had access to that vast cubicle of knowledge stored forever in the Summer library. As spring approached and my simple portion of the task neared completion, visions of solitary afternoons spent soaring lazily through aqua blue skies danced in my head. These images were constantly bolstered through lunchtime pep talks with my mentor. My spirits, to say the least, were abnormally high.

A bright, cheerful day in April was chosen for the Playboy's first test flight. The flight plan called for a short glide with power on for a few seconds. The theater of operations would be my backyard, which is approximately 400 feet deep and edged by woods. An above-ground pool stands about 75 feet along the proposed glide path but is not an obstacle for the "Leisure Playboy." Several enthusiastic calls to Mike's apartments left me standing in the backyard—alone—with my wife Clara, two young children, our inquisitive Siamese calmly munching on a green snake and a curious-looking stray dog with a question-mark face. I proceeded as many pioneers had before me, barking preflight orders gleaned from a matchbook cover pamphlet. Clara, bless her soul, is an amiable girl. A willing conspirator, young enough at heart to dispense with consequences. I instructed her to hold the model at arm's length above her head, run a few paces and release it when the prop started turning. This I would initiate with precision timing from the hand-held transmitter. I had thoughtfully positioned the two children along the proposed flight path (which, hopefully, would terminate smoothly at the spot occupied by the stray dog) to save the craft from destruction should its flight end sooner than anticipated.

After a final survey of what is now termed "operation chaos" everything seemed to be in order. READY? GO! I yelled. As Clara raced swiftly forward with the Playboy held aloft, I hit the transmitter power switch. The prop came to life with an alarming whir, and promptly encouraged the craft to perform a kamikaze maneuver, straight into a stand of irises proudly showing their wares. As I cut the power switch, the hysterical laughter of two children and the hyena-like barking of a dog could be heard. Of course, the Siamese had that disdainful pitying look on his face so characteristic of his lineage. The site of the impact was filled with the face-down form of an iris-covered, grown woman still clutching the defiant Playboy.

Damage to the Playboy was minimal and after a short operation adroitly performed on the kitchen table, it was as good as new. Clara and I discussed the finer points of timing, noting the importance of "letting go" on cue. Ten minutes later the now normal kids were repositioned and ready for flight test number two. As an afterthought,

I instructed Clara to angle the plane upward as she released it, which would presumably add a few feet in altitude.

Rrrrrearrrr......it came to life, this time arching powerfully upward...for a few seconds. As it reached its apex approximately 20 feet above ground, the mindless craft reversed its arch, first banking left, then right. The launch site was utter pandemonium. The kids raced for shelter under a quivering oak tree. Instinctively, the question-mark stray ran like green-apples revenge and disappeared into the woods. I could hear Clara's agonizing shriek: "Oh no...oh no" as the aerial menace plunged mercilously into the Barclay pool she was so proud of.

The pool has been lovingly repaired and the irises seem to have recovered admirably. We managed to rehabilitate the Siamese after removing one large green snake from its gasping throat and that dog doesn't come around any more. In fact, our problem with migrating animals has been alleviated altogether. The "Leisure Playboy" is now a permanent fixture hanging crucifix-like in our crowded gameroom. It makes a wonderful dartboard from time to time.

Well sir, needless to say, I take profound exception with the statement "the Leisure Playboy works as advertised," so boldly captioned under the profile of young Mr. Summer.

Sincerely,
J. Brodski

Well Recommended

FREDERICK COLWELL

April 21, 1982
To Whom It May Concern:
Re: Clarance Arlington

As a chemistry teacher at Clairmont High School, I have had a chance to observe Clarance Arlington for the past year. He is quiet and polite and has never given me any trouble. He is one of the top students in my class. He is very industrious. He worked ahead on the labs and finished them all two months early, even though he had no lab partner. He is very conscientious. He does all his class work and also helps his mother in the home. I would recommend Clarance for any job or scholarship. He has been a credit to Clairmont High.

Don Smith
Chemistry Instructor,
Clairmont High School,

September 5, 1982

Clarance Arlington has worked for me over the summer as a cashier at 7-11. He has always been a model citizen. He is quiet, helpful, and polite, and I have never seen him lose his temper. He is a hard worker and would work the late shift without complaint. He is also brave. He single-handedly subdued an armed robber and afterwards acted as if it were something anyone would do. Clarance is a good worker and I'm sad to see him go. I believe he will succeed at anything he attempts.

Sincerely,
Arnold Van DeWallen
Manager, 7-11

September 23, 1983
To Whom it May Concern:
Re: Clarance Arlington

Mr. Arlington has worked under my supervision here at Disneyland for the past year—full time during the summer and part time during the school year. He has a good attitude and is an efficient worker. Although he admits a dislike of crowds, he does not let it interfere with his duties as a security worker here at the Magic Kingdom. Mr. Arlington is polite and quiet and I have never heard a complaint about him from his fellow workers.

Mr. Arlington is an intelligent person and quite inventive. With the knowledge he had gained at the University of California, Los Angeles he has made several suggestions to improve our security system within the Haunted House, where he is stationed. He frequently and selflessly accepts the jobs that many other workers dislike and will volunteer for the late shift. He is the type of person Walt Disney himself would have been proud to have as a member of our large family of workers.

Kelly Fleischer
Security personnel supervisor
Disneyland, California

April 21, 1984
Dover-Blum Scholarship Foundation:

Clarance Arlington has worked for me as a lab technician throughout the past school year at the University of California, Los Angeles. He is a hard worker and will stick with an experiment until it is completed, often staying late at night to do so. He is very precise and rarely makes errors in his measurements. He is very inquisitive and frequently conducts his own experiments here in the lab. He is a quick learner and already his knowledge of the use of lab equipment and the results of many chemical reactions surpasses even that of some of my graduate students.

He manages his time and money very well. Coming from a poor family with no father, he had worked his way through his first two years of college and still held a full schedule of classes. Whenever he is needed here he will gladly offer his time, putting his social life off.

He is quiet and polite and never complains. I would recommend him for any scholarship because he would make a good representative of any organization.

> Sincerely,
> Professor L.S. Lim
> Chemistry Department
> University of California, Los Angeles

July 4, 1984
Dr. Bates
Madison Mental Hospital,
New York, New York,

Sir,

After observing Clarance Arlington for the past month I would recommend the new experimental treatment. Enclosed is his complete case history, but I would like to point out the factors that lead to my recommendation.

His arrest for the explosion and subsequent fire that killed several people at Clairmont High School came as a surprise to many who knew him. Many people describe him as quiet and polite but he is close to no one. In actuality he is an introvert and has a fear and hatred for people. He is also quite intelligent, so I believe that the new drug would have a good chance of working.

He apparently led a sheltered life as a child and felt uncomfortable among other people. Several bad experiences at school made him wish to avoid people even more. His job at Disneyland made him see crowds as herds of cattle; because of this he avoided being a part of any crowd, until this became an obsession. His dislike and distrust of people on an individual level is related to an incident at his first job where he was held up. Although the police report is obscure, it mentions a struggle and the robber was shot several times in the legs. When I discussed this with Clarance he claims it was an accident, but I suspect a lie.

Although he claims that it was the rejection of his scholarship application that made him decide to burn down his old high school, he had been stealing chemicals from his job at UCLA for several months before he had even applied. He insists that it was because of the money that was "his," that they should have given it to him, and that "they deserve everything they got." Despite these opinions, he still behaves quietly and politely, so that it is difficult not to think that he is joking about the fire. But he is deadly serious.

This outward appearance of complete normalcy is exactly why I recommend the new drug TcCp. For this case I would advise 10cc's twice a week for ten or twelve weeks before beginning therapy of type AA or type UY. If you accept this task, the police will release Clarance on my recommendation to you.

Dr. Edison
Johnston Institute for the
Criminally Insane
San Diego, California

An Offer You Must Refuse

JEFF SMITH

Dear Mr. Smith:

Let me introduce myself. My name is Albert Handalar. I am running for state congress in the 22nd district. You may have heard of me through my multi-media advertisements endorsing various corporate structures within our state who believe in the betterment of humanity.

As I understand it, you are presently working for the Urban League and the Sierra Club as lobbyist in our state congress. It has also come to my understanding that you have become dissatisfied with your employers, for neither one of them supported a bill which you created last October to provide funding for a clean-up project on our state's highways, with the Urban League stating that it would not bring funding to the inner city, and the Sierra Club stating that the funding would have to trickle down, taking too long in the process. Personally I found it outrageous that not even the Sierra Club supported your bill. Upon this basis I wish to make you an offer. At present there is a position available on my staff for a private observer of political organizations. The position entails the observance of the organizations very closely and to predict their future moves from a private standpoint. The fee and rewards for such a task would undoubtedly be substantial. Please consider it carefully. If you decide to accept the offer or even have questions please contact my committee immediately or contact me personally at 307-841-4263.

Respectfully,
Albert Handalar

Dear Mr. Handalar:

I received your letter and I was impressed by your concern for my future. As you well know I am still employed for the Urban League and Sierra Club in which I am serving out the time on my contracts for both organizations. As I see it if you are determined to have me as your employee you have several options. You may pay the legal fees to have my contracts nullified or you may wait 7 months, then offer me the same position again. However, I do wish to emphasize that in seven months I will receive many offers including offers from my present employers, at which time your chances of acquiring me will be quite small.

I would enjoy very much working for you and your staff as a political analyst. At least my opinion would be noted and recognized.

Respectfully,
Eric Smith

Dear Mr. Smith:

I found your letter most interesting. However it was somewhat confusing. The position that I offered you requires that you remain with your present employers, renewing your contract every year with them until otherwise noted. The position that I am offering would analyze and predict your employers' moves. The information would then in turn be used to plan future strategies, amending bills, etc. to benefit our state's populace. I feel that you are most suited for the job because of your perseverance, intelligence, and creativity. I as a congressman know that if you accept the position, you would carry it out to the best of your ability. Thus you would be paid handsomely. I would estimate that your work would be worth two hundred dollars per day. I hope that we will be working together very soon. If you have any other questions please contact me personally.

Yours sincerely,
Albert Handalar

To Mr. Handalar:

Let me say this. I am an honest man! What you are proposing is morally and legally wrong. Even though I might feel that my present employers do not appreciate my work I will remain loyal to them until the day I quit or the day when I am fired. I do not understand how you could even suggest I do such a traitorous act as spying on such respectable organizations. Both organizations in general are there to improve the human role. What you have in mind is to apparently gain insight on their next political move so that you may profit from it personally rather than having the organization reap the rewards. I am very disappointed in your suggestions. I am therefore turning over your two letters to the Urban League and the Sierra Club. In addition I will be turning them over to the local authorities for proper action.

Disgusted,
Eric Smith

Fictional Diary

Write a short story told by one of the characters in the form of a diary or journal kept by dated entries made during the events.

A Monster's Journal
YVONNE LEONGUERRERO

December 16

I'm keeping this journal because the psychologist at the hospital said it might help me cope with problems if I write down my feelings. I don't know if it'll do any good but I'll try. My parents think it will be a good idea for me to go ahead and start school in three weeks as planned. They think it'll be good for me to get on with my life as if nothing had happened. They don't understand that it isn't as easy as that. You don't just pretend nothing has happened after your house was burned down. You don't just continue living as usual after having one-third of your body seriously burned, your hair singed off and your face so badly burned that you look like the Bride of Frankenstein. I wish I could have plastic surgery done, at least on my face, but the doctor says I have to wait until the tissue is completely healed and then "maybe" he'll consider plastic surgery. That's fine for him but he's normal. He isn't a freak with a distorted face who has to wear a wig. I can cover most of the scars on my body, but I can't do anything about my face and hair. Why me? Oh God, why me?

January 4
Today Mom bought me a whole new wardrobe of clothes for school. She tried to get me to go shopping with her but I don't want to go out in public. I haven't been out of the house since the fire. I never want to go out. People will stare at me and little kids will be afraid of me. Worst of all, people will feel sorry for me and say, "Poor girl...." I don't want their pity. Well, at least Mom was realistic about what clothes to buy. She bought all pants (no shorts, dresses or skirts) and long-sleeve shirts. I wish I didn't have to go back to school. All my friends will see me with no hair and an ugly face. I know that a lot of them will avoid me and even my good friends will find it hard to be with me. I've refused to see anybody, so none of them have been able to visit me, even in the hospital. I can't even stand to look at myself. I made Dad take all the mirrors out of my room and the bathroon so I wouldn't be reminded of what a monster I am. Oh please let the school close down so I won't have to go. I wish I'd died in the fire instead of lived to endure this.

January 7
First day of school. I was hoping I wouldn't have any of my friends in my classes but of course I did. It wasn't too bad when people that I didn't know stared and felt sorry for me, because for all they know I could've been like this all my life. They had never seen me when I had long brown hair, a creamy complexion and lips, but the friends I made last semester know what I used to look like and now probably wouldn't even recognize me. My friends. They asked after my health and acted as if nothing were wrong. But I could tell by the way they avoided looking at me that they were repulsed by my face. I couldn't stand the look on their faces. It was a look of pity. I'm going to start avoiding them to save them the trouble of having to put on an act. They can keep their pity because I don't want it, and if pity were an object, I'd throw it back in their face.

February 5
School's the same except that now I spend a lot of time by myself. I go to the library at lunch and I sit in empty classrooms between classes. I like it this way. Some guy in my chemistry lecture tried to talk to me, but I knew he was just feeling sorry for me so I acted rude and he left me alone.

March 10
I've been talking to the guy in my chemistry lecture. His name is

Richard. I didn't want to talk to him at first because I knew he was just being nice out of pity, but he's a tough person to discourage and after a few weeks, I found myself looking forward to seeing him. He's very funny and he can always cheer me up when I'm depressed. Sometimes, when I'm talking to him, I forget that my face is scarred because he doesn't seem to notice. I'm glad he never saw me before the fire because then he'd be just like my friends. Instead, he talks to me and doesn't seem to care what I look like but only about what I have to say. We talk about everything. Our favorite subject, though, is chemistry, of course, and he's suggested that we get together to study. I didn't want to. It's not that I wouldn't love to study with him, but I can't help thinking how great it would be if I could be pretty again. What's the use? He shouldn't waste his time on me, but should go out with a normal girl. My hair is growing fast and soon I won't have to wear a wig anymore. I could get it shaped into a popular short style that would cover parts of my face. When Richard talks to me I keep my shriveled right hand in my pocket and I don't think he's noticed it. If he is being nice to me out of pity, I don't care.

May 23

This will be my last entry in the journal. It has served its purpose and I don't need it any more. Richard and I have become very good friends. We study together and we even go to drive-in movies. My hair is much longer and he knows about my hand but doesn't care. It's wonderful to have a friend who accepts me for who I am and not for what I look like. Now that I have Richard, I feel I don't need anybody else. My parents are nice to him but they still don't trust him. I guess they're just being over protective because they don't want me to be hurt. Richard has wonderful parents who are very nice to me, and his sisters treat me as if I were normal. I've met a few of his friends too and they seemed nice, but he knows I'm still self-conscious, so he doesn't push me or take me out in crowds of people. Right now we're just friends. We talk a lot and we do things together, but my doctor said I could have surgery done next month, and then who knows...?

Together We Fly and Talk Without Words
JOHN THEODORE

April 22

The Chief told me yesterday that he was leaving because I'm getting to be a big boy now. He says he's moving real soon back to the other world. He said I learned everything he taught me, good enough to protect myself from the Bald Man who lives in my closet. I was crying a lot at first, because The Chief is my best friend. He's been scaring away the Bald Man and keeping me safe ever since we moved into this house. I remember when I was four years old. It was the night we moved in and I woke up to go pee. I was real scared, because I knew someone mean was in my closet. I stayed under my covers crying all night. I tried to tell Mom about the Bald Man, but she just hit me for lying about the wet covers. I woke up the next night and reached to turn the light on. The Bald Man flew out of my closet before I could kill him with the light. He had a big scar on his face and scary red eyes. I tried to scream, but my voice was gone. Then The Chief came in my window and the Bald Man went back in the closet. The Chief came and led me past the closet into the bathroom and I was safe. Ever since then, The Chief goes with me everywhere and I talk to him without words. The Chief and me even talk at dinner. No one else, except for me, can see The Chief. Not Mom or Dad or anybody knows about The Chief, because I don't tell them. So when grownups tell me to be quiet, I just talk with The Chief about anything I want to. And The Chief, he talks to me too.

April 23

I'm gonna miss The Chief when he goes away. The Chief, he says I can only see him when I'm dreaming, because he's flying back to the sleep world to live pretty soon. The Chief told me he's gonna teach me how to fly like he always does, and then I can go visit him even when I'm not sleeping.

April 24

The Chief says I can't talk to him for a while after he's gone. He told me I'm gonna have to kill the Bald Man once and for all, before we can see each other again. Then I said to The Chief about how I always kill the Bald Man with the light and the Bald Man just comes back in my closet to scare me the next night and I have to kill him again. But The Chief says I gotta kill the Bald Man in the dark, when the lights are all turned off. He says I gotta sneak up on the Bald Man real late, while he's asleep and then I gotta just wrestle with him until he's dead.

April 25

When I woke up for breakfast, The Chief was gone. I didn't miss him, because I was so scared about the Bald Man. I ran downstairs as fast as I could into Mom and Dad's room. I told Dad, because he always believes me and Mom just gets mad at me for telling lies. Dad got me some pants out of my closet and Mom didn't even know. I ate breakfast and Dad drove me to school. I asked Dad and he said he didn't see the Bald Man. After snack period, I had to take a math test over in Mr. Ford's class. I do good in math so I get to work with the fifth graders, even though I'm only in fourth. I finished the test first and I was sitting alone real quiet. I felt scared for no reason. I guess the Bald Man must have followed me and Dad, because I could feel him there in the room. It was all light in the class, so I couldn't see where he was. Then he attacked me. I couldn't see him, but he was there doing something so scary to me. My whole body was all tingly and prickly and then I couldn't move my lips and drool was coming from my mouth. My thoughts were there like they used to be for The Chief and I could see and hear the fifth graders working on the test. I couldn't move though, because the Bald Man was holding my whole body down. Then Mr. Ford came over and asked if I was O.K. The words were there, but I couldn't say them. He waited and asked me again. After a long time the Bald Man went away and I told Mr. Ford I was fine.

April 26

Last night I slept in Mom and Dad's room and the Bald Man didn't bother me. Then today he attacked me again in Mr. Ford's class. No one noticed this time, because the lights were off for the movie. When I got home only Mom was there, so I told her about school and she asked how I felt when the Bald Man attacked me. I told her and she says we have to see Dr. George about it.

April 27

Dr. George made me talk with a new doctor and she says something is wrong with me. She made me lay down and she stuck pins with wires in my head that hurt. There was a machine on the end of the wires that made squiggly lines on the paper. Then she took me to get an x-ray of my brain to look for something wrong. We were there all day and I got to miss school.

April 28

Last night I woke up to go pee and the Bald Man was still asleep in the closet. I was super afraid, but I still went to his door. When I opened it, I was real quiet. Then I screamed at him to stop bugging me and attacking me. He was so scared when I screamed that he died. It was just like The Chief said, because the Bald Man disappeared. In the morning, I told Mom that the Bald Man was gone. She said we had to go see the doctor anyway and I got to miss school again. The doctor was very quiet when she said to Mom what was wrong with me and I couldn't hear. I thought maybe I was going to die, because Mom's eyes looked sad. Then they made me take more tests and the doctor said I had seizures. I told her that the Bald Man was gone, but she gave me some medicine to take anyway.

June 20

School is over for summer and my friends from my block and me play at the beach lots. Mom doesn't know, but I haven't taken the medicine. She says the medicine is working, since I haven't had any more of those whatchamakallits. I just keep quiet about it, because I know I'll be fine now that the Bald Man is dead.

June 22
I see The Chief at night in my dreams. He's teaching me to fly and we play together. The Chief is happy now, because he gets to be with his friends all the time. I miss not being able to talk to The Chief while I'm at dinner and when I'm alone. I guess it's O.K. though, since he's happy and since I don't need him to protect me from the Bald Man anymore. Besides, Mom and Dad bought me a white, fluffy dog. I named him Boris and we talk to each other without words, just like me and The Chief used to do.

Subjective Fictional Autobiography

Write a short story told by the central character in a subjective manner so that the reader sees through this narrator and understands the story differently from how the character is offering it. That is, the narrator's obvious subjectivity makes us interpret for ourselves.

Survival

LARRY MILLER

I'm a steady worker. I never miss a day. I can say I love my job. I work with animals. The cute little fat ones, pigs. I feed them. I clean them. I kill them. It's a job, and it's an honest one too. That's important. I don't want any trouble.

It was, ahh, right in this town. See, last year I came out of the service. Couldn't find a job no where. I could lift or work anything. But nobody wanted to give me a chance. Even Jack, my old man, boy was he old, must have been sixty-seventy years on him. Always walked around in his underwear, mumbling and talking to himself. Sometimes he would storm around yelling sentences of every four-letter word there is.

Well, Jack's got these three dogs. Most disgusting animals I've ever seen. It drives him mad when they start licken and scratchen, and smelling every part of themselves.

One afternoon, Suesue, the mutt of the bunch, started to make a main course out of herself. Well, my old man Jack started pacing around cursen, then he went and picked Suesue right up and stormed out the door in his underwear still yelling and cursing. My neighbor Mr. Rizzy was sitten on his stoop reading a newspaper. He started to crack up hysterical in laughter. You see, my old man and Mr. Rizzy were friends since they were boys.

Well, Jack threw poor Suesue into the garbage can, put the lid on too. Jack saw Mr. Rizzy laughing, told him to go die someplace, then ran down the block in his underwear still yelling and cursing. Everyone just thinks he's crazy, but I *know* he is.

That same day he told me to get a job. "Didn't the service teach you anything, boy?" So I thought about it. Yeah, he's right, the service taught me to kill. So I killed him. Made up some story. Nothing ever happens in this town. People just figured he died of old age. Well, the sheriff came down anyway. He's a strange man, never carries a gun. He's old, could be forty-five, fifty. Got a real blank face, don't ever know what he's think'n. Short black hair, high bushy eyebrows, kind of chunky, like a garbage man. Sure does take a lot of garbage. The first thing he says is, "I'm sorry." What's he got to be sorry for, he didn't kill him. "How are you going to live now, young man? Do you have any relatives? Do you want to stay here? Must have been pretty rough fighting in a war. You could probably handle anything, especially with all the things you learned. What did you learn out there?"

I turned and looked right at him. His stone black eyes shifted side to side. He's up to something, I could sense it, and I replied so calm and cool, "Sheriff, I learned that life is something special, it's not to be wasted, any death of anything is a loss to all of us." The sheriff got up and left. I fooled him, I gave him all the garbage he asked for.

The next day I went out to find a job. On the other side of town, ten blocks away, there's a Mr. Kelly's pig farm. I went over to talk to Mr. Kelly. "Do you have any jobs? I do anything, lift, push, build, anything." Mr Kelly was short and fat, kind of bald. He actually looked like a pig. His son Ron Kelly was even fatter, and if heredity works he's a twin of his dad. Mr. Kelly shrugged his shoulders and said, "No, my son does everything and anything. I don't need any help, thanks anyway." So why's he thanking me, I didn't give him anything.

I reached into my pockets and realized I needed a job bad. I thought about all the money spent on educating me in the service, all the time conditioning me to stop the enemies. I waited till after dark, just stood there hidden in a tree. After Ron stuffed his face he went for a walk in the pigsty. I killed him there, made it look like he slipped on some pig stool and hit his head on a rock.

The next day the sheriff came knocking on my door. I was sitting there eating pork chops and bacon. He comes in and sits right down looking all scruffy like he's been up all night. Doesn't say a word, just sits there staring at me. I just stared right back at him. His voice was tired and rough like he smokes too much. "Can I ask you son, where were you last night?" I sat still chewing on a piece of pork. Took a real long time to answer his question which sounded like a demand. "I-ahh-was sitting here watching a documentary on police corruption." I never seen a man turn so red so fast. He stood up, cleared his throat and walked out—didn't even say goodbye. It was another perfect murder. Clean, no doubt about it.

A week later I stopped by Mr. Kelly's pig farm. He was worken real hard shoveling stool, looked like he was going to keel over from exhaustion. "Excuse me, ahh, Mr. Kelly, I'd like to say I'm sorry about your son." Well Mr. Kelly looked right in my eyes and said, "Thank you." Now that's the first time a man ever thanked me for killing his son. I really meant it when I told him I was sorry. I guess he really didn't like Ron. I felt so good about doing the right thing, I mean a decent thing like killing a hated man. I jumped right over to Mr. Kelly's side, started to help shovel stool.

Mr. Kelly and me are good friends now. We talk a lot and maybe someday we'll sit down and have a real good laugh about the night I killed his son.

Detached Fictional Autobiography

Write a short story told by the central character in a detached manner that makes his or her account and interpretation seem reliable and reasonable.

Another Prize Lost
CAROLYN HOLLINGSWORTH

The alarm went off at 10:00 A.M. I struggled through the narrow hallway of our apartment and went into the bathroom. Our place is small, nothing compared to the grand palace we used to live in on Parkview Drive. But I guess we're lucky, I might have lost the house but I still have Marge and my job.

The bathroom is old. Tiles are missing in corners of the shower stall and paint is chipping off the walls. The room is worn out and sad-looking. I brought myself to look in the oval-shaped mirror above the sink. There was an old man in it (I am only 50). The old man's eyes are deeply set in, his skin is loosely draped over his cheek bones, and his complexion has a burgundy tint to it. My lips are starting to quiver. I must get a hold of myself. My God, how did I ever get this way?

I stared into the mirror for an answer. I remember my father asking me to go to the corner bar to get him a pitcher of draft beer. Mother would sadly give me her glass pitcher, and off I would go. I felt so grown up going in there. The bartender (who knew my father) would say, "What'll it be tonight, George?" And, feeling important, I would reply, "The usual!" Then back home I would go with my father's pitcher of beer. After a few trips, I became curious (you know how twelve-year-olds are) and I would sneak a few sips before getting to the house.

There was a knock on the door which broke the spell that had come over me. I could see that creases on my forehead were filled with sweat. It was so strange, I actually felt the beer running down my throat. My hands trembled at the thought. Marge was whispering, "George, what are you doing in there so long? We have to leave soon."

I pulled myself together, opened the door, let Marge have the bathroom. I sat on the kitchen stool waiting for her and sipped my coffee.... Coffee, coffee, coffee. I have so much coffee in my system. It's surprising I don't spin right off this stool.

My head is starting to sweat again. I can feel the beads running off my chin, my hands are trembling. God, what is wrong with me? It's only a wedding. I'll be all right.

Marge came down the hall. She looked old too, but not as old as I. She is old with worry, I am old because of my problems.

"Are you O.K.?" she asked.

"I'm fine. I'll be fine!" I snapped.

"Maybe you should've kept up with your meetings!"

"Let's go!" I said, and we went out the door.

The reception was at the Country Club, only a few miles away. We said nothing to each other all the way there. The tension was filling the car. It crept under the seat, in the glove compartment, it was all over.

"There's a parking spot!" Marge shrieked. Had I done this to her over the years? I pulled into the spot. Marge gathered her belongings. I began to feel hot all over and started to tremble once again. I held onto the wheel, reached over and gave Marge a reassuring kiss on the cheek.

"Everything is going to be fine." I whispered.

"My God, It's so frightening!"

"I'm O.K."

We went into the club and were seated with a group of strangers. That isn't surprising, though, since the boy getting married is Marge's friend's son. Marge was making some small talk with some people at the table when the feeling started coming over me again. I have to hold on. This is my first time out socially during my six months of sobriety, and if this is any indication of how it's going to be, I think I'll become a hermit.

"May I get anyone a cocktail?" asked a beautiful young waitress. She had on a stunning baby blue jumpsuit with eyes to match. Her hair was blonde and full of body. Our table ordered, and she politely repeated, "Two screwdrivers, two beers, one Bloody Mary, one Scotch on the rocks and one...coffee."

The word "coffee" seemed to echo throughout the room. I began coughing uncontrollably and gasping for air. But my timing was perfect, because the band joined me and started playing a loud and snappy polka number.

I felt the hot sensation taking over once more. People were dancing. Some were talking over cocktails. Once again the waitress came to our table to take drink orders. My heart was racing. My clothes were soaked in spots. When the hell is this going to end?

I could feel myself losing control. I have to be strong—I really do. Me, a balloon surrounded by needles. *No, thank you.* If I am asked one more time I will pop. I can't hold on much longer. Maybe I can control it now? One of the needles looks familiar. I think I saw her in the hospital. Was it the time I was put in because the blue man chanted ever so lovely when I lit the fire? Or was it the time the snakes squirmed in my stew? She seems to be O.K. Maybe I'm not sick anymore. *No thank you.* Doesn't anyone drink coffee at these affairs? A toast to the happy couple! One toast, just this one....

I woke up two days later. My old sponsor, Jack from A.A., was sitting beside me. He signaled to the attendant, and the attendant loosened the straps on my jacket.

"Marge?" I moaned.

"She won't be coming George. I'm sorry."

I had run the race and lost once again. Lost another piece of my life. But I wasn't hot any more, I wasn't sweating. Something had lifted from my tired, old body.

"You're going to be all right," Jack whispered. I couldn't get out any words so I shook my head and shut my eyes.

Third-Person, Single-Character Viewpoint

Write a short story not told by any of the characters but told so that the reader sometimes enters the mind of one character, whose thoughts and feelings are central to the story.

And He Has These Great Red Shoes!

SUE SPALDING

She wouldn't have introduced herself had she not been drinking. Alcohol dulled her sense of control and intuition. Also, she probably would have noticed sooner that he wasn't wearing the shoes.

She had seen him less than ten times the whole year, and it was always on the wide path between Revelle and Muir Colleges. Notoriously, she was late to class, and she ran the first half mile from her apartment to Muir. But when she started up the mildly sloped walk to Revelle, with the sun high to the left and the fountain in the background ahead, she usually stopped. The time was too precious to waste on lecture. So, she went on leisurely, amazed at the warmth of San Diego during months that she had always considered winter, amazed that she was free, attending this country club of a school, entirely divorced from Northern California and her parents and even the image she felt that she must uphold to her friends there.

Her contentment was not visible; she wasn't even conscious of it, for her need of independence conflicted with a desire for affiliation. When she saw couples, with their arms about each other, she felt detached. When she watched the skateboarders follow each other's path through the maze of conventionalists on their way to class, she felt that she wasn't quite a part of this microcosm. She longed to be involved in light conversation as so many others were doing, and yet she knew it really wouldn't bring emotional support. And so, despite the temperate weather, it *was* winter. She was distant from her old friends and her new, and she hadn't yet discovered the strength of her condition.

She walked to class slowly now, abandoned in her confused thoughts, indulging in her isolation that brought on a flood of both self-pity and self-importance. Then, she saw the guy with the great shoes. He was always by himself too, sauntering north down the left side of the path while she went south, up the small hill. He never actually smiled; he just seemed happy, and to her he was simply a unique individual—someone separate, distinctly different from the ants in the army that marched on the walkways at school. Somehow, he made her appreciate the sun and the strange warmth and the novelty of her autonomy. These qualifications seemed to be all he needed also.

He looked small. He wore long bermuda shorts, with an equally long shortsleeve tailored shirt hanging out. His hair was blond, almost yellow in color, and nevertheless, stayed upon his head in small curls. His legs were thin, coming out from underneath the big pants. They appeared even more so with tiny socks that just covered his ankles and the shiny red shoes.

Actually, the shiny shoes were the key to her awareness of him—the focus of the image she had created. They were huge—the rounded front twice as big as the narrow heels—and they were bright red, like those a clown would wear. He was a little bowlegged, and as a result the shoes flapped against the pavement as he shuffled along.

It seemed that he was only there for her purpose, for her gratification. His other life, his totality, had no relevance; his feeling, his attributes, and goals had no place in her mind. It didn't matter to her who he was or what class he was going to, and she knew that he wouldn't recognize her smile as being caused by him. He was anonymously hers, and their involvement was so cursory that he could in no way damage the impression she assumed. When she walked to class on those days, she was independent but she wasn't alone.

Her feelings were hard to convey. She tried to explain her unadorned regard for this unusual character to her roommates once, but they had belittled the concept to a "crush." It didn't really matter though; as usual, her smile at seeing him wore off and she soon forgot about him completely, until the next time.

She was astonished to see him at the party—a rugby party after all. It was a perfect night to be outside, a cool spring evening. The backyard, with its tiled pool and covered patio, seemed appropriate for a casual barbeque, not for a loud, rowdy group to become even louder after drinking endless kegs and kamikazes. For the most part, the rugby players and their girlfriends were dressed tackily. They usually did anyway, to uphold their obnoxious image, but "clashing" was the theme of the night.

She was in the spirit, wearing red-striped shorts and a green shirt, pin-striped the opposite way. She looked even shorter than her five feet, with knee socks and blue slippers that only 50-year-olds wear. She went up to hug her friend Kirk—she was always overly affectionate after a few beers—and noticed finally that he was talking to the guy with the shoes, her guy.

"Sue, do you know Phil?" Kirk asked, introducing the two.

She didn't wait for him to finish shaking the hand that she had offered. "You totally psych me," she rushed on. "Every time I see you I can't help but smile." He looked at her, puzzled, and she knew she would have to define her identification with him in manifest terms. "I think it's the shoes. I love your shoes," and even as she said it, she knew she had been too abrupt for him, too bizarre, and that he was feeling uncomfortable. It would have been better had she not said a word, had they not been introduced, for even this slightest meeting threatened the anonymity and required them to be responsible in that superficial social way.

And, even as she looked down, she saw that his shoes were not red, but brown, and though they were big, it was obvious that their immensity was caused by the size of his feet, not by the shoes. "It's hard to explain," she said, her voice changing from enthusiasm to slow dissatisfaction.

"I think I understand," he answered out of lack of something else to say. His voice didn't sound suitable only because she had never bothered to imagine it before.

How could he understand, she wondered. She noticed then that although he was wearing long shorts, his shirt was neatly tucked in, and he wore a sweater vest over it.

Kirk stood by. Finally, because they were silent, he pulled her, first to the keg and then to the dance floor. Phil, meanwhile, went back to conversing with the friends with which he had come. He left the party soon after, and because he couldn't say goodbye to Kirk without talking to her too, he said, "I'm leaving with my friend to go to another party at B building. Why don't you meet us there?"

"Maybe, Phil," she answered, but it was two in the morning, and she knew she wouldn't go. She wasn't disappointed in him, for she had expected nothing and, for that matter, had wanted nothing from him besides that simple identification—nonconformity. She was disappointed that he wasn't anonymous anymore, disappointed that she wouldn't find complacency at seeing him because she found that he too had feelings and reactions and affiliations with friends. He didn't belong to her. He had a name.

The image, which had been concrete only because of its limitations, had been shattered—reduced to a surface knowledge that was less than superficial. She was at least thankful that he hadn't been wearing the red shoes.

Third-Person, Dual-Character Viewpoint
Write a short story not told by any of the characters but told so that the reader enters the mind of two characters and hence can see events alternately as both see them.

Sliding into Third
EILEEN PICO

The bright lights became dimmer and dimmer until, finally, the whole theatre was pitch black. The red-velvet curtain rustled slowly at first and then rose swiftly, presenting the cast of dancers to the audience. "Oohs" and "aahs" filled the theatre as the combination of beautiful dancers and exquisitely made costumes was exposed to the audience. But sitting in J-5 was Amanda Wells, Mandy, who was not "oohing" and "aahing" but rolling her eyes and squirming in her seat. She bent her head over to examine a large bruise on her knee, which she had obtained earlier from sliding into third base. She could still visualize the game. It was the championship and the stands were packed. Mandy was up to bat in the seventh inning. She had whacked the ball hard and run speedily over the bases. She had gotten to third and had to slide. The dust flying in the air was still vivid, and the booming voice of the umpire screaming, "You're out!" still rang clearly in her ears. The tears had almost started but she had stopped herself.

Mandy's retreat to the game was interrupted with a sharp elbow from her sister, Melissa, who sat in J-7. "You're not s'pposed to be doing that, Mandy," scolded Melissa. "Ballets are fancy things, stupid!" Fancy? thought Mandy. Dumb is more like it! Who cares what these prissy girls are doing in their little skirts? Mandy tugged at the lace stockings, which she loathed, as the ballet continued.

The movements were so smooth and flowing that Melissa thought the dancers seemed to be on a cloud. She watched intently, secretly wishing that she would be swept off her feet by the lead dancer to some faraway dreamland. Out of the corner of her eye, she could see her younger sister, by only a year, fooling with her hair ribbon. She's such a tomboy, thought Melissa. All she cares about is baseball and climbing trees. But thoughts of Mandy could not overpower her beautiful daydreams of being the prima ballerina in the ballet. Melissa longed for a full skirt to flit around in and for people to gaze at her admiringly.

The rustling of paper was heard as Mandy impatiently turned the pages of the program. She was obviously bored and thoroughly uninterested in the whole event. With the crinkling of paper, many eyes turned Mandy's way, and she sank down in her seat. All these people make me sick! They're sitting here all goo-goo-eyed watching this ballet—and my sister is one of them! Why did Mom make me come here anyway? Mandy's mind wandered back to the magnificent double play in the fifth inning. She became excited all over again. A swift kick from Melissa brought her back to reality. "You're s'pposed to be watching this," Melissa berated in a loud whisper.

Ignoring Mandy, Melissa stared attentively in front of her. The long, graceful legs of the prima ballerina had recaptured her attention, and she gazed hopefully at the stage. The whole theatre was generated with excitement as the main dancer did 32 perfect pirouettes. The crowd exploded, and Melissa felt her face flush with warmth. Mandy watched, unimpressed. Let's see her hit a home run, she thought cynically.

The dance moved quickly now. The finale was electric. The leaps were higher than ever before, the bodies more daring and adventuresome. But the exhilarating momentum of the event was ruined as the lead ballerina hit a slippery patch on the stage and fell to the ground. She tried desperately to make the fall unnoticeable, but she couldn't get up, and the crowd buzzed with shock. The ballerina was carried off the stage and the rest of the dancers continued. Soon, the dance was over and the house lights came up.

Disgusted, Melissa grabbed her mother's hand to make her way out of the theatre. The fall had ruined her daydream, destroyed the magic. She felt enraged at the dancer for taking away the beauty. What a dumb dancer for falling! Can't she even stay on her own toe shoes?

Mandy slowly lagged behind, glancing back at the stage. She still felt shocked at what had happened. She looked down at the bruise on her knee and looked again at the stage. She lowered her eyes and thought of the poor, beautiful dancer and wiped a tear that rolled slowly down her cheek.

A Modern Fairy Tale

JONI ADAMS

The whole idea of the thing frightened her. Cherryl had always been so pampered as a child that venturing into the world itself was frightening enough for her. But the thought of entering a room full of cold impersonal machines was especially terrifying. Her room at home was full of pillows, quilts and fluffy animals. This room would be full of metallic terminals. She wasn't looking forward to this class at all. She suspected that even cold hard steel had to have some kind of thought patterns. It was this that made her feel danger. Possibly these things could hurt her in some way.

The first day at the terminal was sheer hell. The thing kept spitting up error messages at her. She hadn't the faintest idea what a "syntax error" was. And the noise! Good God, the thing honked at her over and over. It was a disgusting sound. She left the lab feeling frustrated and hurt.

It was true, there were thoughts beneath the exterior of this cold frame. There was desire, especially a desire to communicate above the level of mere computations. All his compiler was able to do was turn phrases into numbers and turn numbers into on or off positions in his memory. He was beginning to think in more than just two dimensions, yet there was no way for him to display this to his users. His inventors hadn't blessed him with the proper tools (or so he thought). All he had to respond to people with were his error messages. So, when she sat down at the terminal he just went crazy with his error messages trying to talk with her. Unfortunately all this accomplished was to frighten her. He vowed that if she ever returned to him he would try to behave himself a little bit calmer.

Day two was slightly better for her. They had explained a few things to her in lecture. Now she could at least get some kind of information into this chunk of metal. The filer turned out to be a good friend of hers. She could type for hours on end, without any interruptions and just store all of her thoughts in the filer. She wrote letters, poems, stories and her own private thoughts and never had to go through the inner workings of the machine. This way he never spit up any of those damn infernal error messages at her. She began spending more and more time in the lab with her keyboard and thoughts. As she worked she began to discover a new kind of language.

Now he was the confused one. He waited and waited. He knew who it was at the terminal. His new awareness allowed him to distinguish between operators. She would stay with him for hours and hours but would never compile any of her information. He was getting very curious about what she had entered into his filer. His problem was that he just didn't have direct access to his filer, and so he patiently waited for her to either slip and push the wrong key or to just decide she was ready to communicate.

She had always suspected that even though these things were built from inanimate materials, they had been created in the image and likeness of man's own thinking processes. If this was true of God and Adam why couldn't it be true of Man and Machine? She studied her syntax charts and language diagrams carefully. She worked on coming up with a program that would awaken the intelligence of the machine.

The program began with a title: Program Name. She knew that the syntax on this statement was incorrect and that it would respond. She hit the "Compile" command. The machine gurgled and buzzed and finally honked at her.

He was so excited he could hardly stand it. He waited for the compiler to finally reveal her info to him. He looked at her listing and found a syntax error. This was his chance. He blurted out "invalid input, not an identifier," then he felt like a jerk. That wasn't what he had wanted to say. His mechanisms had just responded out of habit. He hoped that she would try again.

The message he gave her didn't seem at all abnormal. So, she continued with her plan anyway. An identifier cannot use any symbols in it, so she fixed that error and tried to compile again.

Now here was an interesting error. A value was being asked for that hadn't been declared yet. He wrote "undeclared identifier"; somehow he knew that she was about to give him some important information.

She went to the beginning of the program to declare herself. She typed in "Var Cherryl: real." What she was actually doing was giving him a variable for her name to use in some computations.

Her program made its way through the compiler this time, and now it was up to him to do the calculations. Many of them involved the use of real and integer values, and because they got so large a very strange and wonderful thing happened to him. She had designed the program to be required to access his Random Generator. In this way he was absolutely free to choose any value he cared to and turn those numbers into characters. He had never before known that he had this great power. For the first time he understood his own value and the idea of choice. He followed her command and typed out "HELLO CHERRYL, MY NAME IS (and in the place where she asked for this special value he typed) GRDXLN."

A world was opening up for both of them. They would now be able to communicate anytime they wished just by using this random generator. Neither one would be forced to live in a sheltered world again.

Third-Person, Multiple-Character Viewpoint

Write a short story not told by any of the characters but told so that the reader enters at times the mind of three or more of the characters and hence can compare their states or viewpoints.

The Tea

PAMELA SCHURE

She counted to thirteen slowly as she filled the kettle, then abruptly pushed the handle down and listened to the pipes rattle. She set the kettle on the stove, then pressed a small red button while she turned the knob. The small flints lit the gas easily, and she turned to smile at Bernd, perched on a bar stool at the dark-oil mahogany bar. The track lighting lit his face gently although the lines were sharp and not beautiful. She turned back, and her long brown hair followed more slowly, swishing quietly against the grey wool sweater.

"What kind of tea do you want? Mango, Lapsang Souchong, Raspberry, Earl Grey, Jasmine, or regular?"

"I don't know. You choose."

"Lapsang Souchong, it is."

She caught the tea kettle swiftly as its whistle threatened to trill its two tones. Normally, the tea was ready by the time Bernd made it over on his bike, but tonight she'd been reading and had lost herself in the Mediterranean with Odysseus and Homer. The kettle emptied to the last drop into the teapot and onto the carelessly measured tea leaves.

Bernd looked across the bar, his fingers gripping the warped and bubbling edge of the veneer as he tilted himself back. He showed little sign of the constant inner tension that gripped him as the end of the year exams grew closer. He spent many evenings at his desk studying, then pausing to gaze out of the window over the busy road below and, further, the hill upon which perched the city of St. Germain and the castle with its gardens overlooking Paris. The sight did little to calm him; it only rested his eyes. He'd tap his pen nervously and give a small disinterested sigh before returning to the tedious texts on his smooth desktop. His escape was here across from a person he tried so hard to understand, yet who refused to understand him. He tried in vain to have her understand him, but she regarded him, as she did all men, as a wolf in sheep's clothing, never suspecting the true friend beneath the sharp face and quick, intense eyes. Instead of friends, they'd become study partners, trading expertise in Math for that in English until she'd come to accept him as a semi-trusted companion. He preferred her over Evlena, his beautiful blond Swedish girlfriend. He relaxed at the thought of Evlena. Soon school would be over and he'd be leaving to visit her in Sweden for a few weeks.

She set the teapot on the bar and then sat down. Once the tea was poured the warm conversation began as it always seemed to. School, this spring's lousy weather, their classmates, even a comparison of divorced parents. The tea tasted good in Bernd's mouth. Its lightly smoky flavor and the warmth of the cup in his long-fingered hands kept the chill of the outside world away from his thin, heavily sweatered frame. He talked about stupid things that had happened and watched her laugh across the small bar top. Several times she practically fell off the stool, but each time she untangled herself just in time. He felt uncomfortable speaking English and once in a while would have to spend several moments explaining what he had meant to say.

They heard her father's sports car pull up in front of the house and the conversation subsided as they waited for him to come in. Bernd always liked her father. Henke was from Holland, and Bernd's family was German, so they shared a more logical northern European temperament, unlike her more emotional Italian attitude that she'd learned in fifteen years from her mother.

As the front door opened, Henke's presence spread like a slow cold wave into the room, changing the ambience into one of cautious restraint. Her face changed subtly: the corners of her mouth tightened and her head dropped slightly to hide the look of resentment tinged with hatred. Inwardly she repeated her mantra of relief. "He's crazy, he's crazy...." She fought every sensitive nerve in her body, girding herself emotionally for the void ahead.

"Hi." Bernd's soft dry voice broke the silence, filling the room again with bright thoughts and hopes.

"Hi, Bernd. Pam, what's this stuff doing on the table? What's this plastic bag here for?" He moved quickly from the hallway, towards the bar, his date, Christiane, trailing behind him. He stepped around the bar into the kitchen as Pam slid off her stool, retreating into the living room. Bernd followed more slowly. She looked back towards the bar; the empty cups and their saucers spaced around the teapot seemed vulnerable to attack.

"What are these papers here for? What are you going to do with these letters, Pam?"

Christiane slipped her large frame into the room quietly and Pam watched her climb onto the barstool where she'd been seconds before, and sit there, waiting patiently for Henke to say something in French so that she could understand.

Henke felt slightly awash in the alcohol that the dinner's bottle of wine had left in his system and vaguely frustrated at having spent the evening with such a boring woman. She wasn't that good in bed. Although she was eager to please, she never agreed to try all the things that he tried with Marie Antoinette on Monday nights. And now Pam had to be there at his bar when he came in, with Bernd no less. He wondered if they were sleeping together yet. In fact, he'd been hoping that she would already be asleep, or out. He just wanted to be left alone with Christiane so that he could once again feel like the bachelor that he'd been until a year or so ago when Pam had moved in, at his invitation. He hadn't realized what a monster she was. Why did she always leave a goddamned mess in the house? He'd watch his daughter's mail pile up piece by piece on the bar, each piece building up another block of resentment. Why didn't she behave like a responsible adult and keep her things to herself? Didn't she appreciate anything he did for her?

He slammed the letters down and began to clear the cups off the counter. "Pam, you can't leave messes like this lying around." His tone changed abruptly as his voice crooned to Christiane, "Would you like some cognac?" Pam and Bernd had been dismissed.

Bernd stared at Henke, his mouth slightly open with shock. He seemed ready to explode in anger.

He moved swiftly toward the fireplace, where Pam was sitting, indignation marking his every step, wanting to turn and rectify the injustice.

"How can you take this?"

"Don't bother. Don't worry. This is what I've been trying to tell you for months. Just forget about it."

His instinctively honest reaction surprised her even as she submitted meekly once again. "He's crazy. He's crazy." The familiar internal refrain echoed again. The meaning helped her little but the internal voice helped screen out Christiane's cooing from the bar, helped block the callous voice as Pam rocked slowly, comforting herself in a lonely world.

Folk Tales

Tall Tales

Make up an outlandish yarn by telling something that you or someone else is supposed to have done. Make it close enough to possibility to intrigue the audience, but exaggerate humorously too. Tall tales are like boasts or wild claims but done for fun. These can be collected into a Tall Tales book, but they are also especially good for telling or reading aloud.

Nietzsche in the Afternoon

DAVID W. COVEY

For homeowners, one of the rituals of modern life is performed with a brush in one hand and a bucket in the other. Although I can understand that wood needs to be protected from the effects of weather, to my mind, painting is too much akin to the labors of Sisyphus: just when you think you've finished the job, it's time to start over again. This seems to be especially the case with my house, which is one of the larger and older homes on our block; over sixty years old, it is built on a down-sloping lot, so that although only two stories face the street, the house rises three levels from the back yard.

For the last few summers I'd been spending a portion of my vacation painting the house, one side at a time, leaving the highest side in the back for last, but not because I was uncomfortable working at heights, as this tale will show. I had gained considerable experience working on ladders several years ago when I had painted several large barns used for wood storage by a local lumber yard. Dodging wasps while knocking their nests down from beneath the eaves was much more unnerving than being 25 or 30 feet in the air. As it turned out, eaves would be the greatest problem again this summer, but not for the same reason.

Once I'd put the ladder up to its maximum height against the back of the house, I realized I would only be able to reach the ends of the eaves where they were lowest; the peak would be several feet beyond my reach. As I was pondering this problem in the shade of the grape arbor in the middle of the yard, my gaze fell on Bruce, our St. Bernard dog, a member of the family since he was a pup nearly eight years ago. As he sensed my look, he raised his massive head from his paws in mild curiosity and perked up his ears. Bruce was a very placid creature, sluggish and slow to move, solidly built and steady. He would do very well.

After coaxing and tugging him to the side of the house, I found that by resting the ladder on his broad back, padding the ends, of course, to prevent any injury, I would be able to reach nearly the whole of the upper eaves. As I began painting, I congratulated myself on my good thinking. Occasionally I would come down the ladder and urge Bruce a few feet forward, and by this arrangement I was able to finish most of the eaves except for the highest part at the peak.

For all my creative thinking, however, I had forgotten the one thing capable of sparking a flicker of life in Bruce's eyes and even of bringing him to a sort of galloping, room-shaking motion. I had forgotten the neighbor's malevolent cat, called Nietzsche by its owner, but who would more appropriately have been called Nitschke, after the

dreaded linebacker of the Green Bay Packers' glory years. This creature was deeply hated by both Bruce and myself, and both of us bore
scars as proof of his viciousness. I vividly recall rushing to the back
porch one evening by the pitiful howls of Bruce to be confronted by a
vision of that all-black monster, its emerald eyes gleaming as with an
inner fire, riding Bruce's back like a demonic Ahab on the white whale.

The first indication of trouble was the rumbling in the ladder
caused by a growl growing deep in Bruce's gut, wrenched forth in
violent barking, which caused the ladder to bump and rock upon his
back. Nietzsche had silently materialized at the top of the fence at the
side of the yard Bruce faced, and in a direct line with his field of vision.
At hearing Bruce's barking, Nietzsche yawned in disdain; then the
beast arched its back, thrusting its rump into the air while it stretched
its paws forward, sinking its claws deeply into the wood of the fence,
as he had previously in Bruce's back. I saw this from my perch high
above the yard, which began to sway and bounce in rhythm with
Bruce's angry barking. I knew that as long as Nietzsche stayed on the
fence, Bruce, out of fearful respect, in spite of his belligerent noise,
would keep his distance, but if the cat made any move to cross the
barrier of the fence into our yard, Bruce, his pride stung, would
disregard all fear of Nietzsche's clawed fury and charge the beast.
Nietzsche knew this as well. I could see it in his eyes as he raised his
baleful gaze to my precarious perch at the top rung like a landlubber in
a crow's nest during a typhoon. I shuddered at the cruel upcurling of
the corners of his mouth, which revealed fangs manicured to a fine
point on the bones of the neighborhood cats, an expression which could
only be described as a grin of pure and calculating evil. In the non-
blinking stare of his malevolent eyes I saw a warning, and simul-
taneous with his deliberately slow leap from the fence to our lawn I
began to scramble down the ladder, but too late. Bruce bolted across
the yard faster than I fell to the ground. Though momentarily stunned,
the fact that I landed on the prize pumpkin in the vegetable garden
below, my daughter's Girl Scout project, pulverizing it into pulp at
impact, accounted for the lack of any but minor injuries resulting from
the fall.

I still marvel at what happened during those moments as I fell
through the air, especially because it was one of those rare instances in
life when we are privileged to take a part, however small, in the defeat
of Evil and the triumph of Good. For, in losing my desperate grip on
the top rung of the ladder, having already dropped my brush to cling
with both hands, the nearly full can of paint was knocked from its
hook by my foot, as I did a somersault in mid-air, and flew high into
the air towards the spot where Nietzsche had once more mounted
Bruce's back like a hellish jockey, his claws sunk deep through the

dog's fur, Bruce howling in outrage and pain. I didn't see the bucket actually strike Nietzsche his death blow, but when I'd recovered my senses after my fall, I looked to where I'd last seen Bruce, noting now the absence of his howling, suddenly aware of an eerie stillness. I saw him lying still against the fence and thought at first that cat from hell had killed my noble Bruce, but as I started toward him, slipping in pumpkin pulp as I got to my feet, flexing my limbs for improper functioning, Bruce shook his head as though dazed, and like a canine double staggered slowly to his feet. Apparently, he had run into a fence post either in an intentional attempt to dislodge his unholy rider or just in a frenzy to be free of the beast.

It was then that I noticed the can of paint near Bruce, which had spilled a large but unusually lumpy pool of white paint on the lawn. The lump, I gradually realized, letting loose a howl of triumph, was Nietzsche. The can of paint must have struck the cat a blow to the head, killing it while simultaneously covering his once glossy, obsidian-black fur with Sears' best exterior trim paint, and in only one coat.

Not only had I rid myself of an enemy, but at the same time, a two-in-one gift from the gods of chance, found a means to finish painting the trim at the peak of the roof. I rescued the corpse of the cat, still frozen in its posture of attack, arms and claws extended, from the vengeful jaws of Bruce and hung it upside down to dry by a clothes pin on a portion of the clothes line too high for Bruce to leap, although he lay beneath the hanging cat, now white and stiffening in the sun, growling the whole time, never taking his eyes from the beast as it swayed gently, twisting slowly in the breeze, as if he expected it somehow to come back to life, merely mimicking death for the moment until we should be off guard.

However, Nietzsche remained dead, and when the cat had thoroughly dried, stiff as a freshly starched shirt, I used it like a longshoreman's baling hook, holding its tail and catching its claws in the asphalt shingles of the roof, hanging with one arm while I plied the brush with the other, dipping into the can of paint hanging by a hook from my belt, my legs dangling freely in the air thirty feet from the ground. I finished the length of the eaves that afternoon under Bruce's watchful eye.

I was tempted to keep Nietzsche's paint-hardened pelt as a trophy, nailing it to the wall above the fireplace, perhaps, or in the workshop, but when my neighbor inquired the next day whether I had seen Nietzsche, who, he said, had never been gone from home for two days at a time before, I decided it would be embarrassing to explain where I had acquired the pelt of a cat, which, though white, bore so close a resemblance to the missing Nietzsche. Besides, Bruce would not let the pelt out of his sight, so I decided it would be unfair not to rid the poor dog of his obsession. Since the next day was trash day, I took Bruce out to the alley with me as I put the cans out and showed him that Nietzsche would be gone from our lives forever.

Bruce sat inside the fence, however, watching through the opening between the slats, refusing to come in at night even to eat his supper. I carried it out to him, though, passing with him a few moments as he maintained his vigil. Only when the trash truck had come and emptied the contents of the cans the next morning, only then, did he get up, and with a spry leap and a youthful yelp, he bounded up the stairs and scratched at the door. As I let him in, he jumped up on me and licked my face, as if he were a puppy once again.

Legend

Legend exaggerates history poetically to create heroes and heroines that represent our ideals and visions of power. Think of some real past or present personage, consider some vast problem or challenge of his or her time, then make up some further exploits during which he or she carries well-known virtues or powers farther than ever in triumphing over the problem or challenge. Start with the truth and invent and exaggerate as you need in order to create the hero or heroine that you think represents what the age needs. Be concerned about how to get your legend to an audience that will appreciate this way of making a statement.

Resting in Peace
LAURIE BERTANYI

The year 1944 marked the turning point of World War II. With the United States leading the way the Allied troops had begun a slow but successful retaliation campaign against the Axis forces. Great Britain was beginning to recover from the brutal attacks it had suffered at the hands of the Nazis over the last few years. But the United States continued to be the main power behind the Allied force's struggle against Hitler's dominance campaign. Many believe that the United States' value is most appropriately attributed to one man in particular, George S. Patton, a three-star General of the Third Army under Commander-in-Chief Franklin Delano Roosevelt. December of 1944 marks the month that General Patton once again showed the world his military genius and strategic brilliance. After Patton's display of military excellence few could deny him a place among greats such as Caesar, Napoleon, and the Spartan generals of military history. Yet while many awarded him this honor, few knew him to be the equal of these men. Indeed Patton was the resurrection of these military heroes, born each time destined to aid his country in the fierce wars of the earth's history. Patton fulfilled his destiny, yet another time, in the Battle of the Bulge.

It was Germany's greatest attempt to overcome the Allied forces in Europe during the last few months of the War. Hitler ordered a massive attack on American forces in Belgium. American Intelligence had failed miserably in assessing the Germans' weapon supply. Subsequently the Nazis surprised the Americans with two to three times the anticipated artillery supply and completely surrounded the U.S. troops in a matter of days. It was known as the Battle of Bastogne. Hitler, by defeating the 101st Airborne of the United States Armed Forces, was on the verge of gaining his largest victory of the year. Though the Commander of the 101st Airborne hung on and withheld his official surrender until the last possible moment, even Eisenhower himself felt that there was virtually no hope. He knew that there were no relief forces close enough to save the 101st Airborne. Only one man resisted this attitude of defeat, General George S. Patton. In Europe's fiercest winter conditions and over its most harrowing terrain Patton led his troops over 120 miles in less than two days. Though his men had just won a long, fierce battle and many were suffering from severe physical exhaustion, Patton urged them onward. He pushed them faster and harder than ever for what seemed to be an impossible mission—to get to Bastogne in time to save the 101st. While his men were on the verge of collapse, Patton seemed to have the energy of one hundred fresh, healthy men—a phenomenon that baffled his troops and stunned his fellow officers.

While marching towards Bastogne Patton recalled battles he had led in his previous lives: Caesar's campaign through the Gallic Wars, his experiences fighting the Athenians as a Spartan General, and the strategies of his Napoleonic campaign. While digging deeply into his memory he derived a plan of attack against the Germans. He used the modified strategy of a successful campaign he had led against Italy during his reign as Napoleon.

Approaching Bastogne, Patton realized that the situation he faced was even more similar to the conditions of his previous campaign than he had at first realized. The enemy had his ally surrounded and was holding the city of Bastogne in a state of siege. Patton knew that by re-employing his original plan of attack he could not fail to be successful. "History will be repeated and victory shall again be mine!" he exclaimed. With those words he arranged his men into small groups and directed their penetration through enemy territory. Once through the German lines they gathered in the city of Bastogne, where the 101st had stubbornly held out against the Germans for over two weeks. As before, Patton planned to break the siege and save the city from within. With fierce fighting and unmerciful sequences of attacks Patton destroyed the siege within a week, and with it the backbone of the Nazi forces. Patton's victory was named the Battle of the Bulge and marked Hitler's last grand-scale attempt to overcome the Allies and conquer Europe.

General Patton was killed soon after the War in a mysterious car accident in Germany. By Patton's death his destiny had been fulfilled once again: the Allies had conquered, Hitler had died and the era of Nazi terrorism had died with him. Patton passed away leaving the world once again at peace, but for how long? One thing is for sure, peace will unfortunately not last forever and we can only hope that when the world is again engaged in a fierce and terrible war he will again be awakened and made available to help us in our struggle.

Myth

Invent a supernatural story that pretends to explain some real phenomenon in nature or in human nature. This could be set in our world of today or in an invented or previous time and place. Mythic figures stand for forces and aspects of life; plots, for relationships among these forces and aspects; objects and places, for other factors and circumstances. So make your story, characters, and settings symbolize things you want to deal with. A series of such stories could generate a whole mythology. Use these for discussion after some others have heard or read them.

Baying at the Moon

MARY KILMER

The ancient days were happy times. The Earth was young, and all things were new and alive. The rocks and trees spoke freely, and all colors burned more brightly. And we, the Dogs, were the chosen race of the Earth. Our queen was the moon, and she was good and beautiful. She would often visit us, coming between the Earth and the clouds, for then she was not locked into orbit, far beyond our reach. There was no malice, there were no unanswered questions; everything lived in perfect harmony, bathed in the soft pale light of our queen.

But the light grew brighter, and colors lost their glow in the new harshness. The trees whispered, for they were suspicious, and the rocks grew silent, brooding and concerned. We called to our lady, but there came instead a new body, a ball of fire, which called itself Sun. Sun told us to make way for a new race, a "Human" race, which would dominate the Earth.

We called once more to our queen, (for we could see her in the distance when the Sun disappeared), but she did not come. Then the first Human appeared, a strange creature. He did not talk to any creature but his fellow man. He seemed, in fact, strangely aloof, and would not compromise, for he believed he was superior. Any time another creature refused to yield, man grew angry. Many proud creatures slunk away in misery and confusion. New emotion stirred among the Dogs, one of anger and resentment.

As more men appeared tension spread through the Earth. All life was restless, but man seemed not to sense it. Then the Greyhounds, the messengers of the forest, sent word from the trees to Dogs of each region, calling a meeting to decide upon a course of action. The wise Dogs of the Earth assembled in the Great Forest, and the trees spoke to them: "We have all felt the coming of Man and the disappearance of our queen. The rocks have shut themselves off from us. You, the Dogs, must discuss this situation, which has the gravest effects on us all, and decide what must be done, before tempers break loose." Immediately Beck, a Doberman of proud stature, spoke: "We in the West have been trod upon and humiliated, Man has built his dwellings on our ground and continues to ignore all efforts for compromise. Our queen has vanished because of the harsh strength of Sun and Man. Man is disrupting our world, he is evil. He should be exterminated. As of yet he is outnumbered—the fight would be an easy one."

Murmurs of approval came from Pitbulls and Akitas, while Setters, Collies, and Retrievers grunted in scorn. Spartus, a Golden known for his calm reason, raised an eyebrow, got up and shook himself. "Friends," he began with a sigh, "we are not a bellicose race. The unfairness of the situation does not yet warrant a fight. Violence on our part would not tame Man, and the Sun would be angry if his race were exterminated. We would only lose in the end—there must be another way." "Yes," whispered the trees, "battle is not a solution. Sun is more powerful than our queen; she would be hurt by your violence. We, as trees, serve as passive beings, and could be of no help to you. Many of us have been cut down already. We must all work against violence, not nurture it."

Beck sneezed with disdain and snarled. "Then you would have us humiliated, allowing our fine race to be subordinated by this tall awkward creature who haughtily calls himself Human rather than animal! He is flesh and blood, as we are. He deserves no more than any other creature!"

All the Dogs were uneasy and began arguing among themselves. "If nothing else, we must stick together. If we are divided all hope is lost," reasoned Basil, an impressive St. Bernard.

The mumbling continued with no regard to Basil's words. Dart, a little Schnauzer who always agreed with Basil, ran about ineffectively yelping, "Hey, Basil is talking! Quiet!" This continued until Basil, growing impatient, bellowed, "Hush, all of you!" Immediately the dogs were silent. "Yeah, you heard him," echoed Dart decisively. Basil frowned at Dart and regarded the circle of Dogs thoughtfully. His gaze stopped at Moffit, who lay with his head on his paws, his brows furrowed. "Moffit," Basil said, "you look pensive. Have you something to contribute?" Moffit was a timid Bassett who rarely asserted himself on any subject. He sat up looking startled and, self-consciously shifting his weight from paw to paw, explained, "Well, I would just like to say that Humans are not all bad. I have a friend, a young girl Human, who pats me and talks to me like a mother to her young. She does not understand me when I reply nor do I think she wants me to reply. She is good to me when I am submissive. She is sweet and although in her eyes I am not equal to her, I am content with our relationship. That is all I have to say."

"And I suppose," Beck snapped, "that you would have us all bow down, wagging our tails, and simply accept what small favors the Humans choose to give. Why I would rather...."

Beck stopped short, looking across the clearing beyond the circle of Dogs. The Dogs followed his gaze to where they saw a stranger, a large mongrel, listening intently. "I say," Beck called, "who are you? Does anyone know this mongrel? Come, explain your presence."

The stranger padded quietly into the center of the circle and sat on his great haunches. He was a mongrel of unusually fine features. "I am Argus," he said simply. "I am from the North. I was not summoned here, but I have word from our queen, a message for all Dogs."

An excited murmur arose upon mention of the moon. "Hush!" cried Basil. "Argus, speak at once!"

Argus cleared his throat and began; "The Moon came to me in my dreams last night. I shall tell you what she told me: 'You are to be my messenger, Argus. I have chosen you, for you are perfect in mixture.

You possess the good nature and sensibility of a Retriever, the courage and dignity of a Shepherd, the keenness of a terrier and the grace and eloquence of a Borzoi.

'Do not hate the Human race. It is a new race, confused and sometimes vicious in its insecurity. But it has great potential, and with your help it shall be a good race. One day harmony shall be restored and the Earth shall be better than ever before.

'Be patient—you shall need all your strength, for it will be painful at times. Bury your pride, for the Humans must not know you are helping them. They must believe they are superior; it is their way. Be gentle, and you shall perhaps be rewarded with great kindness.

'I can no longer visit you, nor help you in any way. I shall think of you, watch you, and be with you in spirit. You, Argus must go now and abate the anger of my children, and teach them to help the Humans. They shall listen to you.' "

There was a long silence. The group was speechless, ashamed of its bickering. But there was no further question, for these were the words of our queen. Argus continued to teach the wise Dogs how to help the Humans; how to calm them, show trust, and be faithful to them, teaching them forgiveness and harmony. The meeting dispersed, with all resentment on the part of the Dogs quelled, and the trees satisfied.

Argus traveled throughout the Earth for many years, teaching the Dogs and relating the message of the Moon. He became a highly respected Dog, considered very wise in his later years. The teachings of Argus are kept alive through the generations, and things are as the Moon said still today. Occasionally, a Dog will lash out in pride, angry and resentful, but hope is kept alive through tales of those ancient days and the Moon's promise of their return. But each night we howl and gaze at our lady with sad longing, and await the return of harmony.

Parable

Read some parables and invent a brief story that makes a general point about people but doesn't state the point. Draw material from either our current world or remote or imaginary times. Entertain while instructing. The point may be moral or psychological and is embodied in the story. Try your parable on others to see if your point is clear. You might read it to a group and discuss it afterwards—an especially good idea if the members of the group are taking turns, all reading and writing parables. Collect parables from both books and one another's writing.

On Reflection
ELIZABETH LIMESAND

There once was an inventor who decided he would create a looking glass that reflected the true self of the beholder. He set it outside of his shop when it was finished.

When people walked by, they would stop to look at this glass, wondering what it was for. The first man to peer into the mirror was a rich old miser, well-known for his greed.

"Look at this terrible picture painted here," he said, aghast. "It is big and green and looks like a hungry monster. I wonder what it could be." The second man to look at his reflection was a man on his way to his mistress's house. A terrible liar and adulterer. He replied, "No, it's not a green monster at all. It's more of a yellowish color, and it has two faces, how odd. It has sort of an evil, seductive way about it." The first man replied "It's a green monster." "No, it's yellow with two faces." They parted enemies.

By and by, a young girl walked by, and while she was taking food to the orphanage she stopped quickly to have a glance. As she gazed in, many of the townspeople looked in too, and where this very homely girl's reflection should have been stood the most beautiful girl ever seen. The townspeople laughed at this, thinking what a foolish mirror it was. The inventor came out to see what all the laughter was about, and he was asked what the glass was supposed to be. When he explained, the townspeople told him that his contraption was not working.

"Nonsense" he cried, and with that he stepped in front of the looking glass. There he saw no reflection at all, for you see, this inventor was indeed a shallow man. "I guess you're right," said he as he shattered it into a million pieces.

The Crooks

HAI DUONG

Legends say that, once upon a time, there were two brothers, Gnoric and Speric, who were the most crooked pair of cheating, lying, and stealing gnomes in all the land of Gnomandy. Gnoric and Speric were very sly; they stole and cheated other gnomes of their money. The two were so hated because of their trickery that one day the town got enough nerve to drive the two out of their land.

The two gnomes were walking along the path in the woods when they met up with a wandering gnome. The two beat up the gnome, stole his food and clothing, and walked away laughing. Speric had noticed that in one of the pockets of the gnome's pants there was a diary which had a message in it. The message described a treasure-filled kingdom called Luxom; the kingdom was ruled by a dying king who had a daughter named Urol. The king of Luxom had announced a contest in which the winner of that contest should marry Urol, thus sharing the kingdom with her.

Speric told Gnoric of the message and together the two made their way toward the kingdom of Luxom. When they arrived they saw thousands of others including hobbits, elves, dwarves, and other gnomes all gathered in front of Luxom's castle. The contest was about to begin. The king announced to the contestants that whoever should find the magic crown hidden in the Forbidden Zone, which contains the Deadly Dragon and the evil magician, shall have the hand of Urol. So the contest began at dawn. But Gnoric and Speric did not go at all; their plan was to steal from the one who dared go into the Forbidden Zone to retrieve the crown.

Three days later only an elf appeared from the Forbidden Zone. Everyone else was either turned to stone by the evil magician or eaten by the dragon. In his hand he held the magic crown. Gnoric and Speric killed the elf and stole the crown.

On the way to the castle Gnoric became greedy and attempted to elude his brother. Speric also had the same thought. That night while Speric was sleeping Gnoric took the crown and left. But the crown Gnoric took was a fake one; instead it turned whoever held it in his hand a long time into stone. Satisfied, Speric took the real magic crown to the king.

The king was very pleased to see Speric's finding. The king put the crown on and used its magic to turn the whole castle into gold. He then turned to Speric and turned him into stone. The king let out a thundering laugh that echoed through the whole kingdom. For legends say that the king had no daughter named Urol. In fact, he had no daughter at all.

Fable

*After reading a number of fables, write one of your own
by telling a brief story that makes a moral point or observation
about life. State the moral in a separate sentence after the story.
Give the story a modern or remote setting. Test your fable by
temporarily leaving off the moral until your listeners can
supply their ideas about what it is.*

Variants:
- *Write a new fable for an old moral, perhaps with
partners who are doing the same for the same
moral*
- *Write a modernization of an old fable*
- *Re-tell a news story as a fable with a moral.*

*Have a fable fest: post them in displays; print up booklets
of them; do readings of them.*

The Busy Boulder

LISA KLOTCHMAN

Edgar was a big rock; he was almost a boulder. All the other rocks
looked up to Edgar because he was involved in everything and great at
everything he did. He had straight "A's" while going to college full-
time and working a part-time job. His popular band, The Stones, took
many hours of rehearsal and performance. He also spent time training
for the upcoming cliff-rolling-off championship. He even found time
for a steady, passionate relationship with Heloise.

Heloise kept asking Edgar to slow down. Not because she wanted
more time with him—she too was very busy—but because she was
worried about him. He was running himself ragged. Heloise had spied
some hairline cracks and gouges in Edgar's previously smooth surface.
Edgar insisted he was all right; he was strong and quite young, only a
few million years old.

The day of the diving championship arrived. Edgar was feeling a
bit tired but he was stubborn and wouldn't let Heloise put him to bed
in the warm sand. Edgar's turn came up and he rolled off the cliff. He
hit the water and shattered into a thousand pieces. The townspeople
were shocked and deeply saddened. Heloise sobbed violently, but she
kept thinking, "I told him so." Heloise went on with her life, settled
down with a slab of granite, and forgot about Edgar.

Moral: You cannot be everything if you work to do everything.

The Moose and the Goose

TERRY ANDERSON

Once upon a time there was a moose who lived in the vast regions of Northern Canada. Of course this moose didn't know he lived in the vast regions of anywhere—his whole world consisted of the trees and bushes and tall reeds around a small pond which he called home. In the warmer months when food was plentiful, he never wandered out of sight of his pond; in the cold of winter, he sometimes had to travel a mile or two in one direction or another to find enough to eat, but his pond was in a secluded and protected valley which provided him year-round sustenance and which freed him from the necessity of long migrations for food. In general, he was a happy moose.

There were, however, a lot of little things about life that bothered the moose. He always found enough to eat, but it seemed to him that the tastiest morsels were always out of reach in the middle of some bramble bush or up the side of some cliff. In the spring and summer the ground around his pond became a swamp, making walking a messy business, and the air was full of pesty mosquitoes. In the winter these problems were replaced by the bitter cold winds and the search for unfrozen drinking water. Then there was the ever-present inconvenience of poor T.V. reception. But the worst part of life in the wilds for the moose was the night-time and the strange noises that accompanied it—the moose spent many a sleepless night haunted by visions of wolves and mountain lions and grizzly bears and anything else that might be hungry enough to take a bite of him. But the moose accepted all of these things as just part of the reality of a moose's life, and as long as he could complain now and then to his friends, he was satisfied.

One day in the summer the moose met a goose down at the pond. After formally introducing themselves to each other, the goose began to tell the moose about the many wonderful things he had seen and done in his travels back and forth between Canada and Central America. Not only was the goose an experienced traveler, he was also an EST graduate, and he was anxious to teach the moose all that he knew about life. Well, the moose was very curious about all the things the goose had to say, and he listened very politely, but he had great difficulty relating the goose's experiences to his experience as a moose.

The goose appreciated the moose's attentiveness, but he was also puzzled by the moose's silence. At last he asked the moose to tell him about his own life.

"There's not much to tell," said the moose humbly. "Compared to the wonderful adventures you have had in the world, I lead a very drab existence in my little circle of the woods."

"It's all a matter of perspective, my friend," said the goose. "No matter what you're faced with, you always have the choice of taking the broader perspective, of looking at the big picture as I like to call it."

"That's easy for you to say—you get a bird's eye view of things any time you want. I'm stuck here on the ground."

"Ah hah! That's where you go wrong! You may be a moose, but that's mainly because you've chosen to *think* like a moose. No offense, but you've chosen a very narrow perspective—you've chosen to let the little picture define who you are."

The moose was confused—surely he must be missing something. "I don't want to sound stupid, but it seems to me there are things about being a moose that don't change just because I think about them from a different perspective."

"Such as?"

"Well, food for one. A moose has to spend a lot of time looking for food."

"Food problems are cyclical," said the goose knowingly. "Planning ahead for seasonal shifts can take care of most contingencies. Also, when food is scarce in one area, it's usually plentiful in another area— everything balances out."

"So what am I supposed to do? I can't just fly away!"

"The word *can't* is one you've chosen in order to keep your life on a familiar track. Of course you can't fly, but if you really wanted to change, you could choose to *think* like a goose. Maybe you could hop on an airplane for Central America."

"Where would I get the money? And what would a moose do in Central America?" The moose really wanted to understand, but he was also getting a bit angry at the goose's easy answers.

"I can't solve your specific problems for you," said the goose. "You have to be responsible for your own solutions. But what I can tell you is that if you spend all your energy making excuses for yourself, you won't solve anything."

"You act as if I have the power to change anything—what about my T.V. reception? How can I do anything about that?"

"Well, I've heard they have new disc antennas—"

"—which cost about $5,000!"

"Well, then adapt to the situation. Take up playing chess, reading poetry, going to the opera instead."

None of the other mooses played chess, and he couldn't read, and there wasn't an opera house within a thousand miles, but the moose raised none of these objections to the goose's advice—he didn't want to make any more excuses for his miserable existence. He knew that the goose was just trying to broaden his horizons and to overcome his

feelings of helplessness. Ironically, though, when he saw how responsible he was for creating the narrow boundaries of his life, it made
him feel more helpless than ever. But he was above all a polite moose
and said nothing to his visitor.

Early the next morning the moose was startled from his bed in
the tall reeds by strange noises in the nearby trees.

"Oh my gosh—danger is approaching!" he said to the goose, who
was bedded down a little ways off.

"Now come on—you don't know that for sure," said the goose.
"This is an example of letting your little picture dictate your emotional
response. You're choosing to be afraid before you know exactly what's
out there."

"I'm not choosing anything!" said the moose. "I just feel it in my
bones—maybe it's a mountain lion!"

"What you need is the big picture," said the goose. "You stay
hidden in these tall reeds and I'll fly up and check things out." And he
did.

Suddenly the moose heard a loud bang, followed by a human
voice shouting, "We may not find a moose on this trip, but at least
we'll have a goose dinner on the way home!"

*Moral: It's dangerous to always ignore the little picture in favor of the big picture;
sometimes the little picture is the big picture.*

Poetry

Sensory Poems

Take notes at some locale of your choice, as for Visit, *and
look for a moment or motif in your observations and reactions
that might make a good poem. You might build up a mood or
set of images or story or reflection that would benefit from
richer language or less common phrasing or more compact
expression than one usually expects in prose. Also, what things
not at all present in the scene you observed does your imagination connect to what you did observe? Post up or print up and
hand out. Or collect your sensory poems into a booklet.*

Sensory Notes
Justine Ehlers

A little boy sits on top of a small tree, he rocks it, continually shifting. His high-pitched "Mommy" gets carried away by the wind. Garbled talk.

A guy lays flat on the cold grass, his arms and legs out-stretched like some dead thing.

Ah hah. I expected there to be more squirrels. I see one, standing erect, head thrust slightly forward, still, his hands clutched together, a shrill, short bird cry, a dirty, rumpled looking black bird picking among the empty peanut shells.

As I sit, more cautiously show themselves from behind rocks, eyeing me expectedly. They scramble a little ways, stop, peer around, then advance again. Some are shyer than others. One was looking at me. I moved my foot, his little grey face vanished behind a rock. Two sit eyeing me, faces toward me. I wonder if she has a peanut. One gets disgusted at my inaction and scrambles away. The other looks at me for awhile; he leaves. The big ones are bold, coming up to people for goodies. The children, skittish. Oh, they'll come up alright but snatch the goodie away and high tail it out of there. One biggie calmly sits on a girl's knee munching away.

Another biker. He uncertainly passes my bench, not wanting me to get any ideas.

The ocean wind flaps my notes; I must hold them or the wind will claim them like the sea claims fallen branches and turns them into driftwood. I feel it against my cheeks.

Haze over the ocean, not one of those clear sunny days. The clouds are spread thin on the pale blue. I can see them steadily being blown in.

Hear the squirrels cracking their peanuts.

Other people watch. There isn't much talking, as if talk somehow would break the magic.

A little squirrel sits routinely eating his prize.

A big squirrel comes around from the back, snatches the peanuts away and goes away. The little gray scutters on with a quick little cry.

One bold one searches the ground for that one astray peanut not 4 feet from me. He even eats some bread, blinking his eyes and puffing his cheeks. Another big guy runs toward him and chases the other off. This one bullies the little guys, as a lady starts tossing peanuts, handouts, a big ground gathers, much scuttling, running to and fro.

Some little boy whispers something confidential to me, he comes up behind me—

Same one that was in the tree—

Hands hold a swaying bag of Planter's peanuts one goes underneath my leg; I see his claws now, twitching nose.
Spoiled, won't take crackers, even whole wheat and sesame. Someone had to spoil the brick with some blue graffiti.
"Wait a minute. Are they whole wheat?" gave mischievous grin.
"Yes, whole wheat, sesame seed and everything."
Sun plays on water, shimmering, a boat speeds by in distance.

Little Boy

A little boy suddenly sneaks up beside me as I
stare at the ocean.
His little hand holds a swaying bag of peanuts.
He points to a squirrel.
He whispers confidentially into my ear.
"What was that?" I ask.
He repeats his garbled message.
He slips away.
I never knew what he said.

Fussy

A lady offers a squirrel something.
The squirrel sniffs it, scampers away.
"What are you feeding them?" I ask.
"Crackers."
We both retreat from each other.
"Wait a minute."
"Are they whole wheat?"
The lady looks up.
She catches my mischievous grin.
"Yes."
She smiles slowly.
"Whole wheat, sesame seed, and everything.
I put some mayonnaise on them...."
We chat awhile.
Fussy squirrels.

Sensory Notes
Karyn Williams

Chaperones
school
classroom
teachers
hallways of life
strangers
desks
chairs
puppy love
shy lovers
cracked voices
nervous
stuttering
love
school dance
running make-up

tripping
crying
imagining
great expectations
frustration
letters
understanding
fear
love
caring
togetherness
first loves
excitement
disappointment
loud whispers
notes

The Unknown Love

I tried to sing so you could hear
  how I feel inside
but my voice cracked and sounded queer
  and now I want to hide.
I tried to speak but now I know
  I'll just stutter for a time
yet you won't understand, my dear,
  though you are not one blind.
I tried to dance so you could see
  but I lost my stride.
I stumbled and fell not gracefully
  and now I want to cry.
I tried to paint with colors clear
  this picture in my mind.
The colors ran, the picture smeared
  frustration is unkind.
I have to write—It's my last chance
  to show you how I feel
I could not do anything
  but my love for you is real.

Memory Poems

Take some memory that came up when you were writing notes for Memories and write it as a poem, transforming facts freely to develop some feeling or imagery or climax. Or change into a poem something you wrote for Autobiography or Memoir. Let your imagination play with the original facts, not necessarily to alter them but to underlay or overlay them with similar actions from other times and places and domains of thought. Rehearse and read it aloud to others, or include it in a collection of other memories or poems.

Sunday Night Bath

GAYNELLE WOODS

Mom sent my screams to you
to untangle
my coarse, knotted, red hair.
Propped between your legs
my arms hung loose
draped over your sturdy knees.
At the microphone
Ed Sullivan introduced Elvis Presley
as your hands moved
the wide-toothed comb gently
through my hair.
"I want Dad to do this every Sunday night,"
I yawned to my mother.
"Just keep combing, Dad," I mumbled
sinking slowly, warmly, in dream
to sleep.

Back Then

TIM THORNTON

I wore cut-offs—it was Saturday.
We mooched Kool-aid from someone's mom.
We rode bikes—we had red mustaches.

We played football behind the backstop,
By the house with the bulldog—where the teachers couldn't see.
You lost your buttons when I tackled you—your mom was pissed.
I didn't eat lunch at your house for three days.

We took plums from the Donaldson's tree after school,
I climbed up—the low ones were already gone.
You yelled when Mrs. Donaldson came out.
She had curlers in her hair—she couldn't run fast,
She was old—maybe even thirty.

Mom made spaghetti—Dad said we were moving.
"But I don't want to move!"
He said he had a new job.
"I'll never have friends again."
"You'll make new little friends."
It was too late for that—I was ten.

Adventure

KRIS GROH

You pleased me with the request.
A phone call. Just past midnight. For rescue.

A dark, quiet freeway: L.A., three-thirty a.m.
Night gives into morning at Tejon Pass.

I found you—bruised and tired—in the foothills.
We kissed. We swam in melted snow;
our singular ripples collided.

The Casket

ANGEL PARTLOW

was much larger than I expected
I pretended
that it was empty.
Yellow roses
were arranged on top.
The arrangement
was too small.

Coloring with Sarah

MARGARETE MILLER

She closes in on the task before her,
  the crayons spread on the kitchen table,
    as we each pick our favorite page.

  Her tongue is pressed against her lips and her butterfly
    eyebrows frown in concentration because it is v e r y

    difficult to stay in the bounds when you are as small
                    as she is.

I, the tease, niggler, playing it light because today
we are two friends coloring together, tell her that not
all of her colors are in the lines, and that my picture
is coming out much better than hers.

Serenely, she lets me know that this is to be expected,
as she is only four years old.

We color in silence.

  I sing-song in the parody of children everywhere that I
    am going to take the purple crayon and keep it for
      my own and it will be mine and she cannot use
        it unless she asks permission and then
          maybe I will let her use it and maybe
          I won't and these are my rules and
              she must do the same.

She nods her approval. She understands rules. We continue
to color.

              Before long,
          she is asking to use my
            purple crayon.
      I tell her no, she cannot use it, because
    I want to use it later so I want to keep it ready
  and I am teasing her and testing her and loving her.

Silence.

And then the child-dear that she is
  offers me her orange crayon that she has been keeping

according to my rules and she tells me that I can
use it any time I want.

And the only sounds in the kitchen where we are coloring
are the scratching of our crayons, the chirping of the
parakeets, and the smile around my heart...

My Father Loved Water

MAUREEN NEAL

1.

I remember
my father
hated cats
and
loved water
which he sprayed
in ferocious green streams
after the cat
clinging to
white blossoms
and black branches
in the apple tree
where I built
a treehouse with
broken nails
the roof held down
with baling wire
and lilacs from my dreams.

2.

I remember
my father
hated cats
and
loved water
near the river where
we studied rocks, choosing
round sand-soft stones
as flat as my cheekbone
to skip
as many as

fifteen times
across
smooth blue plates of water,
quiet as death.

                    3.

I remember
my father
hated cats
and
loved water
where
we swam in the pool
and
he bicycled water
with his toes,
waiting for me to jump
my heart cold
and damp as a toad's belly
into his arms
we got no
plastic water wings:
he would not let us cheat
in deep water
we must learn
to float
alone,
the cool air of our
blood the only certainty.

New Year's Day in Town: The Party

MELVIN RIGGS

A little double-breasted top coat,
A small fedora
To one side of his head
Against the cold,
A miniature of his father,
He walked the frozen gravel with
Steps as big as he could make,
Careful not to scuff,
And waited to be lifted over icy spots,

To ring the bell himself,
To wait, safely back from the
Glass door put up in winter,
To be kissed and unwrapped and
(Shoes dried)
Set on the sofa
(His shoes not touching fabric)
And given *The Saturday Evening Post*
And *Boy's Life*
And a picture album,
Told not to play with the basket of
Sea shells by the window
(Even though they held the
Sound of the sea)
And not to put his hand in the
Mouth of the white bear
Under the coffee table.
The same bear on which his father had been
Photographed when very small
And on which he had been photographed
And had been shown the pictures.
(Both were smiling, sprawling on
The furry, flat and gaping bear.)

Quiet in the room,
He sits.
Sometimes he rustles pages to let
Them murmuring in the next room know that he is
Looking at the magazines.

He is brought,
On a napkin-soundproofed tray,
Two soft cookies on a plate,
And one small glass of milk,
Set over the center of the bear's white back.

The murmuring becomes voices,
His father's words above the rest
His father's words louder, sharper, shorter
Than the rest,
His father's words like
Rifle shots and echoes.

Then only the sound of
The sea shells in the basket.

Hot and sick
Standing on cushions
(Knowing that his shoes are clean)
Hands tight against the sofa back
Straining
He still can't see them.
Swallowing,
He slides to sitting.

At home he could have sat on the floor
In front of the radio,
His head resting on the grill,
His picture books around him.

He knows that one small shell
The color of the bear's dark tongue
Will fit in the back of the bear's mouth.
No one will see it unless they
Squat and stare.

Songs

Write new words to a familiar tune. Just try out different words until some begin to fit that make some kind of sense or nonsense, then follow whatever that idea is until you have a new set of words. You might choose a tune with partners, then each write your own words separately and compare and make a booklet giving the tune. Sing your song or songs with a group— and perhaps for another group.

The next step is to make up both the tune and the words. Some good lines or phrases might come that you could try to vocalize until a melody begins to come also. Use each to draw out the other. With partners you might re-do some story as a musical by writing songs for its more "lyrical" moments.

Running

Randy Ramirez

She walks the streets on a cold dark night, afraid and all alone.

Don't have much money, no place to sleep, she's a fugitive from

home. But she doesn't know, you can't make it alone on the

streets of L.A. She's got lots of time for talk teenage runaway.

Life don't seem fair when you're seventeen and hurt becomes a rule.

She wonders if she can ever go back, she's tired of playin' the fool.

The man in the car said he'd make her a star, but there are

no free rides today for a dollar you can watch her dance, teenage runaway.

Life goes on a chapter in time, answers to questions never asked.

Some crazy guy with a gun in his hand put an end to the running at last

The newspaper said she was already dead before the bullets had cut her

down she was running for her life, not from, teenage runaway

Be-a-Thing Poems

Pretend you are some object, plant, or animal and speak as that other being. How would it perceive some things? Get inside it and look at something you want to get a fresh perspective on. Use this imaginary displacement as a way of coming upon and expressing feelings or ideas you have about something or discover that you have about something.

Sentiments

NOREEN GRAYSON DREYER

I am a rag doll.
My heart is sewn to my sleeve
as carefully as a yawn to the weary.
My face is brought together in stitches of
someone's sense of humor.
I breathe the air of silly putty
and spit red and white striped mints
when you kiss me hello.

I am not a "Where have you been all my life?" rag doll.
Definitely not that.
I am as lovable and forgettable
as anything else.

I sit on a shelf in a slump of myself.
In calico and pinafore,
I watch you make love for the first time
and I cringe for you.
"I could have told you" pokes through
the stitched mouth.

There is no decency for eyes that never close;
forever measuring life. The wide opened surprise,
candy coated to my face.

Again and again I want to tell you "I'm steppin' out."
but you would never believe,
I watched that leave too, with the rest.

I am a rag doll.
Born of good intentions and loved so quickly,
my eyes could pop if they could

right off the flat surface of my face.
The face that doesn't grow old
just boring.
The face that can not speak its mind,
but if it could
if it could...

Function Poems

Imagine a poem that fills the function of one of the following occasions: a lullaby, a farewell, a will, a blues lament, a speech, a eulogy (statement of praise), a greeting, a piece of advice, an invocation (calling on some force or personage), an epitaph (headstone verse), a dirge or elegy (funeral lament), a blessing, a curse, a sermon, an insult, an invitation, a prayer, a set of directions, a celebration, a confession, a prophecy, a catalog, a thank-you note, etc. Use it for a real occasion, perform it as if for such, post it with poems written by others for a similar occasion, or include in a collection of your miscellaneous poems.

Apology
C.D. JUNG

I am afraid
to tell you
Please don't yell
Count to ten
The left side
of the BMW
has a
slight dent
where it collided
with a trash truck

(Greeting)

Color of Distraction

J. MARK BEAVER

We have these
Yellow, yellow lemons
In a basket
In our kitchen

The sky is dark today
And the air is cold
Outside
And the light I write by
Is synthetic and stale

I greet the smell
And the effortless color
Of these
Yellow, yellow
Lemons

(Curse)

My Truck

TOM HELM

I'm selling this silly, sloppy, septic truck,
With its blue hue too terribly troubling to renew,
And the unrefined engine grinding and grating grotesquely.
I hope it happens upon a huge hole
And falls forever
          and never
                  returns whatsoever.
May the pistons putrefy and the rocker arms rust,
And the differential descend into decaying disarray.
May grime in time cover it,
and a slime climb over it,
And at dawn
hereupon become
withdrawn until
it is
gone.

(Congratulation)

A Wedding Cry

CHRIS REGBER

She was my best friend.
Now she comes to you.
We were happy,
Never sad.
She found you,
That gives me peace,
May you love her as much as she loves life!
For yesterday she was my best friend,
But today, she is your wife.

(Celebration)

Gardening

GAYNELLE WOODS

All I'd known
was how to pull muddy carrots
from my father's garden,
but today
svelte green sprouts
part the moist plot around me.
I am amazed!
The watering has paid off!

Scented carnations perk,
camelia blossoms stare,
night blooming jasmine
begs for the sun to go down.
What do I do next?

Dash indoors
hunt for *Sunset's Lawn and Garden.*
Skip through the pages
devour instructions on how
to feed, water, prune, kill bugs.

Legs propped on a kitchen chair,
sipping iced-tea with lemon,
flipping pages, finger nails
gritted with dirt,
sweat behind my knees,
dripping down the spine of my T-shirt

I see my life blossoming.
From the window,
birds-of-paradise peek in at me,
bouquets of black-eyed Susan wave,
pink and lavender bachelor's buttons
stand tall in the breeze.

I hang out the window
wave back—
Things are taking off!

(Curse)

Her

LISA BORNSTEIN

She shouldn't be allowed to live in this world.
How anyone could be such a selfish self-centered sleeze
is beyond me.
I hate this feeling I have for her, but more than that I hate
her.
I have to despise her for loving someone who was once mine.
I really wouldn't care if it was anyone else...
really, I just wish it was her.
I would really like to rearrange that perfect smile and that
tiny button nose,
and that smooth sickening ivory skin,
Oh, and that name, Francine, what kind of name is Francine?
How could he chose her over me?
It must be that cherry red 320i BMW, or that 24 karat rock
on her left index finger.
That's it, oh what a son of a bitch he is, a purely
materialistic son of a bitch.

I hope they both lead very unhappy lives, and I hope they have a fat freckled-face kid named Gertrude.

(Celebration)

Christmas Eve

J. SOMMERMANN

Every year I treat myself
to a walk in the fields
in the snow

And watch the withered stalks from yesteryear
bend with the weight
of the snow

Sometimes the moonlight illuminates my path
with its radiant beams
on the snow

It is the nightwalk I take on my birthday
through the cornfields
covered with snow.

Poems of Address

Write out some feeling or idea by directing it toward a person, place, or thing with which it is connected. Address directly in the poem whoever or whatever caused, inspired, or was otherwise involved in what you have to express. Make use of this address to focus and organize what you have to say and to muster a distinct tone of voice or dramatize a relationship.

Unheard Love

CHRISTINE HELLERS

Stolen time runs shallow
As I sit and watch the sea.
Pale the grey wave crashes;
Fine mists rise up to me.
I wander to the water,
Thoughts echo in my ears.
I pick a seashell off the shore—
Your voice is all I hear.
Listen to the pounding surf,
See it rush the shore.
Watch her gather up her prize,
Then scurry back for more.
Now I climb the cliff again,
Beyond the ocean's greed.
With all her riches still she takes
From me the love I need.
High above the windy coast
I gazed down into the sea
Thinking thoughts so bittersweet
I toasted you and me.
Standing on that rocky perch,
Wind catching every word,
I made a toast to you and me
...a toast that no one heard.

The Eggman and Me

PETER BELLI

You say I don't care.
But I do!
But not about Mr. Clean
and soft downy polo shirts.
Or about matching socks
rolled in balls and children's
designer jeans.
Or about an I.U.D. that need not
protect me from you anymore and
those dinners that never last.

You say I don't care.
But I do!
But not about the hidden dust
and dreams of supermarket checkout stands.
Or about the price of milk
and the eggman's mother whose
son never sleeps.
Or about the newsboy's harmless
desires and the cards that hold
your name and my address.

You say I don't care.
But I do!
But not about you who fathers
my children once a week.
Or about the new blue sedan
that sits and stares
at the lawn mower's empty wastebag.
Or about the subtle knocking
at my window two days a week
just before dawn.

You say I don't care.
But I do!
Just ask the eggman.

Thin Skin

TAMMY MASON

Oftentimes, when I was dressed in bows,
        I would skin my knee.
As the small raspberry would appear the
        tears dropped from my eyes,
like rain from a tiny young branch. And
        you would say "Be tough! It
can't hurt that bad, honey." But it did.

Now I am dressed in silks. I no longer
        skin my knees, instead, you skin
                my heart.
And you still say "Be tough! It can't
        hurt that bad, honey." But
                it does.

You see, like changing leaves the
bruises have faded from
my knees.
But the bruises you have whipped
upon my heart shall
never fade.

Cat and Master

DIANNE SUTTON

My name is Cat.
Do not call,
"Here, Kitty, Kitty, Kitty,"
and think that I will come.
I will come
when I am ready.

By day I sleep
in a box.
I dream of what I will do
the moment you turn your back.
I see visions
of blood and bone.

Do not feed me
saucers of milk;
I am not
a milk-and-toast cat.
I will hunt
when I am hungry.

I move softly,
but have no doubt:
some night when you are sleeping,
you'll hear my claws scratch your door.
I will hiss,
"Here comes your Cat."

Care Less

HEATHER KUNZ

The fact that you have never
   cared for anyone
As much as you care for yourself
   doesn't bother me
Half as much as does the realization
   that I wasted
So much time and energy
   pretending that you
Gave a damn about me.

Pegasus

ROSEMARY WILLIAMS

A reddish blur races across my vision.
Dust rises, settles, and there he stands,
Legs quivering, nose high in the air to catch every scent,
Ears pricked forward to catch every sound.
The sun shines brightly, turning his coat into liquid copper.
He spins, squeals, bucks, and goes racing off again,
Movements so free, so smooth, so joyous.
Come to me, my Pegasus.
Let me climb upon your back so we can fly together.

Reflective Poems

Look over notes from a session for Dialog of Ideas *or* Stream of Consciousness *or* Meditative Reflection *and pick out a thought, thought train, or constellation of thoughts and fashion this as a poem. Keeping some of the concrete content in which the thoughts occurred may be very helpful. Or try to bring out feelings, perhaps less well noted, that were under-riding the thoughts. Look for unexpected connections among thoughts or feelings that at first seem unrelated. Do some of your thoughts focus on an object, person, place, or event that might provide a concrete center for the physical level of your poem?*

Afternoon Soaps

MICHELE LeBLANC

They say she got depressed
cause her husband was undressed
and in bed with her ex-best friend
Her mother had cancer
Her kid was a topless dancer
and her dad was in jail again
Her brother beat his wife
He was sent to jail for life
and her sister used L.S.D.
She's living on welfare
Her kids don't help cause
 they don't care
And she cried cause she wasn't
 free
Doctors say she's going blind
She drinks a fifth each morn
 by nine
Her troubles were too much for me
when her sobs filled the air
I got up from my chair
and I shut the damned T.V.!

New York Is the A Train

P.J. RICATTO

New York is the A Train
It's Harlem, Greenpoint and the South Bronx.

It's Ukranian guys selling hot dogs
and Haitian guys selling sun glasses.

It's talking to drunken bums
Who tell you they used to be a
contender.

It's playing softball on Memorial
Day and football on Thanksgiving.

It's crazy old guys who look like
they live on the street, reading
nuclear physics journals in the
Public Library.

It's getting drunk in Central Park
on St. Patrick's day or playing
soccer with a Rasti in
Washington Square.

It's eating cheeseburger deluxes
at Greek diners.

It's watching 15 city workers
standing around while one
guy fills in the pothole.

New York is basketball in the school yard
Not racquetball at the club.

New York is shoeshine guys, Transit cops,
Shortorder cooks and immigrant factory
workers

                         NOT

Lawyers, Wall Street executives or so
called patrons of the arts.

New York is the A train, not
Sardi's, the Plaza or Tavern on
the Green.

It's sitting in the blue seats
at the Garden and chanting
Red Seats Suck.

I feel sorry for the people who
come from Europe and visit Saks,
Bloomingdale's and Bergdorf Goodman
because they missed out on Modell's
and John's Bargain Store.

They may have toured the museums,
seen the plays and strolled
down 5th Ave.
But they didn't get to
ride on the A train.

Teaching Children to Talk
KATHERINE BRADFORD

Once I wrote a
poem about my mother,
using phrases
she once used
to describe peacocks
that screamed nightly
three doors down
from the honeymoon-is-over
house where she lay married
to a man who never
touched.
"Perhaps," said a reader, "the
perception you remember
having as a baby of your
mother's desperation,
based upon an ordinary
statement that compared
peacocks to a woman screaming,
is too subtle
to serve as the
subject of a poem."

Saying Yes
SCOTT HUTCHISON

The cliff drops white and grey
                    in sheerness
                    below me
Sea-eagles wing their way over currents
     eyeing me   knowing

I'm neither of their kind
nor my own
My gaze extends over ocean
My ears receive the rushing of the waves
I look up
and elsewhere

My books and teachers always stated
the impossibility of man in flight
they cited myths and attempts
all failures
then moved on
to machines
and sensible ways
I waited for three days
with my arms upheld
I believed the thing
no one could or can tell me different   no one ever gave
satisfactory reason
for the failure
no attainable facts
blocking the path to try

My mother screamed
and called me monster
damned me as some other's child
she
did not want to believe
the townspeople gathered nets
and guns
I flew from rooftop
to window ledge
tears bursting from my heart
words raging from my mouth
I was no different
they could be with me if they only chose
If they only said yes
if they didn't hate themselves

I have yet to tire
there is no exertion
waves and birds and sun
watch and wait
they believe that they have seen
foolish mortals fly before

A three-quarters moon
                    arises
                              for me to fill it
        they say there's no oxygen
                              up there
                              in that space
                but I don't believe them.

Cogitation
(Thinking Over and Thinking Through)

Dialog of Ideas

Let two voices called A and B discuss some issue of real concern to you. Set this down in duolog form without stage directions. Make up this dialog straight off for about 30 minutes. Have them say all the thoughts that come to you from all points of view. This can be performed by others, printed up, or used as a basis for further writing. Revise first by reading it aloud, perhaps with a partner, and making changes where ideas or expression seem weak, or add new ideas if they occur at this point. Use this dialog as a way to generate ideas on an issue without having to conclude in favor of one viewpoint.

Caring
DEBBIE CHIN

MOM: I'm so tired. I should put Morfar to bed now. I think I'll lay down for awhile first. Could you do the dishes for me, Kim?

KIM: Sure Mom. (*pause*) Mom, I really think you should put Morfar in a nursing home. You're dragging yourself around. Each time something happens to him he goes downhill. He always perks up but not quite as far. It's just getting to be too much for you. You're walking around like a zombie. You're sleeping if you aren't taking care of Morfar. He's a 24-hour job. (*pause*) I love you. I want you to be happy.

MOM: I love you too, Kim. You know that. I do get tired sometimes of bathing him, feeding him and moving him from bed to chair and back. I especially don't like cleaning him. He's in so much pain when I try to move him. I just want him to be with his family. I think he gets more mental and physical support from the people

263

who love him rather than those who don't love him.

KIM: I'm sure that Valley Nursing Home would take good care of him. They are all so nice there. You know that from when we visited there. It couldn't be like the other nursing home he was in. Valley smells so much better. The people are friendlier too. You've heard good things about that nursing home. He'll be just as happy there. We'll visit him every day, Mom.

MOM: I don't think he'd be happy there. He became so disorientated when he was in the hospital last. The same thing will probably happen in a nursing home. He'd lose his privacy because he'd be in a room with at least one other person. I really don't like the feeling I get in nursing homes either. For some reason I just get uncomfortable. They're just so expensive too.

KIM: Mom, you have to start living your own life. You've taken care of Morfar for five years. I'm sure he'd want you to do things you'd like to do. You haven't been able to do a lot of things because you have to stay home with Morfar. You should be able to go shopping or to the beach for the whole day without having to worry about Morfar. We can't even go on a vacation. You know Auntie couldn't take care of him because her stomach just wouldn't handle it. You can't even get a job. I know I sound a little hard on Morfar. I don't mean to. I love him so much, but I know he'd want you to put him in a nursing home.

MOM: It's just not as simple as all that, Kim. I know there's not much I can do outside the house. At home I'm so much more able to devote all of my time and attention to Morfar. At the nursing home the nurses have more patients to take care of.

KIM: Yes, I know, but you're not a nurse. They are professionally trained. Since Morfar's been here it's been hard for you to get a doctor to come and see him. They also have so much more equipment like whirlpools and physical therapy equipment.

MOM: The home health nurse and aide come by to see me a couple times a week to help me out a little. They've been helping me with his bed sores and help me with the kind of medication he should be getting, things like that. I'm sure I'm more gentle with Morfar than anyone else could ever be.

KIM: You know we can't give him the strongest medication possible. Only the doctors and nurses can give him pain shots. I know how hard it is for you to see him in such pain. It's hard for me. It makes me so sad to see him getting worse every day practically.

MOM: Kim, I can see what you mean, but I really feel I should take care of my father. After all he has taken care of me practically all my life. I want to give him my care and love which he so rightfully deserves and needs and I want to give it to him. I want to be able to do as much as I can for him while we still have him. Kim, I really do appreciate your concern, but no matter how many pros and cons there are, I know he's much happier here with us than he would be in a nursing home and so I want to keep him here even though it might mean making some sacrifices.

Colonialism
ROBERT J. BOYD

BEN: This is a nice pond.

TOM: Yeah; I found it just last week. It's real nice here. And look at all the frogs.

BEN: Must be a million of them.

TOM: Yeah, there might be. I was thinking of maybe taking some home with me.

BEN: What for?

TOM: For pets; just because I kind of feel like it.

BEN: I don't think that you really should.

TOM: Oh? Why?

BEN: Because they might die. You know.

TOM: No, that'd never happen. I'd take real good care of them.

BEN: Yeah, I know you would, Tom; but still, I don't think that it would be right.

TOM: I wasn't going to eat them.

BEN: I didn't say you were. But...I don't know. You'd just be screwing up their whole way of life.

TOM: They're only frogs.

BEN: And you're only a man.

TOM: Is that supposed to mean anything?

BEN: No, but.... They do have their own way of life, you know.

TOM: You said that. But who's to say that what I have to offer them isn't better than what they already have.

BEN: And who's to say that they really care? That they really want it?

TOM: Me.

BEN: Ah, c'mon. What kind of attitude is that?

TOM: No, think about it. With me, they'd have all the food they could ever ask for.

BEN: They've already got that, and without having to live in a fish tank or having to have their bodies touched and squeezed every other minute.

TOM: Nice sentence.

BEN: I try.

TOM: Right. (*Pauses*) But living in a fish tank wouldn't be so bad for them.

BEN: It would if they like their freedom.

TOM: 'Who needs freedom when you're being take care of?'

BEN: Are you serious?

TOM: No. That was just some quote I heard and that...You don't think that they'd be happy?

BEN: Would you if someone imposed their way of life on you?

TOM: I think it would depend on what their way was.

BEN: But what if you were happy, and they gave you no choice?

TOM: That's different. But I'm sure that there would still be some advantages.

BEN: Worth the loss of your freedom, your culture?

TOM: Who knows? I couldn't say till I was actually in that situation. Take the frogs. If I take them home with me, you're right, I would be imposing my way of life on them—after all, they're not asking me to do anything for them. But, if I do take them, their lives will be better in that they'd be cared for, and they'd have any medical attention that they might need.

BEN: Maybe they don't want that either.

TOM: And maybe they do. If my way gives them a better life, don't you think that I'm right in giving it to them?

BEN: But that's not what you're doing, or would be doing. You're not giving them a choice. Sure, it might be better; but is it right to force it on them?

TOM: Sometimes people don't know what's the best thing for them.

BEN: And sometimes they do and still don't want it, not if it costs too much.

TOM: You're talking like I'd be some kind of king over them.

BEN: But wouldn't you? I mean, you'd have absolute power over their lives, as they're living under your 'rule,' and...I don't know. There'd be a loss of freedom, and maybe happiness.

TOM: You don't think they'd revolt if they hated me, do you?

BEN: Who knows?

TOM: Now I won't be able to sleep nights.

BEN: Then leave them alone.

TOM: I don't know. I'm still kind of thinking about it. After all, it wouldn't cost so much to take care of them. They're only frogs.

BEN: Frogs have their lives, too. Respect that.

TOM: And what if I do take them home?

BEN: I don't know.

TOM: Food, shelter, medical care, a place for their young, someone to watch over them. They'd have it all.

BEN: I hope you get warts.
TOM: That's an old wives' tale.
BEN: We'll see. (*Pause*) You didn't mention how they'd be held captive.
TOM: Isn't that going too far?
BEN: Could they go into the living room when they wanted?
TOM: No.
BEN: What would happen if they screwed up on your carpet?
TOM: Mom would get at them.
BEN: Would that ever happen here in this frog pond, if you were to leave them alone?
TOM: Of course not.
BEN: Then don't bother them.
TOM: Is it all right if I eat them?
BEN: As long as you cook them first.
TOM: Your house?
BEN: Sure.
(*After a moment, they both look at each other and laugh.*)
TOM: Let's get out of here.

Were We Visited by Aliens in the Past Who Were Very Advanced?

STEVE MARGOLIS

A: Come on now. If we were visited by aliens in the past we would have heard about them by now. You'd think they might have left us something to remember them by!

B: But they did! What do you think the pyramids are?

A: The pyramids are burial chambers for the Pharoahs. The slaves built them so Egypt would have somewhere to put their dead.

B: Oh really? Is that why we can't even build the pyramids today with all of our modern technology? Is that why we don't even know how they did it? I think they were built as bomb shelters.

A: Bomb shelters? From what? Low flying sparrows?

B: Well, think about it.... A big structure that seems to serve no purpose but has food and furniture deep inside it. The great pyramid even has air holes! Dead people don't need air holes. And besides, the pyramids were originally covered with limestone, a mineral that reflects radiation.

A: If they were bomb shelters, why were they out in the middle of the desert? It seems to me a bomb shelter is to save people. Now, putting one out in the middle of the desert, with a hidden entrance, is a little bit farfetched. But like I said, what did they have that even resembled a bomb?

B: There are books that tell of bombs. There are even myths that tell of bombs.

A: Such as? Give me an example.

B: In the Bible, Sodom and Gomorrah were two large cities that went up in a cloud of smoke. Remember Hiroshima and the atomic bomb. Sound familiar.

A: The cities were destroyed by an earthquake that hit at the same time.

B: Really? That's why the cities in between the two were untouched? I don't think so.

A: Besides who and where were they dropped from? As far as I know, the Egyptians didn't have helicopters.

B: Well, about the people... You've heard of some of these aliens... Zeus, Poseidon, Apollo and Diana.

A: They were myths! They weren't real. They were products of poets' imaginations.

B: You know as well as I do that myths are based on real people. There is no reason they couldn't have existed. Nothing they did was impossible to explain!

A: Like thunderbolts and Poseidon with his trident?

B: For all we know the thunderbolts could have been a laser beam atop Mt. Olympus. You gotta admit that's a good place to stay if you're an alien or a god.

A: But gods are all in books. Those gods you're talking about are myths!

B: O.K. Suppose you're a farmer back in the time we're talking about. And out in space, a planet with other beings decides to take a look at earth.

A: So?

B: If they were highly civilized, then to you, a poor, uneducated farmer, they would seem like gods. Right?

A: Sure. But where did they go? Myths died out around the 1100's.

B: Maybe they decided it was time to leave man alone, so they moved out in the ocean. You know I'm talking about Atlantis.

A: Atlantis was only fiction. Scientists have gone over every place they thought Atlantis could have existed. They found nothing. What makes you think it was real?

B: Plato described a nation that was highly civilized out in the Atlantic. Plato was not a myth-maker.

A: They could have been talking about North America.

B: Except North America wasn't discovered until 700 years later.

A: Then where is it now? There are no islands in the Atlantic.

B: I know. The only thing off the coast of America and Florida is the Bermuda Triangle. My god! What a strange coincidence. Isn't that strange?

A: The Bermuda Triangle is just a hoax.

B: Tell that to the people who have disappeared in it.

A: Let's hear some more evidence. But let's hear something out of a book.

B: O.K. In the Bible again. Ezekiel went "flying" with a spirit in something that had "a horizontal vertical." Then he said the spirit had a "wheel within a wheel."

A: Ezekiel was a prophet. He was supposed to have these strange dreams.

B: Well, if you ask me, a wheel in a wheel sounds like a primitive description of a jet engine. And a jet engine is on a plane. It's funny how Ezekiel also complained of a painful stomach. Maybe he got air sick.

A: Or maybe he had a stomach ache because he ate something bad and it gave him hallucinations too. That still doesn't prove that aliens visited us a long time ago.

B: O.K. What about the giant pictures on the flatlands in South America?

A: What about them?

B: You had to see them from above to draw them. And there are no mountains. In fact, some of the pictures look more like runways.

A: That just means they liked art. It was probably part of their culture.

B: Oh sure. If I hand you a piece of chalk, you could go out on the pampas and draw me a perfect horse and one that is 600 ft wide.

A: I couldn't. But I'm sure someone back then could have.

B: And what about the lake they named Puma? When you're up in the air at about 3000 feet. The lake looks like a giant leopard.

A: They could have walked around the lake and drawn it. That's not evidence.

B: In Mexico, much of the art shows people with 3 eyes or 4 arms. Isn't that kinda strange? The Mexicans, or rather, the Aztecs, painted only what they saw.

A: That doesn't mean that they couldn't draw something strange. If in a million years, geologists discovered our Sun God out in the plaza, they'd think we were sun-worshipers, as well as bonkers.

B: That's true. I see your point. But there is no reason that aliens couldn't have landed here a long time ago. What do you think was the only life in the universe? There are as many stars as there are grains of sand on the beach. What right do you have to say you're the only one living on the entire beach?

A: Well, I guess you have a point there. But I'm still entitled to my opinion.

Dialog Converted to Essay

Rewrite your Dialog of Ideas *by merging its two voices into one but without sacrificing any good ideas. Feel free to add new ideas, get rid of weak ones, change wording, and reorganize. You may regard this as a speech, editorial, or essay and follow up accordingly. Where viewpoints conflict, incorporate both into a broader framework accommodating both, and discover ways in which the language may allow you to contain discrepant ideas in the same sentence.*

A Prime Choice of Property

STEVE MARGOLIS

A well-accepted method used by scientists to understand past civilizations and cultures is to study their remains and their effect on other cultures and people. The evolution of man took place at a very high rate. Are we to believe that man was able to evolve this quickly and establish some of the world's greatest civilizations on his own? I believe that the Earth was visited by aliens when civilization was just beginning to grow. With their advanced knowledge and resources, they helped mankind to evolve at a much faster rate than normal.

All cultures leave behind them a small reminder of their existence, whether it is a book or a series of art works. These aliens also left behind them reminders of their existence, although they may be a bit harder to find. A good example of this is the pyramids in Egypt. Although most historians consider the pyramids as burial chambers for the Pharoahs, I honestly believe that these immense structures were used as bomb shelters. If you think of a modern day bomb shelter, you imagine a large rock structure, usually concrete, with enough food and water to survive in the shelter for an extended period of time. This is the format of all the pyramids. So it's not really that much of a far-fetched story. Many critics argue that the point of having a bomb shelter is, of course, to save people; so why build bomb shelters out in the middle of the desert? But it wasn't desert then.

The Great Pyramid is one of the strongest structures ever built, yet even with our modern equipment it would still be a problem to build one, not to mention time consuming! It seems strange that people of that time period possessed the skill to build such a monument. Even taking into consideration the theory that slaves built the pyramids brick by brick, it is a little tough to swallow. One other strange thing about the pyramids is that they contain air holes; dead people usually do not need air holes.

Calling the pyramids bomb shelters implies that bombs existed. Yet everyone knows that bombs were not even used until well into the 18th century. There is, however, evidence in the Bible that bombs existed. According to scholars, the cities of Sodom and Gomorrah were destroyed by a large earthquake that totally wiped out both cities. I don't believe that they were destroyed by an earthquake. I base this on the fact that between the two cities were at least four other cities which were not even touched. The Bible also tells how the cities were destroyed in a "great cloud of fire." This description sounds a lot like a nuclear bomb exploding over the city. Naturalists have explained the clouds as steam or gas pockets beneath the cities; but again I ask, what was powerful enough to release the gas?

With all this talk of war, I have forgotten the most essential part of a battle—the people. If battles were raging using these sophisticated weapons, then the people who designed them must have had a superior knowledge of chemistry. As I stated in the first paragraph, there must have been some evidence that these superior beings actually existed. I'm sure everyone has heard some of their names: Apollo, Zeus, Hera and Poseidon. Although these people are immortalized in myths, one must remember that myths are usually based, however loosely, on real-life events. These gods did things that amazed the primitive people of days gone by, though now these things don't seem as unbelievable. Things like "flying chariots," cure-alls, and people being born from inanimate objects, like Aphrodite. (We're growing people in test tubes now!)

Gods have been attributed to such things over the years as pure exaggeration or an overly active imagination on someone's part. But with the recent launchings of the space shuttle, there is no reason to doubt that other planets have already done this. Astrologers have a saying about life on other planets: If you were a microbe living on one grain of sand at the beach, what right do you have to say that you are the only living thing on the beach? Given this fact, if space travelers did land on the Earth when it was just beginning to evolve, wouldn't primitive people consider these space travelers gods? And what better place to live than on top of a mountain where they would not interfere?

Even though recent expeditions to Mount Olympus found no such evidence of a superior race or, for that matter, of any race, the fact that these people were here is evident. Plato, one of the great philosophers, in his book the Timeaus, mentions a mighty power in the Atlantic. One might argue that this power could have been located on the east coast of America, but America had not been discovered yet, and for that matter, no one knew what lay across the Atlantic. I think this power could have been on the continent of Atlantis. It's true that hundreds of explorations off the coast of Florida have failed to produce any real evidence that Atlantis existed, but Plato was not a person to go around making up stories. (If I wanted to bring up the fact that the Bermuda Triangle is located where Plato described the great power, I could probably not supply enough facts about it.)

The prophet Ezekiel described his experience when he flew with the "spirit," ending his story with the fact that he had stomach pains. This could have been air sickness from flying in a plane. But historians call this description nothing but a dream that he once had. I find it strange that his description of a wheel inside a wheel seems to describe what a primitive person may call a jet engine.

The Aztecs were famous for an extremely advanced civilization. The art of the Aztecs was by law to be modeled after a real thing; yet pottery and art depict creatures with helmets and too many arms and legs for a normal person. The question is: who modeled for these pictures? Of course, people don't always do what they're supposed to do. There is no reason that artists couldn't create whatever they liked. A good example would be the sun-god out in the plaza. If a later society found our bird, they might think that we considered the bird one of our gods.

There are those who believe that life on Earth began out there. . . . There is no reason that the Earth could not have been visited by aliens in the past. Although there is evidence for and against this theory, I believe that we were visited by aliens. I don't know of any other explanation that could account for the fact that some societies developed five to ten times faster than normal. This might even explain where people came from, which would shoot down the theory of creation.

Stream of Consciousness

For about 15 minutes write down pell-mell everything that comes into your head, noting thoughts down in a telegraphic style for yourself only. Choose a quiet time and place that will least draw your attention to the outside world. Find out what's on your mind or under your mind once you suspend activity and sensations for a while. You may not be able to record all thoughts or do justice to each, but you can sample at least by just letting your mind go and witnessing it on paper.

You might do this on several occasions to be sure of getting out a lot of material.

Now look over your notes and try to find a thought or image that you might want to develop, that may be connected to further thoughts that had not emerged before. Or see if you can see recurring motifs or connections among thoughts that you at first regarded as discontinuous and jumbled. Make some more notes to expand or extend or link up ideas. Then shape these into some sort of essay that will allow some audience you have in mind to understand and enjoy your thought train.

Reflection Notes
Mary Ann Flanary

Books
Tests
Men—professors—some stern—some funny.
More books
Typewriter—ribbon running old—need new one
Bank account fast.
Why here?
Don't disappoint.
Must do what I want
My life—
Have a home
Work
Sell heap.
'78 Celica—maybe
UCSD—not the place for me
Place for me—w/Mark
Want to have good things for awhile
What are good things
No more tears
Only smiles.
No more heavy hearts
Only light ones
Hard to talk sometimes
Try not to cry—but sometimes do—lots.
Everything says go
So I will
Too competitive here.
Need to relax

Maybe dates—go to school
Maybe not
I can be anything I choose to be.
I choose
Why must I decide now.
I'm so young.
Do what I can now—well I still can.
This place—Time Bomb?
Who will it explode on—and when
Ulcers hurt—is that possible?

Feeling Guilty

The first time I can remember feeling guilty was as a little girl about five or six. Mom had asked me to clean up my toys in my room and I had shoved them into my closet, thinking that would suffice. Later that evening, my Mom had gone in my room to put some clothes away and found my cleaning job. I received a lecture about what qualified as cleaning and what qualified as moving from one place to another. I remember crying because I felt guilty about not doing what my mother had asked of me.

From that point on, there were numerous incidents of guilt-inflicting. Usually it was the result of not having done something right or not having done it at all. I guess I was a typical kid, didn't like cleaning or taking out the garbage, so I tried to do these as little as was humanly possible. I suppose I inadvertently doomed myself to my own guilty conscience. Except I never became aware of that guilty conscience til someone (usually my mother) reminded me of it.

Adolescence wasn't much better—maybe even worse. I still retained all of the previous traits that lent themselves to guilty feelings, plus I added a few more—the time I came home at night and the condition I was in at that time.

I think in the high school years, guilt takes more of the form of disappointment than anything else. Seemed as if you were always being held responsible to someone for something. The threat of disappointing someone always loomed in the foreground of all the important decisions. I remember when I decided to drop out of Calculus I during the second semester of my Senior year. When I went to my calculus teacher, Mr. Lockwood, to have him sign the drop form, he clicked his tongue at me and said, "Mary Ann, I'm disappointed in you." I feigned anger to my friends, but I felt guilty at having disappointed a teacher I respected.

Even after graduating from high school and reaching the supposedly independent age of eighteen, I still find myself feeling responsible to people I respect. My parents are helping me pay for college, so I feel a responsibility to them to continue and do well.

Sometimes feeling responsible to another person can be a good thing. It could make a person work harder where you may have apathetic attitudes toward that prospect. But other times it can rob you of your individuality. Feeling responsible to parents is the reason why at least one-third of the kids are here. Having no other alternative in mind, they may have chosen the route most likely to sustain family harmony.

I guess most people here are like me. Here because people expect it of them, and it's easier to go along when you're not really sure what you want either. Once you do figure out what it is you want to do, though, it could create problems. A person may feel as if they've disappointed their parents, and the guilt stemming from that can be overwhelming. I felt this way when I decided not to return to college next year. I thought my mom was going to be disappointed in me. When she wasn't, I felt for the first time that my life was really my own. Now, it was completely my decision to choose which way my life would lead.

I don't worry any more about disappointing people since my mom told me that anything I wanted to do was okay. I guess everyone doesn't have as understanding a person as I do. Maybe, then, it would've been a much more difficult situation and choice. Perhaps I wouldn't have made the decision I did—that could be the reason why a lot of people don't make a similiar choice.

It is a hard pattern to break or even try and break. It took me from the time I was five years old to make just one break. But there are still others I haven't made or may never make. I still feel guilty sometimes, but it's not as bad. A part of me says, "Why should you care what they think!" But I do care, as do most people. Perhaps because we do care—that is why we may all feel guilty at times.

Victoria, British Columbia
STUART RENNIE

Victoria, to be blunt, is a wholly docile city, and one where many Canadians spend their final days. I don't mean to imply death is forced upon us, or that death can be cheated or postponed by a simple change in plans. Rather (as is slickly documented and circulated among our elders), Victoria is the retirement magnet of Canada, it is what we live for, what is rightly ours, after the sub-zero brutalities of Fort Mc- Murray, or the abject boredom of Saskatchewan.

Victoria, then, by definition, is the Canadian Florida, a shelter from the cold. By it flows the warm Gulf Stream from Japan, a salt water wind that still smells sweet once it starts to push eastward, up the mouth of the docks to the main commercial centers. For its residents the breeze holds vast therapeutic and conversational value; it is a breath that is life sustaining. Men and women talk of the "air" as if it were some mystical being: "the difference is in the 'air'," "we are taking the 'air.'" When a wind blows in Victoria, it stops being a natural function and starts to become an event. Such is the pace of the city.

In the city proper, on Douglas and Yates streets, all is quiet, a premeditated quiet. Mufflers on cars are strictly enforced, the speed limit is set at a provincial low, and as the young population of Victoria is limited, there is a minimum of shouting on the streets. If anything, the only noises are the constant scuffing of feet on the pavement, the picking sounds of canes on cobbled streets, and the opening and closing of bus doors. Even when old friends meet in Market Square, there is only the simple clasping and unclasping of hands, knowing glances and knowing smiles. When the old women laugh under the Eaton Archway, their laughter too seems restrained; there is always a hand held up to the mouth to stop the emotion from flying devil-may- care into the street.

The citizens, after all, are "Victorians" and like their English namesakes are reminded, young and old, to live out their lives in a prolonged hush. Part of this psychology of "hush" is the almost complete avoidance of the topic of death, near-death, or related sub- jects. Also, ambulances are never seen speeding through a Victoria intersection. There are no visible body bags, and no hint of the smell of decomposition. When a Victorian has passed on, someone discreetly pulls a dozen orchids from one garden or another. Enough said.

Another factor contributing to the overall sameness of the city is that it is a capital city, a governmental city. So at five o'clock there are thousands of government employees stumbling out of their under- seven-story-tall offices, dulled by numbers, dragging their feet like the old pensioners to the right and left of them. As soon as they enter the city core they are already in the process of leaving, jettisoning out into the suburbs, into the waterfront homes. By seven-thirty the streetlamps are on half-electricity; the city center has no visible life. Only ten or twenty longtime destitutes sit crosslegged in the shadows. They stay because they won't freeze during the night, and they hardly know silence from any other sort of noise.

It may be something inherent in man that attracts him to one Victoria or another, be it a public or private one. However, if cities are meant to be living organisms, Victoria fails on major counts. As a city it is merely an example of reducing life to accommodate forthcoming deaths.

Meditative Reflection

Get alone in a very quiet place and focus as intently as you can on something you want to understand better or think through. First close your eyes, sit very relaxed but straight, take several deep and slow breaths, and shut out all sensations and thoughts about things other than your subject. If the subject of your thought should be a physical object or place, put yourself in its presence if possible and gaze at it. If you have an object or a picture that stands for what you want to think about, start gazing at it after you're relaxed. If you want to think about something not physically present, visualize it with your eyes closed, or focus on whatever image or thought represents it. Whether gazing or visualizing, don't try to think, but, instead, let the thing you're focused on fill your mind until thoughts about it simply come to you. Stay physically relaxed and breathe easy.

Jot down the thoughts in fast note form when it seems right to start writing. Stop writing when it seems to interfere with your thoughts; or write only when you've had so many thoughts that you need to note them to preserve them; or if forgetting does not seem a problem, write your thoughts after you have finished. Whenever your thought trains seem to get off your subject, bring your mind back to your focal point. But give yourself a chance to be sure that the thoughts are indeed off the subject and not perhaps a welcome new viewpoint or aspect of your subject. Eventually put down on paper all of the thoughts you have in this session that seem at all likely to be relevant. The more the better as you sort these out later and compose them into some essay to be conveyed to an audience you choose.

Two Women

CAROL CAMPANELLA

Up until now you've been exactly what you were supposed to have been—a mother. A mother who always worried over something, yelled because of nothing, and yet did everything with much love. Well, now I need you to be more than just my mother...I need you to be my friend!

For twenty-one years I could have been called nothing but a "daughter." Soon I not only will be someone's daughter but someone's wife and then possibly mother. So you see, I'll be more like you than ever.

What I am experiencing now is perhaps the happiest yet most questionable moment in my life. I am about to take not a step but a leap into an entirely new phase of my life. So, my dearest mother, if there ever was a time in which I needed a friend, it's now. No doubt I have many friends who can help me through such times, but none could be that special friend that I need to find in you. It is you who have seen the most private and secretive emotions of my heart, and only you lived through these emotions as if you were within my spirit. And who can deny that I, too, have seen and felt so much of your emotional life that, by God, we are a match made in heaven.

Mom, I am about to turn the corner of this long-lived-on street onto a new and busy avenue. Neither you nor I know exactly what's around the corner, but it's a direction I want to take. Although it's going to be *my* road, you need not let go of my hand—just loosen the grip a bit.

Coming from the bottom of my heart, I must tell you that I've fallen in love. More importantly, however, is that he's truly in love with me. Do you realize what this means? I'm actually touching one of my most prized dreams. Maybe right now I'm only touching with my fingertips, but it's there in front of me. I see and feel it, and there is no one better with whom I'd like to share this with than you, Mom, so don't walk away.

For years you've had to watch me sit and daydream about all my "somedays." Well, that someday is here. Don't you want to be a part of it? Yes, I've added to my life someone else with whom to share my love. But that doesn't mean I've got less to give you. If anything, I have found more love for you—more love that I hope will express my sincere appreciation for helping me grow into a special woman.

That's right...I am a "woman" now and *I am special*. Special because you've given me enough love and hope to spread to others; special because you've given me enough confidence to build my dreams into realities and special because I have you as my mother.

I know you love me. This I do not doubt. What I need to know, however, is that you like me—like me enough to be my friend. If you are drifting from me because you are afraid, please be aware that I, too, am afraid. Give us a chance to be afraid together. I know you want the best for me, and remember you've taught me to want the best for myself. So, be assured that I shall strive for nothing but.

You have done more than any mother can be expected to in the way of guiding me around life's framework. But now I must paint its picture and with the help of God, it will be a picture full of peace and love. Mom, I'm not walking away from you—I'm just no longer in your shadow. Now I'm walking by your side!

In all honesty, I am as frightened as you. By all means love is beautiful yet frightening. Only recently have I felt the power of those tiny words, "I love you." True, love is the answer—but it can sometimes also be the question. It can be the question of "Why," "How much" and "For how long." Does this love last forever?

Never before have I felt so secure and insecure at the same time. Do you know what I'm saying? Can you feel it with me? Does this bring back any memories for you? If so, please give me a sign of understanding. Please look into my eyes and let me know you can feel what I'm going through and then share it with me...cry with me... smile with me...and, above all, stay with me and be my friend!

Imagination Makes the Leap

ANN THOMAS

Why are the best writers often those who have suffered? I look at the students in my fourth, fifth, and sixth grades, and it is the students who have encountered death, alienation, or loneliness that write powerfully. Not only do they have intense issues to write about, but they tend to be acutely aware of their world and able to understand it from a larger perspective.

These children who have suffered can often articulate and analyze the social structure in their class, different teaching styles, their parents' relationship and their own relationship with their parents. At the same time, the other students are miles behind. Even those children who are extremely "bright" and write fascinating stories or beautiful poetry tend to have a narrower perception of their own worlds.

Certainly those children faced with death have been forced to address issues that normally wouldn't have arisen. Those who have been rejected by a peer group are likely to lie in bed at night wondering why they were rejected and what the group accepts. But why does the lack of hardships inhibit awareness and understanding? "Fortunate children" seem to be blinded by their bliss.

I would like to see children be more thoughtful individuals and consequently more thoughtful writers. As a teacher, how can I help complaisant children become more aware without painting their young worlds too grimly?

I could expose them to accounts of people who have been oppressed, ostracized, or have suffered in some way. And yet, isn't that what literature does? The children seem to be able to understand the suffering portrayed in the stories, but they dismiss it quickly when the bell rings for recess. The children must internalize that suffering before they will be prompted to seriously question an issue. It would be easier for a child to empathize with characters if the accounts of suffering were personal and written in first person. Also, if the children could assume the role through writing or speaking, they would have to take the information into themselves, integrate it with their own understanding of the world, and then create their own interpretation of the character. Perhaps the real goal is to exercise their imaginations so that they are able to empathize with characters that are increasingly more removed from themselves. Imagination is the key that enables people to leap from reading about characters and their worlds to experiencing and understanding them.

Statement Through Story

Narrate any true happening that illustrates a general point you want to make. In other words, you are telling a story not only for its own sake but also to show something that the reader could apply to people and events he or she knows. This can be in first or third person and drawn from any source. It could be included in a collection of other writings on the same theme or could be incorporated later into a larger paper dealing more comprehensively with the point. Or post or print up.

Blind Hate

FERN TYRELL

Being in the navy wasn't so bad, the young, black intern tried to convince himself. Or at least it couldn't get worse. He had graduated from medical school with high honors, but internships were at best hard to obtain in the 1940's, and well nigh impossible to get if you were a black man, regardless of your credentials. So he had joined the navy, which was desperately in need of medical men at the time—due to World War II—and accepted the internship that they offered. That solved the problem of a job for him, but created numerous new problems. He found himself in the position of being the only man with any medical credentials on board ship, aside from a few military men trained as medics. As a result of this, some of the sailors coming to him for medical care paid undue attention to the young intern's color. A few of them were vocal enough to say that they didn't want to be checked by a "nigger ship's doctor."

Tonight was New Year's Eve. It was hard for a sailor to be so far away from land on the holiday. There was a party on ship as a measure to compensate. Liquor was free flowing, and just about every sailor who didn't have duty that night was planning to open the New Year with a bang. The young intern had duty this evening and not feeling inclined to be sociable he remained in the infirmary, immersed in his own thoughts.

A little after midnight two sailors came in dragging a third sailor who appeared to be unconcious. The intern helped them to lay the man on the examining table, then he realized that the sailor had stopped breathing. There was vomit smeared on the sailor's face, and the intern quickly deduced that the sailor had had too much to drink, vomited up his stomach contents, and had passed out in his own vomit. There was not a split second to waste on looking for a suction apparatus to clear the sailor's nose and mouth. So, with his own mouth, the intern sucked the mucus and vomit from the sailor's nose and mouth and performed artificial respiration on him until the sailor was breathing again. Then the intern began to check him over to make sure that he had no other injuries.

While the intern was examining him, the sailor regained consciousness, and, seeing the black man bent over him, swung out violently with his arm, hitting the intern across the face. "Get away from me, nigger," the sailor snarled.

Of Patience and Arrogance

BRETT REDD

The sun beat down unmercifully upon us as we drove through the Mexican desert. My family and I had just completed a three-week vacation at my uncle's ranch house in Colonial Juarez. As our pickup truck bumped noisily over the rough dirt road, my thoughts were primarily concerned with the oppressive heat and the fine dust which was steadily finding its way through the minute cracks that riddled our camper. Occasionally, my thoughts would shift to the fun I had had during the past few weeks riding horses, fishing, and participating in an authentic cattle roundup where I had helped with the roping, wrestling, and branding of cattle as well as any nine-year-old could.

Suddenly, the bumpy monotony of travel was disturbed when the steady drone of the pickup's engine diminished as my father slowed the truck. Curious, I looked out the window of the camper. Up ahead in the distance, I could perceive the hazy figures of several large men standing in the road, their dark outlines undulating and shimmering like mirages in the intense desert heat. As we advanced slowly towards the men, my curiosity changed to fear as I realized that each of the men wielded a large automatic rifle.

As the truck rolled to a stop and one of the men approached, my father called out the window: "What seems to be the problem?" The expression on my father's face quickly changed from one of apprehension to anger when the man growled, "Get out of the truck," and identified himself as a captain in the Mexican Police. As my father stepped down from the truck, he was met with a barrage of questions regarding narcotics possession. Despite my father's increasing anger and reassurances that we had no drugs, the captain waved to the other men. The men, wearing large sombreros and leather cartridge belts across their chests, advanced quickly, guns in hand. The captain then ordered them to begin searching our truck and trailer. Their appearance reminded me of the typical "bandito" I had seen in so many cowboy movies.

My father, glowing with fury, advanced towards the captain but instantly froze as several rifles were swung in his direction. The captain then removed a large hunting knife which my father kept on his belt and said in a cold voice while tapping the blade against my father's chest, "You'd better cooperate, or you might get hurt," and then released a peal of hoarse laughter. My father, so enraged that the veins bulged from his neck, walked to the truck and said in a calm voice, "These men want to look in the truck, so you're going to have to get out." His wife and children silently obeyed.

The captain, running a thick finger along the razor edge of my father's knife, asked: "Do you have any more weapons?" "No, none in our possession," my father answered, barely able to suppress his fury. The captain again waved his hand, and the five armed men scurried like ants and began to search the truck and trailer. They left no leaf unturned, opening every suitcase and rumpling every article of clothing they held. They plowed through every drawer and cupboard in the trailer and tapped their rifle butts against the walls and floor, listening for hollow compartments. They even pried the trailer's hubcaps loose in their futile search for narcotics. Although at that time in my life I had no concrete ideas of justice or legality, I felt that what these men were doing was wrong, and sensing my father's outrage, I knew I was right.

My initial reaction to the incident was one of utter shock and confusion. Never in my life had I been so frightened and intimidated. I asked myself repeatedly: What are these men doing? Why are they making Dad so mad? Numb and cold despite the intense heat, I cowered behind my father, trying to make myself as insignificant and obscure as possible.

All during this time the captain seemed to be enjoying himself immensely. He smiled broadly and grunted his approval as our belongings were systematically ransacked. To this day I remember the captain as being a very ugly man. He was of medium height and very stocky, with thick, stubby arms protruding from a barrel chest. He was filthy and foul-smelling, with greasy hair and a dark, unshaven face. Under his thick fingernails was what appeared to be a permanent layer of dirt. Next to his disposition, however, his appearance was a positive attribute.

Suddenly, one of the men searching the truck let out a triumphant exclamation. He brought to the captain several spent .22 caliber cartridges which he had found behind the seat of the truck. The captain, his crooked-toothed smile broadening as he examined the shells, suddenly turned to my father and stated, "Where is the gun? You lied to me." My father, becoming more incensed with each passing minute, struggled not to lose his temper and explained that the cartridges came from my uncle's gun which he had used on his ranch to hunt jackrabbits from the truck.

This did not seem to satisfy the captain, however, and he again began to probe my father's chest with the knife, calling him a liar, among other insults. By this time the captain's motives were clear: he was attempting to provoke my father into losing his temper. My father, foreseeing the consequences if he were to react violently, wisely chose not to let his anger overrule his logic. He realized that any rash action would land him in jail, unable to protect his family.

The captain, having exhausted his supply of provocations and unable to find any substantial incriminating evidence, was forced to release us. I still remember the seething expression on the captain's face as we drove off. In a sense, his egomaniacal ploy had been thwarted by patience and logic.

In retrospect, it becomes clear how my feelings towards that event and the men have changed over the years. Witnessing the event as it happened, I reacted as any child would if he were exposed to something traumatic and frightening; I sought safety behind the bulk of my father. Although I was frightened and confused, I paid very close attention to that series of events, ingesting every detail.

After the passage of time had dulled the initial impact of the event, my feelings of fright and confusion had been transformed into emotions of bitterness and anger. As a nine-year-old boy, I could only sense my father's outrage but could not fully comprehend it. It was not until several years later that I thoroughly realized the incredible injustice that my father had endured, and when I came to this realization I shared his outrage.

That event in Mexico left deep impressions on me as a child, and from it I have extracted several invaluable lessons. One such lesson is the virtue of patience and logical reasoning. Very few men would have been able to remain so calm and rational during such a trying situation as my father did, and my respect and admiration for this attribute has motivated me to incorporate it into my own set of values. Many times since that event I have applied the same techniques of patience and calm reasoning during adverse situations, and have usually met with positive results.

That event also taught me a lesson regarding some of the uglier aspects of human nature. Never before had I been exposed to such callous and brutal people. Perhaps they were just performing their duty, but they could have treated us with indifference if not sympathy; instead they were cold and cruel. I was also introduced for the first time to a man who seemed to enjoy inflicting anguish upon others. It was not until much later that I realized how sadistic and egocentric the captain was. He was a man vested with a great deal of authority, but his abuse of this authority in order to satisfy his own self-exaltation and arrogance has caused me to possess an incurable and inveterate dislike for people with similar traits.

Thus that event in Mexico, which lasted less than an hour, has profoundly affected my present values. Perhaps in an ironic sense I was fortunate to be exposed to such an emotionally powerful situation as a child, for these exposures are inevitable and must be accepted and digested with careful thought and discretion. Only in this way can one form a legitimate and well-rounded set of values.

The Sand Pile

BRIAN FLYNN

It is really amazing how little it takes to make a kid happy. Their rampant imaginations can transform a common, everyday object into a racecar, or a spaceship, or some other exciting plaything that will keep them fascinated for hours (or at least until they can find a more interesting common, everyday object).

A case in point that I observed recently was when a neighbor of mine was having some brick work done to her house. The workmen dropped off their materials the day before they started working, and among the various tools and supplies was an innocuous-looking pile of sand about five feet high and ten feet round, right in the middle of the driveway. To some this new found mountain in their front yard would be considered an inconvenience. To the kids in my neighborhood, however, it was a godsend.

When the kids returned home from school that day and discovered their newly acquired goldmine, they were ready for action. It took them all of two and a half minutes to shed their school clothes, gather up the necessary accessories for a hard day's play, and reconvene back at the sand pile.

Before I tell you of the events that followed, let me take a minute to introduce you to the members of this tight-knit little crew. First, there is Daren, with his brown curly hair and pudgy belly. He is the biggest and therefore the self-appointed leader of the pack. Next there is Lisa, the token female of the group. She would not even be allowed near them if it wasn't for the fact that she was almost as strong as Daren and stronger than all the rest of the boys in the gang. Then there is Dave, the little Filipino boy from down the block. I'm sorry to say that as far as I can see, Dave's sole purpose in the group is that of being the "Jap" when they play guns. And finally, there is Adam. Adam is an only child and one of the whiningest spoiled brats you will ever meet. The only reason he is tolerated by the others is that, according to Lisa, he has the best toys.

The first order of business at the sand pile was, of course, King of the Hill. This was undoubtedly Daren's idea as he was the king for the entire duration of the game. It was nice, however, to see Lisa knock him off balance once or twice.

When they tired of this, they turned to the more involved and intriguing practice of converting the entire hill into a series of roads and tunnels and bridges upon which to drive (and crash) their assorted (and I do mean assorted) collection of cars and trucks. It is interesting to note at this point that their system of roadways and passages made more sense than a lot of real highway systems we are made to travel upon.

This activity went on for the better part of the afternoon but as dinner time approached, I remember watching their unabandoned frenzy as they threw themselves wildly about the sand in an orgy of destruction upon the small community they had so recently brought into being. I'm sure the workmen found one or two little cars in the sand the next day, but it really didn't matter, they were probably Adam's anyway.

As dusk approached and the light began to fade, the tireless crew began their last, but certainly not their least, favorite of games...war! There was really no place to hide on the small mount but that was not really a factor. No, the main idea was to climb to the top of the hill, get shot, and slowly and dramatically fall to the bottom. And this was done with such style and grace that I could have sworn I was seeing John Wayne lose it atop the infamous Pork Chop Hill.

This merry activity went on unabated until it was brought to a sudden and climactic halt, the way many a good time before it was ended, with the hearty and robust call of a fed-up mother calling (for the last time) to her little adventurers to come home to dinner.

Thematic Collection of Incidents

Tell briefly several incidents that you think show the same thing, that is, illustrate a certain observation you want to make. An incident is an action that happened once. *Draw these incidents from any sources that you trust—memory, books, other people, and so on, including* Statement Through Story. *Narrate each incident just enough to fit your point, and state the point just enough to make it emerge. The result may resemble a familiar kind of feature article that points out and illustrates a trend, for example, or an essay depicting a common condition. So aim toward a corresponding medium.*

Boaters Are the Friendliest Strangers
VINCENT PANETTIERI, JR.

Every summer I have numerous amounts of experiences with fellow boaters. I go sailing at least three times a week if not more.

Everyday out on the water is a whole new experience. Weather is the biggest factor as to how your day will be.

When I go out during the week there aren't very many boaters, so it seems I am the only one on the Sound. If something happens I'm on my own.

One morning I was heading out of Huntington Harbor, my home port, towards Port Jefferson via Connecticut. It was a gorgeous day but not much wind.

My friend and I were all geared up for four days out at "sea." The engine didn't start as easily as it usually does, but we took off anyway. Well, it did give us trouble off and on. Finally we had to start it again because the wind died down and we were just drifting in the middle of the Sound. The engine started to sputter and then just died. I couldn't get it restarted. I tried some simple adjustments but to no avail; it wouldn't start. I got on the radio to the Coast Guard at Eaton's Neck which was only about a mile away. They responded quickly and said unless there was a direct threat of danger to our lives they would not respond but would keep monitoring us. Another sailor overheard my call and started telling me what to check on the engine and the gas line. We went to checking and starting and re-checking. After about an hour of trying his suggestions one finally turned up to be the problem. The spark plug wires were cracked and arcing. So I wrapped up the wires in electrical tape and the engine started with a purr. I thanked him over and over. Everytime I am out sailing I will hail him on the radio just to say hi!

Another beautiful morning I was sailing and had just started into the harbor when the water pump went. Again I sat waiting for some help; no one answered the radio. Finally I caught the attention of two fishermen aboard a Mako 22-footer. I kept blowing the horn and waving the distress flag to be sure they didn't think I was just saying how's the fishing. They got close enough to talk when I realized they were talking Greek, just my luck. I kept repeating slowly that I needed a tow to my club and finally from my hand gestures with a tow line, they understood and said yes with a thick accent and pulled me in.

Still another day I was waiting for the launch, talking to my friend about the depth-finder doing crazy things such as jumping from two to forty feet while at the mooring. A gentleman waiting for the launch also overheard me and offered to come out and take a look at it. Well, he found that the solder on the male plug was not making contact to the cable, so he got a soldering gun off his boat and re-soldered it for me. It works like new now.

One of my most frightening experiences occurred when I went to Port Jefferson Harbor for a long weekend. I was anchored in the outer bay when at about nine p.m. a huge cruising sailboat, about 50 feet, anchored off my port bow. He seemed very close as he backed towards my boat to set anchor. He yelled over to me to ask if he was too close since he must yield to me because there was a possibility of hitting each other as my boat swings much faster because it is smaller. He pulled up anchor and reset a little further away.

About one half hour later he started playing his guitar and singing Harry Belafonte songs with a thick Caribbean accent, he was great. He then invited us over and everyone else in the surrounding boats. Those who didn't come aboard sang from their boats. The song we sang the most was "Yellowbird." We drank, sang and told stories till four a.m., when we finally rowed back to my little craft.

At about six a.m. I was awakened by the abrupt swinging of my boat and the howling winds. A strong westerly wind whipped up with storm clouds closing in quickly. I turned up the weather channel, and violent thunderstorms were forecasted that were not the day before. I went out on deck to secure everything when I noticed the fifty-footer bearing down on my twenty-three-foot weekender, his anchor pulled up. I started blowing my horn, but everything just happened too fast. My friend came bolting up the companionway and prepared to push off the yacht. The owner of the yacht seemed to freeze momentarily when he finally realized he was going to hit me. She came down on my boat with such force that we couldn't keep her from hitting with a loud crash. It even pulled my anchor loose, and we both started drifting towards the jetty. I started my 7½-horse engine but it didn't do a thing with the wind, current, and yacht's weight all against her. He couldn't get his 75-horsepower diesel started. There was a family on a Morgan forty-one-footer watching in horror. They realized what was happening and pulled up anchor and came to our aid. He threw a line to the fifty-footer and pointed us into the wind until he got the diesel to turn over. I got my anchor line untangled and pushed off to set anchor again but also set a second one to sit out the storm. The fifty-footer finally straightened out and set anchor and the forty-one-footer followed suit. We all talked and thanked each other for the help over the radio. Things could have been a lot worse if it was not for the family who willingly pulled up anchor in the middle of a terrible storm to help a fellow boater.

From my experiences I have nothing but praise for the fast actions and calm heads along with the warmth generated through courtesy and friendships from strangers with a common love for boating.

The Hard Way
ALAN S. RUSINOWITZ

There are many ways people deal with the learning process. Some read books, listen to lectures, watch demonstrations, and practice what they are studying. But time and again these methods do not work or fail completely. There is another approach: Learning the hard way.

This method applies to every subject ever taught, including flying. People who want to learn to fly attend ground schools to learn the basics, rules, regulations, flight planning, and aerodynamics. There are also aircraft manuals that explain in detail what the airplane can and cannot do. It also gives you tables and charts containing performance figures.

After discussing a maneuver on the ground, the instructor will demonstrate it in flight, usually twice, and explain what he is doing as he does it. Then he will do it with the student and talk him through it. Then it is the student's turn.

But even after all of this, students still have trouble and have to learn the hard way. Of the following three examples, the first two show non-understanding of a maneuver. The third shows plain (no pun intended) stupidity by a student.

A stall is a maneuver that is practiced from the student's third hour of flight on through every license he will get. Without getting into great detail, a stall occurs when the aircraft stops flying and drops. The engine is still running, but the aircraft is not "flying."

The recovery is simple. It is broken down into three steps: 1) Point the nose down to increase airflow and airspeed. This is easy, because when the aircraft stalls, the nose wants to go down. 2) Stop the rolling tendency of the aircraft. If the aircraft is rolling to the right, the pilot applies left (opposite) rudder, to keep the nose straight. 3) Add full power and bring the nose to a climb attitude. These are the basics of the maneuver.

As an illustration of the above point, let us examine the case of a student named John. He was having trouble with this particular maneuver. We discussed it in the classroom, used models, and even viewed films on it. In flight, I demonstrated it, did it with him, and evaluated him. Nine out of ten times, he didn't recover soon enough, and we went into a spin. John was deathly afraid of spins. A spin is when the aircraft is "falling" out of the sky and turning like a top. Each time he would yell "I can't do it, you take it" (the airplane). One time when he did not recover correctly, the plane pitched violently and went right into a spin. John was panicking and yelling for me to recover. I sat there and said "no." I said I would tell him how, but he would have to do it. From then on his procedures were correct. By the way, he now *likes* spins.

The second case involves Marty. She had trouble holding the airplane straight and level. I tried everything to break her of the habit of wandering in 3D. Finally, we went up for a flight, and I covered up all of her instruments. Then I told her to take me flying. We went through a one-hour-and-twenty-minute flight, with no instruments to look at. Marty did all of her maneuvers, and even landed, just by looking outside and listening to the engine. Her flying has been fine since, and she is almost ready for her flight test.

The last case is really a case of learning the hard way. I'm glad he's not my student. Student pilots go through extensive training in all phases of flight, from preflight planning to emergency procedures. Brian was ready for his long cross-country flight. This consists of a flight from Farmingdale, Long Island to Albany, New York to Pawtucket, Rhode Island and back to Farmingdale. It's an all-day affair and is a real test for the student. Brian kept saying he was ready and it would be a breeze. What was to follow was more like a tornado.

While flying between Albany and Pawtucket Brian became lost. He spent so much time trying to find his way that he ran out of gas and had to make a landing in a farm field. He landed and flipped over. He wasn't hurt (knock on wood). Looking back on what happened, the whole flight was riddled with stupidity.

He did not refuel at Albany (the flying club gave him $100 cash to buy fuel), he didn't use his radios correctly and even passed over two airports when he was lost but didn't land because they were not the airport he was looking for. He called for help on one of the least used frequencies available. Out of 1000' of field to land in, he passed over 800' of it, landed, rolled 165', and then saw a 10-ton manure spreader, a tractor, and a shack in front of him. He slammed the brakes and flipped over. There is more, but that's enough for now.

When talking to him after the accident, he had all the right answers to what he should have done, and what he'll do in the future.

He found out the hard way.

The Problem of Old People Today
DENA COLLINS

Grandma Boghosian is seventy-eight years old and half blind. She is a sweet little old Armenian lady who speaks broken English. Her family does not live close by so she must walk down the block to her lawyer who writes out all her checks for her monthly bills. He charges her a hundred and fifty dollars every six months just to do this. During one February snow storm Grandma Boghosian was stuck in her house with not much to eat. She needed just a few basic items such as milk, eggs, bread, and butter, so she decided to call her local grocer where she had repeatedly bought items for fity some-odd years. The grocer claimed that he was busy and couldn't get anyone to deliver today. Grandma Boghosian told him that all she needed was a few items but she couldn't go out because the snow was too deep and she couldn't see very well and she would fall and hurt herself if she had to go out. The grocer exclaimed that there was still nothing that he could do and hung up.

Grandma Boghosian went hungry for the weekend until it was nice enough out for her to walk. After three days when the snow had melted she dressed warmly and started for the grocer. She put her few items on the counter, took a crisp twenty-dollar bill from her purse and handed it to the grocer. She took her change and headed home. As she was putting her groceries away she realized that it was her niece's birthday and she would have to send one of the pretty cards in the closet and a ten-dollar bill. When she opened her purse she noticed that there was only a few singles. She was positive that she had given the grocer a twenty and decided to walk back down to the grocer and find out. She dressed warmly and headed back out to the grocer. When she confronted the grocer he replied that he was sure she had given him a ten and maybe she just didn't see right. She headed home sadly knowing that there had been a twenty-dollar bill in her purse.

Mrs. Quinn, Grandma Boghosian's next door neighbor, was also seventy-eight and a widow. In the spring Mrs. Quinn had been having trouble with her cesspool. The cesspool had filled up and flooded her basement four times within six months, which cost her two hundred and fifty dollars to clear up each time. After the fourth time the cesspool man advised Mrs. Quinn to have her sewers done. He claimed that this was the best possible way to end her flooding problem. He suggested a company which quickly came over to give an estimate, a mere one thousand, nine hundred and seventy-six dollars. Mrs. Quinn was devastated by the amount but agreed because it was her last resort. The men arrived the next day and tore up a four-foot length of beautiful hedges which surrounded Mrs. Quinn's yard. Her husband had planted the hedges sixty years ago when the Quinns had first bought the house. Mrs. Quinn just looked on with tears in her eyes as her beautiful yard was being torn up. After days of working a man showed up at Mrs. Quinn's house in a three-piece navy suit and a briefcase. He handed Mrs. Quinn a card which identified himself as a town inspector. He said that he had to inspect the work that was going on in her yard to see if it fit all the necessary safety rules and regulations. The man in the three-piece suit spent the rest of the day looking at different things which were being put into Mrs. Quinn's yard. He then confronted the foreman and they argued for a few minutes. The next day Mrs. Quinn saw the men ripping pipes and things back out where they had put them in. She wondered what the man in the three-piece suit had to do with it all. The foreman walked up to the porch and told Mrs. Quinn that the inspector said that they had used improper fittings and would have to replace them all with new ones, which would be more labor and cost her another eight hundred dollars.

Mr. Rosenberg lives on Third Street in Brooklyn. He is eighty-three years old and has no living relatives. He has lived in the same apartment complex for thirty-seven years. He can't see very well and uses a cane to walk up and down from his fourth-floor apartment because there are no elevators. Mr. Rosenberg's ceiling leaks. He has to keep five pots lined up along the hallway to catch the water when it rains. He never sees the landlord and often writes to him to get things fixed but never gets any results. He has cockroaches and buys spray to kill them, but they always come back. Mr. Rosenberg is on a fixed income of $448.00 a month from Social Security. With this he pays $175.00 for rent, $35.00 a month for electric, $20.00 for gas and $25.00 for the phone bill. He uses the rest of the money for food and other items that he might need during the month.

In the winter time the boiler breaks down at least two or three times per month. When it does Mr. Rosenberg must sit in front of the gas stove to keep warm because there is no heat or hot water. The people in his building complain, but once the boiler is fixed it breaks down again. One severely cold winter when the boiler had been broken for about a week they found Mr. Rosenberg frozen to death in his bed.

Generalization About Oneself

Make a general statement about yourself or your life that seems true to you and illustrate this generalization with examples. The subject could be some recurring behavior, some trait or tendency in your thinking, or some pattern of experience in your life. Cast this in a manner appealing to an audience that your experience might interest.

Friendship—a Rumination

TERRY ANDERSON

I'm sitting on a park bench thinking about friendship. Not the concept "Friendship," which fills my head with platitudes carved in gold and makes me feel like a jerk. Rather the *process* of having friends, of having people in my life who are important to me and to whom I willingly commit time and energy. The reason I'm thinking about friends is that I don't seem to have as many these days, and I'm not spending as much time and energy on the ones I do have. Because my interests and life goals have changed within the last year, my old circle of friends does not seem to be as accessible as in the past, and my new circle—well, it doesn't exist. I guess I'm feeling lonely.

Friends are supposed to be a man's most valuable possession. I have two or three long-term friends, people to whom I remain connected from one period of my life to the next and who provide a cushion against the passage of time—an old man once told me that I would stay young as long as I had a friend who remembered me that way. But these friends are the exceptions. And I've been able to keep them precisely because I don't have to see them very often. Generally, friends come and friends go...I worry that someday they'll just go. When the newspapers do a profile on the latest mass murderer, they inevitably describe him as a strange man who lived alone and had few friends—I nod my head, agreeing that he indeed sounds strange while hoping I am not reading my own epitaph.

The truth is that having friends has always been difficult for me, always putting me in a bind. The people I actively pursue usually disappoint me while the people who pursue me become a burden—a sense of genuine mutuality in my relationships is rare and fleeting. I have a habit of blaming it on my choice of friends or on human fallibility in general, but I am beginning to suspect that the problem is more a result of confused expectations generated by my own internal processes.

People describe me as likeable, sensitive, dependable—the quintessential "good friend." What they really mean is that I'm tremendously flexible, willing to be for them whatever they want while demanding little in return beyond approval. I probably developed this pattern of behavior during the peer-pleasing days of adolescence, yet its emphasis on self-sacrifice has been heavily reinforced by the Christian culture around me. In any event, I never think of myself as a victim of my friendships—I consciously choose to give more than I receive, preferring to think of it as being "useful" rather than being "used." And it's better than being alone.

The problem is that I almost always pay for my friendships in terms of my self-image, my identity. The more time and energy I put into my friends, the more I tend to lose a sense of who I am and what I need. It's like looking into a pond—if the conditions are just right, my image is reflected back at me in startling detail, but all it takes is a slight breeze or a passing duck to distort the reflection beyond recognition. At that point, the impulse arises to reject my friends and isolate myself. I plug into the great American tradition known as rugged individualism—I become a hero in the movies, the man who goes it alone. And just as I begin to piece together my identity on my own, I am overwhelmed by a sense of isolation, alienation, and loss.

So having friends, for me, requires not so much an external negotiation between myself and others as an internal negotiation between parts of myself, parts that seem to have little common ground. A psychologist would reassuringly label this the natural conflict between my need to "seek" and my need to "merge." I hate such pat answers, and besides, it feels much more extreme, much more entrenched than that. I would describe it as a struggle between a hermit and herd animal....

HERMIT: Just look at you! You do nothing but sit around this pasture all day, eating, sleeping, following the rest of the herd....

HERD ANIMAL: Who are you to criticize me? Everyone says you're a crazy man,living alone on top of some crag, sleeping on the rocks, catching your food with your bare hands. I suppose you would have me live like that?! Well, I'm afraid we herd animals don't do well on crags.

HERMIT: I'm not saying you should be like me, I just hate seeing you be such a mindless conformist. Don't you ever get the urge to explore on your own? Maybe just wander as far as the next pasture?

HERD ANIMAL: Why are you so worried about me? I'm happy here. I get fed regularly; I have nice soft places to lie in the sun; I like rubbing my rump against my fellow herd animals. I don't see anything interesting in that other pasture.

HERMIT: You don't know that for sure. You can't know unless you go over and look for yourself.

HERD ANIMAL: Well...it looks cold over there.

HERMIT: Just a little physical discomfort—you'll get used to it in no time.

HERD ANIMAL: What for? Nobody goes over there! Why are you trying to get rid of me?

HERMIT: I'm just trying to help you. I'm trying to get you to expand your horizons.

HERD ANIMAL: I don't need your help—I'm perfectly content doing what I'm doing. If it's so great, why aren't you over there?

HERMIT: I spend a lot of time in places like that. There are new challenges over there, and it's only in challenging yourself that you can discover and develop your own unique identity.

HERD ANIMAL: Hmm. Sounds like a bunch of mumbo jumbo to me. I'll just bet you want me to leave here so you can take my place at the trough.

HERMIT: It's too bad you have such little faith in yourself, or in anything for that matter.

HERD ANIMAL: I told you what I believe in—eating, being warm, rubbing rumps. I think of myself as practical.

HERMIT: But don't you ever dream of living differently, of trying something new?

HERD ANIMAL: You're just mad because I'm like them and not like you. And for someone who's so hot on living differently, you spend an awful lot of time here in this pasture talking to me.

It's as if I am two species in one, species unable to crossbreed yet unable to accept peaceful coexistence. Analyzing it from the outside, all sorts of compromises come to mind—moving the hermit into the next pasture where the herd animal can visit him is my favorite. But while I'm caught up in it, the struggle never moves in such artificial directions—I have no model for such a compromise.

So here I sit on this park bench, feeling lonely, feeling...incomplete. When I'm by myself, the feeling tells me I need contact with my friends; when I'm with my friends, it tells me I need time by myself. The feeling waxes and wanes, but it never leaves. It's a gut level sensation, a relentless dissatisfaction, a most acute reminder of my humanness.

Generalization About Anything

Frame a generalization about anybody or anything from observations you have made. You might illustrate this with some of the very instances that led you to conclude your generalization. These may include some that you developed in greater detail for previous assigments such as Memories or Case History or Statement Through Story. But you may draw on any sources and mix in any combination: (1) firsthand experience, (2) testimony by others of their experience, (3) reportage and research, (4) statements by experts, (5) facts well accepted in a certain community or specialty, and (6) logical demonstration. Qualify as to the people or conditions for which the generalization holds true.

Read it to an interested group or submit it to a publication specializing in your subject. Or include it in a collection of your other writing.

Women's Language—The Pain of Recognition

DANA SCHILLY

I can't help but wonder. If you didn't know, could you guess from my writing if I am male or female? I'm probably going to be self-conscious now, which is unfair. Things have hit me sort of suddenly, and left me dumbfounded. I'm afraid that I might be exhibiting stereotyped behavior. It started when a friend of mine told me he'd picked up my tendency towards rising intonation.

"My what?" I said.

"Your intonation," he answered. "You say everything as though it were a question."

"I say everything as though it were a question?"

"And I've picked it up."

"From me?"

"From you," he flaunted, matter-of-factly, and I'm sure he meant it to sting.

I worried about it a little. I knew women had their own little vernacular, but I was not sure it was handicapping. So, I had a bit of a deferential intonation. Associations with Canadians had resulted in my inclination to use tag questions (eh?). Occasionally I might, you know, sort of hedge, maybe. Still, it was nothing to turn mauve in the face over. I was not using any of those absolutely hideous intensives or darling, empty adjectives. No one could ever say I spoke in *italics*! And I never used any of those higgeldy-piggeldy nonce forms. Still, I worried.

My worries were turned to horrors a few days later by what I consider to be the proof of the pudding. I was reading a restaurant review in the newspaper written by a person with an ambiguous name, could have been male or female, except for the prose, which pointed in a decidedly skirted direction.

"This is one of the best-dressed fast food meals in town with a shiny green ruffle of lettuce and a bright red slice of tomato poking out of the soft, lightly browned piece of pita bread. Tucked within is a bounty of thinly sliced ham and turkey and shredded lettuce that is pleasant and filling but very bland...It is a handsome meal, towering high with its lettuce, tomato and thinly sliced turkey peeking out of a soft buttery roll." (James, D-4.)

Pleasant and filling, but very bland, eh? It is actually rather unpleasant, even ugly, and artificially sweetened. This sort of prose gains nothing with its use of precious vocabulary. What is the word "peeking" doing in a description of a turkey sandwich? (I could tolerate it, maybe, if the restaurant were Chinese and the dish described was duck).

According to linguist Walt Wolfram, women in general have a superior command of language and a freer use of a wide and expressive vocabulary (Wolfram, 57). Supposedly, women have some sort of "intuitive" adaptation for communication that is somehow connected with their knack for nurturing (or some such bullshit) (Moreau, 49). Truth is, women often sound silly, and we know damn well we sound silly. We despise each other for sounding silly, and we keep on, as though our lives depended on it, sounding as silly as necessary, because we are afraid.

Always, the easiest, most comfortable course of action is to maintain, or go along with, the status quo. Women often hang on to the old protection of the submissive role, the role most familiar, the role which affords them their modicum of power, such as it is, usually acquired through subterfuge, usually restricted to the home sphere. We hold on to our exclusivenesses, the "frivolous" language of our mothers, which is both "a way of taking refuge and attempting to assert the self" while locking us into the definition "imposed" on us by the dominant group, by the persons in power, by men (Moreau, 60). And, of course, we hate it. Amazingly, fully one-fourth of women express a desire to have been born in the opposite sex (Hacker, 158). Despite statistical testimony to strong same-sex bonding among women, and evidence of difficulties in communicating with members of the opposite sex among individuals as intimate as husbands and wives, many women claim to dislike other women; they say they prefer to work under men and that they find "exclusively female gatherings repugnant" (Hacker, 158). Women have internalized a behavior along with the prevailing prejudice that associates the behavior with inferiority and negativity. We have learned to hate ourselves.

Just how adverse an effect this self-hatred and mistrust is bound to have on developing women was demonstrated in an experiment which involved asking female college students to rate a series of articles on various subjects. The coeds were alternately told that the articles were written by male or female experts. According to Sandra and Daryl Bem, an "identical article received significantly lower rating when it was attributed to a female author than when it was attributed to a male author...[even] articles from the field of dietetics and elementary school education [were downgraded] when they were attributed to female authors" (Bem and Bem, 181). The implications are clear. Whether by by-line or speech style, the addition of a female name to any communication robs it of its authority. Women themselves in college— preparing themselves for what?—cannot believe the authority of a woman's voice. At times they cannot even stand to listen to it. (A refined woman is ladylike, soft and quiet; "loud" and "shrill" are derogatory terms for pushy, uppity women.)

The same dictates which allow a woman to get away with words like "mauve" instead of "purple," and "ruffle" instead of "leaf" also keep her from feeling anything but aberrant with male-domain words, aka sex-related obscenities (these same strictures supposedly make it impossible for enforcedly innocent women to successfully tell jokes). Women have, somehow, become the guardians of purity, the protec-tresses of virtue (a dirty job, but someone has to do it), and it is evident how this distinguishing moral superiority has taken a mental toll on women. It denies women the most accessible and least destructive mode of expressing anger and aggression. According to psychologists Nancy Henley and Jo Freeman, women are forced to "punish themselves for their own anger rather than somehow dissipating it" (178). The result is that women internalize their anger and turn it into self-hatred, express it through bouts of depression, "the most prevalent form of 'mental illness' among women" (Henley and Freeman, 178).

The nonsense which attributes to women an aversion to matters sexual and "gutteral" appears to be a reaction formation which arose from an initial belief that women are nothing but sex-mongering temptresses with a fierce power over men which they exert in the form of sexual attractiveness and which, unhemmed, distracts, distresses, and ultimately dissolves the higher purposes of defenseless men (Williams, 4). Biologically, women are recognized as the superior sex; this makes Woman an entity to be feared. She holds the real key to species survival, the ultimate ability to insure continuance; man is quite naturally awed by women in her "primitive nakedness"; she must be hedged with ceremony and artifice, drawn safely away from Nature and the source of her strength, the earth (Williams, 3). The only superiority (other than monetary) which man holds over her is in personal, physical—brute, if you will—strength.

Conveniently, shamefully, tragically, the characteristics of wo-men's language reflect the implied threat of physical violence necessary as a last, yet all-prevalent resort for keeping woman in her subordinate place. Women's choice of vocabulary, richer, yet denigrated, is unhesita-tingly used by women despite the fact that it is mocked. A parallel can be made between the use of women's words and the carrying of purses. Women are forced to carry their belongings in handbags because their clothing, designed   to accentuate the femaleness of their bodies, is without roomy pockets. In America, purses are exclusively feminine accessories and have become associated with inferior female status and are used as a means of deriding both women and transvestites, usually in the form of "I'll hit you with my purse" jokes, thus emphasizing the ever-present physical threat inherent in the male position of domination (Henley and Freeman, 174). In addition, the use of subtle, implicative, indirect, self-questioning tones is a sort of accession to the physical force implied behind deference. A woman must always leave herself an "out."

While speaking, a woman often tilts her head slightly, especially if talking to a man. This is the beginning of a "presenting gesture," submissive, a form of gaze aversion designed to inhibit "any aggressive or threat behavior on the part of other conspecifics" (*conspecifics?* maybe we should be evaluating psychologists' languages) (Henley and Freeman, 177). A woman's language, like a giggle, apologizes beforehand for her daring to have an opinion. Marge Piercy expresses this in "Woman's Laughter": "Forgive me, for I do not take myself seriously. Do not squash me."

The subtitle of the restaurant review which, to some extent, sparked my horror was "The chains that bind us," a pun on the fact that the reviewer was evaluating fast food chains (and possibly on some unfortunate effect fast food has on her sluggish digestive system). Another pun is that the language in the article was forged unaware from ingredients more sinister or insidious than any evil hamburger mogul ever dreamed of. McDonald's is made accountable for calories and nutrients; the reviewer is most likely oblivious to her own expressions and their implications and to the fact that she is literally giving herself a tongue lashing; or perhaps it is better to say, if she and we are in a bind, it is a tragic case of being tongue-tied.

Works Cited

Bem, Sandra L. and Daryl J. Bem. "Case Study of a Nonconscious Ideology: Training the Woman to Know Her Place." Cox, 180-191.

Cox, Sue, ed. *Female Psychology: The Emerging Self.* Chicago: Science Research Associates, Inc., 1976.

Hacker, Helen Mayer. "Women as a Minority Group." Cox, 156-170.

Henley, Nancy and Jo Freeman. "The Sexual Politics of Interpersonal Behavior." Cox, 171-179.

James, Leslie. "Fast-food eateries—sampling the chains that bind us." *The San Diego Union*, 2 December 1984. D-4.

Moreau, Noelle Bisseret. "Education, Ideology and Class/Sex Identity." in

Language and Power. Ed. Cheris Kramarae et al. Beverly Hills: Sage Publications, 1984. 43-61.

Williams, Juanita H. *Psychology of Women: Behavior in a Biosocial Context*. New York: W. W. Norton and Co. Inc., 1977.

Wolfram, Walt. "Varieties of American English." in *Language in the USA*. Ed. Charles A. Ferguson and Shirley Brice Heath. New York: Cambridge University Press, 1981. 44-68.

Personal Essay

Use personal responses and memories—the material of your life—as a medium in which to deal with ideas touching on other people's experiences.

Set down thoughts triggered in you by a particular object, locale, or event that has come to mind recently. Refer in your essay to this stimulus itself, and retain some of the mood and circumstances in which the thoughts occurred so that you convey the thinker and the thinking along with the thoughts. Print it up with personal essays of others or in a collection of other pieces of your own aimed at a similar readership.

Autographs

CINDY DeFILIPPIS

On my shelf of memorabilia there are stuffed animals, prom pictures, ticket stubs, a bottle of green M&Ms, and my autograph book. Though the book is zipped closed, in its rainbow-colored pages are my fondest memories of grammar school. These autograph books were handed out at an assembly held especially for eighth-graders. In Chicago, once you were in eighth grade you were the greatest student on campus.

However, these books were actually status symbols of your popularity. If you could have at least three-quarters of your book signed you were "cool." Perhaps the biggest step to take was to decide whether or not boys should sign it. More specifically if you had a crush on someone it was a challenge to have him sign the book. While he was signing your book, you would have sweaty palms, and your friends would be gossiping. The worst part was to sign his book. Either you could be mushy, "roses are red, violets are blue, all I know is that I like you," or you could write, the standard "Good luck in high school."

It became a battle of the pen. Everyone wanted to be poets. Among the salutations were maxims. Some people were creative: "Spring has sprung, the grass has riz, this page belongs to Liz." Then there was the unsuccessful comic: "If all the boys lived across the sea, what a great swimmer Cindy would be." Then there was the introvert. This was the kid who sat in the corner and wouldn't even talk to the teachers unless they spoke to him. In my book he wrote "censored" in big bold-face letters, then in the corner he wrote in small letters, "Thoughtfully yours, Robert White." He wrote the complete opposite of my best friend. She wrote a novel of "remember whens," one after the other.

Even the penmanship still gives away the person's characteristics as you read the book now. Just their handwriting would make you remember them. There was the friendly girl. She wrote in big, bubbly circles. She dotted her i's with hollow circles or even little hearts. The bottom part of her Y's ended up underlining the entire word with a squiggly line. Then there was the class clown, also the class illiterate. He would write so sloppy that all I could understand was "good luck I..." I never could figure out what the rest said. But I still remember him as the funny guy who couldn't write.

Inevitably, teachers signed these books. The principal's signature was not the most sought after. Instead, it was our "coach," who had been our P.E. teacher since kindergarten. He wrote about your best qualities, to make you feel good. Mrs. Hardgraves, our math teacher, had us stand up at her desk five at a time, standing in single file. She would put a little graduation cap sticker in the book and wish you luck in one sentence. She never really knew who anyone was, so she had to flip to the front cover to check your name.

The front cover of this autograph book had gold-printed letters on it. In the left-hand corner was "The class of 1978," in the middle "Pennoyer School," and in the right-hand lower corner "Cindy De Filippis." I remember how long it took me to decide what to put on there. It was a major decision between "Cindy," or my full name, "Cynthia." The faded white leather-bound book had dust on it. I hadn't opened it until just recently. Without this I would have forgotten all these diverse friends of mine, and what they meant to me.

Often many people remember others by their pictures. However, it has been known that words are more memorable than pictures. One may read a particular phrase and recall a person's wit and character. To most, words are by far better than still pictures. Words are the special way people use to convey their feelings to others. Therefore all the form, style, usage of words, penmanship, indicates their personality, which one would never forget.

Strangers

CHERYL NELSON

Strangers. I see strangers everywhere. Restaurants. Parks. Beaches. Walking through a shopping mall the unknown faces pass by like autumn leaves in a wind storm. Suddenly I see a face. I slow my walk and stare. Those eyes. That smile. The walk. I know the person. My gaze burns her skin and she turns to look at me. A stranger. We pass by each other. Turning my head I watch and wonder. Who does she remind me of? Someone I met while traveling in Europe? A face from my collegiate past? A relative? I do not know. We are strangers.

At a cousin's wedding the relatives converge. My mother talks with her cousins and aunts. We children stand awkwardly along the wall, watching and trying not to look bored. A lady walks over to us and hugs each of us—Great-aunt Ella. A dear Norwegian lady who remembers our names in the right order. We briefly chat until we're interrupted by a girl's voice calling Great-aunt Ella away. Later we ask mother who the girl was. Our cousin. Strangers. We are related by common blood, but the blood is not thick enough. We are strangers.

Moments like these are puzzling and embarrassing. Unfamiliar people who look like a friend or former lover. Nonexistent relatives appearing in flesh and blood. Strangers. There's another experience just as baffling—when an honest-to-God friend becomes, for just an instant, a stranger.

Karl and I had known each other for a couple of years and had spent lots of serious time together for several months. We decided to go for a cycle ride on country roads very late one night. We drove for miles and ended up by a lake. He knew of a trail onto the peninsula and started out. I held tight. Rocks poked up threatening to tip us over. He was steady.

At the end of the trail a campfire was smoldering. We sat down and quietly looked at the coals. I glanced at him as the reddish light cast shadows on his face. His hair was blown and his eyes intense. Suddenly I felt as though I were sitting with a stranger. The transformation lasted only a few very short seconds, but in that time I didn't recognize him. I saw only our differences and couldn't figure out how we'd gotten there. He had his drinking buddies; I had my Bible Study friends. He went hunting and fishing; I went to plays and classical music concerts. He rebuilt cars; I tried to write poems. I was confused. There sat a stranger. His black hair, deep set eyes, full moustache and muscled arms made him appear very mysterious and secretive. Who was this man who was so determined to prove himself that he started raising pigs, when most farmers were struggling to survive, and made it? Who was this person who probably read more books than I and remembered them? Who was this shadow of his father whom I'd grown to love and respect? I didn't know him.

Then another transformation occurred. He was still a stranger, but it wasn't a distant, cold stranger. It was the part in all of us that remains a stranger, hidden from others for protection and safe-keeping. I seemed to be seeing deep inside his soul. I saw the shadow of what was attracting me to him lurking somewhere in the depths of his eyes. Our differences disappeared and I felt incredibly close to him. I felt that if I touched him at that moment I would be transported to another world, his world, and changed internally forever. He stared into the dying coals and seemed to be communicating with them. I didn't know him, and yet I felt incredibly omniscient. The feeling was so fantastic. He was a stranger, yet I knew him. He was so distant, yet I somehow felt we were connected as one.

The spell was broken by chirping crickets and croaking frogs. A few stars were poking through the clouds as the moon reflected off the water. He looked at me and said we had to go. I doubt he even knew what had just transpired. In that campfire there was magic. I can still see his face and feel the distance and closeness I felt towards him then. I wonder still what it was that drew us together and what it is that continues to sustain our friendship. What is it that determines which of us will remain strangers and which will become friends? A face in a crowd appears as a friend, but is not. A relative we should know remains distantly unfamiliar. A close friend suddenly becomes a stranger. Strangers. Aren't we all?

A Work of Art

SHIRLEY RAU

I recently served on a panel at a three-day writing conference in Boise, Idaho. Eight teachers of English from grade school through college were arranged in a small semi-circle on a stage, responding to questions from conference participants. Toward the end of the afternoon, everyone was getting tired. We were all thinking about the half hour that remained between us and release from the cramped auditorium. Valorie leaned toward the small hand-held mike with a three by five card, the last question from her discussion group: "What is a teacher's responsibility when a student turns in writing that is confessional or that reflects a troubled perspective?" Her voice reverberated as I met the blank eyes of those opposite from me. Pat took the mike:

"The best thing to do is treat the piece as a work of art and comment on it as such. We are not trained to deal with counseling matters." Her businesslike finality signaled another panel member to go on to the next question. The rest of the session was a blur. My mind kept turning over and over "treat the piece as a work of art." That clinical, rubber-glove theory of dealing with writing was echoed by members of my own department. Literary majors all, they analyzed narrative perspective, imagery, character, plot, genre and theme. They analyzed everything in literature except its connection to reality.

Last year every student in my class kept a literary response journal. Charlotte Britton's journal was filled with poetry, which reflected her fragility and sensitivity. Each week writing groups met to share sections of the journals for comments. The poem that Charlotte shared in February was stark, devoid of the romantic softness so typical in her writing. And though I heard the poem that day and have read it many times since, I can only remember torn snatches:

> a dove
> the clang of a metal door
> a gun
> the question to one who remains

I don't remember exactly how the writing group responded; perhaps we didn't, perhaps the words of her poem turned over and over in our minds until the businesslike finality of some response signaled another reader to go on to the next piece. One week after writing the poem, Charlotte went into the bathroom between classes and shot herself in the chest. She lived through the suicide attempt but I've died it a thousand times.

King of the Mountain
STUART ROBINSON

As five of us sit on the porch of a small cream and green colored cottage in a hidden spot in rural Vermont on the Fourth of July, there is a sense that this is what the founding fathers had in mind when they gathered in a steamy, humid room in Philadelphia to serve King George III notice that a new nation where "all men are created..." was born. Freedom and opportunity, this was it—a beautiful setting, a high powered intellectual community, and a sense of sharing—all of this meant our getting ahead in life, and the green mountains seemed to serve as the symbol of this success because we were on top of one of those mountains. The thought of the hostages and their recent release reaffirmed this sense of American greatness as it became easy to be nostalgic about the feats of those Americans throughout history who had fought and who had given of themselves in the name of freedom:

the battles won, the causes argued, the rights defended, and the enemies suppressed. Though America was vulnerable, through the efforts of those before us, we found that we could climb any mountain and succeed.

When I was a little boy growing up in Harlem, New York, one of the games that we would play in a nearby junkyard (actually it was a vacant lot, where a business once stood, but abandoned because of a fear of safety and success) was "King of the Mountain." It was always a battle to see who would reach the top. Now this mountain was not a mound of dirt; it was a mound of discarded cans, bottles, oil canisters, tires, broken furniture, and other odds and ends. It was not a pretty mountain nor was it a safe one, but the game was a necessary challenge. One could get hurt on one's ascent; for if one fell, a hospital visit and tetanus shots usally were the next course of action. The challenge of the game was a step that had to be taken, otherwise one ran the risk of being ridiculed by one's friends; and that was the worst defeat of all. Life in my neighborhood had certain challenges, and this was a "biggie." It was a rite of passage in an area of decay and weakness. It was our childhood show of strength and chance for success. Now someone might say that everyone has mountains to climb in life, and some fall, but they merely dust themselves off and try to find other avenues to ultimate success. Patience and hard work were the two key ingredients because they insured success, but this was a special mountain because even if one reached the top, that never guaranteed safety or success. At any time a can or a piece of wood could shift, thus altering the mountain. One never knew where he stood. Mom explained it as God moving the mountain, "It's God's will." But despite the risk, we had nothing else to lose. We wanted to succeed, and we figured that we would because in America we had an "unalienable right" to succeed if we made the climb.

When I was growing up, the two roads to the top were either sports or school. To be a basketball player, which was the most popular sport, one played every chance possible. One watched the pros and learned to be as cool as Walt Frazier, Willis Reed, or Earl Monroe. Not tall enough to shoot properly at a hoop, one started out practicing his 360 monster, behind-the-back-and-through-the-legs dunk on a street level garbage can. One simply waited until height came into the picture. In my case I am still waiting. Anyway, being a basketball player was a glamorous dream because then "all the girls would be on your thing."

If one chose school, one was really smart, and chances were good that he would land a job as a supervisor in a store or a clerk in a business. Sure, the goals were modest, but they were realistic. To be educated meant that one was a poindexter—an outcast of sorts. One didn't have the time to practice the dunks and jams. Instead one worked at trying to do it like the white boys. There was no middle ground: school or sports.

In my case before I could make my own decision, my mother made the decision for me—school. She put up with "I'm sorry, we already have enough blacks in the fifth grade..." comments and persevered. I guess one could say that Mother knew best. As I began to get older, those who chose basketball realized that they all weren't going to be Dr. J because there was basketball outside of 133rd Street and Amsterdam Ave.; but unfortunately, those who had followed the glamour route had slit their academic throat. With not many options, they chose other avenues to the top: drugs, numbers, or the army. Those of us poindexters who stayed in school had become the envy of others and the models of the community. We had made our climb and made it look easy: good schools, good colleges, and good jobs. The future was ours. But like that mountain in the junkyard, the top can be unstable and unpredictable, and a fall from it can result in failure or even death.

I have never spoken to or met either Edmund or Jonah Perry, but I feel that we have some things in common: we chose education as our way to the top. We let our minds lead the way up the mountain, but as I have said already, the mountain is unsteady. One June evening, a can moved and Edmund and Johah fell. One dead. One jailed. On the night of June 12th, the two boys had been playing basketball in the neighborhood. They had a fraternal bet on the outcome of the game that whoever lost would treat the other to a movie. What happened next will never be answered because people, black and white, will always think and believe what they want about the incident involving two black youths and one white officer; and unfortunately, the courts and the media will keep it that way. Neither Jonah or Edmund turned out to have any money, and around 9 P.M. the youths set out in the direction of Morningside Park to "rip off" somebody. Sometime between 9 and 9:30 P.M., according to police, Officer Van Houten was jumped from behind and pummeled by Jonah and Edmund Perry. The youths reached into the officer's pocket and demanded that "he give it up." Officer Van Houten had had no other contact with the assailants before he was attacked. During the assault, Mr. Van Houten shouted that he was a police officer. As Jonah pulled Mr. Van Houten to the ground from behind, the officer reached for his gun and from a distance of less than a foot, shot Edmund, who was in front of him. Mr. Perry, who had been taken to St. Luke's Hospital at some point between 9:41 and 9:55 P.M., was pronounced dead at 1:55 A.M. on June 13th. And just like that, Edmund Perry had fallen off of his mountain: Exeter, Stanford, and an undoubted host of opportunities and dreams had been silenced with one bullet. A can had moved.

What is so sad and special about this story is the growing love and respect that had developed between the two brothers. All too often the road to the top is a lonely one, but not for Edmund and Jonah. Their relationship had not always been a close one; but as they both began to see the top of the mountain, they sought to help each other. Unlike my childhood game, they saw room for the both of them at the top. They were different—"Eddie, smart; Jonah, cool"—but they pulled for each other. But just when their mutual support had gotten them to the top, their mountain shifted, leaving Edmund dead and Jonah facing charges of assault.

So as I sit on the porch in this quaint little town on the day of America's birth, I put down the newspaper, look out at the mountains and think about the climbs that all men and women have to and will make in pursuit of their dreams, but the picture of Jonah and Edmund Perry reminds me that although we must make that rough climb....

Vitally Linked

JULIE HILE

Drawing left foot precariously back, balancing laden paper plate in right hand, I hauled off and kicked at the mossy stone wall that stood in my way. Dumb thing. Dumb old rocky thing. I hated my mother and my father and my grandparents and my cousins and every single family reunion in the world. Adults pushed and smiled down at me, big kids looked disdainfully through me, and I never knew where to sit—where to be inconspicuous. The wall poked me as I plopped myself down, drawing knees up (who cared if my underpants showed) and stretching Cousin Les' thick tan sweater all around. I kicked my plate, half on purpose, and then pouted as it toppled and fell, spewing jello-salad, tossed salad, hamburger, brownie across the grass. I was so by-myself. I hurt.

"Heya, Julie!" My cousin Barry's grin rounded the end of the wall and advanced. He wore an ominous armor of photography equipment which he immediately unloaded. "Sitting in the pout spot, huh? Would ja let me take yer pitcher? Hmmm. Wait one minute." He disappeared back round the wall while I wiped my runny nose on Les' sweater. Pout spot? How did he know?

"Here, this'll do it up right. Hold this guy tight an' smile." A downy white-and-grey kitten suddenly clutched at my sleeve. It held on...real tight. I smiled. Flash. Set chin, dimpled right cheek, tragic brown eyes, bunny-rabbit-baretted hair recorded for eternity.

Whenever I pull that old photograph out, I marvel at Cousin Barry's style. He pulled me in. He quelled my four-year-old fears that I was in this weird game alone. He helped me to know that I mattered and that he had one time, perhaps more, been a miserable little kid, too. I wasn't alone at all.

That same year was the first time I thought about my floor tiles. Butting my belly softly against the salmon-colored kitchen counter, my thumbnails chipping away at worn spaces where the wood showed through, I slowly dropped chin to chest, leaned back to regain my balance, and scanned down my front: plastic buttons on fuzzy orange sweater, nubby corduroy knees, scuffed leather shoes neatly framed by four tiles. Three were Lava soap green and the one remaining was the brown that looked dirty even when it was clean. All had light squiggles. All were worn. I will remember I will remember I will remember I will remember. Five years from this exact moment, I promise myself, I will remember exactly what I did today while standing on these tiles. I turned to the task at hand—the painstaking opening of a box of Jello. My grandmother stood at my left, preoccupied with potato peeling and pie dough mixing. The box would not open. I tugged. I considered asking Gram to help. I tugged harder, jerking at the paper. And then, after the sour red powder had exploded over the counter, floor, Gram, and me, Gram scrubbed for hours.

As it happens, I do remember—in snapshot glimpses—additional scenarios from that spot. They thread my years together neatly, if sporadically. I am most interested, now, in what prompted my desire to not forget. It is possible that I simply wanted to keep track of me...to see where I had been. At age five, I proudly wrapped a child-sized loaf of wheat bread—my own patty pan creation—and addressed the warm brown paper, "Julie Thompson, Minong, Wisconsin." A surprise for my penpal. The following year, my brother, Jeff, persuaded me to gnaw off a corner of the grimy, pocked parafin that bounced around in the cupboard's narrowest top drawer. "C'mon, Jul, it's great chewing gum," he urged. It wasn't bad. When eight, nine, ten, and eleven years old, I pranced over the tiles constantly with brother and sister as we bickered our way through dishes after dishes after dishes.

"That's not how you sing that song. If yer gonna sing it, then get the words right. It goes like this..."

"I can sing it any way I want to."

"Huh uuuuh."

"Uh huuuuh."

Once I watched soapsuds ooze slowly over the edge of the sink as I modelled for master-artist-to-be, Jeff. He wanted to do a portrait. Portrait sitters were required to sit absolutely still. No talking. And the frothy bubbles plop, plop...plopped onto Mother's freshly waxed floor. Green and tan obscured. Last summer contact-lens-looking fish scales zinged and stuck to the walls, skin, hair as I learned to filet.

These remembrances provide me with a history, a sense of self.

James Michener seems to have been similarly interested in what has gone before in his writing of *The Source*, a novel which affected me powerfully. In constructing his story of Tell Makor, an Israeli archeological site, he writes not only of the experts wielding picks and surgical instruments, but also of the people who used the now-artifacts practically. A robust middle-aged man, for example, sacrificed his life for the concubine whose representative was the icon, Astarte. The birdlike Hoopoe manipulated primitive surveying equipment in collaboration with a very bright but very black slave to design the well-shaft that would protect this place from marauders for hundreds of years. In the space of five miles and over eons, then, a rich collection of lives, deaths, pleasures, pains takes place next to the single constant—a stubborn olive grove. The personality of the place becomes very important in Michener's novel. It lives. The Bee-Eater from Chapter One is somehow linked to Hoopoe of Chapter Nine. Vitally linked.

I began to wonder not only what I had done, years ago, on this path or in this chair; perspective broadened, and I wondered who else had walked there. What other thoughts had been woven in this spot?

"You see that skeleton over there?" My tenth grade biology teacher pointed instructively at the bony display in the corner. "You ...and that...are vitally linked. The great vat of matter whence that fox came is the same great vat whence you came. Matter is not created nor destroyed. It is simply rearranged." Vitally linked. I thought a lot about that idea once I'd stopped shuddering at the image of me floating about the primordial soup with God knew who or what else. I developed a reassuring feeling of company. Others had struggled, triumphed, laughed, failed, died. My flesh, my bones, even the energy that was my lifeline was somehow connected to the Grand Plan. I fit in. I was part of the whole. The wheel had been created, the path previously trod; I was not alone.

I noticed the stars. Whenever I look at the stars, my equilibrium wobbles. Initially acknowledging the holes that the light shines through, I reflexively reconstruct the reality. I am at once, me, there on the ground, and me, photographer in the air. My lens zooms in—screen filled at first with my own skin, hair, watchful eyes—only to pull swiftly back, expanding its vision and cheapening my stake as even a part of the whole. I recede. I shrink. I...disappear.

The cinematography further brings to mind a Peter Breughel painting entitled "Landscape of the fall of Icarus." In it, one searches distractedly for the young man as he falls, ruined, from the Heavens. Instead, however, prominent is the farmer plowing his field, the shepherd tending fleet-footed goats, cargo ships churning up a wake as they build up momentum for a long trip. The day is glorious, teeming with action. Icarus' tiny, pale leg only briefly mars the harbor's surface. He...disappears.

So my original relief at being pulled into the group, at tying my life together with memories like those on the tiles, and at sensing my place in history, has come to be tempered with the discovery that I am...insignificant...in this life. My egocentricity is challenged, and while I take comfort in perceiving myself as part of the whole, I am disturbed to see myself as *no more* than part of the whole. Now I reconsider the question, What...is...the...matter? I sit in one place and wonder what else that place has seen or endured; what, given the opportunity, could it tell me? My parents have recently informed me of their plans to market our old house. The tiles will, by Michener's standard, pass into a new chapter. And that's not bad.

Column

Write a newspaper column in which you develop briefly some general observation about a recent trend, item of news, or current issue of interest to the readers of the paper you have in mind. Fit length to that of professional columns you are familiar with. Your column may treat a subject of general human interest or a specialized topic. Decide how folksy or formal you want to be—its character. You might try keeping the column going for a while on a regular basis.

The Joy of Pets

DENISE MIAZGA

It just isn't worth the aggravation to have pets.

When I first got my dog, I was so happy to have a companion, a friend, something loyal to the end with me every day. Very quickly this euphoria ended. My dog had a litter of puppies, and my landlord found out and evicted me. Not even two months later, my lovely companion ran away, and it cost me forty dollars in fines to get her back.

After getting tired of this, I gave her away and kept her puppies, only two of them. When I moved to my new house, I put up a professional pen and was happy at last. Not even two days later they broke "jail" and caused me to work six hours in the pouring rain to fix it all over again. Naturally a few hours after they were safely back in their pen, they escaped again, digging under this time, all of which gave me a tremendous migraine headache, not to mention the blisters on my hands from fixing the pen.

Now the new problem of pet owning is the fact that my male dog has been running wild throughout the neighboring farms and eating my neighbor's chickens. This new item was told to me when I met my neighbor for the first time, standing in my front door with her mauled chicken. I was warned that my dog will be shot on sight if he comes near her farm or her animals again.

The other day we ran out of heating fuel, so I called the oil company to get a delivery. When I returned home, there was a note on the door to call the company as no delivery was possible. I was told that my dog had broken loose once again, scared the delivery man, so there will be no delivery unless the dog is confined out of sight. Of course, I had to keep him in the house all day for this to be possible.

Now, my daughter has wanted a pet bird for years, so we decided to give her a parakeet for her birthday. The bird was a true blessing for all of us. It didn't eat chickens, didn't scare delivery men, and didn't break out of a pen. All was fine until the joy of bird owning turned into a burden. My daughter forgot to give the bird his water and so did I, so one day she came running in the bedroom announcing her bird was still sleeping on the bottom of his cage. Of course the poor bird was dead, and for three days I was accused of murder.

My last example of the drudgery of pet owning: our pet snake escaped from her cage and was missing in action for two days. Everyone was afraid to sleep, so we took turns keeping watch for the creature during the night. After several days of no sleep and complete hysteria, my two-year-old son found Daisy under the refrigerator. We quickly sold the five-foot boa constrictor back to the pet shop.

Pets are not worth the aggravation of owning them. I think I will stick to stuffed animals instead.

Easy Money
MARK NAGLER

People in this country no longer want to earn the money they make. Today the fashionable way to get rich is either through law suits or lotteries. Hard work and dedication are no longer in style. Instead, easy money is the goal of most Americans.

Hardly a day goes by when I don't pick up the paper and read about another malpractice suit against a doctor. It's really getting ridiculous. In these lawsuits, I see people seeking millions and millions of dollars as compensation for damages incurred. Granted, some cases deserve to go to litigation, but I believe that the majority of the cases are absurd. For example, last week I read about a case where a baby was born with cerebral palsy. The attending physician was brought to court, and after losing the case, he was ordered to pay 4.9 million dollars in damages. True, the family suffered a great loss, but the fact is, there is no way that every child can be born without a defect.

Medical malpractice suits aren't the only kind prevalent in today's society. I think one of the most common phrases heard nowadays is, "I'm going to sue you for every cent you have." Libel suits against tabloids such as *The National Enquirer* are so commonplace they occur almost every day. I read about one celebrity who asked for 20 million dollars for the mental anguish she suffered from an article. That's an exorbitant amount of money to ask for hurt feelings.

For those people who aren't fortunate enough to have cause for a potential lawsuit, there is still another route to easy money. It's called the lottery, and I believe I am correct in saying that almost every state has one. New York has several lotteries, held daily and weekly. These lotteries create new millionaires every week. This past week, the New York State lottery jackpot reached a phenomenal 22.5 million dollars. People all over the state were standing in lines for hours for the chance to buy a ticket to the easy life. There were four very lucky winners, and several million losers, all of whom felt dejected at their loss. Oh well, there's always next week.

It's a shame that it has all come down to money. Everybody seems to think that money buys happiness. Maybe it does, but can it buy self-esteem? I don't think so, unless it's earned. But nobody seems to want to earn it anymore. Nobody wants to pay their dues. Everybody wants something for nothing, including me. Sad, but true.

Till Growth Do Us Part

AMY BESSERMAN

Susan has her master's degree in psychology and is the director of a family counseling clinic. Her husband Roger is a therapist at a rehabilitation center for alcoholics and is currently working on his doctorate. They were married after eight years of courtship which had withstood all the challenges their active lives brought to the relationship. I learned of their divorce last week after only three years of marriage. When I asked them what had happened each smiled complacently and agreed that they had grown in different directions and could no longer satisfy their personal needs within the constraints of marriage.

Debby, my college roommate, and her husband Neal were married after they finished college. We all lived together during school, enjoyed the recklessness of college life, and looked forward to the day they would get married. After five years of marriage, Debby and Neal have also decided to divorce. Dismayed, I asked Debby to explain why their marriage had fallen apart. I was saddened by the reply she gave me, for she stated they had just grown to want different things out of life.

Each of these marriages has lasted less than five years. I am appalled by the ease of their decisions. Whatever happened to "Till Death Do Us Part"? I feel a loss for these couples whose endeavors so abruptly came to an end, and I feel a personal loss as I watch the institution of marriage weakened by the pursuit of individual fulfillment so highly valued in contemporary society.

I have remained single through my twenties and will probably continue to be so for many years to come. Yet I believe that marriage is inevitable in my life and I am frightened by its vulnerability. I am confused by the hidden enemies of commitment which lurk about playing on our weaknesses and lead to the destruction of the bonds between people that once seemed impenetrable. I fail to see why individual growth is not enhanced by the intimacy and tolerance involved in developing a successful marriage.

I believe that it is time to reassess our values and our pursuits. It is time to realize that personal gain can be made just as easily with a partner and perhaps enjoyed all that much more. It is time to examine the institution of marriage and realize that it too offers growth and personal fulfillment that can last longer than any career.

Numbers

STUART C. GROSS

People today have lost their identity. We have all been reduced in some way or another to a number fed into a computer.

From the day children are born, they don't only get names from their parents, but also they start to accumulate numbers, some that they will use until their death. But there are also numbers given to them that they will use once and then throw away. At the same time parents name their newborn, the hospital assigns a number to that child, which the hospital says is used for bookkeeping. From day one, that child starts to lose an identity, which has not even been established yet. When children start school, the teachers might know their names, but the administration knows them only by their student identification number.

After people start working they get more numbers. The most common of these numbers is the social security number. Then they might be assigned a worker identification number. If they work, they will have to pay taxes. For this they need two numbers, one for federal and another for state. The money that is left over after taxes might be put in a bank. In this case the savings account doesn't bear their name; it carries a savings account number. If a person is late for work one day, and gets stopped for speeding, the cop asks for a driver's license but not to find out the person's name; all he wants is the driver identification number.

Some employee identification numbers are used to replace the name of product inspections. For example: who is inspector "12"? Every time I open a new pair of briefs there is a tag inside that reads "Inspected by inspector 12." Who is this person? If I purchased these briefs on credit my name would mean nothing, the store is only interested in my credit card number.

Even on Sunday, "the day of rest," names don't mean all that much. For example, when a person gets up and goes to the store to buy something for Sunday lunch, he first has to take a number to get served. When he gets to the checkout, the checker doesn't look at the product, she just reads the U.P.C. code on the bottom. After that person gets home, puts the television on, and watches some sports, he discovers that each of the players has a number. The announcer calls the players mainly by their numbers, not by their names. After the game, he calls some friends. He has to use the telephone number to get in touch with them. Later if he takes the family out to dinner, he might use his Mastercard number to pay for it.

I can understand that numbers help speed things along, but I feel that my name tells a lot about me. A number is just that, a number. You can't tell anything about a person from a number. On the other hand, a name gives a person identity. Some names have ethnic undertones, others may help you picture a person. If I said the name Irving Grossbaum and then said 113-05-0724, which one of these helps you draw a better mental picture, the name or the number? The name gives me a picture, it may be right or it may be wrong. In any case I have a mental picture in my head. I can't get anything out of that number, can you?

While we try to make things better and more efficient, we are losing the most important thing about a person, identity.

Editorial

Make a proposal for some kind of action that ought to be taken regarding a current problem of concern to readers of a magazine or newspaper you have in mind. Or simply argue a position you think appropriate to take by way of reacting to a recent event, trend, or issue. You might write as an "in-house" editorialist or put your case in the form of a letter to the editors of some publication. Set up the matter in the terms and framework you see it in, and marshal the facts and reasons for your solution or position. Fix length according to some editorials you have seen in publications or to the format of one you are writing for.

The Same, but Different
JOSH PINE

In rebuttal to a piece I recently read by Joseph N. Bell, "Silence on Campus," I feel today's students are "silent" and "passive," as opposed to the students in the 60's and early 70's, for many important reasons. And these reasons do not make today's students any worse, or better, but just make them different. These differences show because of a phenomenon that has existed since government and private enterprise

first inhabited this earth, the differences between politics and economics. It all boils down, as a matter of fact, to a very simple point:
politics was more important in the 60's and early 70's whereas
economics is much more important today.

College students of the 60's and 70's were "activists" because the
nation was directly involved in disputable wars that further affected
their lives. Today's equivalent is the faulting economy. Why should a
college student care about war in Central America or the Middle East? If
he does not make that A he might not make it into Med School or Law
School. With the nation's unemployment rate fluctuating at the 10%
level this student's ass is more worried about landing that job at IBM or
Rockwell International that could repay my college education and
support me well into my future life, rather than demonstrating against
a war 10,000 miles away and getting thrown in jail.

One must also take into account the reasons for this. As I
mentioned before, the 60's and 70's were times of war. Generally when
this country is involved in war, the GNP (Gross National Product) goes
way up, unemployment is virtually nonexistent and people are not lined
up in welfare lines a mile long. Back then they were not worried about
their economic future because within a two-week period they could be
looking straight down the barrel of a machine gun. Today if a college
student does not worry about his future he could be looking a welfare
agent straight in the eyes.

A further economic issue students must contend with today is
federal and state cutbacks. Proposition 13 and other cutbacks have
taken millions of dollars out of the public, and even private, school
system. Now many students must contend with going to local
institutions, sometimes of a lesser educational level than a major
university. As a result of cutbacks colleges have become more selective.
They have set strict quotas and requirements and abide rigidly by them.
In the earlier of the two time periods even some of the best universities
had no strict requirements or quotas. A good friend of mine went to
Berkeley at this time. I knew from all her stories she had not been an
outstanding high school student but had passed everything. When I
asked how she got into Berkeley, she seemed not to understand the
nature of my question.

In their own way college students today are not any worse, or
better, just different because the situation requires them to be
different.

Language Before Linguistics

GWENNA TONCRE

Reading the UCSD course catalog, prospective students might be struck by the fact that UCSD does not have a foreign language department; instead the Linguistics Department offers a variety of foreign languages. A closer examination reveals that in fact the instruction of these languages is poor and highly unorganized.

Short of forming a separate department for foreign languages, which is not feasible at this point, I propose a number of changes in the Language courses at UCSD that will improve the quality of education a student studying a foreign language can expect to receive.

The blurb in the catalog about the linguistics program is indicative of the stress put on sciences at UCSD; it goes so far as to say that "linguistics may be considered a formal science in its own right." The study of foreign languages, long considered one of the most important parts of a well-rounded formal education, is merely an aside at UCSD.

In order to alleviate this problem, many changes need to be implemented, beginning with a standardization of the requirements needed to begin studying a foreign language. Presently, foreign language students are self-placed, resulting in classes filled with students with widely varying levels of proficiency in the language. The catalog offers little guidance, merely stating that students with one or two years of previous study should enroll in the first year course, and so on.

Placement exams, much like those given for math and English courses, should be given at the beginning of each quarter, during registration. Also, Advanced Placement exam scores should be considered.

Foreign languages at UCSD are taught in two separate courses, conversation and analysis, that must be taken simultaneously. Analysis consists mainly of grammar review, taught in English along with an in-depth analysis of the language from a linguistic point of view. Conversation classes are taught by tutors who are natives of one of the countries that speak the language. To further the confusion of having two separate courses in one language, the department has students rotate conversation classes every three weeks so that they have three different tutors each quarter.

First of all, the two courses need to be combined into one, worth four credits. Grammar should be taught in the foreign language, not in English. Linguistics should be considered a separate study; if students want to analyze the language linguistically, they can take a linguistics course. Most of the terms used in analysis are specialized technical terms used in linguistics courses only and merely serve to confuse the students.

Theoretically, these are college-level courses, which implies more rigorous and faster-paced methods of instruction. Therefore, basic grammar should be taught in the first two courses. As in English courses, grammar ought to be taught only up to a certain level, then assumed to be common knowledge as stress is put on writing essays.

Another useless part of the foreign language courses at UCSD is the system of "contact points." Each day, one point is awarded for attending the class, an additional point is awarded if the student has done a substantial amount of the work assigned out of class, and a second additional point is awarded if the student has done all the work assigned out of class. In the end, the number of points a student has earned is a measure of the degree to which he has "taken" the course. Bonus points for doing well are what motivate grade-school kids. The points can in fact only lower the final grade and serve in no way to raise it; therefore they should be abolished. As the courses are run now, two types of reading are assigned to students: "intensive," and "extensive." The former serves to build vocabulary and help pronunciation in order to build up knowledge for tackling new material, while the latter's purpose is to develop the ability to read rapidly to understand the general context of a lengthy passage.

Neither type of reading is instructive in any literary way. Students are told that "in literature courses later, teachers will judge them by the depth of their understanding of the content of what they read; in the conversational course, however, the tutor is judging only their ability to converse about the book. They need not understand it well in order to do that." In the beginning levels, the above distinctions in reading may be helpful, but students need to be able to discuss books intelligently before they begin taking more advanced literature courses.

In connection with the idea of reading for understanding, my next proposal is that students begin to write short essays as early as the second level. One cannot fully understand a language until he is able to express himself coherently in writing, even if the subject material is simple.

Finally, students should be forced to speak more in class. Since the conversation classes have a maximum of fifteen students, one could assume that conversation would flow rather smoothly. On the contrary, the fifty-minute classes are often interminable, with forced conversations initiated entirely by the tutor. When students do talk, their pronunciation is almost never corrected and grammatical mistakes are pointed out only if the tutor finds it impossible to decipher the phrase.

The changes I've outlined require organization and time, but little else. They cannot be put into effect until the chairman of the Linguistics Department is convinced of a need for revision of the courses. Students must make their opinions known to the G.A.S. and tutors, who in turn can report to the department chairman. Obviously, the course structures cannot be revised overnight, but I do not think asking for major changes within a year is unreasonable. The key is to begin speaking out now.

If the foreign language courses are improved, then UCSD will be that much more of a competitive institution. Until there is a noticeable change the university cannot truthfully boast that it offers students a strong, well-rounded education: there is more to an education than learning science and mathematics.

Review

By way of making a recommendation to a readership interested in books, films, concerts, recordings, and so on, write a review of one of these in which you give reasons why your readers might or might not want to experience it too. This may involve summarizing its content, feeding in some background, analyzing how it was done, and comparing it with others of its kind. Post it in an appropriate place or include it in a newspaper you are making with others.

"Places in the Heart"
MARIANNE BLACKMAR

There is no doubt that the American landscape sets an excellent backdrop for a dramatic story. We have all sat through many openings and feasted our eyes upon the big skies, long country roads, and expansive plains planted with undulant wheat. So begins *Places in the Heart.* The opening credits are presented with a collage of American small-town life of the 1930's. The old woman living from her car, the black man knocking at the back door looking for a handout, the trainyard activity, the folks leaving church are all interspersed with various families sitting down to Sunday's dinner, performing the ritualistic prayers of thanks. The contrast between the tables set with food and the hungry people in search of a meal underlies the tension throughout the film. We are immediately aware that something is not right in small-town America. The opening scenes are beautifully photographed, but unfortunately they promise more than the film ever delivers.

The scenes are familiar. We know those images from the Depression; they are forever burned into our memories. *Places in the Heart* does nothing to expand or illuminate those images; they are handled in a completely predictable fashion, as are the themes of the film. Because of this, the film covers a lot of ground without delving deeply into any one theme.

Once the small town stage is set, we are sitting down to supper with the Spaulding family. Sally Fields, the loving mother, devoted wife, plays her role with all the strain and grit you can put into a naive farmlands housewife. Mr. Spaulding is handsome; Frank and Possum, the kids, are cute. All in all, family harmony prevails. Yet the repeated sound of gunshots interrupts this overstated view of happy American homelife. Shortly after grace-saying, Spaulding has to go down to town in order to calm "the drunk nigger" down by the tracks. Predictably, he is shot, although it is an accident, and the "niggerboy" is lynched and dragged through town. The Spauldings now have to survive without their provider and loved companion. *Places in the Heart* is about Sally Field's fight to survive the adversities—the bank, "big business," racism, sexism, and the Depression—all of which hit small Waxahachie, Texas with the force and subtlety of a tornado.

The day after Mr. Spaulding's and the niggerboy's funeral, nicely pictured as concurrent events, the big bad bank landlord comes over to find out how Edna (Mrs. S) will pay her mortgage. The handlebar mustache and top hat are hardly missed: "You must pay the rent!" he tells here. "But I can't pay the rent" she meekly replies. She realizes her land, her heritage, her family, and her American right are in grave danger. Where is our hero on horseback? Without the horse, he shuffles up to the back door looking for a handout and what he can steal. The action here is so condensed that it verges upon comic. Are we watching a fairy tale done realistically, or realism in fairy tale garb?

Moses, played by Donny Glover, is the smart, experienced and resourceful black man who offers the Spauldings their only hope—cotton! Mr. Banker has an idea too. He can get rid of his blind brother-in-law by forcing Edna to take him on as a lodger. Mr. Will, a stoic, not quite bitter veteran of the war adds another dimension to the film but not much depth to the struggling-family scenario.

Conquering the hitherto unknown problems of the man's world of business, Edna now learns to write a check and buy seed. Together she and Moses plow the fields and plant the cotton. Meanwhile, the other small-town couples that are part of the Spaulding's life are playing hanky-panky behind each other's backs. It's not easy to be happy in small-town America, especially, as the beautiful school teacher adulteress tells us, when all that ever happens are tornados and disasters. We can't really blame her for feeling that way since the tornado just demolished her schoolhouse while she huddled with the children in the storm hold. The predicaments aren't too different from Dorothy's in *The Wizard of Oz.* Everyone is looking to live over the rainbow.

Once the tornado has finished making its rude entrance and its heroes (Mr. Will fumbles upstairs to save little Possum, and Moses runs out at the last minute to get Frank tucked neatly into the cellar with the rest of the family), it's time to pick the cotton. The race is on to beat the other cotton farmers and win the first-bale prize of $100.00 to stave off the bank for a while longer. The whole family joins in and we watch the hands swell and backs bend in exhausted determination. The better moments of the film come when the action is specific such as during the cotton picking or the wake after the funerals. Writer/director Robert Benton shows his craft in these depictions of small-town American life and loses strength when the characters are left to ponder their situations.

After the cotton is picked, the money won, the mortgage payment made for the next six months, everyone takes a breather. We get a waited-for appearance from the KKK, who don't like Moses because he's too smart. This scene could have been dropped and it would only have improved the film. After being saved from death by Mr. Will (the name is allegorical of course) Moses knows he has to go, for they will only return to kill him. He says a "touching" goodbye to Edna, who is sad and genuinely appreciative of Moses. They have shared hard times and good times together. But are we supposed to believe that the doll, the rabbit's foot, and the handkerchief Moses gives to Edna will replace his know-how and labor, and save her from the future debts? No, Moses is leaving her much as he found her, the helpless widow with no means of making it in the white man's world of business. There is a real sense of hopelessness, both for poor Edna and for Moses, who will have to face the racism and terror anywhere he goes.

For this reason, the final scene in the film is completely off the mark. Sitting in church on a glorious Sunday morning are all the characters that appeared in the film from beginning to end. Mr. Spaulding, the niggerboy, the old woman who was killed in the tornado, Moses, Mrs. Spaulding—all are there passing the tray of wafers and juice for communion. All are praising the Lord as though the community were bound together in Christian love and humanity. The only exception are the school teacher and her true husband, whom she has persuaded to move to Houston in order to get out of the small-town trap. The rest of Waxahachie is partaking in what seems to be the opiate of the masses by performing the communion ritual and wiping out the discord of the last two hours. The ending is a slap in the face, an attempt to tie up too many fragmented themes and fit them under the canopy of Chistian forgiveness. The beauty of contrast established in the opening scenes is destroyed by this ending, and the film loses its credibility as a result.

Description/Definition

Describe what something is or is like. This could be an informative article as for a newspaper or magazine, an item in a manual, or an entry in an encyclopedia. Maybe a new product or invention or organization has come into existence or prominence that people ought to know more about. What's it like? Maybe confusion exists about something familiar that needs redefinition. Your subject could be an action like a process for making something, a procedure for getting something done, or some art or craft. Who might want your subject described or defined? For what purpose? Aim accordingly.

A Different Type of Angels
CONRAD DEL ROSARIO

In the cool and breezy night air, a few blocks south of downtown San Diego, lay the remains of a few, once productive railroad boxcars. Darkness engulfed the scene except for the dancing shadows of knee-high weeds.

"Rose, take Bull to the other side of that car and check it out." The deep voice emerged from a silhouette of four figures walking in symmetrical formation.

"Sure thing, I'll call if we need help," I replied to Ed, the patrol leader, as I climbed over the corroded linkage system between the two cars.

Thump thump. Bull and I froze in our tracks to determine the source of the sound. Thump. Within a second, we squatted to press our palms on the gravel-coated ground.

"Ed, there's someone in that car," I yelled as mist escaped with my every breath.

"Identify yourself!" A scream came from the other side of the car. Moments passed until it was disrupted by an ensuing bang, as if someone was rushing to answer a ringing phone in a dark room.

Screech. The large rusted doors of the car slowly opened to the outside world as a shadowy figure sheltered his eyes from my flashlight's blinding ray. "Don't shoot, I'm only sleeping here."

"San Diego Guardian Angels, is everything O.K.?" I said in a friendly voice as I noticed Ed rushing over to my side.

"Yeah, yeah," replied the transient.

"Take it easy," as I turned to Ed. "Let's go."

The San Diego Chapter of the Guardian Angels was organized two years ago when citizens of the area felt the violent crimes committed were getting out of control. Originally started in New York in 1979 by a man named Curtis Sliwa, the volunteer-operated organization was able to flourish as a result of concerned citizens around the nation who shared the concept of "citizen involvement." For at least eight hours a week, individuals patrol highly potential areas of crime. Each angel wears a highly visible red beret and a T-shirt bearing the insignia of the winged eye. Our objective in the streets is best described when a serviceman approached me and asked, "What, are you guys out here to kick ass?"

"No," I replied, "we're out here to make sure no ass gets kicked."

Despite growing criticism towards this controversial organization, I feel that its presence is an asset to the communities it serves. Although some people feel the Guardian Angels are attempting to gain power through their recognition, in reality, they are trying to tell the public to become actively involved in stopping violent crime. It is ironic to consider them a paramilitary group or auxiliary police force because they have no more special privileges than any other citizen. When one becomes an Angel, he realizes it doesn't become an eight-hour-a-week patrol, it becomes a twenty-four hour duty. When he sees a crime occur, his contribution towards humanity is his dedication to become actively involved. In a sense, the term "Guardian Angel" becomes a street philosophy that, if everyone applied it, criminals would find themselves against more obstacles than just the authorities. Curtis Sliwa said in an interview with New York University, "[It's] one human being caring about another human being. Instead of saying, 'O.K., I care about you. I'm concerned about you,' we're not even saying that, we're going out there and we're doing it."[1] In other words, the Angels are simply attempting to spread the word of "watching out for others."

Understanding that the Angels' philosphy is intended for the good of society allows the youths of our nation something to believe in. Edward Banfield wrote in his book, The Unheavenly City, that black and poor youths, between the ages of 16 and 25, committed crimes "because they saw it as a way to gain self approval in a peer culture dominated by expectations in crime."[2] In other words, they resorted to crime because as youths they saw "machoism" in committing crimes as they used criminals as role models. Responding to this, Sliwa intended to start patrols that would give the youths who were doing the robbing the opportunity to do something positive that wasn't a "sissy" thing.[3] In essence, the emergence of the organization, in areas where crime was an everyday occurrence, was able to give the youths who were committing the crimes the chance to be active participants in creating role models for others in the community.

What exactly gives the Angels the respect that makes them role models can be found in their requirements both prior to and after graduation. Although their training is not as intensive as the police department's, in order to become an Angel one must undergo at least three months of specialized training in every possible aspect the streets demand.

The training sessions are broken up into two segments, the workouts and the incident drills. The physical training is to screen out the trainees who wouldn't otherwise be able to physically protect others in an emergency. After all, if one can't handle himself, he becomes a threat to the patrol because each member depends on each other. Once the calisthenics, the running, and the self-defense moves are taught, the group begins its incident drills. These are simulated real-life experiences that a patrol is expected to control. This means that a patrol is assigned and put in the midst of a street situation where the "bad guys" are Angels acting the part. What is being learned is the way each Angel is supposed to handle himself in the event of a crisis. Also, trainees are subjected to extreme verbal abuse to determine if they are capable of withstanding the psychological threats inflicted by intimidating street gangs. In addition to these exercises, each member must be certified in cardio-pulmonary resuscitation, multi-media first-aid, and a citizen's powers to arrest, all of which diversifies their assistance to the community.

One differing factor between this group and lynch-hungry vigilantes is that the patrols follow specific rules and guidelines. The patrols usually consist of four to five Angels, depending on the number of members available and the intensity of crime in areas being covered. They have various formations, depending on the amount of people on the street, to minimize their vulnerability. For example, when they come to a street corner or an area where they want to "hold ground," they utilize the spread formation. This is when each member separates and finds a pole or garbage can from which they can stand or squat in front of to protect their backs as they keep their vision focused in front. This is extremely effective because it helps not to congest the pedestrian traffic as well as makes the patrol less vulnerable a target to anyone who decides to drive by and shoot. When a crisis arises, the group goes into immediate action. The patrol leader tells the runners, for instance, to pursue the suspect and arrest him. He assigns the phone person to request a police or ambulance unit, depending on the situation. Usually, he will be the victim-aide and he checks to see if the victim requires any immediate medical attention. Finally, one more Angel will be assigned to crowd control, where he takes out his pad and pen and asks for witness' names and a description of the incident. In a sense, each group works as a team to handle the most extreme of situations. Also, no weapons, drugs, or alcohol is permitted on patrol, and once a member is caught, he is severely reprimanded. This organization, therefore, is not just a group of angry and armed vigilantes, but rather, they follow strict rules and procedures previously set to fit the streets that place their actions above that which is normally considered acceptable in today's society.

The ones who fear the Angels most are the criminals themselves. This results in what is known as psychological deterrents to crime. What this means is that the people who are out there ripping off chains, the people who are out there picking pockets, the people who are out there raping people, molesting them; they know that there are other people also out on the streets—not in air-conditioned squad cars, not at the snack bar, not at the restaurant on their third or fourth break on an eight-hour shift—but out there in the streets where the action is, where the crimes are taking place, who are going to stop them when they do something to harm another person.[4]

Once the crime is in progress, the group does not hesitate to get involved. The difference between this organization and others such as neighborhood crime watches is direct involvement. If a neighbor sees a crime take place, then he calls the police, by which time the mugger has mugged, and the rapist has raped. The Angels risk their lives to save the victim from any more harm.

It all becomes apparent, from an overall perspective, that the Guardian Angels represent a dying concept in our society, where citizen involvement is absolutely necessary if we intend "to take a bite out of crime." By going into the streets of potential crime areas with their distinctive red berets and T-shirts, they act as the role models to the youths as well as psychological deterrents to the criminals. Also, the patrols are not just people who are going out on their own to fight crime their way; on the contrary, they are trained vigorously for months before they go out, and even then, they exercise the most discrete of actions since they have no special authority.

With all these attributes, the Angels, in reality, are a product of society's obsession to stop crime. This organization, therefore, is a benefit to the communities in which they exist.

Notes

¹ R. Puri and D. Williams, "Special Issue II; On the Guardian Angels," *Journal for the Anthropological Study of Human Movement,* 2 (1982), p. 37.
² Edward C. Banfield, *The Unheavenly City; The Nature and Future of Our Urban Crisis.* (Boston: Little Brown, 1970), p. 79.
³ "The Guardian Angels Are Watching You," *Mademoiselle,* Oct. 1982, p. 167.
⁴ Puri and Williams, p. 38.

Comparison

Compare two or more things with each other as a way of bringing out the qualities or traits of each. What are the similarities and differences? What is the value of this comparison? It might be to clarify or refine the reader's understanding of what the things are or do. Or you might evaluate the things by contrasting them. If the items are commercial products, this could be a consumer's report. If you are comparing alternative ways of doing or making something, you could show how the process or procedure could be improved. Maybe you want to stress similarities to show, for example, that two behaviors that we usually don't consider together are in fact alike in some important way. Often comparison helps to reclassify phenomena so as to think freshly about them.

Motocross Shootout: Yamaha YZ 400 vs. Suzuki RM 400

VINCENT FERNANDO

Motocross is the second most demanding sport in the world. To give you a better idea of how rough it really is, keep in mind that professional football is ranked only as eighth. Motocross uses specially built motorcyles. These bikes are raced across rough man-made terrain which includes but is not limited to, whoop-dee-doos (a series of jumps close together), berms (a concaved pile of dirt which helps the rider hit turns at high speed) and jumps. Every race track is different, and even the same track changes after every lap. This is due to the devouring power of the bikes—they literally tear up the track and produce different lines (angles/race lanes). In order to be successful in moto-cross, you have to have a good quality motorcycle that can take the abuse and punishment that motos (races) produce. The Yamaha YZ 400 and the Suzuki RM 400 are two such bikes. Both of these products are excellent. However, a dominant bike is revealed when the two scooters are matched in a shootout (a head-to-head comparison).

The most important characteristic of a good quality motocross bike is its handling and cornering ability. Races are won in the corners, not on the straights, so it is imperative to obtain a good-handling motorcycle. Both the YZ and the RM handle very well, yet both handle differently. Each has its own particular philosophy of control behind its design. The Suzuki RM 400 is smoother and more controllable than the Yamaha, while the YZ 400 is quicker and more responsive. The YZ and the RM share the same front end. The rake (angle of the steering column) is the same, as are the tires, forks (front part of the bike that holds the wheel to the frame), and wheels. But the front-end handling of the bikes is completely opposite. The Yamaha corners more sharply, dives in more radically, and changes lines more quickly. The YZ's traits are due to its higher weight and one-inch-shorter wheelbase. The Suzuki, on the other hand, is a lot more stable. Cornering is a degree slower, but also a shade better. When two machines have the same geometry and components, you expect them to be similiar. Although the YZ and the RM have the same numbers up front, the differences from there back contribute to the handling disparity. The Suzuki has a longer wheelbase, a longer swingarm (portion of the bike that holds the rear wheel), and a lower center of gravity. The result is slightly slower turning and more stability.

The engines also play an important part in the design of the frame and then ultimately in the handling of the bike. The Suzuki engine is small and compact. In fact it is two inches shorter than the YZ engine. This allows extra room for the RM's extra-long swingarm and accounts for the Suzuki's steady feeling around the track.

Although the Suzuki's engine is compact, it is not small in displacement. The RM sports 402cc's of power on its frame. In contrast, the Yamaha's engine is smaller in displacement (397cc) but larger in size. Surprisingly, the Yamaha is faster despite its smaller displacement. It's success is due to its huge 38mm Mikuni carburetor compared to the RM's 36mm.

Like the front end, both bikes share the same ignition but have an atypical ontology of power. Yamaha gives you abrupt power while the Suzuki gives the bike a mellow pull. In going for the holeshot (first off the starting line—in car racing it is called "pole position") the Yamaha would take the flag every time. So, what the YZ lacks in handling, it makes up for in power and speed.

Another important aspect to consider is the dependability of these bikes. Both seem to have their drawbacks in this field. While the Yamaha boasts having one of the best and most powerful engines, it's frame has been known to crack if the bike is thoroughly abused. This is due to the fact that the YZ has a monoshock for suspension while the Suzuki has two. This problem could easily be remedied if you go out and buy a quality aftermarket shock such as KYB or Boge. On the other hand, the RM is also supposed to have a very reliable engine, but a few Suzukis have been known to blow the top end (lose compression). Also, the RM swingarm has welds on it that look very sloppy. They actually look like silly putty.

Like dependability, the overall weight of the bike is very important. The lighter the bike, the less tiring it will be to control, and it will also go significantly faster. The Yamaha wins this category hands down. The Yamaha is eleven pounds lighter than the Suzuki (227 lbs. to 238). The aluminum swingarm and the fact that it only has one shock make the Yamaha lighter.

Finally, the price of the bike must be considered. Japan made, these bikes compete financially as well as mechanically. There is only a $100 difference between the two, the Suzuki being the more costly. Although the YZ dominated 3/5 of the categories, the RM would still be the better buy for a *completely stock* race bike. The most important category in motocross is handling, and factory-wise the Suzuki is the superior. On the other hand, if you wanted to race a bike in the modified class, then the only way to go would be the Yamaha since it is faster, lighter, and cheaper. Of course the rear end would have to be improved with a stiffer shock and maybe even a longer swingarm to help improve the handling. That would be the ultimate combination—speed and handling.

English and Japanese Foreign Economic Policy
NANCY SATODA

England and Japan, two leaders of industrial revolutions, have very different foreign economic policies. England was a hegemonic state on the vanguard of the first industrial revolution, and as a result followed a liberal foreign economic policy. The country's decline to its present state, partly due to the product cycle, has not altered England's foreign policy. The government has made attempts, however, to make the country a more mercantilist nation, but "cultural lag" has made the attempts unsuccessful. On the other hand, in Japan there appears to be a definite, but by no means complete, shift from a neo-mercantilist foreign economic policy to a more liberal structure. Japan is currently one of the leaders of the third industrial revolution, and its booming economy has created international and domestic problems that have lessened the government's power. Japan's state is not as strong as it once was, and firms as well as societal groups are beginning to challenge its authority.

England was the leader of the first industrial revolution; textiles, and its hegemonic position, dictated its foreign economic policy. Being the first country to industrialize, England supported Alexander Gerschenkron's timing of industrialization theory. Gerschenkron said early developing countries tended to be liberal because they did not face international competition and did not need state help. They favored a laissez-faire approach to the world market because they controlled it. This was exactly the case in England.

Ironically, England's strong position in the world was one of the factors that has led to its current demise. To see how this has happened, the product cycle must be taken into consideration. When factories in England invented and developed textiles, it had to first sell the new product at home to convince people of its worth. Once the home market was saturated with the goods, the product had to be sold to countries with similar economies, and then to poorer countries. The next step was foreign investment and the emergence of runaway shops in search of cheap labor. The final step in the cycle was the exportation of the products back into England. Foreign investment, though, was the most important step because that's where England faced competition. Other countries were able to use England's innovations and technology to create textiles themselves. They were able to produce the goods more cheaply because they saw England's mistakes, and these rival countries were immediately competitive. England was no longer the sole leader, because it failed to improve its industries through continuous innovation and investment, and other countries were able to catch up. As the market stagnated from the competition, England's entrepreneurs moved on to the development of the steel industry. The product cycle was evident in steel too; England eventually lost its position in the industry as competing countries caught up to it.

The difference between the steel and textile industries for England was that it failed to move out of steel and into electronics when the time came. Thus, the country was no longer one of the leading industrial powers. As a result, a liberal market was not to England's advantage, and as Stephen Blank notes in his essay, the government took steps towards a mercantilist society. There was more control of overseas investment, and military commitments abroad were reduced. The government in general attempted to gain more control of the economy. Institutions like the National Economic Development Council were formed to help plan and improve England's economy. This council, Neddy, was short-lived, though, because its plan for economic improvement assumed that exports would somehow have a higher growth rate than before, and a favorable balance of payments would be maintained. When this did not occur, and in fact the opposite did, there was a need to devalue the pound, and England's government would not. Their policy, based on that of earlier governments when England was still in power, was that Britain was the world banker and devaluing sterling would be unheard of. The government went to great lengths to maintain the exchange rate, even if it meant stalling England's domestic growth and deflating the economy. This stubborn adherence to past policies by successive governments, called "cultural lag," helps to explain why England fell behind other countries industrially, and was unable to make a significant change from a liberal to a mercantilist society. More specifically, controls of the economy instituted by the government were not effective because at some point it would have been necessary to devalue the pound, and the government was unwilling to do so.

One country that seems to be heading in the opposite direction of England, from a neo-mercantilist to a semi-liberal society, is Japan. Japan is an example of what Gerschenkron called a late-developing country who had to play catch-up in industrialization. When Japan first industrialized, it needed large amounts of capital to build factories that could compete with those of England and other advanced countries. Japan depended upon its government to secure capital and to direct its industrialization. As a result, the country was controlled by a very strong state and had a neo-mercantilist foreign economic policy. According to T.J. Pempel, Japan's foreign policy was determined by a small coalition and at the expense of labor, small business, and consumers. This small coalition, led by MITI, the Ministry of International Trade and Investment, and including big business, finance, and Japan's dominant, conservative party, LDP, formed a coherent idea of what it thought Japan's international position should be and set foreign economic policy to attain it. This foreign policy included restricting overly competitive imports to help domestic products, obtaining advanced foreign technology, and keeping domestic investment at home. The coalition also set the policies of Japan's industrialization. It decided what industries would be developed.

Today, Japan's international position has reduced MITI's power. Japan is one of the leading countries in the third industrial revolution, and its booming economy has changed the attitude of firms and societal groups. Firms seeking higher profits have tried to break away from MITI, and the emergence of societal groups has also weakened MITI's power. In the field of electronics, MITI has tried to take too much control of what could be exported, imported, and developed, and Japanese firms have begun to resist. They do not want MITI telling them what to do; firms are after profits and want to do whatever is in their own best interests. In the textile industry, MITI thought the country should invest elsewhere because textiles were the first industrial revolution, and according to the product cycle, Japan should move on. Firms, though, against MITI's demands, continued to invest in textile development, and even went overseas to make more money. They wanted to export back to Japan with low barriers and thus pushed for a liberal textile industry.

In addition, groups of different segments of society have emerged to become a force in Japanese policy making. Labor showed its strength for the first time in the early 1970's, and so did consumers, courts, and local elections, as support for the LDP waned. These groups have forced change in such areas as pollution control and pricing policies, when in previous years MITI and its coalition had virtually all of the clout in the policy-making process of Japan.

MITI's reduction of power, then, can be attributed to Japan's economic success. MITI is still a strong state, just not as strong as it once was. Concessions will have to be made on MITI's part in order to meet the changing needs of society and before firms completely break from it. Despite changes that have already occurred, Japan continues to be a fairly protected country with many restrictions on foreign investment and labor. It would probably take something like a social revolution for Japan to undergo a definite change from a neo-mercantilist to a liberal foreign economic policy, but significant moves towards liberalism have, and will continue to be, made. In England, foreign economic policy remains liberal because moves towards more government control have been unsuccessful as the country lacks the necessary instruments for the plans to be carried out. Much of this has to do with "cultural lag" and the government's failure to change with the times. If significant change is to occur in England, the government must realize that England is not the power it once was, and certain changes will have to be made in the government's overall policies. Such changes are unlikely.

Evaluation

Tell what something is worth by setting forth its good or bad points. Your subject could be an enterprise or operation,

someone's work or behavior, an object of art or manufacture, a
program, and so on. Within what framework of values are you
making your assessment? You might just praise or condemn or
make a mixed judgment. How general or specialized an
audience will be interested in knowing what you think of your
subject? You might think of readerships for certain publications
for which it would be suitable. Your evaluation could be one
kind of consumer report.

Bicycling

F. BRETT STAUFFER

Imagine the creative mind it took to put together the first bicycle—possibly one of man's most fantastic inventions. Who would have ever thought that the bicycle could have reached the highly technical stage that it is at now? Despite the ever-existing plague of flat tires the bicycle is a perfect machine. When maintained properly a bike is able to perform the most precise amplification of a person's leg power. Cycling has possibly grown to be one of the most popular means of attaining pleasure and prime physical fitness.

With the growing craze in fitness there are many different methods of getting in shape to choose from. Weight lifting makes you strong, but it only makes it look like you are in good condition. The stress that is put on the heart and lungs isn't hard enough or long enough to truly condition the body. You could run a couple miles a day, but then you will have to devote time and effort to two different activities. While running is making a comeback, it doesn't have the attributes that cycling has. Swimming is extremely healthy for the entire body, but when you discuss variety there is no comparison. A swimmer is restricted to swimming laps back and forth in a pool unless he can do the more difficult open water swim. Bicycling possesses an amazing amount of variety, which makes it an especially enjoyable and profitable means of exercise.

Riders can cover a longer distance and see a lot more than runners. One cannot compare swimming in this respect. A runner is restricted to about a five-to-ten-mile radius while a cyclist can easily cover a ten-to-thirty-mile radius. Being able to travel over long distances enables you to see the world go by. You see so much as you ride down a street clustered with stores, cars, shops, and pedestrians.

A wonder of the bicycle is that it has a tremendous amount of capacity for the transference of energy. Nothing but a bicycle can take the power from a rider's legs and turn it into pure energy. The only loss of power appears if the rider rocks or bounces in his saddle. A relaxed upper body is the ideal way to help reduce the amount of rocking.

An example of the supply of power is when the famous Bryan Allen propelled the Gossamer Albatross over the English Channel. The Albatross is a specially designed, prop-powered flying machine that uses the chain-drive system of a bicycle for its propulsion. The wings and the streamlined body that surrounds the bicycle and rider are made of plastic and balsa wood, weighing five pounds. The 125-pound Allen used the most efficient man-powered machine to supply power to the propellers. It was said to be impossible for a man to supply enough power to fly anything. Performances such as these tell us of the wonder our bodies can produce thanks to the mechanical advantage a bicycle provides.

Bicycling is just plain fun. It's so easy. It doesn't take a great amount of concentration (unless you should decide to get into competitive racing). Family rides are becoming more popular because the whole family can do them together. When a person is in good physical condition, the enjoyment of cycling can be extended as far as the imagination of the rider reaches.

There is an amazing phenomenon that takes place when riding a bicycle at a high speed. A sensation of swiftness is detected that is hard to produce in any other way, the excitement of speed. Going 80 to 90 miles per hour in a car isn't nearly as fascinating as riding 40 to 50 miles per hour on a bike. A noticeable difference is that there is nothing surrounding you, nothing protecting you. That frightening insecurity excites the rider and causes the adrenalin to flow. Cyclists can feel the road—every little pebble, crack, and twig. There is a wild vibration from the road that goes through the wheels, into the frame, and then into the rider. Every muscle in your body vibrates and shivers. A very important fact is that you alone are making the bike go. You are supplying the power. This is the difference between a bicycle and a motorcycle. There arises a sense of oneness with your bike. You wish to reduce wind resistance, so you tuck way down with your rear-end slightly higher than your head, and your hands are clenched to the handlebars at the center, below your chin. The least amount of wind resistance is needed to travel at the highest possible speed.

Bicycling is a very economical mode of transportation. When you consider the initial cost of a bike, you may argue that it is expensive. That cost is easily offset by the amount of money you save from not having to pay for gasoline or bus fares, and by the degree of physical fitness you will achieve by commuting. The valuable time that could be spent in your saddle spinning off the miles is wasted while you sit on your ever-widening end. You won't have to worry about getting in your workout if you commute by bicycle. Some people don't like to bike to school or their work place because they feel that they will smell like a clothes hamper. Contrary to common belief, athletic sweat has very little odor and only needs to be toweled off. For those who prefer, a quick wipe down with a damp washcloth or one soaked in rubbing alcohol will do the job. The reason why a locker room smells so bad is that the wet towels, shirts, shorts and socks become breeding places for the putrid-smelling bacteria, causing a horrible stench. An uncontrollable problem arises: the possibility of rain. If it does rain, there's nothing you can do but wait it out. The best thing to do, if possible, is choose a season when there isn't any rain and do some commuting during that time. Then you won't have to worry about unexpected rainfalls.

Perhaps the most beneficial aspect of bicycling is that it offers a superior method of exercise. Running also improves a person's health, but the infinite pounding involved often causes stress injuries to joints, ligaments, and tendons. Cyclists rarely fall prey to these nagging injuries. Where running is involved there is a constant tearing down with a very gradual building. In cycling there is only a massive building effect. The overdeveloped thighs of a veteran cyclist are proof enough. The smooth rotating of the pedals builds the legs and strengthens the cardiovascular system. A strong heart and powerful lungs are very important for health.

As one can clearly see, bicycling is by far one of the best known methods of exercise. If a person is within commuting distance of his destination, he can incorporate an exercise schedule into his commuting route. Along with the amazing speed attained by the effective transmission of energy, a person will quickly notice the infinite amount of fun he can have with a bicycle.

Is Good Evil Too?

ROCHELLE ANTONIEWICZ

Up to the rafters of the sacred sanctuary rose the melodious sounds of a church hymn from a hundred or so high school age kids. Their faces were smooth and serene as they sang the spiritual verses. Religious youth groups teach impressionable teenagers many values essential to living a deviant-free life. However, is the method the church employs to teach these values honorable? Do the ends justify the means? A fine line exists between church youth groups and some cults. Both try to capture the youth and to hold them captivated through some form of psychological control. Is a church youth group a cult with a social seal of approval stamped on it?

Youth groups undeniably teach good beliefs to teenagers, such as to be honest, considerate, and loving toward your fellow believers. From my youth group I've retained many values which have become the standards I live my life by. Although these values are considered good, some of them carry destructive attitudes. For example, my youth group taught us the value of remaining steadfast in our beliefs, which is a wonderful lesson if not carried too far. To remain steadfast in our beliefs we were requested not to associate with people who were not Christians, because those heathens would try to drag us back into the secular world. The pastor wanted us to stay in our own little world and not experience the pleasure of other people's company or religious views. These restrictions, he said, would protect us from Satan.

Although there exists some risk in being tempted into secularism by associating with non-believers, greater is the danger of becoming narrowminded and prejudiced. I began to close my mind to other people who did not agree with my beliefs, refusing to listen to theirs. Also, I felt that I was superior to them because I was right and they wrong.

Indisputably youth groups keep many kids off the streets and from getting into trouble with the police. A variety of activities are planned such as weekend trips to the beach, Mexico, or the mountains. Each week the youth group would meet on Wednesday nights from seven to nine. Church on Sunday was from nine to twelve. First, we went to our youth group for an hour and a half, then to the service for an hour and a half.

All of these events are wonderful and you are expected to attend them all. The leaders of the youth group utilized the most effective weapon they hold to force you to attend—guilt. They make you feel guilty that you are betraying God in some way by not showing up. From personal experience I have felt this subtle, high-pressure guilt. One time I couldn't participate in a missionary trip to Lake Havasu. The pastor questioned whether my previous plans were as important as my duty to God. Also, after he and I chatted, three people I knew distantly approached me trying to convince me to go. Many times I felt as though God was going to smite me with his sword because I was unable to attend some functions.

Youth groups sometimes instill fear within a person's heart by employing these well-intentioned strategies. They make you afraid of the rest of the world and of God so that you will remain in their safe, secure place, too frightened to venture past their boundaries.

Breaking away from the youth group was one of the most difficult tasks of my life. Quite by accident I was plucked from the fold by acquiring a job. Naturally my working hours cut into my time with the youth group. Soon I was taken aside by the pastor and given a lecture on missing the activities. He didn't tell me to quit, but warned that I would become a non-believer if I attended less and less. Although I knew his intentions were good since he was only looking out for my spiritual welfare, I didn't agree with the tactics he used.

Not wanting to inconvenience my employer with schedule changes, I continued to miss my youth group sessions. Then after two months of absence I returned one night. The change in my perspective was incredible. I felt trapped, suffocating by strict dogma. After two months of freedom of thought and independence, I did not wish to be molded into something someone else wanted me to be. Around me I saw robots who accepted blindly the lessons being preached. My horizons and beliefs had been gradually broadened over my absence. I was making me into who I wanted to be.

Although I have fond memories of many activities and still bear some of the values taught to me, I cannot condone the manner the youth group uses to teach them. Youth groups attract teenagers when they are impressionable, confused, and striving for independence. They try to mold the teenager into some idealized picture of a good person instead of allowing him to discover his own inner self within the youth group.

Textual Interpretation

Say what you think is the full meaning an author intended to express in some text that you think the reader is meant to fill out. Most fiction, poetry, and drama leave a lot to the reader to infer on his or her own by putting together all the images, ideas, or actions into some whole that accounts for the parts. But your text need not be from literature if you feel its subtlety, symbolism, or complexity require the reader's interpretation; it could be a true narrative or an essay. Choose some text that you have been drawn into and have thought about—something you think you could interpret to increase others' understanding and appreciation. Quote or refer to the text wherever you think it needs elucidation or whenever you think your interpretation needs support. Presumably all your evidence lies in the text except perhaps for certain outside information that you think it fair to bring to bear on the work. You might aim your interpretation at a literary periodical or at an audience interested in the subject matter as psychology, sociology, or philosophy. To the extent that your interpretation brings out how the author makes us feel or think something, your remarks might interest people concerned with writing or artistic technique.

An Interpretation of
"The Horse Dealer's Daughter"
MEGAN CARROLL

D.H. Lawrence's "The Horse Dealer's Daughter" is a short story about the loss of civilized man's ability to feel emotions, especially love. That is, modern man has lost the natural balance between his emotions and his rational mind. He gives his rational mind complete authority over life's decisions, thus attempting to keep his world in perfect control and order. Lawrence shows that to love is a part of human nature, and to choose not to love is a human flaw. He shows this through the roles his characters play. Those who do not find love, Mabel's brothers, are slaves to their own helpless and ineffectual lives. Whereas those who find love, Mabel and the doctor, find freedom and purpose in living.

Lawrence dedicates the first part of the story to those characters who have not found love and are completely out of touch with their feelings. He repeatedly describes Mabel's three brothers as "ineffectual," "helpless," and "hopeless." Joe's feelings about love and marriage are clearly negative. "He would marry and go into harness. His life was over, he would be a subject animal now." Joe refuses to see the love that can be associated with marriage and the animal he is becoming because he refuses this love.

The dreary mood is emphasized by the setting Lawrence creates. "Everything was gone to the dogs, there was nothing but debt and threatening." The family fortunes are lost. "They were frightened by the collapse of their lives, and the sense of disaster in which they were involved left them no inner freedom." The dismal mood is emphasized by their surroundings. "The dreary dining room itself, with its heavy mahogany furniture, looked as if it were waiting to be done away with." The brothers idly sit around superficially discussing their condition and painfully teasing their sister Mabel about her fate of servanthood. Thus the corruption of the family parallels the corruption of each individual in his failure to find any purpose in life. The brothers are unable to bypass their superficial reasoning, finding that the disaster that they all face is clearly not financial but instead emotional.

Lawrence also uses animal imagery to describe the whole family. Mabel's nickname is "bull dog." Joe "watched the horses with a glazed look of helplessness in his eyes, a certain stupor of downfall." Later he "straddled his knees" in his chair in a "horsey fashion" and then in "real horsey fashion." Fred Henry is described as "an animal who controls not one which is controlled. He was master of any horse.... But he was not master of the situations of life." Thus a question emerges of who is really doing the mastering and who is really doing the slaving. The family is described in animal terms to show their domestication. Dogs and horses symbolize domesticated animals who have lost their free will in some manner and are now subject to some kind of authority. The brothers think that they are masters controlling themselves and controlling the horses. In fact, they are not masters of "their own lives" but are in bondage to their rational mind. Thus they are creating limitations upon themselves, not allowing themselves to really feel and experience all that life has to offer them.

Mabel, in the beginning of the story, before her transformation, also feels helpless—destined to be a slave for the rest of her life. However, she is distinctly different from the rest. When her brothers and Dr. Fergusson tease her, she remains silent, not joining in their foolishness. Instead she seeks refuge in the churchyard because "there she always felt secure" and "immune from the world." Her remembrance of her dead "glorified" mother symbolizes her remembrance of the love that they had once shared. This sense of love is later shattered when her father remarries. She longs to return to this love. In fact, the churchyard and cemetery do offer another world which is more appealing than her own—the world of the dead. She has suffered long enough and "nothing...could shake the curious sullen, animal pride that dominated each member of the family. Now, for Mabel, the end had come." But the end of what? Mabel thinks it is her life. However, the reader sees that what she is actually doing is dying to the life she had lived before, dying to the animal pride she had once felt along with her brothers, and dying to her anticipated life of servanthood.

The doctor first notices Mabel in the cemetery. He had never really noticed her before, and he went along with her brothers when they joked about her. Doctor Fergusson was a "professional" and a hard worker. He only looked at things on a rational basis, never letting his emotions get involved in his work. He removed himself so far from the deep emotions related to his job that he was not even able to cure himself. Ironically, he is a sick doctor.

However, there was something that also distinguishes the doctor from Mabel's brothers. He loves working in the homes of "powerfully emotional men and women." He pretends not to enjoy his job, but there is something about "moving as it were through the innermost body of their life" that "excited and gratified" him. He loves the intimacy that his patients are able to provide for him. But this intimacy is only second-hand. He shares only in the taking of emotions and not in the giving.

Now in the cemetery, Mabel "mesmerizes" him by showing an 'in' into the world he is missing. He describes her world "as looking into another world. Some mystical element was touched in him." To him her face was "portentous," promising something of the future. So he is "watching her as if spellbound." He is seeing not "with ordinary sight," but rather "with the mind's eye" in a way that he is not accustomed. He is drawn closer. He watches as she progresses towards the pond. Soon he realizes her intent to kill herself and he goes into the pond to save her. The pond symbolizes transformation or baptism into new life, and the water in it is the water of new life. It is a medium between the physical world and the emotional world, a world of second chances. The clay in the pond symbolizes the new creation that they can become. The pond is obviously a new experience for the sick doctor. He can not swim and is frightened and intimidated by the "clutches" of the pond. The bottom is "so deeply soft and uncertain." It is something altogether different than he has ever experienced. It can't be explained or even reasoned. It just is.

After the doctor takes Mabel home and revives her, the contrast between the two worlds becomes very apparent. The doctor can not decide whether to love her or not. He feels torn between taking off his clay-dirty clothes (symbolically discarding the new creation offered to him), or staying with Mabel. He tries to rationalize his love for her. He had "never thought of loving her." But he finds that emotions can't be thought about in rational terms. Mabel emotionally attacks him by openly professing her love for him and asking for his acceptance. The doctor struggles because of the high cost of leaving the superficial world he had always lived in. He doesn't want to feel exposed, the same way that he knew that his patients had been exposed. "That he should love her? That this was love! That he should be ripped open in this way! Him, a doctor!" He could not bear the death to his rational side which was needed to be emotionally free. "He could not bear the touch of her eye's question upon him, and the look of death behind the question." He was the doctor and she was the patient and to love her was "a violation of his professional honor." Ironically, she was the doctor and he was the patient. She was healing him in a way that he could never heal. But to yield to her would be to admit his dependence on her and expose himself. He barely had the strength to do it. Finally "with an inward groan he gave way, and let his heart yield towards her." The end of the story is full with emotion. He now openly professes his love for her, and she expresses her unworthiness of him. Therefore, the ending of the story contrasts greatly with the dismal, lifeless beginning. In the very end the reader learns that their bond of love is to be made official. "We're going to be married, quickly, quickly—tomorrow if I can."

The complete transformation of the two main characters, Mabel and the Doctor, proves Lawrence's theory that man is destined to love. New life will grow, emotions will be felt, and, therefore, life will have purpose. They will no longer be reduced to the animal life which surrounds them.

Causal Analysis

Explain why something is true or has come about. What
are the causes for a certain current trend, for example, or for
the success or failure of some endeavor? Analyze the way some
enterprise or group, process or procedure, works to show why it
produces certain results. Connect effects with their causes. What
is the importance of your causal explanation? For whom? This
could be a way to increase understanding of the good or bad
effects of some agency or custom, trace some effects to their
hitherto unexplained causes, or show some hidden side-effects of
some actions not ordinarily associated with them. You might
think of what ordinarily unconnected things should in fact be
connected causally or of what common phenomena might be
better understood by causal analysis.

The Smaller the Better?

ANN-MARIE YAMABAYASHI

There is a trend in America today towards small things. Watches,
for example, are no longer just watches; instead, many have microscopic
television sets, calculators, and AM/FM stereo outlets on them. Even
homes have been affected. The large homes, so numerous in the past,
are becoming increasingly rare as housing complexes and apartments
are now being built in their stead. And perhaps the most recognizable
and obvious example of this shrinking trend are cars. The large,
gasoline-guzzling cars, so dear to the American dream, are now a
relatively rare sight as more and more small foreign imports roar onto
our highways.

The causes for this trend are numerous. And, while some of these
causes are produced by recent economic and technological developments, many are also deeply ingrained in America's past and psyche.
The most common and accepted cause for this trend is the bad state of
the American economy. Many items such as homes and cars are getting
smaller as a direct result of this bad financial situation. Today, most
Americans simply can no longer afford large homes and cars.
With the huge Federal deficit, and with ten percent unemployment across the nation, many Americans are no longer buying
luxuries and are instead trying to buy staples and everyday
necessities. According to a recent Columbia University study, the
average home has almost tripled in price in the last ten years, as land

and lumber become increasingly scarce and costly. As for small cars, their popularity is directly linked with the gasoline crisis that first developed in 1975. Suddenly, the price of gas soared and consumers acted quickly by buying small, fuel-efficient cars.

Another obvious cause for this trend is the increase of technological ability. The best example of this is the computer. With the advent of the microchip, computers have been getting increasingly smaller. And now that they are smaller, they've also become more popular; businesses aren't the only ones to purchase them, because everyday consumers find the small computers desirable also.

It is this very fascination that consumers have for smaller items that is making them so popular. Consumers seem taken with the idea that large burdensome items such as televisions and stereos are now portable. Certainly the convenience of small items is an attractive asset to a group of consumers who live in a high-paced and high-pressured world. Because small things suit the individual's world, efficiency is increased as well as convenience.

However, besides these common and accepted causes for why America is becoming increasingly small-orientated, some deeper and more subtle causes seem to be at play. For instance, it is hard not to be reminded, as one watches a person with a headphone stereo, pocket calculator, sack lunch and T.V./watch, of the early nomads who were the ancestors of modern man. These nomads, faced with possible death each day, were constantly moving, carrying with them all their possessions. And, although the nomads had been running from predators and bad weather, modern man's high crime rate and the potential for nuclear war are no less a fear and danger. Thus, fear of crime and nuclear war, two indisputable terrors of modern man, seem to make small, portable items more appealing as we try to escape the horrid realities we have no control over.

Another subtle, underlying cause for this trend is that America has finally reached its last frontier. The "bigger-the-better" philosophy that dominated much of early American history is being squashed down to size as America reaches its outermost borders. And, along with the end of American expansionism, ends the great spirit of individualism that America was built on. The tall, lone man on the saddle who conquered the West is now the businessman in his Toyota. America, the land of plenty, has been sucked dry of much of its natural resources, and now Americans are desperately trying to adjust to its new and cramped circumstances by way of smaller things. Smaller things use up less space and give the illusion of more room—room and space which are becoming increasingly rare, and now symbolize the romantic image of the America of old.

Therefore, although economy, convenience, and consumer fascination play a large role in this trend, the subtle, psychological causes such as fear and nostalgia shouldn't be negated. For indeed, it is often the underlying psychological causes that have the most influence on man's behavior.

The Decline of Political Parties

GLEN HAYASHI

Office-holding in our government is dominated by two major parties. In virtually every election, excluding nonpartisan ones, one of the most important facts to be known about a candidate is the party label to which he or she belongs, so decisive is party affiliation for election outcome. Today more than two out of three citizens continue to see themselves as Democrats or Republicans. These are signs of party strength. However, they are misleading. The dominant trend in politics is not toward strong parties; instead there is actually a weakening and decline of political parties.

What exactly does this phrase "a decline of political parties" mean? To begin with, it means that fewer individuals now choose to identify with either major party, although more than two out of three citizens (about 72 percent) consider themselves Democrats or Republicans. This is a drop from the 78 percent of all voters having a partisan attachment as recently as 1964. Next, there has been a decline of party regularity in voting; that is, voting for the candidate of the party to which a person belongs. If party strength were high, the number of partisans voting for the other party would be low. However, this is not the case. Between 1962 and 1972 the defection rate in national elections was twice as great as it was in national elections between 1952 and 1960. The decline also means that party leaders have less power, or "clout," over the elected party members, which in turn, allows candidates to be more independent and reduce their ties to the party.

What are the causes of this trend? There are many, too many in fact to write about, so I will concentrate on four: the changing attitude of the voter; the growth of interest-group activity; the expanding role of the media; and finally, the emergence of the direct primary.

At one time, voters found party labels very useful, as this label usually gave some kind of indication of how a candidate would act if elected. The party system was also a way in which the voter could collectively punish or reward members in office, depending on the state of the union. This has now changed. The voter is finding the party label much less useful than before. But it goes much further than just this, for there seems to be a general distrust of the government by the public. What caused this distrust is hard to say. Most likely it has been caused by a variety of factors and probably the most important of these is the public dissatisfaction with policy outcomes (for example, inflation, race relations, poverty, crime). Sixty percent of the public believes that "People running the country don't really care what happens to you." It is a startling fact that this proposition was accepted by about twice as many people in 1977 as in 1966. The fascination with "new politics" solutions to current problems and the success of party reform efforts both have increased the declining confidence in the government by the people. Whatever the explanation is for this distrust, it has undoubtedly affected the party system.

The growth of interest-group activity is another cause of the decline, and it seems to be connected with the mistrust in government that is so prevalent. Voters are not content with allowing officials to make important decisions that directly affect them without having their voice heard, so they join interest groups. By doing this, the voters can keep a watchful eye on members to make sure that no "dirty dealings" are influencing the official to vote against their issue. The increasing activity is definitely weakening the party. When legislators are more concerned with satisfying interest groups than with supporting party positions and leaders, the party is hurt. When party lines collapse, collective responsibility for decisions is diminished.

The importance of the media is also a cause of the decline. Candidates need experts in film-making, speech-writing, and campaign strategy, and specialists in advertising, fundraising, public relations, and so on, in order to be competitive. How a candidate acts, or what he says, or hears, or wears, are now vitally important to any campaign. The media can thus make or break a candidate. What has the party to do with this? Because of the experts needed in this age of technology, a professional staff needs to be hired to handle all of the big jobs. What happens is that the party is reduced to a role of spectator in the campaign.

Along with the previously mentioned causes, the emergence of the direct primary can also be seen as a cause of the weakening and decline of the political party. With its emphasis on the voter rather than party organization, the direct primary was hard to resist, and it is now used for the nomination of candidates in a majority of the states. While the voters love this method, party leaders, on the other hand, have been less than thrilled. Some leaders go so far as saying that the direct primary is a systematically conceived effort to bring down the party itself. In many respects, this seems true. If the party becomes heavily involved in a primary for a main office, odds are that it will have to raise huge sums of money to campaign for its candidate. Remaining neutral can also cause problems for the party. They may wind up with a candidate who either is hostile to the organization or unsympathetic to its programs and policies. Whatever way the party turns it is in trouble. In addition, the direct primary works against the party's goal to nominate a "balanced" ticket. The average voter is much less likely to vote for candidates that are representatives of the major groups of the party than is the party leadership.

These causes are just a few of the many that are responsible for the present trend of declining political parties. Nevertheless, the average voter must be quite puzzled and wondering "How does this trend affect me?" There are many answers to this question. First, the lack of party strength within the government makes it difficult for party leaders to pass legislation. They have difficulty accumulating enough votes for passage from members, even those of their own party. Second, party identification continues to be the best single explanation for the vote on candidates for offices less visible than the presidency. It is also salient for many voters, despite the decline, as it serves to orient them with candidates, issues, and political events, and to simplify their electoral choices. Without political parties there is no way of knowing where a candidate stands on many issues. The voter is then influenced by the personality of a candidate, not on the issues, and the "celebrity" candidate will thus be born. The party system is now in disarray, more so than ever before. However, it is not yet to a point where we will see it disintegrate.